THE TAO OF ABUNDANCE

Laurence G. Boldt, author of the bestselling *Zen and the Art of Making a Living,* is a nationally known writer and career consultant. He has given speeches and conducted workshops across the country and has been featured in such publications as *New Age Journal* and *Newsweek.* His previous books include *How to Find the Work You Love* and *Zen Soup,* both available in Penguin Compass.

Achieve success, but without vanity;
Achieve success, but without aggression;
Achieve success, but without arrogance;
Achieve success, but without gain;
Achieve success, but without force.

—Lao Tzu

THE TAO OF
ABUNDANCE

LAURENCE G. BOLDT

PENGUIN COMPASS

COMPASS
Published by the Penguin Group
Penguin Putnam Inc., 375 Hudson Street,
New York, New York 10014, U.S.A.
Penguin Books Ltd, 27 Wrights Lane,
London W8 5TZ, England
Penguin Books Australia Ltd, Ringwood,
Victoria, Australia
Penguin Books Canada Ltd, 10 Alcorn Avenue,
Toronto, Ontario, Canada M4V 3B2
Penguin Books (N.Z.) Ltd, 182–190 Wairau Road,
Auckland 10, New Zealand

Penguin Books Ltd, Registered Offices:
Harmondsworth, Middlesex, England

First published in Arkana 1999

5 7 9 10 8 6 4

Calligraphy by Steven Jian Chen

Illustration credits
"The Pure and Plain Pavilion" by Liu Chueh, Ming Dynasty, National Palace
Museum, Taipei, Taiwan, Republic of China.
"The Ambassadors" by Hans Holbein the Younger, National Gallery, London.
Two figures from *Taoist Yoga: Alchemy and Immortality* by Lu K'uan Yu
(Charles Luk). By permission of Samuel Weiser, Inc., York Beach, Maine
and Ebury Press, Random House UK Ltd, London.
Images from *Asian Art Motifs from Korea: Ying and Yang* edited
by Ahn Sang-Soo. By permission of Ahn Graphics, Seoul

LIBRARY OF CONGRESS CATALOGING IN PUBLICATION DATA
Boldt, Laurence G.
The tao of abundance / Laurence G. Boldt.
p.   cm.
ISBN 0 14 01.9606 4
1. Philosophy, Taoist. 2. Life. I. Title.
B162.7.B64 1999
181'.114—dc21   99-27726

Printed in the United States of America
Set in Garamond
Designed by Laurence G. Boldt

To Tina, who brings abundant joy to my life

ACKNOWLEDGMENTS

I would like thank several people whose assistance has been indispensable in bringing this book to life. It is difficult to express in mere words how much your help has meant to me or how deeply grateful I am for it. Susan Shapiro did the entire layout of the book. She contributed many good ideas to the interior design as well. Beyond this, her dedication and commitment to the project—expressed in ways too numerous to count—has been a phenomenal help. Also invaluable was the editorial help I received from Kim Grant. Her sharp eye and sensitive ear, combined with her vast knowledge of editorial minutiae, contributed much to the quality of the finished project. Thanks, Kim, for all your help over the years. I also want to thank Tina Kolaas for her help in copyediting, her continued moral support, and—most of all—for being who she is in my life.

Thanks to Steven Jian Chen for the calligraphy. Also thanks to Janet Goldstein, my editor, and her assistant Allison Hastings at Penguin.

Contents

PREFACE

Whether we hear news reports of good economic times or bad, whether we make a lot of money or a little, many of us feel that something is missing in our lives. I wrote this book because I wanted to address the real sense of lack that people feel in their lives today and offer some practical suggestions for bringing greater abundance into them. I think that today, in many ways, we've become confused about what real abundance is. In reducing it to something that can be measured in abstract economic terms, we've substituted a concept of abundance for the experience of it. It is my hope that this book will prompt readers to consider for themselves what real abundance means to them and how they can go about creating it in their own lives. I further hope that it will prompt readers to begin challenging the notion that they live in a world of scarcity and lack. It is not the world that is insufficient. It is the way we relate to it, to one another, and to the deepest parts of ourselves that is the source of our problem.

This is not a book about Taoism. It is a book that applies insights from Taoist philosophy to the situation we in the West find ourselves in at the beginning of the twenty-first century. The question occurs as to why the Taoist philosophy? Apart from my own long-standing interest in the subject, I believe that, for a variety of reasons, the Taoist perspective is particularly relevant to our situation today. In a world that defines abundance in terms of scarce resources and economic abstractions, the Taoist philosophy defines abundance in human terms and sees the world as a naturally abundant place. In a do-oriented society that puts its faith in future progress, it reminds us to be, and that here and now is the only place we live. In a world caught up in glamour and obsessed with consumption, the Taoist perspective offers an appreciation of leisure and beauty in the simple things in life. In a society that values the cerebral and abstract, the Taoists remind us to trust our intuitions and to recognize the power of the unconscious intelligence. In an increasingly narcissistic and artificial society, Taoist philosophy values humility, naturalness, and spontaneity.

In a world facing a major ecological crisis, the Taoist philosophy offers a path to regaining a sense of connection and cooperation with nature. In a world confused about the relationship between the sexes, the Taoist perspective offers a path to harmony and cooperation, based on a mutual respect for the roles that the inner and the outer feminine and masculine play in all of life. In a world obsessed with celebrity and social status, it reminds us to value our own human dignity above any prize or outer recognition. In a world where we too often neglect the inner or spiritual dimension of life, the Taoists remind us to cultivate the treasures that lie within. In a world where people are confused about their place in the world and their own direction in it, the Taoist philosophy tells us that every living thing has a place in the natural order of things and that each has its own destiny to fulfill. I could go on, but all of these things and many more will come out in the course of the book.

For the reader who is new to Taoist philosophy, or for those who would like a concise overview of the same, I've included a chapter entitled "The Five Fingers of the Tao." Because it is not essential to the discussion on the Tao of Abundance, I've placed it at the beginning of the book. Some readers may want to turn to it first, to get a grounding in fundamental Taoist concepts before proceeding to the main body of the work. Others may choose to begin with the introduction and chapter 1 and then, perhaps, come back to it later to reinforce what they have read and place it in a broader context. I've also included a "Tao of Abundance Workbook" at the end of the book. I strongly encourage readers to complete the exercises in it, as a way of integrating and applying the principles in their own lives.

As this is intended to be a popular and not a scholarly book, I've taken a certain license in using phrases such as "from the Taoist perspective, "the Taoists would say," or "the Taoist tells us." In using the word *Taoist,* one runs into the same problem as when using the word *Christian.* By *Christian,* do we mean the sayings of Jesus and the apostles, or do we mean Christianity as taught by the desert fathers or the Christian mystics of the Middle Ages? Even more problematic, do we mean the religion practiced by today's Roman Catholics, Episcopalians, Methodists, Baptists, Pentecostals, Egyptian Coptics, or others who call themselves Christian? Even as "Christian" can mean many different things to different people, so there are many schools, systems, religious sects and cults with a wide variety of teachings that call themselves "Taoist." Like the Christians, today's Taoists have had their own internal squabbles over which faction best represents the "True Church."

When I use the term *Taoist,* I am, by and large, referring to the *Tao Chia,* or the classical Contemplative School of Taoist philosophy, as expressed by its three principal exponents Lao Tzu, Chuang Tzu, and Lieh Tzu. I will sidestep the debate about whether or not these individuals were in fact the sole authors of works traditionally attributed to them. Whether or not any one of these historical figures (assuming all were historical figures) wrote all, part, or none of a particular work traditionally attributed to him may be an interesting question for scholars, yet is not germane to my purpose in applying the philosophy contained in the works. Though I cite other Taoist sources, I rely mainly on the classic texts of *Tao Chia.* These are the *Lao Tzu,* or *Tao Te Ching*, attributed to Lao Tzu, and the *Chuang Tzu* and the *Lieh Tzu,* each attributed to its author of the same name. The reader should be aware that even within these classic Taoist texts, there are significant philosophical differences.

In many ways, this book is a companion to my earlier book *Zen and the Art of Making a Living.* That book addresses the desire that many today have to create an experience of work that reflects who they truly are, one that integrates the calling of their hearts with the practical realities of making a living in today's world. This book addresses the desire to enjoy a balanced and abundant life in the midst of the frenetic and often chaotic society we live in today. I hope that it will serve you, and I wish you the best of luck in charting your own path to total abundance.

Tao

THE FIVE FINGERS OF THE TAO

*The philosophy of the East, although so vastly different from
ours, could be an inestimable treasure for us too; but in order
for us to possess it we must first earn it.* —CARL JUNG

Before considering how to apply principles of Taoist philosophy to enhance
our experience of abundance, it makes sense to ask, What is the Tao? This
is a difficult question for two reasons. First, when we speak of the Tao, we
are talking about that which is transcendent to thought and name. The
Tao—by definition—is beyond definition. As Chuang Tzu put it, "If it
could be talked about, everybody would have told their brother."[1] Second,
the word *Tao* takes on different shades of meaning in different contexts.

The discussion that follows focuses on five distinct "meanings" or applications of the term *Tao*. For purposes of this introduction, each of these meanings will be considered as a referent to a distinct level of consciousness. Yet we should keep in mind that in reality, these levels are not distinct at all. They can be separated in thought, but never in reality. Even as water remains water while taking the form of rivers, clouds, rain, ice, and dew, so the Tao remains the Tao through all levels of consciousness. The Tao is a multidimensional mystery, a cosmic tapestry in which each of the threads is seamlessly woven into the whole.

I call these elements "the five fingers of the Tao."[2] We should never forget that these fingers are part and parcel of the same hand, and fingers and hand together only point at the Tao. They are not It. Still, recognizing each of these aspects will help us to appreciate the subtlety and depth of the Taoist world-view. They also serve as a foundation to the discussion of the Tao of Abundance in the later chapters.

The Five Fingers of the Tao	Dimension	How we relate to:
The Eternal Transcendent Tao	Mystical	Spirit
Mother Tao, Source of All Things	Cosmological	Nature
The Tao of the Great Mergence	Psychological	Soul
The Tao of the Ten Thousand Things	Scientific	Work/Art
The Social Tao, the Way of Humanity	Sociological	Society

The Taoists offer us more than a spiritual philosophy, a path to transcendence. They have a great deal to say about how we relate to nature and our own psyches. They also have much to say about work and interpersonal relationships, about health, sex, the organization of society, and more. Throughout the nineteenth and well into the second half of the twentieth centuries, Western interpreters of Taoist philosophy tended to emphasize the mystical dimension to exclusion of all else. This emphasis gives a distorted view of Taoist philosophy, making it seem otherworldly and remote. One exposed solely to these interpretations might conclude that while the Taoist philosophy may have had relevance for hermits in the mountains of China two thousand years ago, it has little to say to an urban dweller in the twenty-first century.

In more recent years, there have been a number of books that focus almost exclusively on utilitarian applications of the Tao, for example *The Tao of Negotiation*, *The Tao of Teams*, and so on.[3] The dangers of emphasizing utilitarian applications of Taoist thought are two. First, we risk a simple-minded approach to what is an infinitely rich and subtle philosophy. Second, we may try to "use the Tao" in seeking results, rather to seek the Tao and let results take care of themselves. Just so long as we are grasping after it, the Tao will elude us. It is in hopes of avoiding these errors and encouraging readers to pursue a more in-depth study of Taoist philosophy that this introductory material is included in this book.

Below, you will find a brief sketch of each of the five "dimensions" referred to above. Don't be concerned if any of these aspects are not immediately clear to you. For most Westerners, Taoist philosophy presents a radically different way of viewing the world—one that requires an open mind and considerable reflection to be fully appreciated. You will have the opportunity to explore many of these ideas in greater depth and in more concrete terms in the chapters that follow.

道 The Eternal Tao of the Transcendent Mystery

> *The Tao that is spoken of is not the Eternal nature of the Tao.*
> —LAO TZU

In its eternal aspect, the Tao cannot be spoken of. Eternal means transcendent to time and space and, therefore, beyond the reach of the physical senses and the intellections of the mind. The Eternal Tao cannot be seen, tasted, or touched. It cannot be spoken of or reasoned about. It is a transcendent mystery. If we try to speak of it, we get jumbled up in words, and it comes out sounding like a paradox. We could say that the Eternal Tao exists, quite apart from existence, that It lives beyond life and death, or that It is and yet, both is and is not. Yet statements such as this communicate nothing unless one has experience of the transcendent, and if one has the experience, what point is there in talking about it?

Many are familiar with the saying attributed to Lao Tzu that "those who know do not speak, and those who speak do not know." Nevertheless, Lao Tzu himself is purported to have written the five thousand characters we call the *Tao Te Ching*. We have as well, preserved in writing, the sayings attributed to the Buddha, Jesus Christ, the Hebrew Prophets, Zarathustra, Shiva, and Krishna, among others. Presumably, at least some of these "knew." Or are we to think that all of these "teachers" were charlatans and all their "students" fools?

The fundamental difficulty lies, not with the veracity of the scriptures or the realization of the teachers, but with the limitations of language to communicate or express Eternal Reality. As Lao Tzu put it, "The name that can be named is not the true name." Name, words, and language are only symbols of the Reality they seek to represent. This is an obvious point; we know that the word *dog* is a not the living, breathing animal. Yet in practice, and especially in dealing with more abstract concepts, we forget the difference between the word and the reality it stands for. Why then do we bother with the scriptures and the teachers? In Picasso's statement, "Art is a lie that leads to truth," we find a clue. The scriptures, like all great art, are not to be thought of as "truth" but as "lies that lead to truth." So long as we cling to the literal meaning, the letter of what is being said, the Eternal Tao eludes us.

Yet if we can listen with an empty mind and open heart, we may hear the Word (Spirit, Tao) from which the words have originated. The words are gateways to the Mystery. Yet whether or not they swing open for us depends on how we approach them. Chuang Tzu described spiritual teachings and the words used to convey them as fishing baskets. "Fishing baskets are employed to catch fish; but when the fish are got, the men forget the baskets. . . . Words are employed to convey ideas; but when the ideas are grasped, men forget the words."[4] The point is not to collect baskets but to catch fish.

The Eternal Tao by any other name is still the unutterable Eternal. Taoists have no particular claim on the Transcendent Reality that all spiritual traditions have pointed to. Lao Tzu and Chuang Tzu were not members of any formal religion or philosophical school. Indeed, the chief articulators of Taoist philosophy would not have thought of themselves as "Taoists." They were simply enlightened individuals around whom students gathered and whose sayings were in some way preserved.[5] It was only much later that they were classified as belonging to the "Tao Chia," or Taoist school of philosophy.

While there are elements unique to Chinese culture and history within the teachings of Lao Tzu and Chuang Tzu, these texts are better understood as representations of what has been termed "the perennial philosophy" than as the scriptures of a particular religion or culture. In many of the world's great spiritual traditions, we find alongside the popular religion an esoteric or mystic teaching, reserved for a rather more dedicated few. (For example, within Taoism, the "Tao Chiao," or what might be termed "popular Taoist religion and magic" developed alongside the esoteric Tao Chia, or Contemplative School of Taoist philosophy.)

The striking parallels and correspondences within the world's esoteric teachings—across cultures and historical eras—has led some scholars to view these teachings as local representations of a single universal, or perennial, philosophy.[6] Like a single melody fashioned into numerous musical arrangements, the perennial philosophy takes on different inflections in different cultural contexts and historical periods, but is always recognizable as the same tune. As Thomas Aquinas put it, "All that is true, by whomsoever it has been said, has its origin in the Spirit." We could, for example, quite easily confuse the description of the Eternal, given by Jesus in the Gnostic text, The Secret Book of John, with Lao Tzu discoursing on the Tao:

I simply believe that some part of the human Self . . . is not subject to the laws of time and space.

CARL JUNG

It is the invisible Spirit. One should not think of it as a god or like a god.
It is greater than a god, because there is nothing over it and no lord
  above it.
It is unutterable, since nothing could comprehend it to utter it.
It is unnameable, since there was nothing before it to give it a name.

The Eternal Tao cannot properly be equated with the Western notion of God as interpreted by orthodox Christianity, Islam, or Judaism. Still, there are many parallels with the notion of God as understood in the Western esoteric tradition. There are Greek philosophers, Christian and Jewish mystics, and Islamic Sufis, who speak of God in ways not unlike those Lao Tzu might use to refer to the Tao. Yet the Eternal Tao most closely parallels the Hindu notion of "Brahman." Like the Tao, Brahman is recognized as transcendent and immanent, that is, as both prior to, or beyond, the realm of time and space, and manifest in it. In the Bhagavad-Gita, Brahman is described as "beginningless, supreme: beyond what is and is not."[7] Chuang Tzu described the Tao as "the changing changeless and changeless change."

道 The Eternal Tao and Abundance

The man who is not divorced from the essence is the spiritual
man.
— CHUANG TZU

The Eternal Tao, or Transcendent Reality, is central to our discussion of the Tao of Abundance. The world-view of the modern commercial culture recognizes neither the existence of a Transcendent Reality nor the importance of the spiritual dimension in daily human life. For one who takes the prevailing world-view as his own, there is no reality that cannot be measured by time, space, and the ego. Consequently, people today are, as Joseph Campbell put it, "running up against a hard world, that is in no way responsive to [their] spiritual need[s]. . . . When you think of what most people are actually undergoing in our civilization, you realize it is a very grim thing to be a modern human being."[8]

It is the loss of a living spiritual experience in daily life that, more than anything, breeds the alienation and anxiety that plague modern life. Since we have no means of transcending them (nor even the belief that it is possible to do so), we feel pressured by time, restless in space, trapped in ego. Our preoccupation with material possessions and material achievements both reflects and perpetuates our sense of spiritual emptiness. Without an experience of transcendence, the world is, as Wordsworth put it, "too much with us." In a life of getting and spending, we don't just "lay waste our powers"; we miss the wonder and bliss of what it is to be alive.

For many today, there is a growing recognition that the spiritual dimension is fundamental to human life, as much a feature of what it is to be a human being as the capacity for language or the ability to walk erect. It is not, as we have been taught by modern science and psychology, a relic from a superstitious or prescientific past. As Anne Baring and Jules Cashford put it, "'The sacred' is not a stage in human consciousness that people grow out of or into, but it is at least an element in the structure of consciousness, belonging to all people at all times."[9]

Yet for many today, especially for the more well-educated, the traditional portals to a spiritual life no longer seem relevant. For these, neither mythology, with its complex and culture-specific iconography, nor religion, with its antiscientific bias and preachy moralism, offer ready access to an experience of the sacred in daily life. As an articulation of the perennial philosophy, Contemplative Taoism offers a spiritual vision that is neither religious nor mythological, but philosophic in approach and poetic in expression.

In subtle and beautiful poetry, it speaks not of exploits of God or gods but of the reality of an Eternal transcendent consciousness that all of us move in, whether we are conscious of it or not. To access this timeless wisdom, there is no need to learn about or identify with a pantheon of gods or a mythological story about a single all-powerful deity. Recognition of the Eternal Tao does not require that you join an organization or that you subscribe to religious rules and regulations. You needn't call "it" Tao or yourself a Taoist. You need only begin to wonder at the mystery of life.

Mother Tao, Source of All Things

Something is mysteriously brought into existence
Long before Heaven or Earth is made,
It is silent and shapeless,
It is always present, endlessly in motion
From it like a mother every living thing has come.
I do not know what to call it.
So I call it Tao. —LAO TZU

The Tao is also referred to as "the Mother of all things" or as "the what-is-not that is the source of the what-is." In some respects, "Mother Tao" harkens back to the goddess religions that dominated in matriarchal Neolithic cultures throughout the world. Yet Mother Tao is not to be imaged or conceived of as a divine personage, but as a kind of "silent and shapeless" protolife from which "every living thing has come." As Chuang Tzu put it, "Tao makes things what they are, but is not itself a thing"—even a divine thing. Within the "silent and shapeless" womb of Mother Tao, every existing, or potentially existing, thing or event resides.

All cultures are made in the image of their cosmology, that is, in their understanding of the origin and structure of the universe. Cosmology deeply affects not only our relationship to the universe but our notions of time and the creative process. In Western Biblical cosmology, we have a divine per-

The most beautiful thing
we can experience is the
mysterious. . . . He to
whom this emotion is a
stranger, who can no
longer pause to wonder
and stand rapt in awe,
is as good as dead;
his eyes are closed.

ALBERT EINSTEIN

son who wills the universe into existence. As a personality (albeit a divine one), He is subject to loneliness, anger, jealousy, and revenge, as well as goodness, mercy, kindness, and joy. In six days, He made the universe and all the things that fill it. Like so many mudpies, He fashioned the heavens, the earth, the fish in the sea, the birds of the air, the creatures of the earth, and eventually, human beings. All of these were made by deliberate, discreet operations within linear time. First He made this, and then He made that. The Divine Person stands apart from His creation. He is wholly spiritual; His creation, wholly material. He is good; His creation, fallen and corrupt. Man, as a part of this fallen creation, can only be redeemed by His divine intervention.

From the Taoist perspective, there is no Maker or Creator God. Nature (the universe) is not made, but is *tzu-jan* "of itself so." The process of the universe is not one of deliberate manufacture but of organic growth. From the Taoist perspective, everything that now exists (or ever will) came into being when Mother Tao was "mysteriously brought into existence." Everything has grown out of this One source and is latent in it. In the Chuang Tzu we read, "Heaven and Earth were born at the same time I was, and the ten thousand things are one with me."[10] The universe, being without a maker, is also without a cause or a boss. No-thing has caused other things to be; all things have mutually arisen (*hsiang-shan*) and therefore mutually create and sustain one another.

With respect to the origin of the universe, there are striking parallels between Taoist cosmology and the theories of modern physicists. The theory of the big bang suggests that the entire universe began with a single giant explosion. From some "silent and shapeless" stuff (gases), the entire material universe was born. All subsequent effects, including the evolution of animate life and eventually of humankind, can be seen as having been latent in the primordial gasses that produced the big bang.

For many years now, it has been the consensus view among physicists that the universe has been continually expanding since the big bang. More recently, a number of physicists have theorized that it may eventually begin to shrink and collapse upon itself. Research is currently being conducted to test this hypothesis. Should it ultimately prove out, this too would fit the Taoist cosmology. If it turns out that the Universe will eventually collapse back into itself, it may well be that this pattern of expansion and contraction is an endlessly repeating cycle that has been going on for incalculable eons.

The expansion and contraction of the universe could be conceived as the in-breath and out-breath of Mother Tao. Tao is the emptiness out of which all things arose and into which they will again return and arise again . . . and return . . . and arise again . . . and so on. Mother Tao is sometimes referred to as "the Primal Unity" or "the One" and suggests the image of a circle—the going out and the coming in of life. This circle of unity applies not only to the grand cosmological cycle of the universe but more immediately to the life cycle of the individual—all that transpires between the in-breath at birth and the out-breath on dying. In this too, we find parallels between the Mother Tao and the Hindu Brahman.

Tranquil, let one worship It
As that from which he came forth
As that into which he will be dissolved
As that in which he breathes.
                                                                    —UPANISHADS

This is Mother Tao—the womb, tomb, and breath of life—the silent shapeless stuff from which one has arisen, into which he shall return, and in which he lives and breathes. Mother Tao is his past, his present, and his future; and past, present, and future are one in birth, death, and breath. The Greek philosopher, Anaximander, is describing Mother Tao when he says:

The nonlimited is the original material of existing things; further, the source from which existing things derive their existence is also that to which they return at their destruction, according to their necessity.

If all things have mutually arisen, we cannot reject any one thing or condition without rejecting the entire universe. The practice of acceptance, or "seeing perfection," applies to the realm of the Tao as the Mother of all things. In the context of a mutually arising universe, to say that this or that should not be is to say that the entire universe should not exist. Even if we were to make such a claim, it would hardly do us any good. That is why, as Camus put it, "suicide or life" is the only real choice or, as Shakespeare put it, "to be or not to be" is the question. As Shakespeare's Hamlet realized, even death is no escape. We either embrace life in its totality or we split it into an endless number of likes and dislikes. Psychologically separated from the whole, fragmented by our likes and dislikes, we can never find peace. Zen patriarch Seng Ts'an put it like this: "The Perfect Way [Tao] is only difficult for those who pick and choose; Do not like, do not dislike: all will then be clear."

The practice of "seeing perfection" is not an appeal to turn our backs on the world or retreat into passivity. The Taoists have often been accused of advocating this by those who have a limited understanding of their philosophy. On the contrary, the *Tao Te Ching* eloquently and repeatedly expresses concern for social welfare and advocates moral discrimination. Certainly, the great Taoist philosophers were not suggesting that we remain indifferent to the suffering of our fellow creatures. Rather, the cosmology of Primal Unity, or Mother Tao, invites us to move in the world *as* the world, not as a force separate or apart from it. The true power to transform events is realized when we accept the context in which they have arisen. The ultimate context is life itself. Embrace the process of life and you embrace all aspects of it.

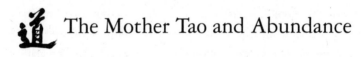 ## The Mother Tao and Abundance

The man who is not divorced from the great source
is the natural man.　　　　　—CHUANG TZU

Mother Tao is relevant to the Tao of Abundance because our cosmology shapes not only our sense of our relationship to the universe but our notions of time and the creative process. Modern alienation, struggle, and hurry can be traced back to our cosmology, and these profoundly affect our economic and social life. These elements of Western religious cosmology were carried over after the scientific revolution and are a part of our shared, or common, sense of the world.

Relationship to the Universe: The God of Western cosmology is in His Heaven. The Tao also has its heavenly dimension in that it is transcendent to the physical universe. Yet it is simultaneously on the Earth, alive in all nature, including human beings. For the Taoists, trusting the Tao is not fundamentally different from trusting ourselves in our deepest nature. On the other hand, Western cosmology gives us the sense that nature is against us. We must trust in a heavenly being who is fundamentally unlike ourselves. The Western religious view is that nature must be overcome in order for us to have a spiritual life; the scientific view, that nature must be conquered by rationality in order for us to realize our full human potential. In either case, we would be foolish to trust in or rely on nature for our support. We could hardly say, with Lao Tzu, "I receive nourishment from the Great Mother."

Creativity: As individuals, we fashion our beliefs about the creative process in the image of our cultural cosmology. Western cosmology gives us the idea that creativity is the result of the active assertion of will (God made the world in six days). For the Taoist, creativity is a natural, spontaneous event (the universe was "mysteriously brought into existence"). Thus, in the image of our cosmologies, we in the West struggle to make things happen and to "make our way in the world," while the Taoist takes the *wu-wei* (p.n. "woo way"), the path of effortless action. In the West, creativity is something we must actively choose. For the Taoist, creativity is an organic process in which we naturally participate, unless we somehow interfere with it.

Time: In Western cosmology, time began at a definite point (when God willed the universe into existence) and ends at a definite point (the Last Judgment). Time progresses or marches on to its inevitable conclusion— the end of time. From the Taoist perspective, there is no beginning, nor any end of time. We have not time lines but time circles. Nothing is ever final; every beginning is an end; every end, a beginning. The Taoist is not interested in the end of time, but in the transformations within time. These cosmological orientations have many practical implications. Because we in the West take the notion of material progress in time as the standard by which we judge individuals and societies, science is primarily interested in technological advances. On the other hand, the Taoist interest in the cyclical transformations within time yielded a fundamentally different, though equally valid, approach to science. As Joseph Needham wrote, "The Taoists were profoundly conscious of the universality of change and transformation—this was one of their deepest scientific insights."[11] (More on this later.)

To embrace all is to be selfless.

LAO TZU

The Tao of the Great Mergence

If there is no other, there can be no I. If there is no I, there
will be none to make distinctions. —CHUANG TZU

The Tao of the Great Mergence is expressed in the term *Ta T'ung*, the Great
Interfusion. The two central metaphysical understandings in the Tao of the
Great Mergence are what the Taoist calls the "identity-of-all-things" and
the "unity-in-opposites." Again, modern physics can aid us, at least by
analogy, in understanding the Great Mergence or Interfusion. Quantum
physics tells us that our experience of a world of separate things is merely a
kind of optical illusion, reinforced by the conventions (indeed, the structure) of language. What we see is a function of our physiology—not reality.
Astrophysicists have recently estimated that more than 90 percent of the
material in the universe is invisible.

Today, physicists recognize that there is no ultimate or final stuff of
matter. Indeed, in chasing down subatomic particles, they discovered, not
the ultimate stuff, but patterns of probability. The Taoists tell us that there
are no finite boundaries between things or events; all things are interfused,
or mixed together, in the great soup of the Tao. This is the principle of the
identity-of-all-things. Things appear distinct on one level; yet from another point of view, they are recognized as being one and the same. Einstein's
general theory of relativity demonstrates this principle. Time and space are
not separate but depend upon each other. Time speeds up or slows down,
depending upon where you are in space. We can separate time and space in
name, but not in reality.

When everyone knows beauty as beautiful, there is already ugliness;
When everyone knows goodness as goodness, there is already evil.
"To be" and "not to be" arise mutually. —LAO TZU

If there is, in fact, no separate thing, why does it appear so to us? The
answer lies in that isolating bubble of consciousness known as "the human
ego." The ego is the subject, the point of view, that turns everything else
into objects. It is the subjective sense of a "me" in here that makes everything else "thems" or "its" "out there." Chuang Tzu referred to this bubble-
making ego consciousness as *ch'eng hsin*, the individualized or separative

heart/mind. In the writing of the Western philosopher Immanuel Kant, we find the suggestion that this separative consciousness results from what he called "the forms of sensibility and the categories of logic," or thought. The limitations of our physical senses and the necessity of language and thought to differentiate, to split hairs, to make distinctions, give the sense of a fragmented world of separate things.

The Taoists believed that this bubble-making ego consciousness could be transcended. Chuang Tzu wrote: "By and by comes the great awakening, and then we find out that life itself is a great dream. All the while the fools think they are awake, and that they have knowledge."[12] We find echoes of this in East Indian philosophy, where the great dream, or illusion, is referred to as "maya." Maya has been defined as "the continually changing, phenomenal world of appearances and forms, which an unenlightened mind takes as the only reality."[13] In the Upanishads, we read that all knowledge acquired within maya is "name only." Chuang Tzu calls this "small knowledge." "Great knowledge sees all in one. Small knowledge breaks down into the many."[14] I will have much more to say about the ego and the limitations of its "small knowledge" in the chapters that follow.

> *Before I heard this, I was certain that I was Hui but now that I have heard there is no more Hui.*[15]

If there are no separate, discreet things, then there is no ego; indeed, there is no-thing that we can attach a name to, for example, a body, a sensation, an emotion, a mind. At this level of consciousness, I am not a human being, a male, a writer, or an American. I am not good or bad, moral or immoral, gaining or losing, growing or decaying, advancing or retreating. Having once realized the Great Interfusion, or interpenetration, one can never again take the ego seriously, which is to say, as something real. From this point forward, all of the ego's concerns and ambitions are rightly seen as "much ado about nothing."

The structure of the ego relies on a concrete and limited sense of time and space. The action of the ego is comparison. The ego is always comparing this time against that time, over here against over there. It is always trying to get to the good time over there and constantly being shadowed by the bad time over here. In the good times over here, it fears the return of the bad times that lie over there. In the bad times over here, it longs for the

Only the truly intelligent understand this principle of the identity of all things. They do not view things as apprehended by themselves, subjectively, but transfer themselves into the position of the things viewed.

CHUANG TZU

good times over there. While in the ego consciousness, we miss the here-and-now, and thus, we can never truly relax or find peace. It is this restless, anxious ego consciousness that modern commercial culture takes as the final term of the self (a point that will be developed in the chapters that follow).

道 The Tao of the Great Mergence, and Abundance

What is this place where thought is useless?
Knowledge and emotion cannot fathom it!
—YUMEN

The Tao of the Great Mergence relates to the Tao of Abundance because, as we will see, the separative ego consciousness is the psychological source of poverty, lack, conflict, human degradation, competitive hostility, craving, and exploitation. In the West, we have identified the ego as the final term of the self. The modern economic view of life, which pervades our culture, assumes the psychology of the ego, that is, the feeling of lack and the struggle for self-preservation. We have, more than any culture in human history, committed ourselves to the ego and its consciousness of lack. As a result, we are haunted by a prevailing sense of spiritual and psychological poverty in the midst of unprecedented material prosperity. We have elevated the ego to the status of a god and sought our happiness in its endless desires. Modern economic life demands the continuous expansion of these desires. Yet no matter how much we acquire, it never seems to be enough. We are never satisfied.

To the mind that is still, the whole universe surrenders.
—LIEH TZU

We in the West can learn a great deal from Eastern philosophy in general and the Taoist philosophy in particular with respect to transcending the ego consciousness. As the German writer Karlfried Graf Dürckheim put it, "The West says, If this ego ceases to be, then meaningful reality disappears with it. But the East says, It is not until this ego and the reality it has shaped has ceased to be that humanity's 'true nature' is released and true reality dawns—and only from this reality can . . . the true self emerge."[16] Throughout this book, a contrast will be made between an economics based upon the psychology of the ego (Egonomics) and an experience of abundance based upon the psychology of the Self (The Tao of Abundance).

The ego cannot acknowledge the transcendent, recognize its biological source, experience the unity of life, or give up its fight for self-justification, without feeling itself diminished. Ego is an affirmation of separation that is constantly at war—both with its own negation, what Carl Jung termed the "shadow," as well with the Transcendent (Tao, Spirit, God). The psychological experience of abundance requires that we transcend, or break the bubble, of the ego consciousness and identify ourselves with the Tao, or the Self that is the Self in all things.

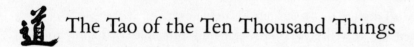 The Tao of the Ten Thousand Things

The great Tao flows everywhere,
to the left and to the right,
All things depend upon it to exist,
and it does not abandon them.
To its accomplishments it lays no claim.
It loves and nourishes all things,
but does not lord it over them.

—LAO TZU

The Tao of the Ten Thousand Things is the Tao expressing itself through the myriad forms manifest in the physical universe. At this level, difference is recognized: a dog is a dog, a man is a man, a tree is a tree; yet all reside within the Tao as Transcendent Mystery, Mother Tao, and Great Mergence. The potential for "tree" exists within the Mother Tao; a tree is one with (not different from) all things, by the Tao the Great Mergence, and yet expresses in its unique "thingness," according to its own organic pattern, or principle (The Tao of Ten Thousand Things). In looking at a tree, you may perceive the unique principle of the tree, while at the same time recognizing its non-being, or interfusion, with everything else.

When things have their principles, the one {thing} cannot be the other . . . . All things have each their own different principle, whereas Tao brings the principles of all things into single agreement. Therefore, it can be both one thing and another, and is not in one thing only.

—HAN FEI TZU

Everything that exists expresses the Tao according to its own principle, *li*. (The term *li* will be defined and developed in chapter 8.) At the level of the Ten Thousand Things, the principles of the human being are qualitatively different from those of monkeys or minnows, of grass or star systems, of mountains or pear trees, for each has its own *li*. The human body and psyche have their own *li*, or organic patterns, which are a kind of microcosm of principles, or patterns, appearing throughout the universe. For example, the four limbs of the human body correspond to the four seasons of earth and the four directions of space. In addition to shared organic patterns, each individual human life has a unique principle of organization, an individual destiny that is entirely his or her own.

There are as well general or overarching principles that apply to the entire manifest universe. These principles help us understand the dynamic process of change within the manifest universe. One of the key overarching principles of transformation is the interplay of yin and yang, which will be considered at length in chapter 6. The selfsame, ever-Mysterious Tao resides within the Earth and the myriad forms that populate it—as well as in the form-less Heaven, the emptiness of nondifferentiation. Where the realization of the Tao of the Great Mergence is "out of many, one"—the realization of the Tao of the Ten Thousand Things is "within the many, one." As Chuang Tzu put it: "That which is One is One. That which is not One is also One."[17]

Though the emphasis is different, the realization "out of many, one" and the realization "within the many, one" are equally important. The first takes us out of the world (the illusory ego). The second brings us back to the world with a sense of loving participation in it. Zen teachers admonish students who believe that the realization of non-being or the identity-of-all-things has brought them enlightenment, not to cling to the Emptiness. Even as the attachment to being (form) must be let go of, so too the attachment to non-being (emptiness) must be released. As Chuang Tzu put it, "The Way cannot be thought of as being, nor can it be thought of as nonbeing."[18] Like all opposites, being and non-being are united in the Tao.

Having realized Emptiness, one must return again to the world of form and act according to the principle of his own nature.

> *Let everything be allowed to do what it naturally does, so*
> *that its nature will be satisfied.* —CHUANG TZU

The early Taoists were interested in understanding the nature of things and in acting in harmony with them. As Chuang Tzu wrote, "The spiritual man . . . follows the nature of things." In the *Huai Nan Tzu*, we read, "Those who follow the natural order flow in the current of Tao." It is this practice of following the nature of things, the "Tao of Ten Thousands Things," that gives a scientific character to the Taoist tradition. In volume II of his remarkable work *Science and Civilization in China*, Joseph Needham pointed out the extraordinary contributions of the early Taoist philosophy to Chinese science (many of which have yet to be fully appreciated in the West). Needham notes that the Taoists did not, as most Western interpreters have concluded, view scientific knowledge and technology as inherently evil. Rather, their approach to science was so fundamentally different from that of the modern, that Western interpreters confuse a difference in motive and method with a rejection of science *in toto*.

 ## The Taoist Scientific Motive and Method

> *Technology is destructive only in the hands of people who do*
> *not realize that they are one and the same process as the*
> *universe.* —ALAN WATTS

The Taoist approach to science and technology was not, as René Descartes, Francis Bacon, and other early modern scientific philosophers advocated, one of exploiting or conquering nature, but of working with nature, as a part of nature. Descartes argued that scientific knowledge should serve to "render ourselves the masters and possessors of nature." On the other hand, the Sung scholar, Lin Ching-Hsi wrote, "Scholars of old time said that the mind is originally empty, and only because of this can it respond to natural things without prejudices. Only the empty mind can respond to the things of nature." For the Taoist, the use of science and technology is not a matter of better imposing man's will upon nature, but of more effectively responding to, or harmonizing with, nature.

Indeed, for the Taoist, the capacity to respond requires that one let go of the will to dominate. Just to the extent that one accepts the world as it is (embracing Mother Tao) and empties the mind of all attachments (merging in the Formless Tao) is one able to see into the nature of things and behold the patterns (*li*) of things, great and small. This is not only the basis of Taoist science, but of its arts and crafts and well.

Creativity (scientific or artistic) is not, then, a matter of the assertion of the separative self, but of "following the natural order of things." As the modern scientist R. G. H. Sui put it, "An original concept . . . prefers the mind imbued with the love of Nature, untainted with hidden plans for Her exploitation."[19] Simply put, working for rewards spoils creativity, while working with love opens vistas hidden to those harboring ulterior motives. Precisely because the Taoists were not interested in lording it over nature, they were able to recognize its order. Mozart made essentially the same point about the origin of creative work. "Neither lofty intelligence nor imagination nor both together go into the making of genius. Love, love, love, that is the soul of genius."

There is nothing that will not reveal its secrets if you love it enough.
—GEORGE WASHINGTON CARVER

Western and Taoist science differ, not only in their motive for scientific discovery (dominance vs. accord), but also in their methods. Both the modern Western and ancient Taoist scientist endeavor to see the world free from prejudice. Yet because they begin with different sets of metaphysical assumptions, their methods are as different as night and day. The Western scientist seeks freedom from prejudice (objectivity) by collecting vast amounts of empirical evidence and subjecting it to rigorous intellectual analysis. The method of the Taoist is the concentrated observation of natural phenomena in the state of *kuan* or empty-minded contemplation. The empty mind, also called "the uncarved block" or "perfect mirror," reflects the world as it is, without the distortion of intellectual bias or opinion.

The Taoist scientific philosophy of responding to nature, and the Taoist method of *kuan*, or empty-minded contemplation, provide an alternative vision of science as valid as the Western approach. Where Western science has been used as a tool to dominate and control nature, Taoist science sought accord, to "follow the way of nature." Where the Taoist method prefers knowledge gleaned from the passive, or intuitive, intelligence, the Western scientific method prefers that gained by the active intelligence—compilation, analysis, and reason.

Today, we need not make a choice with respect to method; indeed, both methods have already made significant contributions to ancient and modern science.[20] Albert Einstein, arguably the greatest scientist of the twentieth century, was a self-professed "intuitive" scientist whose love of nature lead him to certain elegant (which is to say "simple") principles. He was more than content to let others do what he called "the detail work" of experimentation and analysis. On the other hand, with respect to the motive for science, clearly that put forth by Bacon and Descartes (dominance and control) must be recognized—in the era of the nuclear bomb, massive environmental degradation, and commercial exploitation—as hopelessly obsolete.

道 The Tao of the Ten Thousand Things and Abundance

Having examined the appearance of the thing,
one seizes upon its essence. —CHING HAO

In an attempt to be scientific in its approach, modern economics has sought to define abundance in terms of quantifiable sums that can be readily subjected to analysis and projection and thus form the basis of rational decisions—those made in terms of the proverbial bottom line. This has given us a distorted view of wealth and abundance. One who makes decisions and takes actions solely on the basis of "sound economics" blinds himself to the impact that these decisions and actions have on human life and happiness. What is good from the standpoint of the bottom line doesn't necessarily promote real abundance. In fact, because of the artificiality of the economic standard, as often as not, these two are in conflict. The Taoists offer an alternative view of abundance, one that values maintaining human dignity above acquiring social position, and values the free use of time over the acquisition of money in measuring quality of life. In chapters 5 and 7, these themes will be explored in greater depth.

The spiritual is not something that descends from above, rather it is an illumination that is to be discovered within.

AJIT MOOKERJEE

Embracing the Tao of the Ten Thousand Things moves us out of an adversarial relationship with nature, allowing us to tap into the love and spontaneity that is the source of human creativity. Moving in accord with nature is first and foremost a matter of recognizing the human nature we all share, as well as our unique capacities as individuals. When we embrace our unique gifts and capacities as individuals and put them into expression, the road to true abundance opens before us. As we give our gifts, we receive in time the compensation we are due. Moreover, we experience the greatest feeling of abundance there is—that which comes with being who we are. Perhaps the greatest poverty of all is to go through life feeling as though we have never expressed or given what we have come to this earth to give and express. The Taoists were not so much interested in explaining why things work as they were interested in discovering what *does* work and how things relate to one another. Later chapters will consider some of the very practical insights of Taoist science, and how we can apply these in our own lives.

 The Social Tao,

the Way of Humanity

I take no action and people are reformed.
I enjoy peace and people become honest.
I use no force and people become rich.

—Lao Tzu

The term *Tao* is also used to indicate a pedagogy, a way for human beings to live in accord with the way of the Universe. While this use of *Tao* is perhaps more closely identified with the Confucians, the classical Taoists also had much to say about the Way of Humanity. At the level of human affairs, there is a way for people to act that is in accord with the Tao, and there is a way for people to act that is not. In saying this, we recognize that everyone, no matter how he or she thinks or acts, is living in and by the Tao. Whether we recognize it or not, we are a part of the transcendent eternal mystery. You and I, along with everyone and everything else, have arisen from the One source of the universe; we are therefore one in essence with everything (and not separate or different from anything). The world we live in, including our human bodies, are animated by Tao, and each of us expresses the Tao according to the organic pattern of our lives. The Tao of Humanity, then, is simply a matter of living in the consciousness of Tao.

Among the Taoist writings, the *Tao Te Ching* is especially concerned with political philosophy. The *Tao Te Ching* suggests that the ideal political system is one in which those in authority avoid, as much as possible, interference in the lives of ordinary people. Rulers are admonished to govern a country as one "cooks a small fish," which is to say, to rule with an extremely light touch.

The Taoist concern for political economy presents an apparent contradiction, one which many Western interpreters have had a difficult time reconciling. They note the logical inconsistency of a philosophy that, on the one hand, eschews moralistic comparisons and assertions and, on the other, advocates a political ideal and clearly condemns those who violate it. The *Tao Te Ching* instructs that it is only after the Tao has been lost that we have concern for "goodness" and "righteousness." The previously mentioned core concept of unity-in-opposites clearly demonstrates the folly of insisting on the good over the bad or in asserting a "right" over a "wrong."

Yet in the *Tao Te Ching*, we also find statements such as: "The people are hungry because the rulers devour too much in taxes. The court is corrupt, the fields are overgrown with weeds. The granaries are empty, yet there are those dressed in finery with swords at their sides, their bellies are filled with food and drink." This is but a small sampling of the moralistic commendations throughout the *Tao Te Ching*. In the *Chuang Tzu*, Man Kou-Tê is given to say, "The shameless become rich, and good talkers become high officials. . . . Small robbers are put in prison, but great robbers become feudal lords, and there in the gates of the feudal lords will your righteous scholars be found."[21]

Why do the Taoists descend from the rarified air of identity-in-all-things and unity-in-opposites to offer a political ideal or to condemn the misuse of power? This apparent contradiction is resolved by keeping in mind the various dimensions of consciousness referred to above. At each of these levels—different principles apply, and yet within the awakened individual, they are all subsumed in a holistic integrity. If we say that to act in this manner is to act in the way of the Tao, or that to act in that manner is to act in the way inconsistent with the Tao—without recognition or experience of the other levels—we have only ethical judgments. In this case, we have

I go on working for the same reason that a hen goes on laying eggs.

H. L. MENCKEN

first (to borrow a metaphor from a different tradition) to remove the log from our own eyes before we concern ourselves with the mote in our brother's. The log is, of course, the separative ego.

On the other hand, the enlightened individual cannot ignore the political, economic, and social levels of human life. His interest in these matters is a natural outgrowth of his innate compassion, what the Taoists refer to as *Tzu*, the Great Sympathy. It is precisely because the Tao has been lost (i.e., most people do not live in consciousness of it) that there is a need for an interest in politics, economics, and the social order. Early Taoists, including the author (or authors) of the *Tao Te Ching*, clearly had such an interest. While they were adverse to ethical rules and regulations, there is implicit in the Taoist approach a kind of natural ethics. The origin and effect of this kind of ethics, Albert Schweitzer describes below:

> Ethics is born of physical life, out of the linking of life with life. It is therefore the result of our recognizing the solidarity of life which nature gives us. And as it grows more profound, it teaches us sympathy with all of life . . . This material-born ethic becomes engraved upon our hearts, and culminates in spiritual union and harmony with the creative Will which is in and through all.[22]

If the classical Taoists were in fact interested in the social order of their day, why does the image of the Taoist as a reclusive hermit persist in popular imagination? The standard textbook description of Chinese philosophy has the Confucians interested in society and its future, and the Taoists rejecting society and seeking refuge in nature and in mystical contemplation. This makes an easy and tidy division for purposes of comparison, even if it doesn't quite fit the facts. The oft-recounted refusal of Chuang Tzu to accept government service and the later tradition of eremitism are often cited as evidence of Taoist indifference to the life of society. To properly address this question, we must understand something of the broader context of the existing social order, as well as the particular historical context of the time.

First, not only in China, but throughout the civilized as well as the "primitive" or nonliterate cultures, there was a long tradition of the spiritual seers playing the role of advisors to the political leaders. The political authorities, in turn, were expected to seek and accept the counsel of the spiritual leaders. The typical pattern in nonliterate cultures was for the village chief or warrior leader to be advised by one or more shamans. We find this pattern appearing again with the priesthood of ancient Egypt and the Chaldean astrologers advising the pharaohs and kings. In the European tradition, we have the legend of King Arthur receiving counsel from the wizard Merlin. We know that Alexander the Great was a student of the sage philosopher Aristotle, and that Brahman priests advised the rulers of India.

There is ample literary evidence that political leaders also accepted the advice of sages and prophets—individuals who, while not members of any official priesthood, were recognized for their spiritual power, or what the Taoists call *"Te."* Alexander recognized the spiritual power of Diogenes; Rama's father King Dasaratha, that of Viswamitra; and the biblical Saul (at least at times), that of Samuel. Yet throughout this relationship, whether it was based on the psychic abilities of the shaman, the official authority of the priest, or the spiritual power, or *Te*, of the sage, there remained a clear separation of "church" and state. In many cultures, spiritual leaders were explicitly barred from accepting positions of political authority. In others, the separation was a matter of long-standing custom.

It is in this context that we should view Chuang Tzu's refusal to accept government service. Nevertheless, the early Taoists were interested in the social order, though they were not, as the Confucians were wont to do, ready to assume a role in government. (Though, like Chuang Tzu, Confucius himself refused government service.) This was in keeping with prevailing tradition. Lao Tzu and Chuang Tzu lived in a period of great political, economic, and social turmoil known as the era of the "Warring States." China had only recently abandoned matriarchal Neolithic collectivism in favor of the patriarchal feudal state. Lao Tzu recognized many problems with the new system and was not above offering advice to the political leadership of the day. Joseph Needham argues that it was only after they were effectively locked out of political influence by Confucian and feudal interests that the Taoists retreated into eremitism.

Within the *Tao Te Ching*, statements concerning the political economy are addressed, not to the masses, but to the ruling elite. The *Tao Te Ching* is not alone in recognizing a greater responsibility for those who accept political authority or who have achieved some measure of spiritual enlightenment. The New Testament Christ, who urged us to "love thine enemies," "not to cast the first stone," "to forgive forty-nine times," "to turn the other cheek," etc., had very harsh words indeed (e.g., "vipers," "serpents," "hypocrites") for the religious authorities of the day whom he perceived as

To be selfless is to be all-pervading.
To be all-pervading is to be transcendent.

LAO TZU

leading people astray. Those who accept political or spiritual authority are apparently to be held to a higher standard than the great mass of people.

Sages and wise political leaders seek to establish a social order that encourages the enlightenment of individuals who are so inclined, and one that brings the greatest possible happiness and least possible suffering to the people as a whole. Those who have no interest in, or aptitude for, more advanced spiritual practice ought to be allowed, as much as possible, to follow their own natures and fulfill their own destinies. Interference in the lives of ordinary people from those in political or economic authority ought to be kept to an absolute minimum. In this way, the people remain close to the Tao in spirit, even if they have never heard the word *Tao*. The Taoists offer concrete recommendations for a society organized around these principles. Later chapters will explore these themes.

道 The Social Tao and Abundance

The sage has no mind of his own.
He is aware of the needs of others.
—LAO TZU

True abundance takes into account the commonwealth, that is, the well-being of the entire society. The Taoists recognize that no one person can find true abundance at the expense of others. Attaining wealth without regard to the means employed—or hoarding up riches behind walls or security fences—have nothing to do with real abundance. Being defined by the Self and not the ego, genuine abundance is expansive and inclusive. Implicit in the Tao of Abundance are a sense of social responsibility and a commitment to social justice. The Social Tao respects the dignity and values the natural gifts of every individual, and emphasizes social harmony and cooperation. The chapters that follow will include considerations of the existing social order, its impacts on our experience of abundance, and steps we can take to deal with limiting social restrictions.

The Hand of the Tao

From the unutterable Mystery of Eternal Tao
Arises Mother Tao, shapeless source of all-that-is.
Residing within the womb of the Universe
All are interfused.
In the Great Mergence of Tao
Not-one-thing is separate or distinct.
Yet each expresses its own nature, or principle
According to the Tao of the Ten Thousand Things.
By cultivating the Tao in the affairs of humankind
The people live in harmony and real abundance.

Tao, it cannot be spoken of,
Yet every name is its own.
It is the source of all things
And yet is nothing.
It lives in everything
But few live in it.
Therefore, it is rightly called
Mystery.

INTRODUCTION

*The more you learn what to do with yourself, and the more
you do for others, the more you will enjoy the abundant life.*
—William J. H. Boetcker

Before I say anything about what this book is, I want to begin by saying
something about what it is not. This is a not a "get rich quick" or "think
your way to riches" book. You will not be admonished to "think like a
millionaire," "dress for success," or "climb the corporate ladder." You will
find no advice in this book on managing your investment portfolio or planning for your retirement. There are more than enough books of this kind
already. In this book, the emphasis will be on a deeper experience of abundance than can be realized by the mere accumulation of goods or by amass-
ing an impressive balance sheet.

To be sure, many readers will find that applying the eight principles contained in this book will, in time, bring greater material abundance into their lives. Certainly, applying these principles will assist you in opening to receive the creative ideas from which all wealth ultimately springs. Yet this increased material abundance will come not from struggling to attain it as a goal in itself, but rather as a natural by-product of experiencing a deeper state of psychological abundance. The new feeling of abundance that you enjoy within will come to be reflected in all aspects of your outer life, including your finances. Yet even if you make not one dime more, or even a few less, but come to earn your money in a way that truly reflects your nature and expresses who you are, your experience of abundance will be enhanced. Indeed, some may find that a truer experience of abundance requires that they relinquish their attachment to social status or excessive material consumption.

Real abundance is about so much more than money. A "healthy bottom line" does not equate with a healthy and abundant state of mind. Evidence of the psychological and spiritual poverty of the rich and famous fills our newspapers, magazines, tabloids, and television programs and hardly needs repeating here. Suffice to say that many who own great stockpiles of material possessions, and who are, to all outer appearances, extremely wealthy individuals, do not enjoy real abundance. They are never content with what they have, and live in fear of losing it. Clearly, real abundance must be something more than having a lot of money and things. But then how do we approach it?

The fundamental premise of this book is that the universe is you and is for you. If you put yourself in accord with the way of the universe, it will take care of you abundantly. To experience this abundance, there is nothing you need do first. It is not necessary for you to earn one more dollar, get a better job, buy a new home or car, or go back to school. All that is required is that you become aware of the inner process through which you create an experience of lack and struggle in your life, and refrain from doing it. Feelings of abundance and gratitude are natural to the human being; they do not need to be added or put on. We have only to become aware of how we are resisting and inhibiting this natural state.

Throughout this book, you will be asked to accept responsibility for creating your own experience of abundance or lack. Of course, no individual operates in a vacuum. It would be absurd to deny the impact that the values and organization of the broader society have on us as individuals. In an effort to secure the ever-expanding productivity and consumption upon which its "health" depends, modern commercial culture vigorously promotes a "lack consciousness." We buy things we don't need (or even want), because we have become convinced that we will be somehow lacking or inferior without them. We do work we don't want to do, because we have become convinced that there is a scarcity of good jobs and that we can't create our own work. Thus, even while we amass more and more stuff, the feeling of abundance keeps eluding us. In addition to the role that the values of the broader society have in promoting a psychology of lack within the individual, the current organization of society poses institutional barriers to his or her creative development and financial independence.

Nevertheless, ultimate responsibility for the individual's experience lies with the individual, not with the culture into which he or she has been born. Awareness of the broader social dynamics that promote a consciousness of lack, as well as the inner ego drives that bind us to them, empowers us to break, once and for all, the chains of psychological poverty and lack. This book will address the root causes of the psychology of lack, and how these can be overcome.

Ultimately, *the system* is the ego. Freeing ourselves from the dominance and control of this system will be our primary concern. What we see reflected in the broader social and economic system—alienation, attachment, struggle, resentment, craving for approval, competitive hostility, pride, greed, and chaos—originate within the ego. We *are* the system, or, as J. Krishnamurti put it, long before the popular song: "We are the world." This book will contrast the way of the Tao with the way of the ego. The way of the ego necessarily produces a psychology of lack—one that cannot be overcome, regardless of the quantity of money or goods we accumulate. Alternatively, the way of the Tao naturally yields a feeling of abundance, regardless of how great or meager our accumulation of money and goods may be. Though he was often without money, and at times even food, William Blake's poetry exudes abundance. As he put it:

I have mental joys and mental health,
Mental friends and mental wealth,
I've a wife that I love and that loves me;
I've all but riches bodily.

This is not to say that we should reject material wealth or shun the blessings that come with it. With money, much good can be done and much unnecessary suffering avoided or eliminated. Moreover, in the culture we live in today, time is money and money is power. It takes time to appreciate and enjoy life and all of its simple beauties. It takes time to stop and listen to the voice of our true selves. It takes time to develop our gifts and talents. It takes time to learn and grow. It takes time to develop and nurture meaningful relationships. And in making time for all of these, money is a great help.

Money can also give us a measure of freedom from the control of others and in this respect is more important today than ever. Throughout most of human history, one did not need money to live, that is, for the basic necessities of life. For one unable or unwilling to fit into society's mold, there was always the option of retreating to some remote place and subsisting on the land—an option that isn't really feasible today.

The Taoist values freedom and preserving the dignity of the human spirit, and in this respect, would not object to Humphrey Bogart's assertion that "the only point in making money is, you can tell some big shot where to go." The idea here is not to express (or harbor) hostility toward others but to affirm and follow your own path, free from intimidation or the control of others. The big shot might be a boss for whom you do soul-draining, monotonous work—or a landlord or mortgage-holding bank, whom you must pay for the privilege of a little peace and quiet. In as much as money is an important factor in determining the time we have to enjoy life and the power and freedom we have in it, the pursuit of money is a worthy goal. On the other hand, if we are looking to money to fulfill or satisfy us, we are sure to be disappointed.

In lacking money, we too often think a lack of money is our only problem. Money can give us the time to appreciate the simple things in life more fully, but not the spirit of innocence and wonder necessary to do so. Money can give us the time to develop our gifts and talents, but not the courage and discipline to do so. Money can give us the power to make a difference in the lives of others, but not the desire to do so. Money can give us the time to develop and nurture our relationships, but not the love and caring necessary to do so. Money can just as easily make us more jaded, escapist, selfish, and lonely. In short, money can help to free or enslave us, depending on why we want it and what we do with it. In this respect, nothing has changed in the two thousand years since Horace wrote, "Riches either serve or govern the possessor."

Money is a relatively simple issue. There are only two important questions: (1) How much do you need? (2) What is it going to cost you to get it? It is keeping these two questions in mind that gives us a true sense of money's relationship to abundance. If we have less than what we need, or if what we have is costing us too much—in either case, our experience of abundance will be incomplete. As things stand in the modern world, you need money to eat, sleep, dress, work, play, relate, heal, move about, and keep the government off your back. In what style you choose to do each of these will determine how much money you need, that is, your lifestyle. Remember in choosing your style that it comes with a price tag. How much money it costs is not the issue, but how much the money costs *you* is of critical importance. Keep in mind:

Money should not cost you your soul.
Money should not cost you your relationships.
Money should not cost you your dignity.
Money should not cost you your health.
Money should not cost you your intelligence.
Money should not cost you your joy.

When it comes to determining how much you need, there are two important catagories to keep in mind. First, there are the material things you need to keep body and soul together. Second are the areas of "need" related to social status and position. With both, you have a great deal of discretion. The ancient Taoist masters were keenly aware of the cost of money and were particularly skeptical of the cost of attaining social status and position. In the *Lieh Tzu,* Yang Chu says:

[People] realize happiness is not simply having their material needs met. Thus, society has set up a system of rewards that go beyond material goods. These include titles, social recognition, status, and political power, all wrapped up in a package called self-fulfillment. Attracted by these prizes and goaded on by social pressure, people spend their short lives tiring mind and body to chase after these goals. Perhaps this gives them the feeling that they have achieved something in their lives, but in reality they have sacrificed a lot in life. They can no longer see, hear, act, feel, or think from their hearts. Everything they do is dictated by whether it can get them social gains. In the end, they've spent their lives follow-

ing other people's demands and never lived a life of their own. How different is this from the life of a prisoner or slave? . . .

In the short time we are here, we should listen to our own voices and follow our own hearts. Why not be free and live your own life? Why follow other people's rules and live to please others?

Why, indeed? In a recent study, 48 percent of the male corporate executives surveyed admitted that they felt their lives were empty and meaningless. When one considers the cultural taboos against such an admission, the figure is surprisingly high and leads one to conclude that the real number must be higher still. Yet these are the ones who have the money and status so many others desperately crave. Napoleon Hill, who wrote the classic "success" book *Think and Grow Rich*, learned the hard way that true riches can never be equated to dollars and cents. In a later work entitled *Grow Rich! With Peace of Mind*, he described how his own obsession with money and material success had indeed made him rich but had cost him his peace of mind, health, relationships, and ultimately, even his financial fortune. He acknowledged the spiritual dimension of true and lasting prosperity and determined that in reacquiring wealth, he would keep money in its proper place as but one of the many abundances of life.

Many think they'd be happy if they had enough money to give up working altogether. Yet this is often only a reaction to the drudgery of working day after day at things they find meaningless or even absurd. In response to my previous books *Zen and the Art of Making a Living* and *How to Find the Work You Love*, I receive many communications from people about their experience of work. One day, I received a phone call from a man halfway around the world who, at forty-five, had never worked a day in his life. As a beneficiary of a sizable inheritance, he was free of the need to earn his daily bread. Yet he was not a happy man. Indeed, he was deeply troubled by the fact that so much of his life had gone by without his having expressed his own talents or made a difference in the lives of others. Like good health, spiritual growth, and nourishing relationships, meaningful work is one of the abundances of life, that we neglect at our peril. It is this kind of wholistic approach to abundance that I will be taking throughout this book.

To begin with, it's worthwhile to ask whether the world we live in is one of natural abundance or scarcity. The way we answer this question depends in large part on how we define wealth. Traditionally, economists have defined wealth in terms of scarcity. In fact, economics itself is defined as "a science concerned with choosing among alternatives involving scarce resources."[1] The first economists viewed land as the basis of wealth. While land provides sustenance and often an abundance of food to exchange for other items, there is a definite limit to the amount of land available for cultivation. Next came the mercantilists, who viewed gold and silver as the basis of wealth. Gold and silver are valuable *because* they are scarce. This conception of wealth spurred the colonial expansion of European nations, resulting in what remains to this day worldwide cultural and economic dominance by the West. Later economists viewed labor as the basis of wealth. Early industrial development required vast numbers of "cheap" laborers. Generally, the more people one employed, the richer he became. Yet there is a finite number of workers and a finite number of hours each can work. All of these definitions of "wealth" (land, gold, and labor) then are based on limited, that is, scarce resources. Now, to state the obvious, if wealth is based on owning scarce resources, a relative few can be considered wealthy.

If a man says money can do anything, that settles it: he hasn't any.

EDGAR HOWE

The noted architect, inventor, and futurist Buckminster Fuller begins with a fundamentally different definition of wealth. For Fuller, wealth equals physical energy (as matter or radiation) plus "metaphysical know-what and know-how."[2] This conception of wealth as "all energy available to planet earth and ever-growing-human-knowledge" makes us all, as Fuller puts it, "billionaires." This is so since physical energy, as we know from physics, is always in some way conserved and since the application of knowledge brings ever greater knowledge. From Fuller's conception, then, the basis of wealth is virtually infinite. We live in an abundant world.

After many years of compiling and evaluating data on global resources and technologies, Fuller concluded that "humanity can carry on handsomely and adequately when advantaged of only its daily energy income from the Sun-gravity system." In other words, there is enough for everyone to live comfortably without exhausting the earth's natural resources. (I haven't space here to examine the research on which Fuller based his conclusions, though I encourage interested readers to investigate his findings.[3]) While their approach was naturalistic and intuitive, not empirical and methodical, the Taoists arrived at essentially the same conclusion: We live in an abundant world. Their assertion that "if all things are allowed to fulfill their natures, all will be happy" assumes a natural state of abundance—one that comes from being at one with the process that is the universe.

If we live in an abundant world, if we are all, as Buckminster Fuller puts it, billionaires, why do we see so many examples of scarcity and lack? Beyond issues of economic and political control and the distribution of wealth, most people believe in and operate from a psychology of scarcity and lack. *The psychology of lack relies upon wide acceptance of the belief in physical scarcity.* To be sure, there are powerful interests that have a stake in promoting and perpetuating this view. As Fuller puts it, "With their game of making money with money, the money-makers and their economists continue to exploit the general political and religious world's assumptions that a fundamental inadequacy of human life support exists around our planet."[4] People who believe in lack are more likely to become lackeys for those who would manipulate them for their own purposes.

Whether or not we accept Fuller's findings, or even his definition of wealth, the important point here is to recognize that the way we define wealth has a great deal to do with our individual and collective experience of abundance or lack. Moreover, each of us can benefit from challenging the assumption that we live in a world of scarcity and lack. On a more immediate level, we each might ask ourselves, if we don't *already* live in abundance. Certainly, on a material level, most of us enjoy an abundance unprecedented in human history. Think about all you have and enjoy. First and foremost, you have your life. I'm willing to guess that you have enough to eat, ample clothing, and a place to sleep, out of the elements. Beyond the basics, the average middle-class person in the developed world has a higher standard of living than the kings and queens of earlier eras enjoyed. We have running water and indoor toilets; we have central heat and air conditioning, and refrigeration. We eat exotic foods from all over the world. In the dead of winter in New York city, one can enjoy bananas and other tropical foods, something even Queen Elizabeth I would have been unable to do. In addition, we have means of communication and transportation that would have seemed fantastic even a century ago. Through most of their time on this planet, the life expectancy of *homo sapiens* was about forty years. Today, a good many will live twice that long.

Regardless of the *facts* of abundance on an individual or planetary level, for many, a *feeling* of lack persists. To be sure, the psychological factor is critical in determining our experience of abundance or lack. Even hardheaded economists recognize the psychological component to wealth creation and valuation. When economists use terms such as "consumer confidence" or "investor confidence," they are recognizing the importance of the psychological dimension in economic life. In the fluctuations of the stock markets or in the individual valuation of a particular company, psychological factors often play a significant role. The perception of, or belief in, the strength or weakness of a given market or company may override the "economic fundamentals" in the determination of value. Even the paper money we use—backed as it is by absolutely nothing—depends on our collective belief in it. If believing in the reality of planetary and individual abundance is an act of faith, it is certainly no less an act of faith than believing in the real value of the paper money we use everyday.

Because the psychological dimension is so important to our experience of abundance, this book will address it at length. The Taoist principles examined here will provide powerful keys to embracing and integrating a psychology of abundance. In the first two chapters, a groundwork will be laid for overcoming the sense of alienation and separation that are the underpinnings of a psychology of lack. Again, for most of us, the feeling of lack is not a result of a lack of things or material stuff. It is a sense of struggle and a lack of ease; a lack of energy; a feeling of powerlessness and blocked expression; a lack of harmony and connection in relationship; a lack of time to be, grow, and relate; and a lack of opportunity to fully appreciate and celebrate the beauty in life—that give a sense of deficiency to our existence. Each of these "lacks" will be considered respectively in chapters 3 through 8, both in terms of understanding their causes, and in terms of practical suggestions for creating greater abundance in each of these areas. The exercises at the end of the book will help you to integrate and apply the information you encounter in the text.

The Eight Principles of Abundant Living: The dynamics of the psychology of lack go like this: Simultaneous to the formation of the individual ego there arises a profound sense of lack, a feeling of *separation* from everything else in life. This sense of separation brings a feeling of contraction and a sense of incompleteness, which we try to mitigate through mental, physical, and emotional *attachments*. The perceived need to defend and expand our attachments, in turn, creates a feeling of *struggle*. Struggle brings *resentment,* ingratitude, and withholding, which rob us of joy and keep the energy from flowing freely in our lives. This leads us away from the path of our inborn destinies. Instead of following our own paths, we *crave the approval* and attention of others. This craving for approval, in turn, produces *competitive hostility* and envy. Envy, in turn, provokes *greed,* which agitates our minds and sends us on the mad chase that today we call the "rat race." In the process, we lose the ability to appreciate the simple enjoyments that come with leisure. Ultimately, this leads to a sense of *chaos* and confusion that obfuscates our innate intelligence and robs us of our capacity to appreciate the beauty in life.

On the other hand, a psychology of abundance flows naturally from the Tao, the way of life. Moving from the *unity* of the *Tao*, from the experience of oneness with all of life, we receive the *natural* abundance of the universe with *ease* in a spirit of gratitude and joy. Thus, the energy *flows* freely in our lives, and we fulfill our innate destinies. Recognizing the innate *power* and dignity of all of life, we live in *harmony* with it and its natural cycles. Respecting our humanity above any outer goal or reward, we cultivate the sense of *leisure* and peace necessary to appreciate the *beauty* and order inherent in life, and thus, allow it to express itself through us in all we do. (For more on the eight principles and their counterpoints, see the highlights at the end of this introductory chapter.)

In addition to the inner or psychological dimension, *The Tao of Abundance* will address some of the social and economic factors that contribute to an individual and collective experience of lack, and offer suggestions for how we can mitigate these effects in our own lives. This book purports to apply ancient wisdom to modern times, and in this, the modern times are as important as the ancient wisdom. I have no interest in spouting spiritual platitudes divorced from the social and economic context in which we live today. Rather, I will attempt to apply ancient, really, universal, principles to the situation we find ourselves in at the beginning of the twenty-first century. The classical Taoists were keen social observers. Lao Tzu, in particular, often had harsh words for those individuals and systems that oppress people or lead them away from their true natures and thus from the fulfillment of their inborn destinies. In the spirit of this tradition, I will address social and economic factors that contribute to a mass psychology of lack, as well as institutional barriers that limit the natural creative development of individuals.

You may reject the values of the broader society; you may even be actively working to transform them. Still, you needn't make your own experience of abundance contingent on that change. To view the economic system as an enemy that must be overcome before you can prosper and be happy is to put yourself in a position of powerlessness, frustration, and resentment. While there is a place for collective action, in this book, the emphasis will be on what we as individuals can do to enhance our own experience of wealth and well-being within the system as it now exists. By becoming living examples of genuine abundance in our own lives, we participate in the transformation of the broader culture. While no individual can single-handedly change the global economic system, each of us can transform our own experience of abundance. Where once we saw lack, debt, and conflict, we can begin to see gifts, opportunities, and mutual support. We can each, in our own way, challenge the widespread belief that we live in a world of lack.

By now, you're probably getting the idea that what I mean by the "Tao of Abundance" is something altogether different from the Dow Jones version of abundance. The Tao of Abundance is more wholistic in its scope, addressing the entire issue of quality of life, and not simply financial goals. It assumes an innate order in life, one that we as individuals realize as we fulfill our inborn destinies. It further assumes that the world we live in, the world we grow out of, is an abundant one.

Now, if in fact, we live in an abundant world, there are three primary tasks for us on the journey to a life of total abundance. The first task is to recognize the inner and outer forces that conspire to make us believe in scarcity and thus to feel lack. Awareness of these factors will help us to overcome their influence over us. The second task is to cultivate a spirit of abundance in our lives, celebrating the gift of life with joy and thanksgiving. As we focus in our thoughts and actions on things that bring a feeling of connection with all life, we begin to move with the flow of the Tao. In this way, we allow blessings to come to us as a part of the "overflow" of an abundant spirit—not as things we crave and struggle for from a sense of lack or desperation. To come from lack can only bring lack, even when we get what we think we need. On the other hand, when we come from the spirit of abundance, we attract ever greater abundance.

Finally, as we move in the world from the spirit of abundance, we become a liberating and empowering force in the lives of those we interact with. We help them see, not by preaching, but by example, that we all live in an abundant world and that they as well can free themselves from lack consciousness. Together, we can unite in a spirit of abundance and create new patterns of community and social organization, new lifestyles, and new ways of relating, based on cooperation rather than competition. As envy, greed, and competition flow from lack, so do compassion, service, and cooperation flow from a spirit of abundance. It is this spirit of abundance that will be our guide as we embark on the journey to creating total abundance in our lives.

The Eight Principles
of Abundant Living

The principles of abundance are stated in English. The corresponding Chinese term is often not, nor is it intended to be, a direct translation of the principle as expressed in English. Rather, the Chinese terms give the essence or active ingredient of the principle. For example, when I use yin/yang in correspondence with the harmony of abundance, I do not mean that yin/yang literally translates as "harmony." Rather, I mean that an awareness and understanding of yin/yang dynamics will help us to find greater harmony in our own lives.

Principle 1   The Nameless Tao   *Wu-ming*   Recognizing the unity of all things starts you on the path to true abundance.

Principle 2   Nature   *Tzu-jan*   Learning to receive opens the door to your greatest good.

Principle 3   Ease   *Wu-wei*   Following the path of least resistance brings success with ease.

Principle 4   Flow   *Ch'i*   Circulating the energy in your life strengthens health, deepens relationships, and generates wealth.

Principle 5   Power   *Te*   Honoring your innate dignity and actualizing your inborn abilities is the road to authentic power.

Principle 6   Harmony   *Yin/Yang*   Balancing yin and yang eliminates stress and brings peace of mind.

Principle 7   Leisure   *Jen*   Taking time to be, to grow, and to nurture your relationships gives you the strength to persevere.

Principle 8   Beauty   *Li*   Achieving your destiny is a matter of trusting and embracing the organic pattern of your life.

The Way of the Tao

Throughout this book, a contrast will be made between the Way of the Tao and the Way of the Ego.

THE WAY OF THE TAO	THE WAY OF THE EGO
1. The Unity of the Nameless Tao	The Separation of the Ego (lack of connection, alienation)
2. The Nature/Receptivity of the Tao	The Attachments of the Ego (lack of spontaneity and inspiration)
3. The Ease of the Tao	The Struggle of the Ego (lack of ease—tension, stress)
4. The Flow/Joy of the Tao	The Resentment of the Ego (lack of energy and zest for life)
5. The Power/Dignity of the Tao	The Craving for Approval of the Ego (lack of power and inner direction)
6. The Harmony of the Tao	The Competitive Hostility (Envy) of the Ego (lack of inner and outer peace and harmony)
7. The Leisure of the Tao	The Greed of the Ego (lack of time and rest)
8. The Beauty of the Tao	The Chaos of the Ego (lack of meaning, nihilism)

CHAPTER ONE

Wu-ming

The Unity of the Tao

Wealth is not only what you have but it is also what you are.
                                        —Sterling W. Still

Abundance has been defined in a variety of ways, by different people at different times and in different cultures. This chapter explores how we can enjoy the deep experience of abundance that comes with trusting in and moving with the flow of the Tao. It is based on the realization of our essential oneness with all things. The ego's insistence on separation cuts us off from our natural state of abundance. We become committed to the idea of ownership and so, to the feeling of being owed and owned. As a result, we are haunted by a profound sense of lack, even as we acquire more material things. This chapter explores how we can break this cycle once and for all. You'll discover how you can learn to use and enjoy all the things of this world without getting trapped in the lack-inducing feeling of possession. You'll also have the opportunity to examine your motivation for wanting more. This awareness will help insure that your efforts will bring you greater real abundance—not simply more stuff. In the related exercises at the end of the book, you will have the opportunity to define your own vision of abundance and begin charting a path toward realizing it.

Today, we typically measure abundance in terms of the money and objects we possess. We think that those who possess the most are the most free and powerful individuals and that they therefore enjoy the most abundant lifestyle. Yet for Plato, Aristotle, and the Roman Stoic philosophers, the most free and powerful individuals were those who could be happy with the fewest things. While our culture values those who earn and hoard the most, among certain tribes in New Guinea, the most valued members of society were those who gave away the most. Apart from the material side of abundance, we can have an abundance of ideas, of friends, of energy, and of courage—or feel a sense of lack in any of these areas.

In the end, we could say that *abundance is the feeling of enough and to spare.* Well, all right, but how much is enough? Does a man with a "net worth" in the millions, whose mood fluctuates with the stock market and who feels himself to be lacking relative to his country club companions, experience abundance? What about a "primitive" in the rainforests of the Amazon who, with the simplest of technologies and a leaky temporary hut for a shelter, feels himself blessed by the bounty of the forest? Clearly, having no quantifiable frame of reference, abundance is a state of mind, or more precisely, of being.

In attempting to define abundance, a look at the origin of the word itself as well as those of other terms we associate with wealth and prosperity will help. The word *abundance* is derived from the Latin *abundāre,* meaning "to overflow." *Wealth* is derived from the Old English *wel* or *wela*, meaning "well" or "well-being." Well is to wealth, as heal is to health. The word *prosperity* is derived from the Latin *prosperāre,* meaning "to render fortunate." *Rich* comes from the Old English *rice,* meaning "strong," "powerful." While today we associate all these terms almost exclusively with money and material gain, in their origins all had meanings that address quality of life in broader terms.

To live in abundance is to be fully alive, free of any sense of lack or desperation. The following little story gives the essence of abundance. A man leaves the remote peasant village of his birth and travels the wide world. After many years, he returns home. His friends, relatives, and neighbors gather round him and ask, "How is life in the world?" He replies, "Same as here. It is good for those who know how to live."

The art of abundance is not the art of making money, but the art of knowing how to live. Is abundance, then, simply a matter of recognizing, appreciating, and celebrating life as it is? Ultimately, yes, but we must in the same breath acknowledge that this is not something we can do by any inner coercion or force of will. It is not a matter of positive thinking or of telling ourselves that we *should* be grateful and have a good attitude. It is a matter of trust, which only comes with understanding and experience.

On every American dollar bill, we read the words "In God We Trust." Yet is it God that we trust as the source of our supply and experience of abundance? Or do we trust the economy, the stock market, our employer, or our current net worth for our feeling of abundance or lack? The Taoist would tell us to trust, not in a personal god as conceived in the West, nor in the machinery of the economy, but in the Tao, the innate intelligence of the universe.

To be sure, trusting the Tao as the source of our abundance will give us a fundamentally different experience of the world than seeing the source of our supply in the economy, the employer, the government, or even in our own efforts. But we are naturally and rightfully skeptical. Trusting the Tao may have been fine for people living a simple agrarian lifestyle two thousand years ago. Yet is it possible that we can learn to trust the Tao in the highly commercial and technologically complex society in which we live today? Can we, as Lao Tzu put it, grasp "the Tao that was of old" and in so doing "master the present era of private property"?[1]

By grasping the Tao that was of old, you can master the present era of private property.

LAO TZU

無名 Trusting the Tao; or, Swimming in What Is

All the fish needs to do is get lost in the water.
All man needs to do is get lost in the Tao.
—CHUANG TZU

Before you can learn to swim, you must first learn to float. Be it water or the natural world, you must trust the stuff you are in. If you fight against it, you are going to gasp and struggle. You may even drown. Yet when you learn to trust it, you see that the water wants to hold you up, not pull you down. In the same way, the universe wants to hold you up, not pull you under. This is not because it is nice and cares about you, but because it *is* you, in the same way that you float because you *are* water. To swim in water or the Tao, you must let go of control in order to find real control. Insisting on control from the outset will cause you to lose it.

We should also recognize that floating is not swimming. Floating is a necessary condition for swimming, but not the same thing. To swim is to move with intention, while letting the water keep you afloat. In the same way, trusting the Tao doesn't mean sitting on your rear, waiting for something to happen; it just means that in your action, you're flowing with, not fighting against, the universe. D. T. Suzuki described the experience of enlightenment as "ordinary life, two inches off the ground." This is what is meant by swimming in the Tao.

Okay, it's all well and good to say we should trust the nature, or Tao, of life. But does this mean we are to go around with rose-colored glasses on? Does trusting human nature, for example, mean that we are to trust that people are always going to be kind, considerate, sensitive, and caring in their dealings with us? Certainly not. It means that we can trust people to be people, capable of the worst greed, ignorance, cruelty, and indifference as well as the most sublime beauty, compassion, creativity, and joy. To blindly trust in the goodness of people or to cynically trust in their badness—each is equally simpleminded. We can trust people to be people and accept the totality of their (and our own) "peopleness" as basically good. Similarly, we can trust nature to be nature in the aspects we find pleasing as well as those we find disagreeable and accept that in its "natureness," it too is basically good.

Can we trust the world as it is? The only reasonable answer is yes and no. If we mean by "the world," society, with its rules and regulations, its laws and moral judgments, its obsession with money, position, and power, then, no, we can't trust the world. As Albert Schweitzer put it, "Never for a moment do we lay aside our mistrust of the ideals established by society, and of the convictions which are kept by it in circulation. We always know that society is full of folly and will deceive us in the matter of humanity. It is an unreliable horse, and blind in the bargain. Woe to the driver if he falls asleep."[2]

Yet if we mean by "the world," life and its organic processes as manifest in the natural world and our own human nature, then indeed, trust is appropriate. In fact, we have no real choice but to trust it, for we *are* it. As Lao Tzu put it, "Stop analyzing, dividing, making distinctions between one thing and another. Simply see that you are at the center of the universe, and accept all things and beings as parts of your infinite body."[3]

Who's in Charge Around Here Anyway?

The universe came into being with us together; with us, all things are one. —CHUANG TZU

Is it mere superstition or wishful thinking to trust that there is an overarching intelligence in the universe, in life itself? For many today, it is difficult to trust in God in the way that we in the West are used to thinking about God. For long centuries, we had been taught to believe in a father-figure god who was in charge of everything. Like Santa Claus, he knew everything we were doing and thinking and wrote it all down in some big book. He made the world in six days and thereafter personally decided each and every thing that happened in it. In the nineteenth century, Biblical scholars placed the date of the creation of the universe at 4004 B.C.E. Because the orthodox Western religions tenaciously held onto such literal and legalistic interpretations of their scriptures, even as scientific knowledge was expanding, faith in this God fell into disrepute, first with the intellectuals and later with the masses. Today, though most people say they *believe* in God, few are ready to *trust* Him in the way their medieval ancestors did. For all but the fundamentalist die-hards, Biblical cosmology, the notion of the Creator who made Heaven and Earth in six days, six thousand years ago is hardly believable today.

In the nineteenth and twentieth centuries, belief in a universe made and controlled by God gave way to a belief in a view of the universe as given to us by Western science. The consensus view of modern science is that the whole of the material universe is but the debris from one gigantic cosmic explosion—the big bang. (The latest estimates place the occurrence of this event at somewhere between ten and fourteen billion years ago.) Every material thing is this one stuff taking an endless variety of forms—constantly transforming itself into planets and pigeons, stars and starfish, horses and humans, crystals and computers. Astrophysicists tell us that the very atoms that comprise our bodies were generated by reactions within distant stars that were scattered across the universe when the stars later exploded. As the big bang eventually produced stars, so the birth and death of stars eventually produced the material substances that constitute our bodies.

The scientific view did away with the creator/boss, but it also did away with any sense of an intelligence and order in the universe. Life was an

If God is not within us, then God never existed.

VOLTAIRE

accident, a random, if fortunate, set of genetic mutations made possible by another random, if fortunate, set of celestial phenomena that supplied the raw materials of life. When scientists ask questions like, "Are we humans the only intelligent life in the universe?" one can hardly keep from being amused. We needn't look to sightings of little green (or gray) men, or await humankind's capacity to travel beyond the solar system for an answer. Indeed, what life is *not* intelligent? Yet, because most scientists confuse intelligence with the cerebral function, they value the thinking brain and belittle the intelligence that produced it. We are to believe that somehow dumb stuff produced intelligent life.

In the West, we have a difficult time recognizing any intelligence that is not self-assertive and willful. Scientists tell us, for instance, the birds and turtles, which migrate hundreds or thousands of miles through the air and sea, returning to the same spots to lay their eggs, are merely operating on instinct and, therefore, show no signs of intelligence. Because they do not recognize any intelligence that is not volitional, scientists likewise tend to view all mystical or intuitive knowledge as so much mumbo-jumbo. Of course, all scientists do not personally hold such views. Indeed, many of the greatest (e.g., Newton and Einstein) have recognized an intelligence at work within the structure and processes of the universe, as well as the role of intuition in scientific discovery. Nevertheless, the conventional view remains committed to the idea of life as an accident. Even more to the point, this is the view taught to young people forming their understanding of the universe.

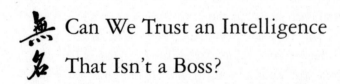

Can We Trust an Intelligence That Isn't a Boss?

It {the Tao} loves and nourishes all things but it doesn't lord it over them. —LAO TZU

Taoist cosmology fits our current scientific understanding of the origins of the universe without throwing out the baby (intelligence) with the bath water (creator/boss). To the question, "Can there be intelligence and order in the universe without a creator/boss?" the Taoist gives a resounding yes.

From the Taoist perspective, there is no Maker or Creator God. Nature (the universe) is not made, but is *tzu-jan* "of itself so." The process of the universe is not one of deliberate manufacture but of organic growth. From the Taoist perspective, everything that now exists (or ever will) came into being when the universe was "mysteriously brought into existence."[4] Everything has grown out of this One source and is latent in it. Things are not made by an outside force but expand from within. In the *Chuang Tzu,* we read, "Heaven and Earth were born at the same time I was, and the ten thousand things are one with me."[5] The universe, being without a maker, is also without a cause or a boss. No-thing has caused other things to be; all things have mutually arisen *(hsiang-shan)* and therefore mutually create and support one another.

*What is springs from
what is not.*

LAO TZU

The notion of *hsiang sheng,* or "mutual arising," is central to Taoist cosmology. For the Taoist, the world was not made by a God who stands apart from it; rather, all conditions are seen as having mutually arisen. For the Taoist, there is an overarching intelligence within the universe (the Tao), and there is a means within human beings, of accessing or becoming conscious of this intelligence, called "cultivating the Tao." (For a more complete discussion of Taoist and Western religious and scientific cosmologies, see "The Five Fingers of the Tao" at the beginning of this book.)

The Taoist would say that the way the universe works is the way we work, for we *are* the universe, temporarily taking the form of human beings. Everything has mutually arisen. I wouldn't be here if you weren't here. This book wouldn't be here if the consciousness reading it were not here. Implicit in the idea of mutual arising is the notion of interpenetration—that what happens here affects there. What I am writing now is affecting the dust on the moons of Jupiter—or is it that the winds of Venus are affecting me? Kuo Hsiang expressed it like this: "However trivial his life may be, [a man] needs the whole universe to be the condition of his existence. All things in the universe, all that exists, cannot cease to exist without having some effect on him. If one condition is lacking, he may not have existed."[6]

The Taoist would say that before the universe was, the Tao is. If the universe arose from one primal (gaseous) stuff that banged its way into various forms, that stuff arose from the Tao. Yet it was not caused or made by the Tao. If algae grows in a mountain lake, can we say the lake caused or made this algae? We can only say that conditions were such that algae arose within the lake. In the same way, the Taoist would say the universe arose from the Tao. For the Taoist, there is no First Cause because there is nothing wholly "other" or "apart" from anything else to cause it. The Tao is not the Maker so much as the Ground of Being and Non-being from which all things arise. Some things are not caused by other things—all things are related, one to the other. The Taoists call this principle *Ta T'ung*, or the Great Interfusion.

Again, the notion of an interrelated universe is one consistent with the current understanding of quantum physics. Heisenburg's uncertainty principle states that the act of observing (even the presence of the observer) changes the thing or event observed. The idea of a separate subject observing a separate object is but a mental abstraction, without reality in the world of physical events. Were our physical eyes capable of "seeing" on a subatomic level, we doubtless would be relieved of the notion that there is any such thing as a separate thing. Yet we don't have to get as complicated as this. We have simply to realize that we cannot describe any one thing without relating it to something else. For every foreground, there is a background or, to borrow a term from the visual arts, for every positive space, there is a negative space. You couldn't read these letters without the white space that surrounds the black. You couldn't hear music without the silence between the notes.

From the Taoist perspective, we could say that subject and object depend upon one another and, therefore, are but two sides of the same coin. In the same way, right and wrong, loss and gain, being and non-being, emptiness and form create one another, or better said, arise together. The Taoists call this the principle of unity-in-opposites. As Chuang Tzu wrote, "Affirmation arises from negation, and negation from affirmation. . . . The 'this' has its right and wrong and 'that' also has its right and wrong. Not to determine 'this' and 'that' as opposites is the very essence of Tao."[7]

Antagonistic or Unified Universe

The Taoist moral is that people who mistrust themselves and one another are doomed.
                                                                —ALAN WATTS

Clearly, the Tao is not to be confused with the Western "One God, Maker of Heaven and Earth." As we have said, for the Taoist, there is no Maker, and Tao is prior to one. As Ch'eng Hao put it, "The Tao has no opposite."[8] "One"

World View	Cosmological Conflict	Inner Conflict	Moral Code
Religious	God/ Devil	Spiritual/ Carnal	Saint/ Sinner
Scientific	Man/ Nature	Conscious Mind/ Unconscious Mind	Rational/ Irrational
Commercial	Market/ Barriers	Productive/ Unproductive	Rich/ Poor

is a thought that immediately suggests its opposite, that is, something which is "not-one." The One God of the orthodox Western religions spends a great deal of time fighting an evil number two: Ahura Mazda vs. Angara Mainyu, Jehovah vs. Lucifer, Allah vs. Iblis. One against not-one is the beginning of ethics, right vs. wrong, good vs. bad, sacred vs. profane, and so on.

In the Western scientific view, this antagonistic dualism of God against the devil survived as man against nature. The spiritual against the carnal became the conscious against the unconscious, and the test of virtue became not saintliness but rationality. The purpose of modern science as explicitly stated by its intellectual founding fathers (e.g., Bacon and Descartes) was to bring nature into submission. Nature must be made to serve the will of man and do his bidding, and the rational mind provides the means of doing so.

Yet it would be a mistake to think that the dominant world-view today is the one given to us by science. For all the lip service we pay to science, everyone knows that is it commerce that runs the show. As the Spanish proverb goes, "He who gives the bread lays down the law." Science today typically serves the large corporate commercial interests that fund it. In a world conceived by the financial and corporate leadership who effectively rule it, the purpose of the human being is to contribute to the economy as an increasingly efficient unit of production and as an increasingly efficient unit of consumption. The financial and corporate elite establish effective social policy, and commercially funded science gives them the technological wherewithal to execute it.

The world today is viewed as a battleground—not between God and the devil, but between the rational, efficient Market and the irrational, ineffi-

COSMOLOGIES

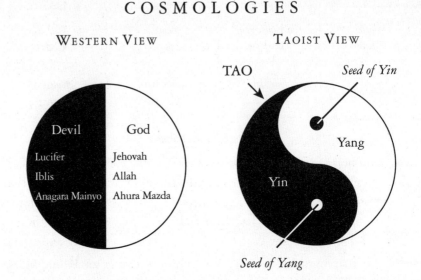

WESTERN VIEW   TAOIST VIEW

cient, market barriers. The productive, i.e., economically profitable (good) must overcome the unproductive, unprofitable (bad). As a result, mountains and oceans are viewed as little more than storehouses of mineral "natural resources," awaiting ever more efficient exploitation or, alternatively, as dumping grounds for the residues of production. Animals become "food resources" to be genetically and hormonally "enhanced" and efficiently housed and fed in factory farms and feedlots before being "harvested" in giant "processing plants." Thanks to "scientific management," human beings have become "human resources" to be manipulated into ever greater productivity with the aid of the new science of organizational psychology. With the science of applied psychology, they can as well be manipulated into ever greater consumption.

Today, the most valued members of society are not the most saintly, nor the most rational or intellectually developed, but the richest. We are told by the commercial media (even if not in so many words) that we are to cheer news reports of increased productivity and consumption, accepting these as unqualified social gains. Yet the Taoist would tell us that the "this" (increased production) has its good and bad, and that the "that" (increased consumption) also has its good and bad.

For the Taoist, the dual, or sexual, character of the universe is recognized in the concept of yin/yang. Yet these are seen as complementary, not antagonistic forces. Moreover, there is no sense that one of these is all good and the other, all bad. They are not rightly conceived of as opposites, for each contains the seed of the other within itself. Neither are these static forces; yin in time transforms itself into yang; yang, into yin. The interplay of these two forces exists within the Tao. The Tao has no devil to defeat, no enemy it must destroy. Being the ground of nature, it is not opposed to it. All things have arisen mutually and are mutually supportive, in the sense that they require one another as a condition of their existence. The man requires the woman; the woman, the man; the night requires the day; the day, the night; the good, the bad; the bad, the good, and so on.

No genuine Taoist would think of asking, "Why does God (or the Tao) let bad things happen?" or even more to the point, "Why does God (or the Tao) let bad things happen to 'good' people?" The Taoist accepts along with the Greek philosopher Heraclitus that "to God (the Tao), all things are fair and good and right, but men hold some things wrong and some right." The agency of our ethical judgments is, of course, thought. As Shakespeare put it, "Nothing is good or bad but thinking makes it so."[9]

Perhaps now we are beginning to get some sense of what we mean by trusting the Tao—or rather what we don't mean. We are not talking about trusting in a creator/boss, nor in the powers of the rational mind, nor in the market system. We are talking about trusting what is, the innate intelligence within all life. The whole thing comes down to this: Is the Universe for you or against you?—a point that will be developed at length in chapter 3.

無 The Separation of the Ego;
名 or, Why It Cannot Trust the Tao

The perfect man has no self, because he has transcended the finite and identified himself with the universe. —CHUANG TZU

Now if the Taoists are right and there is innate intelligence in life, Tao, why do we feel separate from it? Our original experience of separation, the first separate thing in our world is, of course, ourselves—that is, our egos. In fact, the ego can be defined as the propensity to separate or differentiate consciousness. While we may, with the aid of Taoist philosophy or quantum mechanics, understand that we live in a world without boundary or separation, in our daily lives, the limits of our physical senses and the conventions of thought give us an experience of a world of sharp lines and hard boundaries, a world of separate things and events. We may conceptually recognize the unity of all things, yet our actual experience of life comes to us through the separating filter of the ego.

We are told by developmental psychologists that the newborn baby experiences an undifferentiated consciousness—having no sense of a boundary between what is "me" and what is "not me," between what is "mine" and "not-mine." The sense of an individual ego or separate "I" is a learned response, acquired within the first several months during which the child comes to respond to his or her own name. Having once established an "I" ego, the child begins to experience the world through the separating forms of time and space. Now, here can be distinguished from there, you from me, now from then, and so on.

When we began responding to a given name (a Bill or Susie), we started the process of associating memories and characteristics with that name. We moved from an undifferentiated consciousness to a selective one, paying particular attention to memories, characteristics, and objects associated with that name. In time, we came to believe that we *were* the name and, by extension, the memories, characteristics, and objects associated with it. The sound of one's own name has a kind of hypnotizing effect upon the psyche, as do the personal pronouns I, me, my, mine. These conjure up associated memories of pleasure and pain. The English poet Alfred Lord Tennyson described a profound mystical experience, which he realized through the simple process of repeating his own given name. By continually repeating his name, he broke its spell and returned, if only momentarily, to a more expansive, undifferentiated consciousness.

The Tao is said to be *wu ming,* nameless, a unity without separation or differentiation. As Lao Tzu put it, "The Tao that can be named is not the true name."[10] We rely on name to build the illusion of separation. William James said, *"The word 'I' is really a position like 'this' or 'here.'"* Okay, but where is it? Is "I" my body? If it is, then "I" digest my food, "I" beat my heart, "I" make red blood cells, and "I" do all the other things the body does. Yet we don't typically think of it like this. We don't think "I am the body"; we think "I have a body." We think "I am somewhere inside my brain." Yet "I" can't be the whole brain, for most of it is busy with all of these involuntary processes "I" am not aware of or in control of. So for us, "I" is a portion of the brain. Everything else, even the rest of "my" body, is "other." Having defined myself in such a limited way, is it any wonder I feel defensive and afraid in the world? Is it surprising that, from this perspective, I feel as though I must struggle to be happy—or that I must struggle to survive?

Why Do We Need An Ego?

You are amused that other things never remain the same, but do not know that you yourself never remain the same. —LIEH TZU

If the ego blocks us from the perception of the totality of consciousness, from the experience of ourselves as one with everything else, why do we need one at all? The ego and its means of perception—the world-dividing realm of name and thought and the world-limiting forms of sensibility (physical senses)—have, like all things in the universe, arisen from the Tao and have their place in the natural order of things. They are, metaphorically speaking, the training wheels of conscious development, which, while useful in their function, are not meant to be relied on solely or indefinitely.

The development of an ego consciousness is critical to the process of socialization—the system of social learning and control required to establish and maintain human societies. Societies apply external sanctions and rewards to prohibit and elicit certain behaviors and modes of thought, but rely primarily upon the individual to regulate him- or herself according to the local customs and mores. Self-regulation would be impossible without an ego or boundary consciousness, for each individual must have the sense that he or she controls and is responsible for an inner and outer domain called "mine." The birth of the ego is celebrated in many societies with a naming ceremony of some kind. Even as the physical birth is celebrated as a triumph of nature in the continuance of the species, so, in the naming ceremony, the birth of the child into society is celebrated as the triumph of society in perpetuation. Christening, baptism, confirmation, and bar mitzvah have their origins in these ancient traditions.

Yet the development of the ego is also recognized as a loss. It is represented poetically as the original fall from grace, the expulsion from Paradise; for once we become identified with the ego, our consciousness seems locked in a world of separation and struggle. The "I" or ego, taking itself as a thing apart from all else, seems to be at odds with the world. Here, then,

The Taoist sees the ego as a hard core, which can be broken only by the energy of the unconscious, which penetrates it, turns it inside out.

CHANG CHUNG-YUAN

we have one of the fundamental dilemmas of human existence: *we require an ego to function as social beings, and yet the ego puts us into an experience of separation, isolation, and conflict.*

The problem we are dealing with is one of the part's relationship to the whole. As Leonardo da Vinci put it, "The part always has a tendency to reunite with its whole in order to escape from its imperfection." Whether we choose to do so by reuniting in consciousness with the ground of being (Tao) or by attempting to enlarge the ego through mental, emotional, and physical attachments will make all the difference in the world. It will, among other things, determine whether or not we come to know what true and lasting abundance is.

The Eastern spiritual tradition, generally, and Taoist philosophy, in particular, recognizes both a desire and a capacity to return (while living) to our "original nature" i.e., the undifferentiated consciousness that we experienced before we knew that we were a Tom, Dick, or Harry, a Jane, Jill, or Mary. In the Western tradition, beginning already with the ancient Sumerian Epic of Gilgamesh (circa 2500 B.C.E.), there is the sense that we can never return—that we must take for our comforts in this life what we can find within fortress ego. Later came the notion that we could escape the isolation of the ego only at death or with the Last Judgment, when we would be reunited with God, and all the mysteries of the universe would at last be revealed to us.

 ## Three Eyes on the World

If you realize what the real problem is—losing yourself—you realize that this itself is the ultimate trial.

—JOSEPH CAMPBELL

To help us to better understand the problem of the ego and its integration, we will draw on a metaphorical construct from the teachings of Buddhism. Throughout this discussion, we should keep in mind that we are talking about an insight into the resolution of a universal human problem and not the dogma of a particular religion. We could have as easily used terms from a different spiritual tradition, though this one is extremely clear and elegant. As a means of conceptualizing three distinct levels of consciousness that mark the path of awakening, certain Buddhist teachings employ the concept of three eyes, or ways of seeing the world. These are the *Dharma Eye,* the *Wisdom Eye,* and the *Buddha Eye.* They correspond to the recognition, transcendence, and integration of the ego.

The Dharma Eye: Name, Form, and Ego

*Forget about being separated from others and from
the Divine Source.* —LAO TZU

It is with the *Dharma Eye* that we typically see the world. Through this eye, we see a world of separate things, where everything is different from everything else and the boundaries between them are clear and distinct. It is the eye of the ego, of subject/object, of I/you, of this/that. With the *Dharma Eye,* we see what the Buddhists call the world of *"nama* and *rupa,"* (name and form), what the Taoists call "the ten thousand things." This "eye" is the only one recognized and acknowledged in the modern world. Indeed, it is because we have put the other two eyes out of our awareness that we have rendered ourselves spiritually blind. It is the psychological origin of the feeling lack, for we, as a part, or ego, feel a sense of loss in our separation from the whole, the Tao.

The Wisdom Eye: A Totally Thoughtless Being

*To embrace all things means also that one rids oneself of any
concept of separation: male and female, self and other, life
and death. Division is contrary to the nature of the Tao.*
—LAO TZU

With the *Wisdom Eye,* we see the unity of all things, undifferentiated emptiness. Seen from this eye, everything is one and the same. Nothing exists as a separate, distinct identify or form. Even without real experience of it, we can begin to understand the reality of a level of consciousness where things are not as they seem. Do things really exist at all the way we think of them—in solid, concrete terms—or are they better conceived of as events? An event called a "mountain" lasts longer, to be sure, than an event called a "man" or a "spider." Still, in the vast expanse of time, even the life of a mountain is but a blip.

Conditions arise such that an event called a "planet" occurs. Within this global event, smaller events are constantly occurring, so that at any moment, the planet is not the same as it was the moment before. And is the event we call the "human body" any different from planetary ones? Do you have the same body you had as an infant or teenager? Is it, in fact, the same body you had five years ago or even yesterday? As a scientific fact, it is not.

How much less solid and real, then, is this mental structure we call "I," the ego? What indeed is it? Is it the fleeting desires of the moment? Is it the pool of memories that give me the sense of identity distinguishable from all others? Is it not in the sense of the ego that my story is different from your story? And is this not, too, only a result of a limited view of time and space? To the question, "When did I begin?" most of us would answer, "At conception or birth," or perhaps, "With the beginning of memory." A religious person in the West might say, "I began with Adam and Eve, when God created human beings; the story of humanity's fall and redemption is my story." A scientist who believed his cosmology might reply, "I began with the big bang, for all the physical processes that result in this body commenced at this time. The story of the expanding universe is my story." Now these stories give a more expanded sense of time but, nevertheless, they are still bound to it. The question itself is the problem. "When," "begin," and "I" are all time referents. Ultimately, no cosmology or system of thought can free us from the temporal trap. It is thought itself that locks us in time. As the modern Indian philosopher J. Krishnamurti put it, "Time has a stop only when thought has a stop."[11] To stop thought is to stop time. It is to put an end to the hold of ego consciousness. It is to see with the Wisdom Eye. As the apparent solidity of forms is but an effect of our limited view of time and space, so time and space themselves are forms, which the Wisdom Eye sees through.

In the West, the ego and the Self are thought to be one and the same. It is hardly surprising, then, that most of us are not particularly interested in breaking the ego-bubble of separation and letting the world come rushing in. We are so closely identified with the ego that we equate the release of this identification with complete obliteration. We can hardly be blamed for not desiring our own extinction.

In the Eastern traditions, it is widely recognized that there is life beyond the ego and that "beyond the ego" need not be "beyond the grave." Within the Eastern traditions, various names are given to the consciousness that transcends ego. In the yogic tradition, the "goal" of meditation is to unite with the *Atman* (Self) or *Paramatman* (Super-Self or Oversoul), which is the Self in all things. On the other hand, the critical realization in Buddhist practice is called *anatman*, literally, "no Atman," or no-self. Here, the "goal" is not to merge with the Atman or with what in the West is sometimes called the "Higher Self," but simply to release identification with separative ego consciousness and, in so doing, merge with the totality of consciousness. Whether the path to enlightenment is conceived of as gaining unity with the Atman or Tao, or subtracting the separation of ego identification (the lower self), the destination is the same and, finally, no destination at all, but simply the realization of the ever-existing underlying reality.

The Taoists advocated the practice of mindful breathing as a means of opening the Wisdom Eye, transcending thought, breaking the ego-bubble, identifying with the universe, whatever you want to call it. From the *Tao Te Ching*, we read, "Can you concentrate on your breathing to reach harmony and become as an innocent babe?"[12] Chuang Tzu wrote: "Concentrate on the goal of meditation. Do not listen with your ear, but listen with your mind; not with your mind but listen with your breath, let hearing stop with your ear, let the mind stop with its images. Breathing means to empty oneself and to wait for Tao."[13] Then we can say with delight, "The universe is my mind. My mind is the universe."[14]

Yet my mind is the universe only when I have reached the state the Chinese call *"wu-nien,"* "without thought." To experience the innate intelligence of the universe, the Tao, I must let go of thinking. I must, in effect, trust that the innate intelligence of the universe that has produced so many wonders, including my human body with its capacity for cerebral intellection—that this intelligence—is greater than that available to me through conscious thought. If I drop my reliance on separative thought, I can join or merge with this greater intelligence that lives in and animates all things.

But now, wait a minute. Think of it—we are being told that through breathing, we can awaken to a transcendent level of consciousness and merge with the universe. What could be easier than breathing? Who doesn't do it? Yet we are afraid to breathe—to really let the universe in and ourselves out. To do so, we must give up control. We must stop breathing and let the universe breathe through us. We must trust things as they are. So it is with cultivating the Tao in every aspect of our lives. We must stop doing and let the universe do us.

The highest sage shares his moral possessions with others. The next in wisdom shares his material possessions with others.

LIEH TZU

The Buddha Eye; or, The Marriage of Heaven and Earth

As you return to the Oneness, do not think of it or be in awe of it.
This is just another way of separating from it.
Simply merge into truth, and allow it to surround you.

—LAO TZU

With the *Buddha Eye,* we see both form and emptiness and recognize, as the heart sutra instructs, that "form is no other than emptiness, emptiness no other than form." We can also say that the Buddha Eye sees the world with and without time, with and without thinking, and with and without ego. Within many Eastern traditions, great emphasis is placed on the importance of egolessness on the path to enlightenment. Yet even the Enlightened ones—the Buddha, the Bodhisattvas, and the Taoist masters cannot be said to have been without ego. One without an ego would find it impossible to have any personal memory or recollection. "I" would not know what "I" had for breakfast, let alone what "I" did as a child.

Nevertheless, there *are* two senses in which the enlightened individual can be said to be without ego. First, he or she possesses the ability to temporarily suspend the mundane consciousness of name and form and enter into a more total or "cosmic" consciousness. This practice, called entering *samadhi,* may take a variety of forms, depending on the expanse of the consciousness realized and on one's ability to control or direct this expansion or *samadhi.* The *masts* of India represent an extreme example of this type of ego-release. They spend the greater part of their lives in *samadhi* and maintain only the slimmest connection with mundane consciousness. As a consequence, they are virtually incapable of functioning in society and often cannot maintain their physical bodies without the aid of others. They are caught in the Wisdom Eye.

A second type of ego-release, and one more in keeping with a Taoist perspective, is in some respects similar to the Buddhist concept of *nirvana.* In Mahayana Buddhism, *nirvana* doesn't signify a place or time, a heaven or hereafter, nor is it an otherworldly state of perpetual *samadhi.* Rather, it represents a psychological disengagement from the ego. The word *nirvana* means literally "to extinguish." What is extinguished is the cravings that result from the identification with a limited I, ego.

Ego consciousness represents a limitation or contraction of the totality of consciousness that craves something it calls "more" (love, approval, attention, status, pleasure, etc.) Release is not to be found in the acquisitions of the "more" but in letting go of the identification with the original contraction or limitation of consciousness, namely, the ego itself. This brings of its own accord the three jewels of awakening: *sat, chit, ananda,* or being, pure consciousness, and bliss.

In the first chapter of the *Tao Te Ching,* the three levels of ego recognition, transcendence, and integration are expressed in this way:

> Oftentimes without intention I see the wonder of the Tao *(The Wisdom Eye).*
> Oftentimes with intention I see its manifestations *(The Dharma Eye).*
> Both of these are the same in origin *(The Buddha Eye).*

The same idea is expressed in the following Zenrin:

> *First there is a mountain.*
> *Then there is no mountain.*
> *Then there is.*

Or we might say:

> *First there is an ego.*
> *Then there is no ego.*
> *Then there is.*

 # Integrating the Ego

> *The only difference between a wise man and a fool is that the wise man knows he's playing.* —FRITZ PERLS

Within the context of psychological release, an ego may be employed for purposes of social engagement *(dharma),* without identifying with it as the final term of the self. This "dharma (or social) ego" is "with desire," yet it is the Buddha (literally, *enlightened*) desire to lead others to the path of enlightenment. The ego is recognized, not as an ultimate identity, but as a vehicle for easing suffering and spreading Enlightenment. The spell of identification having been broken when the Wisdom Eye opened, the ego is recognized as the social fiction or mask that it is. Yet it is also recognized as indispensable to active engagement in the social world.

The situation is not unlike that of an actor who is playing a part—indeed, totally engaged in *being* the role he is playing. Yet all the while, behind this surface consciousness of engagement, there is a deeper consciousness that recognizes that he is not really this role—that it is all an act. If an actor somehow lost contact with the deeper consciousness and, having access only to the surface consciousness, came to believe that he *was* the role he was playing, we would think that he had gone mad. In the same way, if we think that we are our egos, which after all are only socially conditioned roles, we have likewise lost it (contact with a deeper consciousness) and have indeed gone mad. (One may play Santa Claus to join the fun without believing he *is* Santa Claus.) From an Eastern perspective, ego roles, like acting roles, are recognized as temporary occupations.

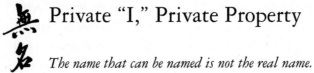

Private "I," Private Property

The name that can be named is not the real name.
—LAO TZU

The primary or original consciousness, the Tao—the innate intelligence of the universe—is there all the while, whether we are aware of it or not. The man who has amnesia has not become someone else—he has simply forgotten who he is. In the Western world, which is today (in a cultural sense) most of the world, we have a collective amnesia regarding the unnameable Tao—we have lost touch with a consciousness that is prior to the ego. It is not only that we have failed to open the Wisdom Eye; we have forgotten that it even exists. As a result, the field of consciousness available to us is limited to that defined by the ego.

One manifestation of our collective amnesia regarding transcendence is our unwavering commitment to the concept of private property. Like the ego, private property may well serve a useful social function. Yet if we take a man-made social convention and confuse it with the underlying reality, we are sure to go astray. Standing out in the middle of the desert, a sign marks an imaginary line that separates the states of Arizona and New Mexico. Nothing in the landscape distinguishes this side from that. The boundary line is clearly arbitrary and imaginary. In truth, this is the case with all property. The boundary lines are always arbitrary and imaginary. They exist as a function of belief—not in the physical world, and much less in the transcendent unity of all things. This is an obvious and easily demonstrable fact of life, yet one which, in our daily living, we choose to ignore.

> *We fail to understand that a particular* thing *is merely an artificial* definition *by our senses, of some indefinable . . . infinitely surpassing that thing.*
> —P. D. OUSPENSKY

Despite the implications that our belief in private property has on our experience of abundance or lack, we seldom, if ever, hold it up to critical analysis. The concept of ownership is meaningless without a name to attach the object to. Name is, as we have said, the original seed of the ego. It is through names that we distinguish differences, and it is by identifying with and clinging to our own names and their associations that we stake out our personal territory. (We forget too easily that *persona* means "mask," which implies both an illusion and a cover.) Having marked the territory, we look for how what is inside the boundaries can be distinguished from what is outside. This territory is the original, and the most private, property. Name (and its associations) is the first thing that we own.

Since name is the core of the ego, we seek to enlarge, protect, and preserve our names. We feel pleasure when "good" things are said about our names, and pain when "bad" things are said about them. From this comes the sense of gain and loss, the psychological origins of credit and debt. Mentally attaching an object to your name gives the sense of possession. Preserving possessions is a way of preserving your name, that is, the ego. Since we realize that we as egos are destined to die, we want somehow to extend our ego identities beyond the scant seventy, eighty, or perhaps ninety years we are normally allotted. One device for achieving an illusion of ego life-extension is the conception of the inheritance of private property. It allows us to pass on the possessions (objects attached to our names) to our offspring, and in so doing, preserve our names and ego identities beyond the grave. It is an attempt of the ego to find security and permanence in a world of constant change.

The universal human problem of recognizing, transcending, and integrating the ego is compounded by the artificiality of modern life. One who lives in nature is constantly in touch with, and immediately aware of, a

The perfect man has no self; the spiritual man has no achievement; the sage has no name.

CHUANG TZU

field of power and experience transcendent to the life of ego and society. People in most traditional cultures tried to live in accord with the cycles, seasons, and powers inherent in the natural world. Today, we try as much as we can to insulate and isolate ourselves in an artificial man-made world. Like no other in human history, our society tries to project and protect the illusion that we are separate from nature and its universal life processes. Wrapped up in the complexity of modern technological society, we find it difficult to see that the order of nature governs our own lives collectively and individually, and therefore to put our trust in the Tao.

> *The Taoists, then, condemned the differentiation of society into classes. Rightly they associated the process with increasing artificiality and complexity of life. . . .*   —JOSEPH NEEDHAM

If there is anything like a law of consciousness, it is this: **whatever we focus our attention on expands in our lives**. Every major spiritual tradition in the world employs this fundamental principle of consciousness as an essential part of its path to liberation. The first of Christ's two commandments is to love (focus on) the Lord with all of thy mind and heart and strength. The yoga tradition of India, from the sutras of Patanjali to the Bhagavad-Gita, tells us that awakening is achieved through the focus of attention—be it on the individual's own higher self, or *Atman*, the impersonal universal Brahman, or the personal deity forms of God, *Bhagavan*. Similarly, the Taoist teachings of Lao Tzu and Chuang Tzu instruct us that we are to cultivate (become more aware of) the Tao.

In traditional cultures, myth, ritual, and art provided points of focus on transcendent symbols as means of projecting or pitching the consciousness beyond the field of the ego. For the society, this served two primary functions: First, it provided the mass of people with authentic rituals that promoted a temporary release from the ego state—a peek into the beyond. Second, it gave a relative few individuals a general blueprint for, or path to, enlightenment. The awakening of these individuals in turn enriched the whole society.

無名 Mastering the Present Era of Private Property

The chief value of money lies in the fact that one lives in a world in which it is overestimated.   —H. L. MENCKEN

In our modern commercial culture, we have effectively done away with all of this. The world of symbols is no longer the realm of artists yearning to lead us to transcendence, but of advertisers yearning to make a buck. The symbols they employ refer us back to the ego, not beyond it. The symbolic images of our daily lives are those supplied by the commercial media, which most recently have taken to employing even traditional symbols of transcendence in their efforts to promote consumption. Their purpose is to excite us to buy, and in order to do so, they must stimulate the feeling that we are lacking something, which ownership of the products being promoted will give us. As a consequence, our imaginative lives are filled with images that reinforce the illusion of ego, and are nearly devoid of those that point toward its transcendence.

What is true for the inner landscape, if anything, applies even more to the physical environment. The urban environment, in which (now, for the first time) most human beings live, is a landscape of virtually constant ego-reinforcement. Think of the psychological effect of the vast sense of space in which most beings lived throughout human history. To be in the fields and forests, the vast deserts and open savannas, to behold above you the vast canopy of the clear night sky is to feel a sense of expansion. In traditional civilizations, sacred architecture dominated the landscape, as sacred rituals dominated the calendar of events. Whether they lived in ancient cities or in remote jungles, people were in their daily lives being reminded of levels of reality transcendent to the life of the ego.

Do you imagine the universe is agitated?
Go into the desert at night and look out at the stars.
This practice should answer the question.   —LAO TZU

Alternatively, consider the psychological effect of the modern urban environment. We move in a crowded environment, where space is at a

How can I forget "me"
when everything is
designed to remember me
to myself?

premium, the horizon is blocked, and everything around us is owned by someone. Large glass towers dedicated to banks and insurance companies dominate the skylines of the major American cities. If the suburban communities can be said to be organized around anything, it is the shopping malls. Life in the modern world is awash in a sea of paperwork, all of which reminds us of our names and positions in society.

Both in our imaginative lives, filled with images supplied by the commercial media, and the physical environments in which we move, we are constantly being reminded of our position, place, and status in society. As much as anything, getting away from it all means forgetting who we are as egos. When I am hiking and camping alone in the woods, there is precious little to remind me of who I am in society (once, of course, I have filled out the necessary forms and received the appropriate license or permit). This allows for at least the possibility of a deeper experience of reality.

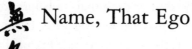 Name, That Ego

The un-named is heaven and earth's origin;
Naming is the mother of ten thousand things.
—LAO TZU

The more one is compelled by his society to focus attention on his name, social position, and possessions, the more strongly he is likely to become identified with the ego level of consciousness. This is particularly true if he has never been made aware that any other levels of consciousness even exist—let alone provided with any encouragement or effective vehicles for accessing them. Having no exit from the barriers of time, space, and ego, he feels trapped. He seeks release through attachments and experiences that only serve to remind him of, and thus further encase him in, his ego.

We have organized our society on the basis of economics. Our economics, in turn, hinges on the idea of the ownership of private property. We take this so much for granted, as a natural part of the order of things, that we forget that it is a product of thought and social convention. We forget that there is no intrinsic, incontrovertible, or universal criteria of ownership and that ownership is finally a product of thought and not a part of the natural world. We are so caught in the myth of private ownership that we can scarcely imagine a world without it.

To be sure, even in so-called primitive collective societies, there is a sense of "mine" not only with respect to personal ego (memory, and where it applies, social position) but also with respect to objects. Yet many traditional cultures survived quite nicely for thousands of years without needing to resort to the concept of property in land or "real" estate. Peoples in matriarchal Neolithic cultures typically did not conceive of nature as a commodity that could be owned.

The extension of the concept of private property is a fascinating one. The historical pattern is one of moving from, among matriarchal agrarian Neolithic cultures, the ownership of personal objects such as clothing, ornaments, weapons, and utensils to, among patriarchal herding peoples (e.g., Indo-European and Semitic peoples), the ownership of domesticated animals: sheep, goats, cattle, and later horses. (The word "chattel," or personal property, and the word "cattle" are in their origins one and the same.) The concept of personal property became extended by patriarchal herding peoples from the animals themselves to the lands in which they grazed and, following their subjugation of matriarchal agrarian communities, to the land on which the crops were grown. The concept of private property was further extended to include the husband's ownership of his wife (or wives) and minor children as well as conquered foes or slave workers.

Descendants of these patriarchal herding peoples, the seafaring Phoenicians and Greeks developed the widespread use of money. Coined money served as a substitute for the trading of cattle, which were difficult to transport in seagoing vessels. The word "capital" itself comes from *captia* (Latin for "head" as in "a head of cattle"). The early coins were often marked with images of cattle, and we still say "heads" and "tails" when we flip a coin. Finally, from the herding cultures, we derived as well the concept of interest payments. The idea of loaning money at interest originated from the practice of repaying one who had lent a bull for stud with some number of the offspring produced from its mating.

From the personal ownership of artifacts, animals, land, people, money, and interest, the concept of ownership was further extended in the capitalist era to include a wide range of abstract financial "instruments." One can, for instance, "own" the future right to buy at, a given price, a share (a stock option) of a fictional person (corporation). Today these "rights" are traded in their own "markets" the way fish and vegetables have been traded for centuries, which is to say, as though they were real. While nothing real is traded in markets such as these (there are numerous others equally or even more abstract), they do have real impact on people's daily lives.

We have created a culture in which virtually everything can be bought and sold. Today, a whole class of specialists (lawyers) is required to determine who really owns what and who really owes what to whom. We've come a long way from trading bulls and have to put up with a lot of bull as a result. *In any society, as the concept of ownership becomes increasingly abstract, life in that society becomes increasing artificial and complex*—a point the Taoists well understood.

In *Science and Civilization in China,* Joseph Needham describes the social disruption that attended the shift in Chinese society from a matriarchal Neolithic communal culture to a patriarchal feudal state. The Taoists, to put it mildly, were not enamored with either the advent of the feudal state nor with the increasing technological complexity that arose alongside of it. Needham writes, "If the power of feudalism rested, as it must certainly have done, on certain specific crafts, such as bronze working and irrigation engineering; if, as we have seen, the Taoists generalized their complaint against the society of their time so that it became a hatred of all 'artificiality'; if the differentiation of classes had gone hand in hand with technical inventions—was it not natural that these should be included in the condemnation?"[15]

Implicit in the idea of ownership of nature is the psychology of scarcity and poverty. With ownership, the emphasis shifts from one of receiving the bounty and abundance as a gift from nature (or God or gods or the ancestors or what have you) to a concern for exercising one's property rights. To think that we own nature makes us feel we are owed something from it. If we think we "own land" and our crop yields are off from our calculations, we feel disappointed. We feel cheated—like we are due something we haven't received. If, on the other hand, we view the earth as a living being, not unlike ourselves, we are able to appreciate and receive its fruits as gifts. When we view life itself as a gift, we are free to receive all of the gifts of nature, of family, friends, and community, and of our own talents and abilities, with genuine joy and appreciation. We are free to move in a world of plenty, with a spirit of thanksgiving.

The conception "own" sets up the feeling "owed." More than any culture in human history, we are obsessed with ownership. Consequently, people in the West tend to go about feeling owed. Life owes us, nature owes us, society owes us, our parents or children owe us, our mates owe us. It is difficult for us then to feel real joy, for we cannot simply receive. If you think you are owed and you receive, it is only the fulfillment of an obligation, and if you don't get what you think you are owed, you feel cheated.

Most of us feel owned as well as owed. We feel owned by our employers, owned by our landlords, owned by the mortgage-holding bank, the credit companies, and so on. Even if we are financially well off, we feel owned in the sense of having to do many things we would prefer not to in order to maintain our status or position in society. So we go about feeling owned and owed. It is any wonder that the feeling of abundance eludes us?

As we have seen, the concept "to own" creates its opposite "to be owned" as well as its corollary "to be owed"; all of these reinforce the psychology of lack engendered by the original separation or differentiation of consciousness, ego. Yet to function in the modern commercial culture, we must have at our disposal a great many things. Even as an ego is required to function in the world of society, so for all but a few yogis in caves, money and material possessions are required to survive in the physical world, not to mention to contribute to the life of society.

Using without Possessing

My body is not my possession; yet once born, I have no choice but to keep it intact. Other things are not my possessions; yet once I exist, I cannot dispense with them. . . . Although I keep life and body intact, I cannot possess this body; although I may not dispense with things, I cannot possess these things. To possess these things, possess this body, would be violently to reserve for oneself body and things which belong to the world. —LIEH TZU

The key to an "enlightened" approach is to be found, not in the literal renunciation of money or things, but in psychological disengagement from the concept of ownership of them. Just as I may employ an ego to function in society, without believing that I ultimately "am" one, so I may employ the things in my care without believing that I, in fact, own them. Even as we may employ an ego identity for purposes of social engagement, so we can use money and things for purposes of creative action.

The critical question and one that warrants continued awareness and self-examination is: What is the motivation behind my desire to acquire money and the things that come with it? The motivation behind any action determines its ultimate effect, which is to say, whether that action will serve to free or enslave us. With respect to the acquisition and spending of money, there are two motivations that bring happiness: pure enjoyment and the desire to serve or help others.

Pure Enjoyment: By *pure enjoyment* we mean, as Leonardo da Vinci put it, "to love a thing for its own sake and no other reason." What makes enjoyment less than pure is "the other reasons," in others words, ulterior motives. Will Rogers described just such a motive when he said, "Too many people spend money they haven't earned, to buy things they don't want, to impress people they don't like." On the other hand, any true enjoyment serves to make us feel more deeply connected with everything else. Enjoying good food, music, sex, and books, enjoying pleasant physical surroundings and beautiful things, traveling to interesting places—all these enrich and enliven us.

In the West, spirituality has been long associated with self-denial, poverty, and the shunning of worldly enjoyments. While there is a similar emphasis in certain Eastern teachings, there is as well a tradition that places the emphasis on self-awareness, not denial. The Taoists could be considered a part of this tradition. While ancient Taoists were not interested in status for its own sake nor in technological wizardry, they certainly knew how to enjoy life. The Taoists refined the arts of love-making and the maintenance of physical health. They cultivated beauty in the arts and had a rare appreciation of nature. They knew how to enjoy food, conversation, and solitude. They cultivated the sensitivity of feeling that allows for the full enjoyment of simple things.

Service to Others: The other motive that brings happiness is the desire to benefit others. In the *Hua Hu Ching,* Lao Tzu describes it as one of the four cardinal virtues. "The fourth [virtue] is supportiveness; this manifests as service to others without expectation of reward."[16] This, as he put it, is not "an external dogma, but a part of your original nature." In your original nature, you are one with everything; in your human nature, you are a social being; therefore, being yourself means being helpful to others. To deny this desire its fullest expression is to go against your own nature, which can only bring pain and unhappiness. If money is required to fulfill this desire (and in today's world, it usually is), then by all means, acquire it. Of course, it is best if you can acquire it in a way that in itself benefits others.

Acquiring status as well cannot be rejected out of hand. Status in, and the respect of, society may be necessary to fulfilling your natural desire to help others. It may be a part of what the Buddhist calls "skillful means." If you must gain status or credentials in order for people to see and value the gifts you have to offer, then again, by all means, do so. Indeed, it would be selfish not to—as selfish as seeking status for its own sake. The test of any desire is: Does it serve to make you feel more isolated or more connected with all of life?

CHAPTER TWO

Tzu-jan

The Nature of Abundance

The universe is a single life comprising one substance and one soul.
                                                    —Marcus Aurelius

From the perspective of the Taoists, if we all lived in the Tao, all would live in abundance. Abundance is the natural way of the universe. We see this natural abundance reflected in the fruit-bearing plant that provides us with nourishment, yet in its seed retains the power of regeneration. The bounty is given, yet nothing is lost. The first step to putting ourselves in touch with this natural abundance is to develop our innate receptive capacities. Receptivity brings a feeling of participation in life and a sense of gratitude for it, an openness to creative ideas and inspirations, a spontaneous joy and zest for life, an experience of the love that pervades the universe, and so much more. In short, receptivity is essential to an inner experience of abundance. This chapter will explore how you can open to receive the natural abundance of the universe and let go of attachments that keep you from experiencing it. The related exercises at the end of the book will help you to integrate and apply the principles discussed here in your everyday life.

From the perspective of the Taoists, the universe has no creator or boss. It is *tzu-jan*, of-itself-so. According to Wang Pi, "Heaven and earth abide by *tzu-jan*. Without their doing or making anything, the ten thousand things themselves govern one another and put their affairs in order."[1] For the classical Taoists, there is a natural order and harmony in nature. There is nothing we as human beings can do to add to it or improve upon it. We can, however, and naturally do, participate in it. As a part of nature, human beings collectively have a place in the natural order of things. As individuals, we each have a natural destiny to fulfill, according to our individual natures. By recognizing and fulfilling our collective and individual destinies, we participate in the natural abundance of the universe.

> *The Universe is sacred*
> *You cannot improve it*
> *If you try to change it, you will ruin it.*
> *If you try to hold it, you will lose it.*
> —LAO TZU

Tzu-jan is usually translated "naturalness," or "spontaneity." Spontaneity is, of course, a response. *We can only respond spontaneously when our receptive capacities are open.* A skilled martial artist responds to what his opponent is actually doing, not to what he thinks his opponent will do. By fully receiving his opponent, becoming one with him in spirit, the martial artist effortlessly and spontaneously responds to his opponent's every move. In the same way, we respond spontaneously and naturally to life when we are fully open and receptive to it.

The Taoists tell us that it is our psychological commitment to separation (ego) that blocks our innate receptive capacities. It not only makes us stiff and unnatural, but it keeps us from participating in and celebrating the natural abundance of the universe. Having rejected the unity and natural abundance of the Tao, the ego seeks security by attaching itself to what it thinks it needs to survive. Ironically, it is the psychological commitment to separation and the attachments of the ego that give the feeling and appearance of lack. After all, if we were experiencing ourselves as one with all of life, how could we know any lack?

In considering how we can apply the principle of *tzu-jan* to our own lives, we find ourselves face to face with a number of important questions, among them: Are human beings better off trying to straighten out nature, or is there something to be gained from wiggling with it? Does nature have an intelligence of its own, or is it some wild and stupid stuff that must be subjugated and forced into doing the intelligent thing (what we want)? If this natural intelligence exists, how we do access it?

In modern Western culture, we've gotten very good at straightening things out. The Taoist would tell us it's time we learned how to wiggle. In a culture where the ego has been enshrined as a god, the be-all and end-all of consciousness and the final arbitrator of reality, we put our faith in what we call "progress." Never content to leave well enough alone, the ego is forever trying to improve upon the universe. Be it personal self-improvement, economic growth, or scientific and technological advances, we are obsessed with the notion of progress.

Personal improvement has its place, but it is no substitute for the realization of that which lies beyond and beneath the ego consciousness. Economic growth is an abstract concept, which in the end has little to do with whether or not we enjoy a living experience of abundance. Technological progress is not an unqualified good but a double-edged sword, cutting losses as well as gains. We needn't reject progress to recognize that there is something to be gained by more fully appreciating things as they are. We needn't reject plans for the future to recognize that life can only be lived in the here and now.

More Blessed to Receive

There is a power above and behind us and we are the channel of its communication.   —EMERSON

Many of us take pride in what giving people we are; yet it seldom occurs to us to consider how receptive we are. Certainly, receptivity is not promoted as a cultural ideal in the way giving is. In the West, we often equate giving with being generous and spiritual, and receiving with being selfish and greedy. In truth, giving often provides an ego gratification that receiving doesn't allow. When we are giving, we are in control in a way that we are not when receiving. Receiving requires a humility and letting go that can make us feel uncomfortable. Often, we feel much more secure when we think we are in control, running the show.

Though we tend to underrate its value, our ability to receive is as important as our ability to give. In fact, we can only give to others what we are willing to receive for ourselves. *Receive and you must give*: this is a spiritual law of the universe. When we allow ourselves to open and receive, our giving takes care of itself. It is then pure giving, free of self-consciousness and inner coercion. It is a natural overflow (abundance), spontaneously spilling forth in the way a river floods its banks when it's full.

On the other hand, when we try to give from lack, our giving is corrupted by ulterior motives. Whether this "giving" is motivated by a perceived lack of things or a craving for approval, it comes out of feeling separate from those who are the intended recipients of our gifts. This separation is the beginning of manipulation. For example, a lack of self-esteem may prompt a desire to prove that we are morally superior, with demonstrations of how good or giving we are. We may puff ourselves up in self-congratulations, yet fail to see that, as Confucius put it, "The goody-goodies are the thieves of virtue."

Genuine giving flows naturally out of who we are. There is no sense of doing good or trying to be good in it. What is true of giving under the guise of moral superiority applies to all kinds of giving based on the idea of receiving some material or ego benefit. Premeditated manipulations born of separation and lack are never to be confused with spontaneous gifts given in a spirit of abundance.

While our Western ideal holds that it is *always* more blessed to give than to receive, the Bhagavad-Gita puts a much finer point on it, distinguishing different kinds of giving according to the motive behind each. It recognizes that to give from lack—which is to say to give with the desire for benefit, be it ego gratification or material or spiritual gain—is altogether different from giving for its own sake. In truth, giving mixed with ulterior motives is not giving at all, but merely a means to a self-serving end. Again, genuine giving is always and only the result of having first received. When we first receive, our giving is without effort, which is another way of saying without ego.

When Walt Whitman said, "To have great poets, there must be great audiences," he was recognizing the creative power of receptivity. Receiving, far from doing nothing, is activity. Yet it is an activity that we in the West don't appreciate enough. We want to know who gave it, did it, or created it, not who received it, much less how deeply it was received. When you open to receive the love of a friend, you are giving them the

Who paints a figure, if he cannot be it, cannot draw it.

Dante

greatest gift you can give. When you open to receive without hindrance the energy of the universe, you are giving the world a gift. When you open to receive an inspiration or creative idea, you are giving. In truth, receiving is giving.

Receiving Is an Intentional Act

The things that are really for thee, gravitate to thee.
—EMERSON

We recognize giving as an intentional act. We have a conscious desire to give to others—and so we do. Yet we often fail to realize that receiving is also a conscious act. In order to receive, we must be willing to receive, which is another way of saying we must intend to receive. Intention implies both belief and action. With respect to receiving, the belief is that we will indeed receive, and the action is that of becoming one with what we want to receive. In practice, belief and action are one and the same. When we are one in spirit with a person, object, or experience, there is nothing between it and ourselves. What separates us is only the belief that we are different from someone, something, or some experience that we are making "other."

We can define receptivity as "the ability to be at one with." Here, then, is a practical key to receiving more of what you want in your life: Become one with what you want. If you want to receive more joy in your life, become one with the joy all around you. Don't separate yourself in your consciousness from joy or from those who fully enjoy themselves. If you want more wealth, become one with the experience of wealth. Don't separate yourself in your consciousness from wealth or those who possess it. If you want to receive more love in your life, become one in consciousness with love. Don't separate yourself in consciousness from the love that pervades the universe or from those who are loved and loving.

You want to be loved because you do not love; but the moment you love, it is finished, you are no longer inquiring whether or not somebody loves you.
—J. KRISHNAMURTI

Receptivity is the ability to merge in consciousness with whatever your awareness is focused on. You can hear a piece of music, you can listen to piece of music, or you can become one with the music. You can hear a friend talking; you can listen to a friend talking, paying careful attention to each and every word; or you can be at one with a friend, listening not merely to her words, but to the whole of her being. Hearing is a sensual experience; listening, a mental one; receiving, a spiritual experience. Ultimate receptivity is the ability to be at one with the process of the universe. We can hear about the unity of the universe as a spiritual concept; we can, by deductive reasoning, conclude that everything is essentially the same stuff and that everything affects everything else; or we can experience ourselves as being at one with all.

Receptivity can be learned or, more accurately, we can learn how we inhibit or block our natural receptivity, then cease these blocking efforts. We block our understanding by struggling to figure things out. We block our capacity to perform by ignoring our natural strengths or by fretting too much about how we are doing. We block our capacity to feel love by concerning ourselves too much with whether or not our love is being appreciated or reciprocated.

Spiritually, mentally, emotionally, and physically—the human being is a receiver set. Yet we often manage to jam up the works with a lot of static. Typically, we do not experience ourselves as being at one with the natural intelligence that is the universe and so feel alienated and confused. We do not experience ourselves as being at one with our natural abilities and so—feel that our lives lack direction or try to impose a sense of purpose based on some abstract notion of what we ought to do.

We do not experience ourselves as being at one with the love that pervades the universe, and so confuse love with approval, which we try to earn by our efforts. We cannot demand, earn, or negotiate love; we can only open to receive the love that is the universe. We cannot make up the truth or discover it by mere intellect alone; finally, we can only open to receive or recognize it. We cannot make ourselves into something we are not; we can only open to receive and embrace what we are. All of the important things in life come to us by receiving what is, not by struggling to get what we think we need. In any area of your life where you are feeling lack, consider how you may be blocking the natural flow of abundance and how you can open to receive more. (See the exercises at the end of the book.)

Receptivity and Intelligence

*Intelligence is whatever is valued, in terms of performance
and behavior, within a given society.*

—FLOYD WATSON

If receptivity is so important to our experience of abundance, why is it
generally so underrated? While masculine values have long dominated in
the West, traditional Eastern cultures in general and the Taoists in particular have placed (or, more accurately, retained) a greater emphasis on the
feminine values. In the *I Ching,* "The Receptive" is recognized and honored
as the quintessence of the feminine, or yin, spirit. It is the living power of
empty space, be it the vast celestial emptiness from which galaxies, stars,
and planets are born or the emptiness of the womb in which we ourselves
take shape.

Lao Tzu reminds us that the useful part of the pot is not the outer rim
that gives it form but the empty space within; the useful part of the house
is the empty space within the walls, not the walls themselves. He tells us
that while advantage springs from forms, or what is, usefulness arises from
emptiness, or what is not. While we in the West tend to think of emptiness
as dead nothingness, the *Tao Te Ching* instructs that "The valley spirit is
not dead: /They say it is the mystic female. . . . Use her without labor." It
tells us to remain open and empty that the Tao may flow through us without hindrance.

The Way of the Tao is to live in openness to this valley spirit, which Lao
Tzu calls the "mystic female." Of course, we cannot say that the Tao *is*
feminine. Indeed, the Tao is beyond the pairs of opposites. Yet it is represented in this way to indicate that it is only through a feminine, or receptive, spirit that it may be approached. We cannot will the Tao into our
lives. We can only open to receive what is of-itself-so and, in so doing,
consciously participate in its mystery.

The Taoists were not alone in conceiving the spiritual intelligence as
feminine. In mystical Judaism, it is called *Shekhinah;* by the Greeks, *Sophia.*
It is the descending dove of the Mother Goddess religion, seen again in
Christian symbology as the Holy Spirit. It is Dante's Beatrice that leads
him to the Heavenly realms. The ancient Egyptians called it "the intelligence of the heart" to distinguish it from the cerebral intelligence.

*Alone I am and different
Because I prize and seek
My sustenance from the
Mother (Tao)*

LAO TZU

As individuals and as societies, what we consider intelligent is a reflection of our values. What one society views as the height of intelligence, another may see as pure insanity. For example, while we locate intelligence in the head and brain, among certain Native American tribes, to say that one was thinking with his head (instead of his heart) was a way of indicating that he had gone crazy. Our modern Western culture has come to rely on *masculine intelligences* or values (analytical judgment, will, and conscious, one-at-a-time awareness) and to suppress the *feminine intelligences* or values (intuition, acceptance, and instinctual intelligence).

By using the terms *masculine* and *feminine*, I do not mean to equate these intelligences with gender. Both men and women possess masculine and feminine intelligences. Perhaps better terms would be *focused* and *diffuse*, or *yang* and *yin* intelligences. The critical point to the present discussion is that the diffuse, or yin, intelligences arise from the feminine mode of being, which is to say, from receptivity.

YIN INTELLIGENCES	YANG INTELLIGENCES
Intuition	Analytical Judgment
Acceptance	Will
Wisdom of the Body	Conscious Attention

YIN INTELLIGENCES

Intuition: Direct knowing: the wisdom of the heart—that intelligence which seems to be heard or known (not thought) when consciousness comes to reside in the human heart.

Acceptance: The recognition of the existing perfection or the "suchness" of things (events, people, etc.) as they are.

Wisdom of the Body: The instinctual innate intelligence in life seen manifest everywhere in nature—that intelligence which grows, maintains, and in time, disintegrates galactic, planetary, mineral, plant, animal, and human bodies.

YANG INTELLIGENCES

Analytical Judgment: The ability to reason and discern, to make decisions on the basis of value choices. It is through this intelligence that we discriminate between what is and is not moral, wise, cost-effective, and so on.

Will: The power to achieve an aim or transform circumstances through intention, concentration, and effort.

Conscious Attention: A linear, one-at-a-time, bit-by-bit, thought-by-thought perception of reality.

At each of the three levels, the feminine, or yin, intelligence is more comprehensive or "expanded" than the corresponding masculine, or yang, intelligence. For example, the intuitive intelligence that spontaneously arises from an experience of oneness with all of life is superior to reasoned, ethical judgment. There is no good that is always or only good, no single virtue appropriate to every situation. Lao tzu tells us that it is only when we lose contact with our innate intuitive intelligence that we resort to "goodness" and "righteousness" as the ethical guideposts of our lives. It is only when real love is lost that we resort to "filial piety" or "family values." It is in this spirit that we can understand St. Thomas Aquinas' dictum, "Love God and do as you please." Love is superior to any ethical code. When we open ourselves to receive the innate, intuitive intelligence of the heart, we can respond freely and spontaneously to the events of our lives. We can, as well, free ourselves from the guilt, self-righteousness, and hypocrisy that attend moralistic thinking.

From the feminine mode of being, we receive not only intuitions about what to do in each moment but visions for the directions of our lives. Creative inspirations as well come in this way. In its origin, the word *author* meant "obedient," signifying that the true author (or any genuine artist) is one who is obedient to what he or she has received from the spirit or muse. He or she has become a vessel through which a universal intelligence may express. In the same way, when you free your mind of clutter, you make

Know the masculine, but keep to the feminine.

LAO TZU

55

yourself an empty vessel into which intuitions and inspirations may freely flow. You don't have to struggle to figure things out. You can respond spontaneously to the impulses of inspiration.

Even as intuition is more direct than analytical judgment, so acceptance is more inclusive than will. There is more in life that we must accept than there is that we can change by acts of will. First and foremost, we must accept the human body and the limitations that result from it. We must accept the confines of time and space and all of the limitations of the natural world. Of course, there is a place for asserting the will to transform, to shape the world in the image of our creative visions. Yet even the visions that we do realize have a measure of imperfection and an impermanence that we must accept. Moreover, without an underlying acceptance of the world as it is, the will to transform often takes the form of an egotistical battle with reality.

> *There are joys which long to be ours. God sends ten thousand truths, which come about us like birds seeking inlet; but we are shut up to them, and so they bring us nothing, but sit and sing awhile upon the roof, and then fly away.*
> —HENRY WARD BEECHER

Finally, the wisdom of the body is greater than that perceived by the conscious mind. First, through procreation, digestion, respiration, circulation, elimination, the immune function, and a variety of other subconscious processes, the instinctual intelligence maintains the life of the body. *In a very real sense, the conscious mind is an attribute of the subconscious wisdom of the body.* Second, conscious attention is selective, whereas instinctual intelligence is global. The power of recall under hypnosis demonstrates that the subconscious mind is aware of far more than we notice with our selective, conscious, one-at-a-time awareness. If we had to stop and think about how to do all of the things our subconscious instinctive intelligence does for us, we would do nothing else.

The Taoist relies principally on the feminine intelligences: intuition, acceptance, and the wisdom of the body. All of these are wholistic intelligences, accessed from a receptive mode of being. On the other hand, the masculine intelligences are self-assertive and fragmenting, which is to say, they function by differentiating this from that and comparing this with that. It is by the lights of the masculine intelligences that we make our way in modern commercial culture. The feminine intelligences are hardly recognized, much less revered. When Lao Tzu tells us to "know the masculine, but keep to the feminine," he is telling us to be on guard against the tendencies to dissect and fragment consciousness, to force our wills on nature and others, and to limit our perception of reality to what can be discerned by the physical senses.

> *It goes beyond a single world creation myth to an almost universal conception of mankind that the right side is regarded as male and the left side as female.* —HERMANN BAUMANN

There is a Hopi saying that further elucidates the meaning of Lao Tzu's injunction to "know the masculine, but keep to the feminine." It goes: "The left side is good for it contains the heart. The right side is evil for it has no heart. The left side is awkward, but wise. The right side is clever and strong, but it lacks wisdom." It is our task to be both strong and wise, to integrate and use the masculine strengths, without letting them dominate or overwhelm the "mystic female." We are to achieve a balance that recognizes and honors both the masculine and feminine intelligences, while keeping first things first. We must first learn to *be,* that our doing may be at one with the deepest energies of the universe. We must learn to receive, that our giving may be guided by the intelligence of the heart (Tao).

On a psychological level, failure to open to the feminine intelligences results from the fear of yielding to sources of energy and information that we cannot consciously control or direct with our egos. Whether we go "beneath" the ego, into the wisdom of the body or "above" it into spiritual intuition, we must (at least temporarily) release the ego's hold on consciousness in order to access the feminine intelligences. Yet when we do, we find the sense of connection with all life that is the true basis for the feeling of abundance.

It is worth emphasizing that from the Taoist perspective, the feminine intelligences are innate abilities that naturally (without conscious effort) and organically (from the inside out) evolve throughout the life of the human being. It is only because we are caught up in the desires of the ego and live in an artificial society that is constantly reinforcing and expanding these desires that the natural development of these intelligences has been stunted. A fruit-bearing tree growing in poor soil may survive, yet it will not produce the quality of fruit that it would naturally develop in more favorable circumstances. It is only in this context that we can speak of

> *Universal consciousness, intuition, that is, is the origin of all art.*
>
> PIET MONDRIAN

consciously developing the innate feminine intelligences. Later chapters will explore practical suggestions for how we can develop these abilities. The section that follows explores the role societal influences play in blocking the development of our innate receptive capacities—and steps we can take to mitigate these effects.

 ## The Nature of Receptivity

The old Lakota was wise. He knew that man's heart away from nature becomes hard; he knew that lack of respect for growing, living things soon led to lack of respect for humans too. So he kept his youth close to its softening influence.
—CHIEF LUTHER STANDING BEAR

In the *Tao Te Ching*, Lao Tzu tells us that as Tao is the model for Heaven, and Heaven is the model for Earth, so Earth is the model for human beings.[2] Today, we have lost touch with our "model." In our artificial society, we have removed ourselves from the earth and from the lessons of nature. Nature teaches lessons about change, the organic processes of birth, growth, decay, and death—lessons that today we have largely forgotten. As we move away from daily contact with the earth, we lose touch with our receptive capacities and the feminine intelligences. In the West, we have for a long time been in an adversarial relationship with nature and, consequently, with the receptive, the inner feminine. We have, as Chuang Tzu put it, "for[gotten] what we have received from nature."[3]

Among traditional peoples—and by "traditional peoples" we mean people who live in nature—it is difficult to find any who have an ungrateful or bitter attitude toward life. They cannot, so easily as we, forget what they have received from nature. Indeed, their ability to survive depends on the gifts of nature. Receptivity, the capacity to be open and alert to the world around them, is a necessary and integral part of their daily living. In the Amazon jungles, native people track jaguars by the smell of their urine. The anthropologist Claude Levi-Strauss reported on tribes who claimed to be able to see the planet Venus in the *daytime* sky. What we call *primitive peoples* are able to feel and sense their environment much more acutely than we do today. They *have* to remain open and alert in their senses and feelings.

When one's feeling capacity is open, one realizes—not as a thought, but as an ongoing felt experience—that one is being nourished by all of life. One has the *experience* of the gift, the feeling that one is constantly receiving. Virtually without exception, we find traditional peoples giving thanks for the sun and rain, thanks for the plants and animals that nourish them, thanks for the earth, thanks for the human community.

Real fearlessness is the product of our tenderness. It comes from letting the world tickle your raw and beautiful heart.

—CHÖGYAM TRUNGPA

On the other hand, many of us in today's technologically advanced societies take all of this for granted. We begin placing demands and conditions on life, without having first received it as a gift. We go about thinking that we are lacking, that we have failed to receive what we deserve. In recent years, there has been a trend toward idealizing victimhood. It has become all the rage to assert that you are in some way more unfortunate than the next person, to vie for the honor (sic) of being the greatest victim. As the life of society has grown increasingly artificial, ingratitude has become the order of the day. Ingratitude steals our happiness and robs us of the inner experience of abundance that those living in simpler societies often enjoyed.

Yet we must resist the temptation to romanticize the "noble savage" as a superior being. People from traditional cultures are not intrinsically better than us. Time and again, we have seen examples of traditional peoples who have adopted (more often than not, been forced to adopt) Western lifestyles and economics. In a very short time, often in a single generation, the spirit of thanksgiving is lost. With it goes a sense of the sacred in life, and the experience of being at one with all things.

As Native American chief Luther Standing Bear put it, "The man who sat on the ground in his tipi meditating on life and its meaning, accepting the kinship of all creatures and acknowledging the unity of all things was infusing into his being the true essence of civilization. And when native man left off this form of development, his humanization was retarded in growth."[4] In the late twentieth century, as China rushed to commercialize, one old man on the south coast remarked to a journalist, "Before, people acted according to ethics of Confucianism, then according to the precepts of Communism; today, people are just greedy."[5]

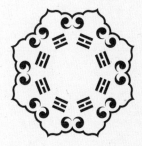

An old pine tree preaches wisdom
And a wild bird is crying out truth.

ZEN SAYING

Shall I not have intelligence with the earth? Am I not part leaves and vegetable mould myself?

THOREAU

As economics based on cooperation with nature tends to bring a sense of humility and gratitude, so economics based on monetary abstractions tends to incite pride and greed (see chapter 5). With the whole of our society organized as it is around money, we should not be surprised that "today, people are just greedy." The "health" of our economy depends on the continual manufacture of what the Taoists called "artificial desires." The Taoists distinguished between the desires of body and soul, and the artificial desires of the ego. Desires for food, sex, progeny, and so on, grow out of the body and as such are a part of the natural order of things. The same is true of what we could call "soul desires," desires related to the fulfillment of our inborn destinies. On the other hand, the desires of the ego originate in and reinforce the feeling of separation and as such move us away from the true abundance of living in the Tao.

In modern commercial culture, the excitement of these artificial desires is indispensable to the endless quest to "develop new markets" and keep the economy booming. As Akio Morita, founder of the Sony corporation, put it, "We do not market a product that has been developed already, but develop a market for the product we make."[6] In other words, first create a desire, then build a product that will seem to fulfill it. This kind of market development relies on what Lao Tzu called the "incitement to envy," which he decried as the worst of all sins:

> *No sin can exceed*
> *Incitement to envy;*
> *No calamity's worse*
> *Than to be discontented.*
> —LAO TZU

It is the avowed mission of the commercial advertiser to insure that we are never content with what we have. While ego desires have been around for as long as human beings, never before in human history has there been such a massive and organized effort to promote them. Anyone who doubts the impact of advertising in shaping world culture simply needs to travel more. The large corporations who fund it certainly believe they are getting their money's worth. Recently, it was reported that one large manufacturer of athletic shoes paid more to a single celebrity athlete who endorsed its products than it did to its entire third world workforce who actually made the shoes. By 1990, global advertising expenditures had reached an estimated $256 billion. This was more than the entire gross national product of the nation of India for the same year and breaks down to nearly $50 for every man, woman, and child on the face of the earth.[7]

In advancing a global culture of discontent, television plays an indispensable role. In third world countries, the television often makes its appearance before running water. In a relatively poor country like Mexico, 99 percent of all households have televisions.[8] As commercial television has come to dominate the imaginative life of human beings around the globe, we should keep in mind that it is, as Fred Friendly, former president of CBS News put it, "the mercantile advertising system that controls television."[9] The values of the "mercantile advertising system" (incitement to envy and discontent) are reflected not only in the endless and often inane commercials themselves but, more importantly, in determining the programs that serve as bait to lure viewers to them.

While the world of advertising and commercial television offers an abundant array of material objects, it relies on a psychology of lack to promote and sell them. The message is clear: without the products being sold, you are not enough, your life is incomplete. Each time we buy something on this basis, we reinforce the feeling of lack. We can never get to a feeling of abundance starting from a feeling of lack. To free ourselves from this kind of influence, it isn't necessary to reject the material objects themselves, only the idea that we aren't good enough without them.

Desensitization in the Machine Civilization

The more a man lays stress on false possessions,
and the less sensitivity he has for what is essential,
the less satisfying his life is. —CARL JUNG

In addition to its dependence on the excitation of ego desires, modern commercial culture is unprecedented in its reliance on technology. We have transformed the world with our technologies. Yet we often forget how profoundly our technologies have transformed us. Perhaps the simplest way to understand these effects is to observe the impact of modern machine technologies on traditional cultures. The introduction of modern machine technologies into traditional cultures has three major effects. First, machines tend to remove people from the natural environment: cities instead of villages, motor scooters or cars instead of walking, factories and offices instead of fields, and so on. Second, the introduction of machines tends to eliminate the traditional, local land-based economics (the hunting, herding, or planting culture) and create dependence on money and employment.

Finally, by eliminating traditional ways of doing and making, that is, the hunting, herding, or planting way of life and the production of crafts, the introduction of machines tends to suppress or eliminate the traditional cultural life of the people. The spiritual or mythic life of traditional peoples is oriented around these practical events—the hunt, the harvest, and the making of the artifacts of everyday life. The native culture of the people of the Great Plains of North America died with the buffalo. In third world countries today, many feel a spiritual void when they are forced to leave the villages of their ancestors and move to the cities to find employment.

The spiritual life of traditional peoples was tied to the practical arts of everyday living; these, in turn, were deeply rooted in nature. On the other hand, in the modern West, we have tried our best to create an artificial world, free from dependence on nature. In the West, nature was perceived as corrupt and evil by religion and as a dirty, disordered mess by technology-driven science. The machine would provide the means with which to defeat nature, to organize and clean up the mess. As the influential twentieth century Swiss architect, Charles Le Corbusier, extolled, "Sweep away the refuse with which life is soiled, clogged, and encumbered, let us undertake the great tasks of the new machine civilization." While no one can deny the benefits that modern machines have brought, we have to recognize that these have not come without a cost. Chief among these costs is the desensitization of human beings.

If you spend the better part of a day tracking and hunting an animal and then watch it suffering as it dies from your arrow or spear, you are going to have a different feeling for that food than if you go to a crowded supermarket, pick up a piece of cellophane-wrapped meat, and throw it in the shopping cart. The same is true of the cereal grain you spent months planting, protecting, and harvesting vs. the box of processed and sugar-frosted cereal or the minute rice you find in the brightly colored box on aisle twelve. Hunting and planting are sensitizing and gratitude inducing in a way that the modern experience of food is not. Though we haven't the space to go into it here, a similar desensitization results from the way we travel, work, play, and relate, relative to that of our more "primitive" counterparts. We take this so much for granted in our common sense of the world that we have turned "touchy-feely" into a pejorative.

In a variety of ways, we've sacrificed our humanity for a sense of security in mechanical order. As Lewis Mumford writes: "As soon as man loses faith in his own potential significance and value, he reduces himself to the status of an animal who has lost the sureness of his elemental instinctual responses and must therefore take refuge in some even simpler mechanical pattern of order." Having lost the confidence in intuition and instinct, we seize on the rational mind as a means of gaining control. Yet by its nature, the rational mind is always in doubt. It can never have the certainty of intuition or instinct. Isolated and defensive, mired in doubt, we turn to the machine for salvation. The culture that does not affirm the value of instinctual and intuitive intelligences must take refuge in the machine, be it the machine of dogmatic beliefs, the machine of corporate organization and production, or the machines of consumptive pleasure.

At the beginning of the twenty-first century, the dominant forms of our lives are machine forms. Today, the typical person awakens, not to the light of the sun or the singing of birds, but to the alarm of a machine. He drives to work in a machine, where he works on a machine as a replaceable part in a large corporate or governmental machine. His leisure hours are spent playing on machines or watching a machine that advertises more machines. Most of the things we see around us are either machines or things made by machines. As we meditate on machine forms, we have a tendency to become machinelike. Now, to state the obvious, machines don't have any feelings. They don't respond the way living, growing things do.

In many of the world's great civilizations, the loss of the sensitizing influence of nature was mitigated by the uplifting influence of art. The architecture and artifacts of everyday life produced by a given people reveal a great deal about the way they experience life. From the greatest building to the smallest piece of jewelry, all manufacture is simply the stuff of nature transformed in the image of the consciousness of the worker or artisan. When work is done in a spirit of love, the objects produced retain the beauty of their intrinsic nature, while being enhanced by the skill and loving attention of the artisan. When goods are produced solely or principally for profit, this consciousness too is indelibly stamped on them. Today,

If you fall in love with a machine there is something wrong with your love life. If you worship a machine there is something wrong with your religion.

LEWIS MUMFORD

Industry without art is brutality.

ANANDA K. COOMARASWAMY

the mass-produced objects of our everyday lives lack the sensitizing quality of the human touch. We've lost the sensitizing and vivifying influences of art in our everyday lives.

The quantity as well as the quality of forms and symbols we encounter have their effect in sensitizing or desensitizing us. The constant bombardment of stimuli and the overwhelming volume of information to which we are daily subjected assault and deaden our senses. The psychic armor we put up against them robs our energy and further desensitizes us. Today, the pace of life is such that we scarcely have time to relate to one another or enjoy the simple beauty in things. We are constantly rushing here and there. It goes without saying that hurrying and receiving are mutually exclusive. Receiving requires relaxing and opening, while hurrying causes us to tense up and shut down.

The point of this entire discussion is simply this: the ideas, things, people, and pace of life around us have a profound effect in sensitizing or desensitizing us, and thus in opening us up or shutting us down to the deeper feelings in life. In modern commercial culture, the "new machine civilization," we've lost touch with our capacity for feeling and receiving the gift of life. Our lack of sensitivity, our inability to receive the gift—indeed, the rapture—of life itself prompts us to seek relief in a variety of entertainments and diversions which, in turn, further weaken our feeling capacity. In our separation from nature, we've lost what chief Luther Standing Bear called its "softening" influence. Our hearts have grown hard. Hard hearts find it difficult to trust, to open, to receive.

Genius is nothing more or less than childhood recovered . . . a childhood now equipped for self-expression with an adult's capacities.
—CHARLES BAUDELAIRE

Genuine receptivity requires an almost childlike innocence. For the individual today, cultivating the Tao is, in certain respects, a matter of attaining the kind of simplicity and naturalness that people in so-called "primitive" cultures knew from birth. Yet there is a different level of consciousness required to realize this kind of receptivity in today's technologically advanced and commercially dominated culture. For the "primitive," born into a culture whose values and way of life supported a sense of participation in nature, the development of his or her receptive capacities came without effort. For us, it must be consciously and deliberately pursued.

Beware your masculine nature;
But by keeping the feminine way,
You shall be to the world like a canyon
Where the Virtue eternal abides.
And go back to become as a child.

—LAO TZU

Freidrich Nietzsche described a threefold process in the maturation of consciousness. He said that in the first stage, we are like a *camel* bending down to have hoisted upon us the load of social conditioning, habit, and convention. In the second stage, we are like a *lion* roaring against the "thou shalts" of society. Only after we have completed the work of the lion do we become the child, which is to say, a fully human being, capable of spontaneously, intuitively, and competently responding to the world. The point is this: there is a path back to trust, naturalness, and receptivity. It is the path of letting go of psychological commitment to the attachments and conditioning we formed as a part of our socialization. As we let go of attachments, we regain the spontaneity of what the Taoists call the "uncarved block." As we become empty, so are we filled. The remainder of this chapter is devoted to a consideration of how the ego blocks our natural receptive capacities by forming attachments, and how we can let them go.

Receptivity and the Ego

When we're not attached to anything, all things are as they are: With activity there is no going, no staying.

—SENG TS'AN

In the denial of the feminine intelligences, in our removal from the softening influences of nature and art, and in the frenetic pace of modern life, we see cultural elements that contribute to a lack of receptivity. Yet we should keep in mind that the primary block on our receptive capacities is the ego itself. *Ego is an artificial boundary in a world of interconnectedness.* The ego cannot open to receive awareness or experience of anything greater than itself without feeling its very existence threatened. Cultural elements apply only in as much as they reinforce the ego and limit access to transcendence. For example, implicit in all of the feminine intelligences discussed above is an awareness of a consciousness that transcends ego; yet as a society, we have closed ourselves off from them. In a variety of ways, we have constructed a society designed to shelter ourselves from any experience that might allow or induce a breakthrough beyond the ego consciousness.

By definition, ego consciousness means limitation, separation, isolation, and alienation. Having committed ourselves to the restricted consciousness of the ego, we long for the expanded, undifferentiated consciousness we have separated ourselves from. Metaphorically speaking, we have rejected the vast expanse of infinite space and have confined ourselves to little rooms. Feeling this confinement as a restriction, we naturally seek escape or at least escape from the boredom that confinement brings.

Attachment is the vehicle through which we attempt to return to the sense of freedom and bliss we enjoyed in the whole or undifferentiated consciousness, while at the same time holding onto the ego. Attachment gives the illusion of ego expansion—that by attaching myself (ego) to some object, person, title, or event, I have become something more. I am now less constricted. My little room has gotten bigger. Yet since attachment keeps our attention riveted on the original contraction of awareness (the ego), the sense of limitation and restriction never leaves us, regardless of the quantity or quality of our attachments. Inevitably, frustration sets in as our efforts to get out of the room only seem to harden and reinforce its walls.

An elegant and poignant statement of this problem is given by the Biblical poet/king Solomon in Ecclesiastes. We feel his sense of exasperation and futility as he faces the realization that all of his efforts to expand his ego, whether by means of authority, conquest, or sensual indulgence, whether through territories, treasures, or monuments, whether through the pleasures of his hundreds of wives and concubines or the parental joys of fatherhood were in vain. He says over and again: "Vanity of vanities; all is vanity." All of his efforts to expand his ego had come to naught. They were in the end nothing but, as he put it, a "vexation of the spirit."

What keeps us from being as wise as Solomon is that we don't have the opportunity to acquire all the things we desire with the relative speed and ease of a powerful absolute monarch. As he put it, "What can the man *do* that cometh after the king? *even* that which hath been already done." Instead of concluding that attachment itself is the problem, we decide that we have only failed to get the *right* attachments. This possession didn't do it, but perhaps that one will; this relationship didn't do it, perhaps that one will. Perhaps that position or power, or those riches or honors, will do it. In this way, we go on—never really understanding the nature of the trap we've gotten ourselves into or that it is we ourselves who make the lock and hold the key.

Seek ye first the kingdom of god and all things will be added unto you.
                                                                —LUKE 12:31

We are like the monkey with his hand caught in the jar while grasping for peanuts. We do not realize that we can pull our hand free of the jar at any time, but that to do so, we must first unclench the fist and let go of the nuts. The clenched fist is the ego's desire for expansion through attachment; the peanut is the object of our attachment. If we want to participate in the natural abundance of the Tao, we must let go of our identification with lack (the ego). We must come to life with hands and hearts open.

The problem of attachment is one that every spiritual or religious philosophy in some way addresses. While these philosophies differ in their particulars, in general, there are only two basic approaches to this problem: (1) Renunciation and (2) Release in Engagement.

Renunciation: Renunciation is the approach favored not only by the yogis of India but by classical Greek philosophers such as Plato and Aristotle, the Roman Stoics, and the desert fathers of the early Christian church, who developed the ideal of the ascetic monk as the penultimate spiritual path. The idea is perhaps best expressed by Plato, who said in essence: That one is happiest, who needs the fewest things (requires the fewest attachments) to be happy. The reduce-your-attachments model is based on the idea of starving or shrinking the ego by reducing its opportunities for expansion through attachment. If we put no more air in a balloon, it will eventually deflate.

In today's commercial culture, this requires that we move in a direction precisely opposite to that taken by the rest of society. While going against the societal grain has, to a greater or lesser degree, always been a part of the renunciate's life, there are certain factors that make it an even greater challenge today. Though the use of money dates back to the ancient Phoenicians and Greeks, it is only in very recent years that it has become a requisite for the maintenance of life itself. Never before has space been at such a premium. Today, virtually all land is owned by individuals, corporations, or

*By letting go,
it all gets done.
The world is won
by those who let it go!*

LAO TZU

governments. There are no open spaces. One cannot simply retreat to the forest as in days of old. Today, "renunciates" typically live in ashrams and monasteries, where they must conform to a highly organized and regimented way of life, which is not without its own entanglements.

Yet as difficult and as important a factor as the cultural component of this problem is, it pales before the more fundamental and universal one, namely: *Attachment is not essentially a physical, but rather a mental and emotional phenomenon.* Ego is a mental structure built on name. (See chapter 1.) Having no basis in physical reality, it is an abstraction of thought. Manipulations of the external physical world—such as reducing one's physical possessions or human entanglements—are only significant to the degree that they alter the internal mechanics of attachment.

It doesn't follow that a reduction of the quantity of possessions or responsibilities will correspond with freedom from ego attachment. On the contrary, it's quite possible to develop an expansion or inflation of the ego, based on how "unattached" or "spiritual" we perceive ourselves to be. The "spiritual ego" can be a more difficult nut to crack than the strictly materially oriented ego. While a simple lifestyle is preferable for those seeking spiritual enlightenment, it by no means guarantees freedom from attachment.

There are, then, two problems with the path of renunciation. First, it requires that we remove ourselves from the life of society. Not only are we to eschew material possessions but also relationships with the opposite sex, as well as any responsible position in society. Second, we are as likely to develop egoic pride in our status as renunciates as we are from the engagement in the life of society.

Release in Engagement: A second alternative is the path of psychological release from the ego, while engaged in the activities of everyday life. Release in engagement is the middle-way path of the Mahayana Buddhists, the path urged on Arjuna by Krishna in the Bhagavad-Gita, as well as that of the classical Taoists. Yet of all the world's great spiritual traditions, the Taoist seems most comfortable with being on earth. As historian Henri Maspero wrote, "The Chinese never separated Spirit and Matter, and for them the world was a continuum passing from the Void at one end to the grossest matter at the other, hence 'soul' never took up this antithetical character in relation to matter."[10]

The classical Taoists did not see a dichotomy or inherent conflict between spirit and nature. On the contrary, they viewed the spiritual life as the full flowering of human nature. For example, while many spiritual traditions have great difficulty reconciling spiritual life with the sexual impulse, the Taoists developed the sexual arts as a means of enhancing physical health while cultivating spiritual potency. As with sex, so too with the everyday business of making a living. The practical arts were viewed as a means of cultivating spiritual life, not as something that must be given up in order to pursue the spiritual path.

For example, Chuang Tzu married and raised a family. He did not choose to live in a monastery or wander the countryside with the begging bowl of the mendicant monk. While much is made of the fact that he refused government service, Chuang Tzu did practice a trade. He made his wares and sold them in the marketplace. Again, what is significant is not the outer circumstances of our lives but the inner freedom from attachment.

We don't have to adopt the trappings of spirituality to live in freedom. We can hold jobs, marry, have children, participate in society, and enjoy material comforts. All of the apparent attachments of the ego, including name, memory, possessions, relationships, and so on, may be enjoyed without identifying with them as part and parcel of who we are. The key is to remain psychologically free.

When we are told that enlightened beings are unmoved by praise or blame, it is precisely because they no longer inwardly identify with names. The release from the psychological commitment to ego creates a nonstick surface upon which anything may appear but to which nothing can attach. In the Buddhist Heart Sutra, we read that "the Bodhisattva of Compassion sundered all bonds that caused him suffering." In other words, he released identification with the ego and, in so doing, severed all of its attachments.

We too should make ourselves empty, that the great soul of the universe may fill us with its breath.

LAWRENCE BINYON

> *Can you support the spiritual energy and material soul and embrace the One without letting go?* —WANG PI

Up to now, we've considered attachments in terms of the possessive attachments that arise from the original attachment to name, for example, memories, physical possessions, and so on. Most people are aware of, and indeed take a certain pride in, these kinds of attachments. Yet not all attachments are as obvious as these. Our receptive capacities and our ability to respond spontaneously in the moment are also blocked by *unconscious associative attachments (mental triggers)* as well as *conscious* and *unconscious proscriptive at-*

tachments (limiting beliefs). By *unconscious associative attachments,* we mean the conditioned responses that interfere with our ability to be here and now in the moment. *Conscious* and *unconscious proscriptive attachments* are any limiting or separating beliefs that we consciously and unconsciously hold about life, ourselves, or others. Below, we will examine these more subtle attachments and how we can release them.

Mental Triggers: Conditioned Responses

*It is our less conscious thoughts and our less conscious
actions which mainly mould our lives and the lives of
those who spring from us.* —SAMUEL BUTLER

Responding spontaneously to life requires that we be in the moment, present with the people and circumstances in our lives. Yet often we are lost in a world inside our heads. How is it that your attention suddenly moves out of the moment and drifts into a daydream? Why is it that you suddenly feel fearful, angry, or uneasy for no apparent reason? Why do you find yourself going round and round in a circle of thoughts you haven't intended to think? These are just some of the effects of mental triggers, otherwise known as "conditioned responses."

The pioneering behaviorist John Watson conducted some rather bizarre classical conditioning studies at the University of Chicago. A famous one involved an eleven-month-old subject named Albert. In this experiment, Watson introduced a white rat to Albert by placing it on or near the child. At first, Albert showed no fear of the rat. Next, Watson began to accompany the introduction of the rat with a loud noise that startled and frightened the child. Every time the rat appeared, Watson subjected the infant to the noise. Albert would become upset and begin to cry.

After repeatedly conditioning the child in this fashion, introducing the rat without the noise produced the same fearful response. Next, Watson exposed the infant to rabbits, cats, and small dogs. Even without the reintroduction of the startling noise, Albert generalized the conditioned fear onto these small animals. Thus, in a surprisingly short period of time, a previously fearless child had been conditioned to fear a number of perfectly harmless creatures.

While Waston's methods were cruel in their deliberateness, it is easy to see that in the course of everyday life, similar kinds of associative phenomena occur *naturally*. Sensations of pleasure as well as pain are generated by associative triggers that we often remain unconscious of. A smell, sight, or sound may trigger emotions that have nothing whatever to do with the situation at hand. We might wonder how many of these associative memories each of us has formed by the time we've reached adulthood. We can think of these mental triggers as our unconscious attachments.

Imagine you are observing an event or trying to concentrate on a task, while one or more aspects of it are triggering associative memories within your mind. A sound, a smell, a tone of voice, or an object sets your mind to running. Though you remain physically present, mentally, you have checked out. You are no longer observing what is actually before you, but have become mentally and emotionally engaged in your memory banks. You see the situation through a distorted filter of associative memory and lose the power of clear observation and effective concentration. In this state, you may jump to erroneous conclusions based, not on the facts of the situation, but on emotional reactions to your associative memories. You may find it all but impossible to concentrate, and conclude that you lack discipline or will power.

A similar process occurs in our encounter with ideas. It's unconscious associative attachments that make certain words so highly charged for some people. For many, the word *God* is loaded with associative attachments. Hearing this word brings to mind guilt, fear, or anger—not because this is the way they rationally or objectively think about God, but because of their associative memories. In your casual conversations, you may have been surprised or startled when the mention of some word or idea produced a strong emotional reaction from the other party. At best, the triggering of these kinds of associative attachments confound and thwart communication. At worst, they can produce highly emotional or even violent reactions.

All men desire to free themselves solely from death; they do not know how to free themselves from life.

LAO TZU

Examining Your Associations with Money

To recognize what is beyond your ability to change, and to be content with this as your destiny —that is truly a sign of virtue.

CHUANG TZU

Unconscious associative attachments may be affecting your relationship with money—blocking your ability to receive the natural abundance of the universe. Today, money is the great remaining taboo of social discourse. People are generally more reticent to talk about money than they are politics, religion, or even sex. Yet there is much to be gained by breaking the taboo and exploring your beliefs about money.

Many people have been conditioned to associate making money with struggle and pain, and thus have come to believe that they can only earn it by doing things they don't want to do. In my work as a career consultant, I have encountered this belief many times. One man, who was financially successful but very unhappy in his job, told me that he knew there was no way that he could possibly make as much money doing something that he loved as he was making in his present job. When I asked him what he would really enjoy doing, he said he didn't know. He had to chuckle when I pointed out to him that it was impossible to compare a known with an unknown. He realized that his limiting ideas about money were not based on objective reality but were, in fact powerful associations that he held deep in his subconscious mind. When we probed a little deeper, he told me that his parents' struggles with money had greatly affected his own feelings about it.

As children, many people heard their parents worry about or argue over money. They came to associate money management with conflict and stress. They may have inculcated a sense of guilt and shame around expressing what they want. In a variety of ways, many of us have come to associate money with pain, or to think of it as something dirty or bad. If, in your childhood, you repeatedly heard statements like: "There is never enough money," "We can't afford it," "Everything costs too much," and so on, these beliefs could well be affecting your relationship with money today. In the exercises at the end of the book, you will have the opportunity to examine your beliefs about money and how they might be keeping you from receiving all you deserve, or from earning it with less struggle.

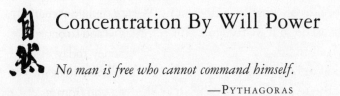

Breaking Through the Mental Fog

The true value of the human being is determined by the measure and the sense in which one has attained liberation from the self.
—ALBERT EINSTEIN

There are many ways to free yourself from the influence of unconscious associative attachments. Yet there is a single test for measuring their influence on your life: The degree to which you are free of unconscious associative attachments is the degree to which you can concentrate your attention. If your conscious mind is focused on A while your subconscious is focused on B, you can't bring to bear the same mental energy that you would were the whole of your mind and being concentrated on a single thing.

Most of us are subject to a kind of mental chatterbox, an inner dialogue of thoughts that we do not consciously intend. This is not the still, clear voice of intuition but the associative ramblings of the subconscious mind. In pop-psychology circles, this inner dialogue is sometimes referred to as *self-talk*. There are a variety of ways in which we can improve the quality of our self-talk to make it more supportive and constructive (see the exercises at the end of the book). Yet we are far better off if we can turn it off altogether. When your mind is empty, you are free to respond spontaneously and naturally to the world around you. Below, we will explore and contrast two kinds of concentration, a yang concentration by will power and a more yin process of absorption, which we could call *merge consciousness*.

Concentration By Will Power

No man is free who cannot command himself.
—PYTHAGORAS

Concentration means exerting the energy necessary to focus and maintain attention on some object, symbol, or experience to the exclusion of all else. In many Eastern spiritual traditions, the development of concentration skills is viewed as a preliminary step to meditation and contemplation. If your subconscious mind is full of thoughts and images, it will be difficult to meditate or to follow a philosophical inquiry to its end. As we develop our powers of concentration, we reduce the background noise of the mental chatterbox. In time, we come to silence it altogether. In so doing, we eliminate the separating (through the triggering of unconscious associative attachments) influence of the subconscious mind while retaining, and indeed greatly improving, our ability to take advantage of its extraordinary capacity for memory. Concentration can be thought of as a mental fire that consumes unconscious attachments.

Boredom is a symptom of an inability to concentrate. When we are bored, it is always first and foremost with ourselves. We bore ourselves with the wearisome and repetitive round of often inane and sometimes frightful thoughts and images that the subconscious generates on the screens of our minds. When our attention is concentrated and fully engaged in the moment, our psychic energy is so fully utilized that none remains for unconscious chatter.

Most of us have experienced a temporary stilling of the mind after vigorous exercise. There are times when intense, even raging, passion can lead to a profound and deep peace. Many of us have experienced this during or after making love. The "high" associated with many adventure sports results from the concentration of the mind. When we are in a free-fall skydive or scaling the rock face of a cliff, all of our attention is riveted to the moment.

Yet we can strengthen our ability to concentrate in less dramatic ways. Our everyday work can provide opportunities to sharpen our concentration skills. We can simply go through the motions, or we can bring our fullest attention to the task at hand. Of course, it helps if our work is something we truly love and enjoy. Yet there are always ways in which we can bring more attention to bear on what is in front of us. We are much more likely to make the effort to do so if we recognize the act of concentrating itself as one from which we benefit.

The idea behind the *dō* practices associated with Zen Buddhism, such as the martial arts, the tea ceremony, or the art of flower arrangement, is to create an encounter with ourselves. In attempting to do anything with full concentration, we become aware of all the places we are not present in our lives. Your *dō* might be painting or writing, performing music, or repairing autos. By learning to do any one thing with total focus, you bring a clarity and simplicity to the whole of your life. Along the way, you will discover that you have left behind countless unconscious associative attachments. Ironically, consistent concentrated effort brings a relaxed effortlessness and spontaneity. At first, you exert great energy to focus on what you are doing. In time, it just comes naturally. This is the process of mastery in any of the arts. Those who fail to exert the energy to concentrate never know the ease that comes to one who has become the task. There is a saying among Chinese painters: *Meditate on bamboo for ten years, become bamboo, and then paint yourself.* This is the path of spontaneity through concentration.

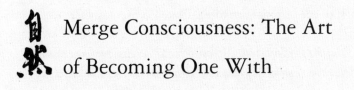

Merge Consciousness: The Art of Becoming One With

How can I be still?
By flowing with the stream.
　　　　　　—LAO TZU

Concentration by will power destroys unconscious attachments yet retains self-consciousness, the sense that "I" am concentrating. In merge consciousness, the awareness of self is gone. Merge consciousness is qualitatively different from both ordinary conscious attention and the subconscious chatterbox that typically dominate mental awareness. From the perspective of conscious attention, one experiences oneself as separate from the "object" of focus and experiences all else as separate, distant, and "out there" in relation to the self "in here." Conscious attention is extremely narrow, working much like a spotlight, bringing illumination to a tiny area of focus. The subconscious mind is more inclusive. Yet because it reduces all experience to memories that are sorted, organized, and stored, these memory files can be easily and automatically triggered in ways that remove us from our immediate experience. On the other hand, merge consciousness takes us into the experience of the moment, while at the same time removing the sense of separation in the subject/object relationship.

　　Absorption, or merge consciousness, is the state of being so completely absorbed in an object, experience, or event that all sense of time, space, and self are lost. The German philosopher Freidrich Von Schelling put it like this, "When the perceiving self merges in the self-perceived . . . at that moment, we annihilate time." In merge consciousness, we experience what

Those whose happiness is attached within the finite sphere will certainly have limitation.

KUO HSIANG

Ananda K. Coomarswamy calls "the destruction of the mental and affective barriers behind which the natural manifestation of the spirit is concealed." We penetrate through the forms of things to the essence, or Tao.

In merge consciousness, the separation between self and other has been overcome. In Sanskrit, this experience is called *yoyata,* or self-identification, meaning that one becomes (united in consciousness with) the object of his attention. To truly become the other is to become all others or to have become nothing at all. This is the mystical experience. It is the essence of religion in the truest sense of the word from *religio* (literally, "to link back"). It is linking back to the original, undifferentiated consciousness.

> *Everything about me is identified. My eye becomes my ear, my ear becomes my nose, my nose my mouth. My mind is highly integrated and my body dissolves. My bone and my flesh melt away. I cannot tell by what my body is supported or what my feet walk upon. I am blowing away, east and west, as a dry leaf torn from a tree. I cannot even make out whether the wind is riding on me or I am riding on the wind.* —LIEH TZU

Mind Traps: Unexamined Beliefs

Attachment is the greatest fabricator of illusions; reality can be attained only be someone who is detached. —SIMONE WEIL

The interest of the classical Taoists was never in abstract concepts of what ought to be, but in discovering and affirming what is. They were never so arrogant as to suggest that the separative ego could ever invent a way better than the way that is of-itself-so. Always trusting in and affirming naturalness, the Taoists encouraged us to free ourselves from all the culturally conditioned and/or idiosyncratic beliefs that limit and frustrate us.

We impede our capacity to receive by holding limiting beliefs about what, when, and how we should receive. For example, if we believe that it is morally superior to be poor than financially comfortable, we limit our capacity to receive wealth. If we believe that it is a sign of weakness to show vulnerability, we limit our capacity to be loved as we are. If we believe that men and women are supposed to act in certain ways, we confine ourselves to culturally sanctioned gender roles. Of course, the same applies when we react against how we think we are supposed to act. Either way, we are letting ourselves be controlled by limiting beliefs. The way of *tzu-jan* means following our natures in each and every moment, however politically correct or incorrect we may appear to others.

Often, we limit our capacity to receive by confusing the roles that we ourselves play with who we really are. Defining yourself or others in role-playing terms limits your capacity to respond spontaneously in the moment. Think of how happy you were when you first fell in love. You received and appreciated every attention and kindness the new lover gave to you as wonderful and exciting gifts. Your openness to the other made you extremely sensitive to the subtlest nuances of mood or feeling. This sensitivity made you feel fully alive.

Yet all too soon, most of us begin to take the gifts for granted and come to expect them as an obligation due us. As our receptivity diminishes, so does our sensitivity, and often before we know it, the thrill is gone. One of the keys to maintaining a loving relationship is never to forget that what we receive from the other is truly a gift. The same applies to all of our relationships. All too often, we don't relate human to human, soul to soul. We relate conventionally, role to role. To be free of the mental attachment to roles is to treat those whom society defines as our betters or inferiors, not according to their respective ranks or roles, but as fellow human beings. Seeing through the illusory nature of role, we have understanding and compassion for the boss and treat the waitress or cab driver with the fullest dignity and respect.

I once had an encounter with Hopi tribal leaders, which illustrates the value of keeping an open mind, free of prejudices. After centuries of abuse, lies, and manipulations, they were justifiably skeptical of white people and of letting them too close to their authentic teachings. A middle-aged leader was telling me as much, when a wise old man brought him up short. He said, "In the old way, we were taught to listen to each one's heart and respond to each accordingly." This is the essence of the principle of *tzu-jan*, to respond spontaneously to each and every situation or person before us. It means to avoid lumping people into groups of any kind, to divest ourselves of preconceived notions of who someone is or what to expect from them, and to respond freely and spontaneously—human to human.

Limiting beliefs can also take the form of "if, then" statements. Only if this happens can that happen. Only if I do what I don't want to do can I make a good living. Only if I deny who I really am can I find love. Only if

When the Great Tao is lost, we have "goodness" and "righteousness." When "wisdom" and "sagacity" arise we have great hypocrites.

LAO TZU

Renunciation means looking upon the universe as essentially Pure Consciousness.

APAROKSANUBHUTI

I obtain xyz degree will people take me seriously. Only when I have earned enough money can I relax and enjoy life. The truth is that the love that pervades the universe is of-itself-so. Nothing must happen first before you can receive it. Nothing must happen before you can receive the abundance of the universe.

We limit our capacity to receive by holding limiting beliefs about how the abundance of the universe must come to us. For example, if we believe that money can only come to us through employment income, we might miss opportunities for making money that are right in front of us. If we believe that all of our needs must be met by our mates, we limit ourselves from seeking or recognizing other opportunities to express and grow. The Eternal Tao is everywhere, and its natural abundance may come to us in an infinite variety of forms, if we are open to receiving them.

There is a story of a deeply pious man caught in a flood. As the waters rise, his neighbors encourage him to leave with them. He dismisses their warnings and tells them that he is not worried. "God will save me," he declares. The waters continue to rise, and soon a rescue crew in a boat is approaching the man's house. "Get in!" they yell. The man waves them off shouting, "God will save me. God will save me." Finally, sitting perched on the roof of his house as it floats along in a raging torrent, the man sees a helicopter hovering overhead. The men above drop down a rope ladder and entreat the man to grab the rope and climb up. He refuses and bravely shouts to them, "Don't worry. God will save me." As they begin to run out of fuel, the chopper rescue crew departs and the man drowns. When he arrives in heaven, the man indignantly confronts God. "I had faith in you. Why didn't you save me?" he demands. Stroking his long, white beard, God quietly replies, "I tried to save you three times, but you wouldn't listen." Too often, we are like the man in the story, limiting ourselves by insisting that things come to us in certain ways. Releasing these kinds of limiting beliefs allows us to respond spontaneously to the world around us and to recognize support from the universe that we might otherwise miss.

Observing and Directing the Mind

To be awake is to walk the border between control and abandon.
— CARLOS CASTENADA

The key to overcoming attachment to limiting beliefs is awareness. Awareness transforms. As Maurice Maeterlinck put it, "It is far more important that one's life should be perceived than that it should be transformed; for no sooner has it been perceived, than it transforms itself of its own accord." Below, we will consider two methods for the practice of awareness. The first is a yin, or receptive, method that relies solely on awareness; the second, a more yang approach that relies on awareness and will.

Mindfulness: Mindfulness simply means bringing full consciousness to whatever you are doing, be it sitting or standing, walking or thinking. If concentration is focusing your mind as though you were looking through a microscope, mindfulness is looking at your mind as though through a telescope—from a distance. Mindful meditation is the practice of observing with full consciousness your thoughts and reactions to the people, things, and experiences of your life. Do not judge or try to change these thoughts and feelings. Simply observe them in a detached manner, as though they were images appearing on a screen. Learn to see your thoughts with an equal mind, which is to say, for what they are, feeling neither attraction for nor repulsion against them. This may take a good deal of patience and focus, as well as some considerable practice, but it will give you a tremendous sense of freedom. In time, you will find yourself developing a deep peace. You will be able to confront the pressures and stresses of life while remaining calm and steady within.

The first rule is to keep an untroubled spirit. The second is to look things in the face and know them for what they are. — MARCUS AURELIUS

At first, you may only notice your reactions of attraction and repulsion *after* you have become caught up in them. In time, you will begin to notice them as they begin to stir the waters of your mind but before they become a whirlpool. You will feel yourself starting to lose your balance, but will catch yourself before you fall into the abyss. Eventually, you will notice

these thoughts and feelings *before* you become emotionally or intellectually identified with them. You will notice as well that a thought always precedes a feeling. You react emotionally because you have identified with a thought that provokes this reaction. Let go of the identification with the thought and you short-circuit the emotional reaction. After some practice, you may find yourself having a good laugh at self-conscious thoughts that previously wound you up in knots. Awareness robs destructive thoughts of their power to make us react. As Seng Ts'an put it, "When all things are seen with an equal mind, they return to their nature."

Intervention: A second method also relies on awareness, but additionally requires that you actively intervene by mentally replacing, canceling, or reversing thoughts that agitate and pull you away from your center. For example, you find yourself thinking thoughts that are producing feelings of jealousy and mistrust. You command that your subconscious mind stop thinking these thoughts and replace them with thoughts that remind you of all you have to be grateful for. You remind yourself that you are safe.

> *Anyone who has insight into his own actions and has thus found access to the unconscious, involuntary exercises an influence on his environment.*
> —CARL JUNG

In an instant, you can grab the reins of a mind running out of control. Perhaps you find yourself thinking low self-esteem thoughts about yourself, thinking in a disparaging way about others, or thinking fearfully about some future outcome. Command your subconscious to knock it off by immediately saying aloud or thinking to yourself: *Cancel! Cancel!* or *Stop! Not this!* Finally, you can mentally reverse a situation that has gone badly for you. Suppose you have gotten into a heated argument with a friend or loved one. You replay the situation in your mind, paying particular attention to the moment things got out of hand. Next, imagine yourself and the other party in the same situation, only this time, each of you is responding in a way consistent with your best. In this imagined scenario, the blowup never occurs and love and respect for one another is reaffirmed. This exercise will help clear your mind of any lasting impressions from the event and help you to mentally let go of it.

Those who really seek the path to enlightenment dictate terms to their mind. They then proceed with strong determination.

BUDDHA

Turning Off the Mind

Stop thinking that meditation is anything special.
Stop thinking altogether. —SURYA SINGER

It is when the mind is empty, in the state the Taoists call *"wu-nein,"* literally "no thought" that receptivity and the capacity to respond spontaneously are at their zenith. This state of alertness without attachment is the natural state of our "original mind." Lieh Tzu said, "When the mind is still, the whole universe surrenders." Now, there is no question of abundance or lack, no separation or unity. We have become the universe and all of its treasures are ours.

Stilling the mind is the sole purpose of all meditation. Later chapters will have much more to say about the ways and means of meditation. Here, the point is simply to recognize that when the mind is still, we are at one with the natural intelligence of the universe. This is the intelligence we generally call "intuition." It isn't really "your" intuition but simply the intelligence of the universe (Tao), aware of itself in a particular location. When we allow ourselves to be guided by this intelligence, our responses are truly spontaneous. They are in the spirit of *tzu-jan*—natural, unpremeditated, and authentic.

Abundance means "to overflow," and to overflow, we must first be filled. This chapter explored the importance of opening to receive. It said, in essence, first receive, then give; first be, then do. Move into the world from the psychology of abundance but not from lack. The next chapter will explore how we can move, act, and create in the world from a spirit of abundance. We can create with ease by following the path of least resistance, what the Taoists call *wu-wei*. *Wu-wei,* or effortless action, is the subject of the next chapter.

Ego Attachments

Conscious Possessive Attachments
(My Stuff)

Anything that we consciously hold onto as distinguishing and separating "possessions." It is not the things themselves, but the sense of possession of them that makes these attachments. Conscious possessive attachments may, among others, include:

"MY" Things	"MY" Relationships	"MY" Problems
"MY" Personality	"MY" Body	"MY" Career Role
"MY" Social Status	"MY" Knowledge	"MY" Race or Nationality
"MY" Money	"MY" Sex	"MY" Religion

Unconscious Associative Attachments
(My Background Noise)

Any thoughts, feelings, or sensations generated by the subconscious mind that remove us from our immediate experience. Includes:

- The mental chatterbox
- Certain fantasies or daydreams
- The store of conditioned responses

Conscious & Unconscious Proscriptive Attachments
(My Limiting Beliefs)

Cultural and idiosyncratic limiting or separative beliefs about life, self, work, or others, including ideas such as:

- Spirit and nature are in conflict.
- Technology will solve all the problems of humankind.
- You can't do what you want in life.
- People in group x, y, or z are always stupid, lazy, or deceitful.
- What matters most is what other people think of you.
- Might is right.
- Rich people are better than poor people because they are more ambitious and industrious.
- Poor people are better than rich people because money is evil and only evil people have a lot of it.

The Law of the Vacuum: Out with the Old, Make Way for the New

Nature abhors a vacuum. When we exhale fully and deeply, the inhale takes care of itself. If you want to bring more into your life, let more out of it. By discarding what no longer works in your life, you make way to receive more of what you do want.

Out with Old Grudges and Grievances: Make peace with the world and everyone in it. Forgiveness releases tremendous energy attached to painful memories. What we do not forgive we have a tendency to relive, in one way or another. The spiritual law is: we receive for ourselves the forgiveness we give to others. Through forgiveness you free yourself from the resentment you hold toward others and the guilt you hold against yourself. Forgive everyone and everything and you too are forgiven all.

Out with Old Ways of Doing Things: Wake up from the sleep of habit and routine. Try things you haven't done before. Find different ways of doing things you always do. Even minor changes in routine can knock you out of the sleepwalk of the automatic. By putting yourself in situations that demand your total presence, you thrust yourself into the here-and-now moment, which, after all, is the only place you can truly receive anything.

Out with Old Ways of Relating: Break out of automatic patterns of relating. For example, if you are chronically shy, try acting in an outgoing or outrageous manner. If you are used to taking control and running the show, try relating in a more passive and receptive way. Demonstrate to yourself that you are not locked into limited concepts of who you are. Remember, you are a free being, capable of responding in a variety of ways, not a personality package of limited conditioned responses.

Out with Old Things: Avoid the pack-rat syndrome. Give away things you no longer need or use. Psychologically, as well as literally, you are making space whenever you give things away. The empty space you create can be filled with the things you really want in your life.

Out with Old Limiting Ideas: Identify and examine limiting beliefs about life, yourself, work, and others. Eliminate tired and worn-out ways of thinking, that you have accepted without critical evaluation.

CHAPTER THREE

Wu-wei

THE EASE OF ABUNDANCE

Use what is naturally useful; do what you spontaneously can do. . . .This is the most easy matter of nonaction. When you are in accordance with the principle of nonaction, your life cannot but be perfect. —CHUANG TZU

No matter how materially successful we are, if our lives are filled with struggle and stress, the experience of abundance has eluded us. Abundant living has an easy and effortless quality to it. If you recognize yourself as being at one with the process that is the universe, if you have opened to receive the bounteous gifts of life and of your own nature, you are free to act with ease in a world you feel at home in. On the other hand, from the standpoint of the ego, the universe is seen as "other." The ego concludes that this "other" is against it and, therefore, that it must struggle to survive. This chapter will explore how the ego consciousness creates the illusion of a world against us—one which we must struggle to overcome. Awareness of these dynamics can keep us from falling into patterns of unnecessary struggle and stress. Also in this chapter, you will find suggestions on how you can follow the path of least resistance, including practical strategies for creating with ease. In the related exercises at the end of the book, you will have the opportunity to integrate and apply the principles discussed here and, in so doing, go with the flow of your deepest desires in an easy, effortless manner.

The *I Ching* tells us that as the Receptive is the principle of the Earth, so the Creative is the principle of Heaven. The creativity of the universe, that intelligence and energy which grows life all around us, including our own bodies, lives within us. From the perspective of the Taoists, we are naturally creative beings. As one living in the Tao is open and receptive to life and its natural intelligence, he or she acts freely in an unforced and effortless manner, devoid of inner coercion or struggle. This is called acting in the spirit of *wu-wei*. Though literally translated "not action," or "nonaction," the terms "effortless action" or "unforced action" gives us a truer sense of how we can apply the principle of *wu-wei* to our own lives.[1] We could say that *wu-wei* is the principle of least resistance if we mean by this, using the least amount of energy necessary and not mere passivity or avoidance.

A baby falls from a window; a drunk man, from a cart; yet both escape without injury. Having no fear, they do not tense or brace themselves; they offer no resistance to the fall and come away unharmed. From this, the Taoists drew a lesson: the way of least resistance provides a way of moving safely in a world full of dangers. Unlike the baby or the drunk man, most of us tense when we feel out of control. We brace ourselves and struggle and effort our way through the world. Action in the spirit of *wu-wei* is free of this underlying tension. It implies a fundamental trust in life, self, and the universe, which results from recognizing these as one in the same process.

We could say that *wu-wei* is receptivity in action. Unforced or effortless action arises from what Chuang Tzu called "the center of the circle." This "center of the circle," like the center of a hurricane or the center of a clock, is still. From stillness comes clarity. Effortless action assumes the capacity to open and receive and thus to see into the essence of things and their principles. Effortless action is action in harmony with the intelligence of the universe. It is this intuitive intelligence that guides us on the way. It is this intelligence or awareness that makes the action easy or effortless.

Kuan-yin said:

If nothing within you stays rigid,
Outward things will disclose themselves.[2]

Observing nature, the Taoists noticed that young and growing things are soft, supple, and yielding, while old and dying things are hard, brittle, and rigid. Attaching ourselves to preconceived ideas makes us stiff, rigid, and brittle. Then we are left with struggling to figure things out and struggling to make things happen. By remaining inwardly soft, receptive, and open, we allow things to reveal themselves to us. In the words of an Estonian proverb: The work will teach you how to do it. This is the heart of Taoist creativity. It serves as the fundamental method of all Taoist art and science. (See "The Five Fingers of the Tao.")

Wu-wei, or unforced action, means letting things come to us. Even more, it means letting things become us, or—more prosaically—become reflected in us. We become the empty mirror in which the innate intelligence in all things is reflected. As Chuang Tzu said, "The mind of the sage being in repose becomes the mirror of the universe." Thus, we don't struggle to figure things out but allow things to speak to us and tell us what to do with them. This is an aspect of intelligence that we in the modern world have lost contact with. When native peoples discovered the healing properties of certain plants, it wasn't the result of systematically testing the chemical compounds of each. It was, as has often been recounted to inquiring ethnographers or botanists, because the spirit of the plant told them.

The Taoists repeatedly advise us to move like water. Water conforms to the shape of things, yet retains its own innate and effortless power. In time, it reduces even great mountains to rubble. Thus *wu-wei* lets things be as they are and, at the same time, transforms them. The leader leads by embracing and effortlessly guiding the forces of human nature. She does not differentiate between right and wrong but lets people be as they are. She brings both what we think of as their good and their bad qualities into accord with the Way. She has no need to idealize or deny, to condemn or correct and does not struggle against what they are. Released of self, free of egoic attachments, she has no position to defend, no opinion to ram down the throats of others. Thus, in an effortless, almost invisible way, she leads without leading. She directs the attentions and actions of others, but they do not feel forced to go her way. As she has no way, no agenda of her own, she is free to guide them in the Way.

> *The sage never follows his own heart;*
> *He takes the people's heart as his own heart.*
> —LAO TZU

Like the flow of water, effortless action is fluid, unhesitating. Spontaneous free action arises from the emptiness. As Chuang Tzu put it, "The man

The greatest effect of the Spirit is to elicit the spirit.

GOETHE

of perfect virtue in repose has no thoughts, in action no anxiety."[3] As was discussed in the previous chapter, it is from attachments, which are ultimately only thoughts, that anxiety arises. We worry that we might lose face or a job, a mate or a healthy body, a financial fortune or our very lives. We struggle to get and fear to lose, and thus are never at ease. When we act from anxiety, which is another way of saying when we fear to lose, we are never at our best.

Anxiety brings hesitation or desperation, and both confound action. Again, *wu-wei* is easy, unforced action, not laziness or passivity. To block action on an inspiration or intuition with the hesitation or paralysis of self-conscious thinking is missing the spirit of *wu-wei* every bit as much as pushing and forcing a result. Spontaneous easy action is free of ulterior motives and attachment to results. It walks without leaving tracks, leads without force, achieves without leaving a mark. When the Buddhist Pali Canon tells us to make money like a bee, it is telling us to earn our living in the spirit of *wu-wei*.

> *The wise and moral man*
> *Shines like a fire on a hilltop,*
> *Making money like the bee,*
> *Who does not hurt the flower.*
> —THE PALI CANON (500–250 B.C.E.)

Again, to be free of attachments is to be without thoughts when still and without anxiety when acting. In one of the classics of Tai Ch'i Chuan, the same meaning is poetically rendered: Be still as a mountain, move like a great river.[4] Being free of attachments, the mind is fluid and flexible. Stuck to nothing, it flows freely and responds spontaneously. The sixth patriarch of Ch'an Buddhism called this principle "awakening the mind without fixing it anywhere." When our minds are fully aware and awake, yet fluid and relaxed, our actions have a simplicity and clarity to them. We are capable of spontaneous, decisive action, what Zen (Ch'an) calls "going ahead without hesitation" *("mo chich ch'u").*

The Struggle for Survival Revisited

Tao abides in non-action
Yet nothing is left undone.
—LAO TZU

When Voltaire said, "Men argue, nature acts," he was giving an insight into the principle of *wu-wei*. The arguing man is the ego; the natural man or woman is the man or woman of Tao. The ego argues its way through life, struggling unnecessarily with everything and everyone. The world we see is a reflection of the conditions of our minds, and the ego sees the world as a battlefield. It coats itself in an armor of defensiveness and goes off to meet the world, prepared for a struggle to the end. And indeed it finds one. Yet most of its difficulties, certainly the most tragic, are of its own making. As Sophocles put it, "The greatest griefs are those we cause ourselves." When we go against the grain of the wood or the current of the river, are we not making things unnecessarily difficult? In much the same way, the ego, always ready for a fight, makes life much more difficult than it need be.

A sense of struggle born out of the illusion of separation is critical to a psychology of poverty. In order to maintain the illusion of separation, we must make an effort to deny, reject, and repel the natural abundance of the Tao. This effort is called struggle. The *idea* of separation, then, inevitably brings the *feeling* of struggle. We feel a need to gain control, to assert ourselves as masters of whatever narrow domains (our egos and their attachments) we lay claim to. The ego becomes heavily involved in the game of struggling to get. It struggles to get love or money, approval or attention—whatever it thinks it needs to be whole and complete. Ego is always struggling to get what it can never have without relinquishing itself, namely, wholeness, peace, bliss. The more we struggle, the more substantial the ego seems to be, which is another way of saying, the more we reinforce the illusion of separation and lack.

When we open to receive the natural abundance of the Tao, we act with ease, for we are acting from a feeling of oneness with all things. We are not trying to build an artificial sense of security based on attaching ourselves to some person, position, title, or thing. Rather, we trust the natural bounty and intelligence of the Universe and move in accord with it. Opening to

In walking, just walk.
In sitting, just sit.
Above all, don't
wobble.

YUN-MEN

receive allows the continuous free flow of energy and the revelation of inborn or innate intelligence. It is effortless.

On the other hand, when we mentally hold on, we block the free flow of creative, emotional, and physical energy and confound our innate intuitive intelligence. With our innate intelligence blinded by a sandstorm of thoughts and emotions, we travel with clouded vision through a world we perceive as hostile and menacing. We knock against this and bang against that, reinforcing, as we go, the feeling of frustration, struggle, and woe.

The ego creates struggle in endless variety and often in rather ingenious ways. For the sake of discussion, we can lump these into several broad categories: The universe (or "cosmic other" God) is against "me," they (other people, society, etc.) are against "me," "you" (the immediate other) are against "me," and I (the inner other) am against "me." Believing all of this, it is not surprising that the ego feels defensive and concludes: "I must struggle to survive." The whole thing begins and ends with this: Is the Universe for you or against you? The ego starts with the assumption that it is against you; the Tao says that it is for you. If you identify with the universe, then clearly it is for you because it is you. It is here "for you" in the sense of providing you with a stage to play with and on and "for you" in the sense of an intrinsic benevolence. On the other hand, if you identify with the ego, it is easy to conclude that the universe is against you and that you must struggle.

The Ego's Struggle

1. The Universe Is Against "Me."
2. They Are Against "Me."
3. You Are Against "Me."
4. I Am Against "Me."

The Universe Is Against "Me"

Oh, isn't life a terrible thing, thank God.
—DYLAN THOMAS

A reporter once asked Albert Einstein, "Is a there a single crucial question which mankind must answer?" Einstein replied, "Yes, it is this: Is the universe friendly?"[5] From the standpoint of the ego, there are plenty of "reasons" to conclude that the Universe is an unfriendly place. It is clearly against "me" and out to get "me." Take death, for instance: The fact that I (the ego consciousness) will die shows me that the universe is against me. From the moment I was conceived, it was conspiring to get rid of me and will do so in relatively few years. Of the six billion people now living on earth, how many will be alive in one hundred years? Not I, and I dare say, not you either, dear reader. If the universe is, as we are told, billions of years old, why is it in such a hurry to get rid of me? It must be against me.

Take the endless complexity and variety within the universe, so far beyond my powers of comprehension. The universe must be conspiring to make "me" feel stupid and inadequate. Take change: "Everything," as Heraclitus said, "is in flux." Just when I think I have things figured out or have achieved some situation I desire, things begin to change. Clearly, the universe must be conspiring to make "me" feel insecure and unsure of myself.

The discoveries of quantum mechanics aside, most of us in the West live by cosmological myths first articulated long ago. The first is that expressed in the Biblical story of creation; the second, the mechanical clockwork of Newtonian science. Neither gives us the feeling that we have much in common with the rest of the universe. Neither gives us the sense that this is a "friendly universe." Both see the universe as "other" and nature as something to be overcome and conquered. Whether it is through the overcoming power of the spirit or by the overcoming power of the rational mind and its technological inventions, nature must be defeated. Consequently, many in the West take an approach to the world like that expressed by the poet A. E. Housman:

I, a stranger and afraid
In a world I never made

In describing orthodox Western religion, Zen writer D. T. Suzuki once remarked, "Man against God. God against Man. Man against nature. Nature, against man. God against nature. Nature against God. Very funny religion."[6] This very funny religion is precisely that of the ego. From this perspective, life is a war, with everything and everyone battling everything and everyone else. On the other hand, from a Taoist perspective, Heaven, Earth, and Man are naturally in harmony; all reside in the nameless Tao. To experience this, we don't have to win the war; we have only to release our identification with the ego.

Of course, the ego knows that it cannot (allow consciousness to) identify with the universe without shattering the illusion of its own reality. As Chögyam Trungpa put it, "The attainment of enlightenment from the ego's point of view is extreme death." As much as it complains about the struggle that it creates for itself, the ego cannot give up the struggle without giving up itself. Recognizing the ego's proclivity for struggle, certain spiritual traditions attempt to compound it until finally, from sheer exhaustion, the ego must give up its grip on consciousness. The process is analogous to starting a backfire to put out an already existing blaze.

This was not the path of the classical Taoists. Unlike later enthusiasts of Zen, the classical Taoists were not enamored with the idea of a single climactic moment of realization, a satori experience. They viewed the spiritual path as an ongoing unfoldment, more a matter of gradual sensitizing than of dramatic transformation. If the classical Taoists saw a different path, it was because they were starting from a different place. More than any surviving spiritual tradition, Classical Taoism embraces nature and human nature.

From the Taoist perspective, the universe is for us. We needn't beat it or ourselves into submission. The Taoists offer us a way of seeing the universe as a friendly place. For example, while we typically think of a mountain as an obstacle to be assaulted and overcome, from a Taoist perspective, we thank the mountain for lifting us up high. For the Taoist, we do not come into the world but out of it. In much the same way that acorns come out of oak trees, people come out of the world. When our season of living has come to an end, we return again from whence we came. Throughout, in death as much as in life, the universe is for us. As Chuang Tzu put it, "The universe carries us in our bodies, toils us through our life, gives us repose with our old age and rests us in our death. That which makes our life good makes our death good also. . . ."[7]

"They" Are Against "Me"

I suffer most because
Of me and selfishness.
If I were selfless, than
What suffering would I bear

—LAO TZU

The structure of the ego, built as it is on thought, is dual. It divides the world into "me" and "not-me," which, in turn, becomes "like-me" and "not-like-me." Like-me is good and pleasant, not-like-me is bad and dis-agreeable. This is why the poor tend to hate the rich and the rich, the poor. The beautiful hate the ugly, the ugly the beautiful; the smart hate the stupid, the stupid the smart, and so on. Not-like-me is disagreeable and bad and ought to be corrected or eliminated. Then the world would be more like me, and that would be agreeable and good. I become irritated or dis-agreeable in the face of what I am unable to agree with, that is, what I perceive as not-like-me.

Collectively, not-like-me becomes people of other races or religions, nationalities or ethnic backgrounds, cultures or political affiliations, income or education levels, sexes or sexual orientations, and so on. These not-like-me (-us) people are sooner or later turned into the evil enemies. The Taoists tells us that the fight against evil is a fight we will never win, and it is manifestly so. Indeed, it is one of the great and tragic ironies of human history that the worst crimes have been committed in the name of the fight against evil. As long as armed conflict was based on mere greed, viz., "We want your crops, livestock, treasures, or labor," warfare, for all its cruelty, maintained a certain humanity. When it came to be fought over religion or ideology, when it came to be a matter of stamping out evil, all bets were off. Now it was possible to contemplate and execute the wholesale slaughter of entire peoples. Now it became both expedient and necessary to develop the technologies by which all life as we know it on this planet could be rendered extinct.

As an ego, I identify with my biography, not my biology. My biography, which is to say, my personal memories, beliefs, and experiences, separates me from the rest. It is particular to "me." I cannot rightly expect "them" to understand "me" because they have not experienced what I have experi-

Perfect happiness is the absence of striving for happiness.

CHUANG TZU

93

enced, seen what I have seen, been where I have been. The best I can hope for from them is that they will resonate with certain elements of "my" story. Likewise, I cannot expect to know others too deeply or intimately. All I can hope for is that I might identify with certain elements of their stories. All this makes "me" feel lonely and alienated from "them." Feeling such a wide gulf between "me" in here and "them" out there, makes communicating with "them" seem a terrible struggle.

If I identify with my biology, my human nature, there is a great deal I can understand about others, without knowing anything about their stories. First and foremost, I know they suffer. Because they are human, they suffer. Those who have a better story, a "healthier" childhood, a more impressive résumé, better looks, connections, or education, suffer. Those who are less fortunate than "me" also suffer. Those who are able or good suffer as do those who are weak or mean. Identification at the level of our biology, our humanity, keeps us from getting lost in comparing stories (see chapter 5). In this way, the individual story becomes the vehicle for the revelation of the universal human condition. The word *compassion* means literally "to suffer with." Instead of the dividing and separating influence of individual stories, I can feel united in sharing with all the common story of humankind.

Now the interesting thing is that as soon as you realize that you are not your biographical story, you have the possibility of consciously creating a story, which is to say, playing with ego, rather than struggling with it. Identifying with our stories as who we are locks us into the past, a past we are constantly trying to overcome, to forget, to redeem, or to live up to—in other words, to struggle with. Releasing ourselves from our stories means we have nothing to protect or defend. This goes a long way in giving us a sense of being at ease in the world we live in. In the words of a classic Taoist text, "What you must do is bury your past: cut off the time that has already gone by and don't ask about it."[8]

"You" Are Against "Me"

The man who is in harmony is absolutely the same as other things,
and nothing succeeds in wounding or obstructing him.

—LAO TZU

The "you" in "you are against me" is, of course, not really you, which is to say, a living, breathing being, but you as an icon, you standing in as a localized representative of "they" or "them." "They" are fuzzy and vague, but "you" have a face and "me" puts on that face whatever it projects from within itself in the moment. "Me" tends to get into it a lot more with "you" than with "them." After all, "they" are too big, too nebulous to deal with, but "you"; "you" are right here. "You" are likely to get the brunt of "me"'s frustration, resentment, and struggle. "Me" is often willing to say and do to "you" (a mate, close friend, or family member) things it would never think of saying or doing to "them," i.e., strangers.

"Me," being no more than a fleeting rush of thoughts, images, and memories, is extremely volatile. Being a highly unstable and rather melodramatic chap, "me" is likely to alternatively idealize and demonize you. The problem is that "me" cannot trust "you" because "you" are not "me," but also because "you" are like "me." You see, one of the big problems that "me" has with "you" is that "you" remind "me" of my bad side, which brings us to our next point.

"I" Am Against "Me"

If I repent of anything,
it is very likely to be my good behavior.

—THOREAU

From the standpoint of the ego, there are two sides to everything, including "me." This means that "I" am not always on my side. More precisely, it means that sometimes "I" am on "my good side" and sometimes "I" am on "my bad side." Remember, "me" is the association of memories, characteristics, and objects related to my name. Sometimes things, events, or people remind "me" of "my good side," or positive associations and memories. Sometimes things, events, or people remind "me" of "my bad side," or negative associations and memories. Now from the Taoist perspective, nothing I do is right or wrong because everything I do is simply what I do. From the ego's perspective, this will never do. "Me" has got to be right! But the minute I call this right, wrong starts chasing me around. The more I insist on being good, the more I invoke its opposite, bad. "Me" then goes about trying to be really good, to prove that it's not really bad. It is not unlike a dog chasing a tail it can never quite reach.

Again, our ideas of human nature play a significant role. Look at the theories of human nature that prevail in the West. There's the idea from religion that human beings are all born corrupt participants in original sin. Fresh from the womb, you are rotten to the core. From this perspective, to "give in" to your corrupt nature is to be slave to every base and carnal desire. From Western political and economic theories, we get the idea that human beings are greedy and barbarous creatures, driven by self-interest and concerned only with their self-preservation. It is only the law of the state and the fear of punishment by it that keep us from reverting to the barbarous "law of the jungle." It is only the "invisible hand" of the market, based on unbridled greed, that can provide "the wealth of nations."

Then we have the Freudian notion of human nature, which even to this day dominates much of Western psychiatry and pop psychology. According to Freud, if we let our natural unconscious *libido* have its way, we'd be sucking or _ucking everything that moves. As luck would have it, we also have an ego and super-ego to keep the horny little devil in check. It is the restraint of this lustful libido that makes love and art and indeed civilization itself, possible. Yet since it all depends on the repression of our innate nature, the whole thing is extremely precarious. At any moment, repressed libido might break through and overwhelm the individual or society itself.

Now, you don't get the idea of trusting yourself from any of these conceptions of human nature. All of these say, in effect, that who you are in your deepest nature is a nasty little creature that must be grabbed by the scruff of the neck and made or forced to be "good." We can't really accept any of these ideas of human nature without feeling, somewhere in the inner recesses of our being, self-loathing and contempt.

A film called *The Edge* is about the trials of three men lost in the Alaskan wilderness. In the film, one of the characters recounts to his companions a fact he read—that most people lost in the wilderness die of shame.

Shame and guilt about the condition they are in prevents them from keeping their wits about them and acting intelligently enough to survive. Most of us die of shame, not dramatically or all at once—but slowly, little by little, day by day. Like those lost in the wilderness, our inner shame and self-loathing prevent us from trusting our basic instincts. Like those lost in the wilderness, we find ourselves in jeopardy, not so much because the universe is against us, but because we are against ourselves.

The classical Taoists take a much more positive view of human nature. For the Taoist, all depraved or perverse manifestations of human behavior result from rejecting our deepest nature, not from following it. It is by denying the unity of all life and committing to the attachments of the ego that we go astray. Believing the "universe," "they," "you," and "I" are all against it, the ego has little choice but to struggle to survive. The section below considers another approach, one that starts with unity and ends at ease.

Creating With Ease

Do not struggle. Go with the flow of things, and you will find yourself at one with the mysterious unity of the universe.

—CHUANG TZU

The ego tells me that I must struggle to survive. I must struggle against life; I must struggle against you and them; I must even struggle against me. Consequently, the struggle to change the world, them, you, and me occupies the lion's share of the ego's time and energy. It has precious little energy left over for genuine creative work. Thus it misses an essential element of the human experience. After all, what do human beings do? What marks human beings from other creatures? Perhaps more than anything, it is the human capacity to consciously relate and create. Real creativity is merely conscious participation in the natural transformations of nature. From a Taoist perspective, we begin with the realization that creativity is nothing special. Human creativity is a natural part of what the universe is doing. It is as natural for human beings to create as it is for birds to fly or fish to swim. We are all blessed with innate creative ability. As Einstein said, "Every child is born a genius."

Sensible people get paid for playing—that is the art of life.

ALAN WATTS

God gives every bird its food, but he doesn't throw it in the nest.

J. G. HOLLAND

We can, however, impede our natural creativity by refusing to accept it. In studies designed to uncover the critical variables that predict creativity—what makes one person more creative than the next—researchers looked at IQ, socioeconomic background, education, and a host of other factors. They were surprised to discover that the only variable that could reliably predict whether or not an individual would demonstrate creative ability was the individual's belief that he or she was a creative person. People who believe they are creative actually are more so. The first step, then, to unleashing your creative power is to accept, no, to embrace and celebrate that you (like everyone else in their deepest nature) *are* a creative person.

The next step to creating with ease is *knowing* what to do. Trying to figure things out by mere intellect alone always leaves us in doubt. We can only *know* by intuition—by listening to the innate intelligence within. When an inspiration arises, we recognize it as the voice in the innate intelligence that pervades the whole of the universe. We know that the idea is at one with the process of the universe; therefore, its means and support also lie within the universe. The idea has mutually arisen with the means and support necessary to accomplish it.

Knowing what to do brings confidence and staying power, in other words, ease. When we *know* what to do, we eliminate the inner struggle that inevitably becomes reflected in our outer behavior. We are not fighting with ourselves—"Maybe I shouldn't be doing this; maybe I should be doing something else instead." When we know what we are doing, we look at difficulties in a different way than when we are unsure of ourselves. We see them not as a sign to quit but as an opportunity to strengthen our resolve and persevere. The *Tao Te Ching* instructs, "Those who proceed resolutely have great force of will."[9] When we create in the spirit of the Tao, when we are not impatient for or attached to results, we can continue long after those needing more immediate gratification have given up. We can relax and enjoy the work for its own sake and not merely as a means to an end.

> *People often fail on the verge of success.*
> *By giving as much care to the end as to the beginning,*
> *There will be few failures.*
>
> —LAO TZU

How do we prepare ourselves to receive the intuitions that give us this powerful sense of knowing? The Taoists would say: Quiet your mind, be happy, and wait. As the empty space of the womb attracts the creative seed, so the empty mind naturally attracts creative ideas. Struggling or straining won't improve, and can only impede, your ability to receive ideas.

The great and prolific composer Wolfgang Amadeus Mozart was said to have written many of his finest works as if taking dictation. He described the state of mind that best facilitated his capacity to receive ideas. He said, "[It is] when I am, as it were, completely myself, entirely alone, and of good cheer . . . that ideas flow best and most abundantly. Whence they come, I know not, nor can I force them." As Mozart said, being alone, quieting your mind, getting away from the noisy hubbub of modern life, the stresses and distractions that typically occupy you, puts you in a frame of mind that encourages the reception of creative ideas.

Notice he also said that he couldn't force ideas and that it was when he was of good cheer that they flowed best and most abundantly. Many people fail to recognize the importance of this emotional aspect of creativity. They think they are not creative people but fail to recognize how negative emotions block the natural flow of ideas. You're not going to be creative when you feel jealous, angry, or resentful. Nor are feeling worried, stressed, or depressed conducive to receiving creative ideas. These emotions throw us out of harmony and jam our natural capacity to recognize the voice of innate intelligence bubbling up from within. If you want to be in harmony with life and your natural creative power, put aside negative emotions. In the words of a classic Taoist text, "To preserve basic harmony, nothing takes precedence over detachment from emotional consciousness."[10]

When we bless the world and all in it, when we feel of good cheer and at peace, we relax into the depth of our being, the fount of all creative ideas. A combination of energy and relaxation, of alertness and peace, is most conducive to creative discovery. Creative visions naturally germinate in a mind that is relaxed and alert.

> *Man was born to be rich,*
> *Or grow rich by use of his faculties,*
> *By the union of thought with nature.*
> —EMERSON

When you receive a creative idea, give it your attention. Abandoned babies in crowded orphanages die for lack of attention and affection. Plants grow big and strong when lovingly spoken to or bathed in uplifting music.[11] Living things grow from receiving loving attention or wither and die without it. The easy way of creating is to give your attention to your creative inspirations. Feed and nourish them with loving attention. With daily consistent attention, they begin to take shape in the world of form. In time, they begin to take on a life of their own, which in turn makes it even easier to remain focused on them. This is an aspect of a creative principle sometimes referred to as the "Law of Attraction." It is not only birds of a feather that flock together but also like-minded ideas and people. Attract what you require to accomplish your visions by staying focused on them.

When you receive an idea, see it in your mind's eye as already accomplished—know that it is done. Often we neglect the all-important inner elements of creating and then struggle about on the physical plane. We may project fear and doubt into our visions and creative intuitions, without realizing how unnecessarily difficult we are making things for ourselves in the process. Overcome this self-defeating pattern by learning to still the mind and/or by projecting positive energy and imaginings into the results you seek. Harmonize your energy by uniting mind and body around the same purpose. Refuse to send your body to do any task without uniting heart and mind firmly behind it, and you will be amazed at how easily you can accomplish even seemingly difficult tasks. Jefferson said, "Nothing is troublesome that we do willingly." On the other hand, in the words of Terence, "There is nothing so easy but that it becomes difficult when you do it reluctantly." The Taoists would have us understand the creative powers of the human mind and put them to work for us. Don't struggle with your imagination; put it to work for you.

The great masters long ago understood what modern Olympic athletes have only discovered in the last quarter century—namely, that visualization is the easy and effective way to enhance performance. As a Ch'an (Zen) master once put it, "When the task is done beforehand, then it is easy."[12] The task is done beforehand when it is done first in the mind, that is, when you visualize the result you seek. Many years ago at the University of Chicago, a study was conducted to measure the effects of visualization on the performance of a simple repeatable task. In the study, three groups were selected and their ability at shooting for basketball free throws was recorded. The first group was told to practice shooting for one hour each day for twenty days. The second group was told to imagine shooting baskets for one hour each day for the same twenty-day period. The third group was told to refrain from mental or actual shooting during the time of the test.

The results were startling! Performance improved 24 percent in the first group and 23 percent in the second, while the performance of the control group remained unchanged. The subconscious mind could not tell the difference between real and imagined practice! Similar studies have reinforced the conclusion that the subconscious cannot tell the difference between real and imagined experience. Think of the implications of this principle in your daily life. How much easier we can make things for ourselves if we will take the time to visualize or mentally experience the results we desire?

Yet doing the task beforehand is not only a matter of visualizing a happy ending. It is also a matter of mentally surveying the landscape before you. In the Chinese classic, *The Art of War*, Sun Tzu wrote, "The considerations of the intelligent always include both benefit and harm. As they consider benefit, their work can expand; as they consider harm, their troubles can be resolved."[13] Observing things in your mind's eye prior to taking action allows you to make the most out of the effort you expend. You can head trouble off at the pass, avoid unnecessary efforts, and fully capitalize on opportunities as they present themselves.

Be patient. Stop and think about things first, and you will save yourself a lot of trouble later on. Ask yourself, what are the possible "benefits" or "harms" of a particular action or major course of action you are considering? Remember, there is no gain without loss, no advantage without disadvantages. There are trade-offs in everything. Just make sure that you are conscious of the ones you are making and that you can live with them. When we learn to, as the Taoists say, "bury the past"—to get our imaginations out of the habit of reliving the traumas, foibles, or successes of our pasts—we discover how to send them out ahead of us to pave the way for our success.

Moreover, we can embrace difficulties and opposition, drawing from them the lessons they are there to teach. As Shakespeare said, "There is some soul of goodness in things evil,/Would men observingly distill it out." This is the essence of spiritual alchemy—taking the lead of painful or seemingly negative experience and transmuting it into the gold of wisdom and understanding. If the universe is truly for us, there is something for us in the bitter as well as the sweet of life. Back of every apparent failure, there is an equal or greater benefit, if we can but learn to see it.

When we run into difficulties, we can trust the universe to supply the answers to the challenges that face us. It is ironic, amusing, and at times even tragic, that thinking makes us stupid. A Taoist classic advises, when

Where do I get my ideas? That I cannot with certainty say. They come uncalled, directly and indirectly.

BEETHOVEN

using spirit, "use the basic spirit, not the thinking spirit."[14] In other words, use innate intelligence, let the preconscious intuitive intelligence guide you. Rather than struggling to figure things out, step back, formulate the question you are seeking to answer, and wait upon the universal intelligence to supply the answer. Act as though you have already received what you have asked for, be it an answer to a question or an object or circumstance you require to accomplish your vision. Then act accordingly.

There is a Chinese proverb that goes, "If I keep a green bough in my heart, the singing bird will come." The simple message: Be happy and you attract good fortune. Life is much easier, must less of a struggle when we meet it with a smile. Prepare yourself for success. If you ask for success but prepare for failure, you will get failure. You will get the situation you expect, the one you have prepared yourself for. Expect to receive what you require, even when there's not the slightest sign of it in sight, and act on that expectation. The universe is an abundant place. It's natural for you to have plenty. Don't make a virtue out of poverty or struggle. The Taoists reject the belief that poverty is a sign of holiness. They tell us life is to be enjoyed.

> *{The man of Tao} does not struggle to make money*
> *And does not make a virtue of poverty.*
> —CHUANG TZU

They also tell us not to resist, fight, or struggle against circumstances we don't like. For example, as long as we resist poverty, we cannot be free from it. If we run from lack, it will follow us. If it doesn't show up immediately in our material circumstances, it will make itself known in our fears of it. Agree to experience apparently negative situations without becoming negatively affected or emotionally drawn into them. In this way, you transcend them. Every condition of inharmony or lack we experience in the outer world reflects an inharmony within ourselves. When you stop reacting to lack or inharmony in outer circumstances, you will meet them less and less often. When, without changing anything else, you change your attitude, you change everything. Be happy, see the good you desire, don't resist or struggle with the things you don't like, and inevitably your "green bough" will attract singing birds.

> *If I keep a green bough in my heart, the singing bird will come.*
> —CHINESE PROVERB

At Ease with Yourself

But do your thing and I shall know you.
—EMERSON

If abundance means anything, it means being at ease with yourself. We are at ease with ourselves when we feel like we don't have anything to prove. When we accept that in our deepest nature we are no better, no worse, and no different from anyone else, we are free to be who we are as unique individuals. If we try it the other way around, if we try to prove how unique, special, or different we are, without accepting our unity with the rest of life, we are always in a battle.

When it comes right down to it, the ego's game is about trying to prove that it is worthy of love. Yet the only way that we can truly experience love is to step outside of the isolation and separation of the ego. We cannot receive love or acceptance for ourselves without at the same time giving it to (really, acknowledging it for) everyone else. This is not simply an abstract spiritual concept or nicety but a logical necessity.

If my "loveability" is based on a physical attribute, say, my looks or strength, I may lose these with age. If my loveability is based on my accomplishments, my ethics, my knowledge, my charm, my status, my power—it is equally precarious. Finally, the only thing upon which my loveability ultimately depends is my existence itself. Yet I cannot separate "my" existence from the existence of everything else. Recognizing this, we can give up the struggle to prove that we are worthy of love and say with Whitman, "I exist as I am, that is enough." Since we no longer have anything to prove, we can simply be and express what we are. Our natural strengths, talents, and abilities can then shine through, unimpeded by the struggle to prove we are worthy. We can embrace our natural gifts and put them to work.

In summary, we can say that ease comes with acting in harmony with the Tao in recognition of the unity of all things. Ease comes with respecting the way of nature and your own human nature. Ease comes with honoring the voice of intuition. Ease comes with a spirit of thanksgiving, of blessing and blessedness. Ease comes with moving from our innate strengths and gifts. Ease comes from doing what we are doing without using it as a means of trying to do or get something else.

CHAPTER FOUR

Ch'i

The Flow of Abundance

*There is nothing which does not require ch'i to remain
alive.*
                                              —Ko Hung

Abundant living requires an abundance of energy and the free circulation
of that energy. The free flow of life energy (*ch'i*) brings spiritual, emotional,
physical, even financial health. When the energy is flowing freely in your
life, you give freely and without hesitation of yourself, your love, and your
inborn gifts. The energy you put out returns to you, a rich and plentiful
harvest of the seeds you have sown. On the other hand, the ego in its separation and attachment struggles to get ahead and defend. In due course,
struggle brings resentment, which blocks the natural flow of energy and
produces symptoms of lack in various areas of our lives. This lack may
manifest as illness in the physical body, a block on creative self-expression,
a withholding of love in personal relationships, or in a variety of other
ways. In this chapter, you will have the opportunity to explore attitudes,
skills, and techniques that will help you to keep the energy flowing freely
in your life. In the related exercises at the end of the book, you will have a
chance to integrate and apply the principles discussed here.

Today, many in the West have become familiar with the term *ch'i* through exposure to Chinese medicine or martial arts.[1] While these disciplines are principally concerned with the movement of *ch'i* within the human body, it is important to recognize that the classical Taoists viewed *ch'i* as a universal force, or energy, that pervades the whole of existence. As the modern Chinese scholar Fung Yu-Lan has written, "The tendency in ancient times with regard to any thing or force which is invisible and intangible was to describe it as *ch'i*."[2]

For the Taoists, the human being is a microcosm of the universe. He or she exemplifies, in body and being, cosmological forces that pervade the whole of the universe. For the Taoists, *ch'i* is the central unifying force, running through all of life. In its aspect of invisible, all-pervading life energy, "*ch'i*" parallels the Hindu term *prana*, the Greek *pneuma*, and the Latin *spiritus*, from which our word *spirit* is derived. All of these terms, including *ch'i*, are related to the breath. Yet in this aspect, we cannot say that *ch'i is* breath; rather, we might call it the essence of breath.

Defining *ch'i* is like defining the wind. All depends on which way it is blowing. Like the word *Tao* itself, "*ch'i*" escapes translation because it does not submit to precise definition. We could say that *ch'i* is the bridge between spirit and matter. Yet *bridge* does not convey *ch'i's* dynamic quality. We could say that *ch'i* is the means by which Tao animates matter. But this suggests that matter is separate from the energy that sustains it and gives it form. Like Einstein, the classical Taoist viewed matter as a manifestation of energy and not as something distinct. Efforts to define *ch'i* are further compounded by the fact that, like *Tao,* it is used to refer to different things at different times and in different contexts. As we might speak of the Tao of Heaven, the Tao of Earth, and the Tao of Man, while recognizing the universal Tao in which all reside, so can we speak of the *ch'i* of Heaven, the *ch'i* of Earth, and the *ch'i* of Man, while recognizing the universal *ch'i* pervading all. In modern usage, *ch'i* can refer to air, vapor, breath, ether, and energy, even temperament. For the purposes of this discussion, *ch'i* will be defined as "life force" or "vital energy."

Originally, the term *ch'i* meant "no fire," and in this sense, it parallels the word *nirvana,* which means "to extinguish," or literally "no wind." When the fires of desire have been extinguished, when the winds of egoic cravings have ceased, the Original Self is recognized. When there is "no fire," our *ch'i* or vital energy is at its zenith. It is our attachments that fuel the fire and our attachments that produce anxiety and struggle, lust and ambition. It is this fire that must be extinguished if we are to realize the fullness of the cosmic life force.

In chapter 40 of the *Tao Te Ching,* we read, "Returning is the motion of the Tao." All things return. In the macrocosmic sense, all manifest things return to the unmanifest, nameless Tao. Likewise, within the time-bound realm, a circular pattern pervades the whole of life—from womb and tomb to the cycles of the moon, from day and night to the passages of the sea-

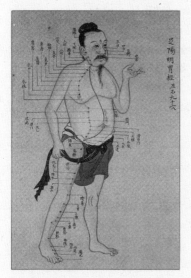

sons—the wheel of life moves in a circle. Similarly, the action of *ch'i* is circulation, a returning circle, or cycle of energy. Within the human body, the *ch'i,* or vital energy, is said to circulate through meridians.

Though not employed by Taoists until much later, the concept of karma as well suggests a circle, or returning cycle of energy.[3] The Taoists would certainly agree with the popular expression that what goes around comes around. Since all things are interconnected, no action can be viewed as isolated or self-contained. Everything we do generates waves or ripples of energy that move out into the world and at last return to us. As every exhale requires an inhale, so whatever we put out into the world—be it thought, feeling, or action—in due course, returns to us. We can think of this circle of energy as our soul *ch'i* or life force. This soul *ch'i,* in turn, is not separate from the *ch'i* within the physical body. From this understanding, sin (though the Taoists would avoid such a loaded term) is not a matter of disobeying a father-figure god, but of violating the immutable natural laws of the universe. And in this respect, the wages of sin *is* death.

Ch'i is also said to be one of the "Three Treasures," a central concept in Taoist philosophy, medicine, and esoteric arts. The Taoists believe that as the human form is taking shape in the womb, it begins to be differentiated from the Eternal Tao. At birth, the internal energy is separated into three primary elements: *ching, ch'i,* and *shen. Ching* is the energy of Earth, of the generative power and the bodily fluids. *Shen* is the energy of Heaven, of the spiritual power, and is associated with the eyes and liver. *Ch'i* (in this context) is the energy of Humanity, of vitality, and is associated with the breath. *Ching* is said to flow through the bones; *ch'i,* through the meridians (per-

What descends to earth as the breath of passion returns to heaven in the spirit of contemplation.

EDGAR WIND

haps best known in the West through acupuncture); and *shen,* through the eight "Strange Flow" meridians.

The importance of preserving, nourishing, and circulating the Three Treasures is a fundamental Taoist concept. These energies are to be preserved and collected from within and gathered from external sources. *Ching* can be gathered through proper diet and the exchange of sexual energies; *ch'i,* through breath; and *shen,* through meditation. In Taoist yoga or alchemy (*nei kung*), the idea is to refine *ching* into *ch'i, ch'i* into *shen,* and refine *shen* to reach the Void. Ultimately, the goal is to merge back with the Eternal Tao from which one was apparently separated at birth.

 ## Circulation of *Ch'i*

Man is in ch'i *and* ch'i *is within each human being. Heaven and earth and the ten thousand things require* ch'i *to stay alive. A person that knows how to allow his* ch'i *to circulate will preserve himself and banish illnesses that might cause him harm.*

—KO HUNG

The circulation of *ch'i* is a fundamental concept in traditional Chinese medicine. Physical disease is recognized as a symptomatic manifestation of an underlying disruption in the natural flow or circulation of *ch'i.* While Western medicine does not admit the existence of the invisible *ch'i,* it does recognize the importance of circulation to good health. Blockages in the flow of the blood or breath, of hormones or waste substances, have long been recognized as precursors to disease.

Beyond the physical body, all dis-ease, including poverty, can be conceived of as an interruption of the free flow or circulation of energy. Our word "affluence" comes to us from the Latin *affluēns,* meaning "flowing." As abundance is a part of the natural order of things, poverty is a indication that energy has somehow been blocked or impeded. Poverty may result from a lack of fruitfulness. If we are lazy or if we fail to give the gifts that are ours to give, material lack may appear as a prod to do what we are naturally here to do. Even if we are making plenty of money, but are neglecting to give our gifts, the energy is not flowing freely. An inner sense of lack, or poverty of the soul, is often the result. On a social level, the Taoists recognize that poverty can also result from interference by those in political or economic authority in the lives of ordinary people (see chapter 5).

The principle of the circulation of energy is also essential to Taoist arts such as *ch'i kung* or "energy work"; to Taoist physical exercises, such as T'ai Ch'i Chuan; to the Taoist alchemy or internal work (*nei kung*); to the Taoist sexual arts, as well as to various schools of Taoist meditation.[4] The principle of the circulation of energy is likewise integral to practical arts such as feng shui as well as to fine arts, including Chinese painting and calligraphy. All the arts mentioned above, and many more that I haven't space to address here, rely in one way or another on the principle of the circulation of energy.

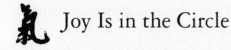 ## Joy Is in the Circle

The soul is a circle.
—PLATO

Application of the principle, then, is simple: to increase joy, the experience of abundance, increase circulation. This principle applies across the board. From the abundance of ultimate spiritual liberation, to the abundance of health and longevity; from the abundance of happy interpersonal relationships, to the abundance of material prosperity—circulation is key. Abundance results from the free flow of energy. Lack is an indication of an interference in natural energy flows. Joy is the feeling associated with freely circulating energy. Pain is the feeling associated with a block or interruption in the free flow of energy.

We can say, with William Blake, "Energy is Bliss." But energy is also pain. How we experience energy depends upon how open we are to letting it flow through us. Because the ego is, by definition, a contraction of awareness, it is also a limitation of energy. Often we resist energy because we feel that it is more than we can handle or control. We fear being overwhelmed by it. We resist energy and block the flow of *ch'i* by holding on.

- Holding onto the breath impedes the circulation of oxygen and produces pain.
- Holding our muscles in place (chronic tension) impedes circulation and produces pain.

- Holding onto limiting beliefs impedes mental circulation and produces pain.
- Holding onto grudges or resentments impedes the circulation of emotional energy and produces pain.
- Holding onto (withholding) our natural gifts impedes circulation and produces pain.

In the West, we know a great deal about lines, but we have forgotten the power of the circle. We know about lines of reasoning and logic but discount the circle of intuition. We know about deadlines, timelines, and lines of history but discount the cosmic cycle of return. We know about getting in line and conforming to the will of society but have discounted knowledge related to the cyclic seasons of the human life revealed in traditional mythology and ritual. We have lines of concrete and pavement, and our homes are square boxes, but we have lost touch with nature and our own biorhythms. Of course, first and foremost, we know about chasing the bottom line, but do we know how to sit still and really listen to the circle of our own breath? Now lines have their place, but life is a circle—and the way of life is circulation.

- Healthy bodies result from the unimpeded circulation of energy, blood, and oxygen.
- Happy relationships result from good communication, and communication is circulation—the free flow of energy, ideas, and feelings between people.
- Peace of mind results from proper mental circulation, which is to say, from being in the moment—neither holding onto the past nor grasping for the future, but letting experience move through us.
- Creative expression results from circulating our natural gifts.

The Taoist says life is bliss. The Buddhist says life is suffering. Both are right—it's just a matter of where we are starting from. If by "life," we mean pure energy and consciousness, it is bliss. If we mean by "life," the humdrum of human attachment and struggle, then indeed, it *is* suffering. One approach assumes an identification with nature as the starting point; the other, identification with the ego. Our planet spins round the sun, while the entire galaxy whirls about. We live and die and are born again. Some say, "If life is just going round in a circle, in a cycle of rebirth, then what's the point?" Indeed, it has many points, but that is not really the point. The point is that all points are connected in the circle of life. Nothing can be isolated from anything else. We have but to merge with the circle and go merrily, not grudgingly, around. The joy is in the circle.

 ## The Circulation of Wealth

A man there was, and they called him mad; the more he gave,
the more he had.   —JOHN BUNYAN

When it comes to material abundance, the principle of circulation applies as well. Circulation is as important to financial health as it is to physical, mental, and emotional health. Generally, as you increase circulation, you increase wealth. Networking, advertising, and promotion are vehicles for putting yourself or your product or service in greater circulation. We could say that the more widgets a manufacturer sells, the more books an author sells, or the more recordings a musician sells, the greater circulation his or her offerings have achieved. Likewise, at their best, investments are vehicles for recirculating money and the energy it represents.

Have you noticed that everything an Indian does is in a circle, and that
is because the Power of the World always works in circles, and every-
thing tries to be round . . . everything the Power of the World does is
done in a circle.   —BLACK ELK

Because energy moves in a circle, because what goes around comes around, we can open ourselves up to more of the good we want in our lives by giving what we want to receive. If you want more understanding, be more understanding of others. If you want people to listen to you, make a point of listening more carefully to others. If you want greater material abundance, focus on giving your innate gifts and abilities. Give real service and value to others, and in time, you will reap the benefits. Believe in your gifts and trust that there is a place for them in the world.

Bottled-up creative energy can be a great source of stress. It is energy that wants to circulate and find expression. When it is not released in the outer world, it builds up within, generating tension, anxiety, and dis-ease.

We cannot know deep inner peace until we develop our own channels for creative release. As Abraham Maslow put it, "A musician must make his music, an artist must paint, a poet must write if he is to ultimately be at peace with himself." Expressing our innate talents feels so good because we enjoy doing what we are naturally good at. To go through life without expressing your innate talents or sharing your natural gifts is the worst form of poverty and self-denial. People who have never known the pleasure of expressing their own unique talents often associate work with pain and struggle or, at best, think of it as a duty that must be performed in order to achieve some benefit or result. They have never known the joy of working for its own sake.

When economists talk about money supply, they refer to specific technical measures related to the amount of money in circulation. Leaving aside for now how money comes into circulation (see chapter 5), what keeps it circulating is economic activity—in other words, buying and selling. When it comes to our personal money supply, many of us conceive of the act of purchasing products or services as spending, not circulating, money. Here are a few of the definitions of the word *spend* from my dictionary: "To use up or consume; to wear out, exhaust; to throw away, squander." Given these definitions, is it any wonder that the idea of spending money is often associated with the feeling of resentment? We enjoy the good we receive, the things we buy. Yet if we resent having to give up something in exchange for it, if we are mentally holding onto it, we are not allowing money to circulate freely in our lives.

Every time you purchase something or give money away, release it with a blessing. Be glad to prosper others, and be happy that you have the money on hand to pay for what you need and want. If whenever you receive money, you receive it as a blessing, and whenever you give it away, you give it with a blessing, you will allow money to freely circulate in your life. Wish others prosperity and success; do not resent the good or wealth that others enjoy. Be at one with the success of others and you allow yourself to receive more.

Another key to circulating money in your life is the principle of tithing. While, admittedly, tithing is most strongly identified with the Judeo-Christian tradition, the principle is a universal one. The idea is to devote a certain portion (*tithe* means literally "a tenth part") of your monthly or annual income in support of individuals, groups, or causes that are in alignment with your spiritual values. Giving money away in this fashion not only does good in supporting the causes of your choice, but it also frees your consciousness from the commitment to the belief that there isn't enough. It's an act of faith, affirming the belief that what goes around comes around.

 ## Resentment: The Great *Ch'i* Robber

Heavy thoughts bring on physical maladies;
when the soul is oppressed, so is the body.
—MARTIN LUTHER

Resentment brings guilt and cuts us off from the innate bounty of the Tao. When we resent others or the circumstances of our own lives, we are bound to feel guilty. Guilt, in turn, makes us feel unworthy and undeserving. It saps our strength and robs us of our destinies. When Jesus said, "Forgive us our trespasses as we forgive those who trespass against us," he was not stating a wish or hope but a metaphysical reality. We hold against ourselves the judgments we make of others. Withholding love and forgiveness keeps energy from circulating. This blocked energy is experienced as pain. In defining the word *resentment*, the authors of my dictionary chose the words "ill will." Ill will suggests sickness as well as hostility. Ill will robs us of our peace of mind. It creates physical tension, emotional dryness, and mental stagnation; in other words, it blocks the flow of *ch'i*.

Gratitude and ill will cannot reside simultaneously in the same heart. We cannot bring good to ourselves while wishing ill to others. As gratitude can bring only good fortune, so ill will can only bring misfortune. As resentment blocks the flow of *ch'i*, so gratitude gets it circulating again. We can stop a downward spiral at any point by practicing gratitude. Think of one thing you are genuinely happy about or grateful for. Hold it in your mind's eye while focusing feelings of love and gratitude onto it. Then transfer that feeling onto people, circumstances, or events that you find more difficult to love. Reclaim energy lost on resentment and guilt. Make a list of your resentments and practice bringing love to them. (See the exercises at the back of the book.) In so doing, you break the cycle of resentment, guilt, and self-sabotage. You get that energy working for, instead of against, you. Remember that circumstances that appear as obstacles or barriers, or people who are opposed to us in purpose or even hate us, have something to teach us. Find that something and you can't help but be grateful.

Blessed is he who has
found his work. Let him
ask no other blessing.

THOMAS CARLYLE

Gratitude is the feeling of abundance. We are grateful for what we have. We resent what we think we lack. Even before the inspirations you are working toward have become manifest realities in your life, be grateful for them. In so doing, you will begin to convince your subconscious mind that you have already accomplished or received them. We've all heard people say, after they have achieved a measure of success, that they knew it was going to happen all along. We act differently when we *know* that we will achieve a result than when we are merely wishing or hoping for it. Imagine that the results you seek are already accomplished, and be grateful for them. Ask yourself, What can I do now to show myself, when I look back over my actions, that I knew all along that I was going to be successful?

> *It is gratefulness which makes the soul great.*
> —ABRAHAM HERSCHEL

The noted American philosopher and pioneer psychologist William James advocated this *act-as-if* principle as a powerful tool for transforming consciousness. According to James, it is easier to act your way into a new kind of thinking than to think yourself into a new way of acting. As you begin taking definite actions toward the accomplishment of your goals, you demonstrate to your subconscious mind that you are serious about attaining them. If you want to be a writer or a painter, begin writing or painting, even if you can only do it part time. The body of work you amass will convince your subconscious mind that you are indeed serious about your new career and on your way to manifesting it.

If you want to start a business of your own, put together a business plan, even if you don't know where you are going to get the start-up capital. *If you always go as far as you can with what you have, you will find that you can always go further.* As the German poet Schiller put it, "Who dares nothing need hope for nothing." Dare to begin taking immediate action toward the results you seek, and you get energy moving in that direction. You build a force of momentum toward the results you desire.

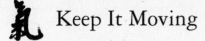 Keep It Moving

Possession of the Way is thus a capacity for dealing effortlessly
with external things. —LIEH TZU

If you want to keep the energy circulating in your life, put your whole self into your efforts. Don't hold back. When we close the back doors of escape, we open the front door of total commitment. Successful people know that if they try to play it safe, they will hold part of themselves back—often the very part needed to accomplish their goals. In any field, the people who achieve the most are the ones who are not afraid to take chances. Experiment with new ways of thinking and acting. Try acting in ways that seem counter to your personality. Remember that *persona* means "mask," and try on some new ones. Anything you can do to break out of routine can be extremely energizing.

Another way we can increase circulation is to free energy bogged down in incompletion. Incompletes disperse and diffuse our energy and leave us feeling scattered and confused. Collect and focus this energy. Make a list of the incompletes in your life. Then, for each item on your list, determine why you stopped taking action. Next, decide what you want to do about each. Will you take action? If so, what? and when? or perhaps you will decide this goal is no longer important to you. The point is to confront each item on your list and make a definite decision about what to do with it. This psychic housecleaning can free up tremendous energy. It can give you a renewed sense of purpose and sharpen your focus.

Communication problems result from a lack of circulation. Good communication requires a free exchange of energy, ideas, and feelings. The communication cycle is broken when we block our free expression or jam our ability to receive. We may withhold things that we want to express because we fear how others will respond or how we will look in their eyes. On the other hand, we may resist hearing and receiving what others, or the events and circumstances of our lives, are trying to tell us. Gaining awareness of where in the communication cycle we are blocked and then releasing these impediments can be extremely energizing. (See the exercises at the end of the book.)

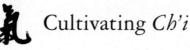

Cultivating *Ch'i*

Energy is bliss. —WILLIAM BLAKE

The classical Taoists rejected the search for physical immortality that occupied so much of the attention of later Taoist religious sects and schools. Chuang Tzu repeatedly ridiculed such practices as vain, futile, and contrary to nature. Nevertheless, the classical Taoists recognized the need to preserve and cultivate one's natural *ch'i*. Just as life should not be clung to, neither should it be recklessly cut short. In the best of the alchemical Taoist tradition, the pursuit of longevity, or the cultivation of nature, is intended to provide a strong physical platform from which to cultivate the spiritual life.

The next chapter explores the principle of *Te,* or innate power and ability. There is no power without energy and vitality. *Ch'i* is synonymous with vitality of mind, body, and spirit. This *ch'i* energy can be preserved, gathered, and stored. A Taoist master with an abundance of *ch'i* may help heal another by projecting her *ch'i* into his or her body. A Kung Fu master can project his *ch'i* in such a way that he can throw a much larger opponent across a room.

Yet one of the great joys of *ch'i* cultivation is increased sensitivity to life. There is a story about Chuang Tzu that illustrates the point. While watching fish swimming about in a pond, Chuang Tzu remarked to a companion, "The fish are happy when they wiggle." Thinking himself quite witty, his companion replied, "How do you know the fish are happy? You are not a fish!" Not missing a beat, Chuang Tzu responded, "How do you know that I don't know? You are not me!" When we have awakened, strengthened, and harmonized our own *ch'i*, we become much more sensitive to the energies of life all around us. We *feel* the innate joy in life. We have less need for and interest in artificial stimulations.

There are various methods for cultivating *ch'i*. Many require years of practice and the careful supervision of a master teacher. Yet all of us can become more aware of how we use, and often misuse, our energies. Starting with a few simple understandings, we can become more conscious of how we typically deplete our energies and how we can preserve and generate our *ch'i*. Below are techniques that anyone can use, without special training, to cultivate their *ch'i*.

Simple Steps to Cultivating *Ch'i*

1. Be cheerful.
2. Breathe.
3. Move your body.
4. Rest your body.
5. Master your emotions.
6. Meditate.
7. Simplify.
8. Spend time in nature.
9. Eat well.
10. Cultivate an awareness of your surroundings.

These methods will not only help you to preserve and strengthen your *ch'i*, but they will also help you to reduce stress, the great malady of modern life. Stress robs even the materially affluent of the feeling of abundance. Anything you can do to increase your energy while reducing your stress will greatly enhance your experience of abundance.

Be Cheerful

We shall never know all the good that a simple smile can do.
—MOTHER TERESA

For a time, I had occasion to live in a small town where the pace of life was slow and easy. After many years of living in cities, I was surprised to find myself in a place where strangers actually (and repeatedly!) smiled at me. The people I encountered on the street and in the shops, coffee bars, and restaurants were genuinely friendly. I discovered that when virtually everywhere you go, people greet you with a smile, you begin to relax in places that you didn't know were tense.

In the same way, the cold and indifferent attitudes of the modern city breed isolation and mistrust. Here, we don't smile at strangers. We fear that a smile might be misinterpreted, ignored, or met with a disapproving scowl. Seeing all these dour and indifferent faces before us, we get the idea that life is a very serious affair. In the city, to be outwardly friendly toward strangers or to exhibit real joy is to stick out like a sore thumb. Most of us don't want to risk it. Peter Brook said, "We don't know how to celebrate because we don't know what to celebrate." The Taoists have no such problem. They tell us to celebrate life—pure and simple. They recognize that expressions of joy, such as laughing, smiling, and playing, release and expand energy.

Contentment produces a genuine smile; and a genuine smile cannot be forced.

CHUANG TZU

Some Taoists practice a method known as the "inner smile" in which one "smiles" into the internal organs and along the meridians through which *ch'i* circulates within the body. An inner smile relaxes and revitalizes areas of the body to which it is directed. Similarly, though it sounds simplistic or even childlike to the average Westerner, smiling into the problems and challenges we face in life is a powerful tool for transforming them. When someone smiles at you, it puts you at ease and makes you feel happy. Think of approaching a person, situation, or event in life with a grumpy, indifferent, or resentful attitude. Now think of smiling at the person, thing, or event before you. Can you feel tension and defensiveness melt away?

> *Half the beds in our hospitals are filled with people who worried themselves into them.*
> —DR. CHARLES H. MAYO (FOUNDER, MAYO CLINIC)

John Ruskin said, "Cheerfulness is as natural to the heart of a man in strong health as color is to his cheeks." It also works the other way around: a cheerful state of mind, a loving and joyous feeling toward life helps keep us healthy. In a book entitled *Anatomy of an Illness,* Norman Cousins described how he used laughter and humor as part of his regimen for overcoming a serious and supposedly irreversible disease. Since that book was first published in the late 1980s, numerous studies have confirmed the mind/body connection in relation to health and healing. The ancient Taoists needed no confirming empirical studies to recognize that one's attitude toward, and enjoyment of, life plays an important role in health and vitality.

Breathe: Respiration Is Inspiration

> *There is one common flow, one common breathing, all things are in sympathy.*
> —HIPPOCRATES

Breath is life. Human beings can live for weeks without food, for days without water, but for only a few minutes at most without oxygen. The way we breathe either impedes or expands the flow of *ch'i* in our bodies. Proper breathing awakens the subtle *ch'i* and increases the levels of oxygen in the brain and blood. On the other hand, an inadequate oxygen supply slows mental performance and puts added stress on the heart and circulatory system. There are literally dozens of breathing techniques prescribed by various Taoist schools and sects. Many of these should only be attempted while under the guidance of a real master. Yet there are a few general understandings from which all of us can profit.

Awareness: As with most things in life, when it comes to breathing, awareness is more important than mental control. Practice focusing on your breath as a kind of meditation. The idea is simply to become aware of the way you are breathing throughout the day. Where in your body does your breath begin and end? Is it shallow or deep? Fast or slow? Do certain thoughts or feelings accelerate respiration or cause you to hold your breath? Maintain an awareness of your breath by "checking in" with it periodically throughout the day.

Through the nose: Unless illness prevents it, it's best to keep your mouth closed and breathe through the nose. The nose comes equipped with a kind of natural filtration system, which the mouth lacks. The hairs (*cilia*) and mucus membranes within the nose trap bacteria and airborne particulates before they enter the respiratory tract. Since you don't have to open and close your nose, it's easier to relax and concentrate on the flow of breath itself than to concern yourself with the manipulation of the breathing mechanism. Also, with the mouth closed, it will be easy to touch the palate with the tip of your tongue, a practice prescribed by a number of schools of "Taoist yoga."

Long and slow: Many of us associate breathing techniques with rapid, deep breathing or even hyperventilation. The Taoists tell us that rather than to force deep breathing, we do better to gently lengthen and slow the breath. When we are breathing naturally, the diaphragm contracts on the inhale and expands on the exhale. This allows the lungs to fill to capacity and, at the same time, gently massages the internal organs. Watch an infant breathe and you will get the idea—long and slow.

Effortlessness: As with all things, the Taoist masters emphasize naturalness and effortlessness in our breathing. Don't worry about doing it right. Ultimately, the goal, if we can call it that, is not to breathe at all but to let the

Wise people breathe from deep within them, whereas most people breathe with their throats.

CHUANG TZU

breath breathe you, which is to say, to become one with it. In a sense, you are returning to the simplicity you knew before you left the womb. If breathing like an infant will fill us with *ch'i*, then breathing like an embryo in the womb will take us beyond the body itself. In easy breathing, as in all things, a quiet mind is most important.

Eat Well

The ancient Taoists believed that one of the key factors determining the strength of our *ching* (bodily essence) is the quality of the food we eat. In the last twenty years, modern medical research has made huge advances in understanding the nutritional foundations of health and illness. Whole grains, legumes, and vegetables should comprise (as now even the USDA recognizes) the bulk of the human diet. The intake of meat, poultry, and fish should be kept to a minimum. Many find they can eliminate animal foods altogether. In so doing, they can eliminate food that is difficult to digest, loaded with excess fat, and often contaminated with toxic chemicals. If you feel you must eat animal foods, eat more poultry than meat, more fish than poultry. It's also best to avoid fried foods, excessive fat and sodium, white flour, processed and chemical-laden foods, and stimulants such as sugar, coffee, alcohol, and tobacco. It is essential to drink plenty of pure, preferably spring, water.

Eat organic foods, whenever possible. This will help you avoid the toxic buildup of pesticides and herbicides in your body. Moreover, you will be getting greater levels of nutrition than can be derived from the "fertilized" fare found in most supermarkets. After World War II, chemical manufacturers found themselves with huge stockpiles of the nitrates used in explosives. In a brilliant marketing move, they began peddling these "fertilizers" as a necessary and essential component of modern farming. The result is the nutritionally depleted food that fills our supermarkets. Healthy, nutrient-rich foods grow in living soil that is full of microorganisms. Long-term use of fertilizers and pesticides destroys these microorganisms. Because it takes many years to rebuild damaged soil, even organic foods may lack adequate nutrition. Therefore, vitamin and mineral supplementation is a good idea for most people. In addition to providing greater nutrition and freedom from toxic pesticides, organic foods taste much better. Anyone who compares the taste of a chemically grown carrot or peach with their organic counterparts will be convinced at once of the difference.

Food is the chief of all medicines.
—THE UPANISHADS

While organic foods do cost more and are often harder to find, they are worth the effort and additional cost. Fortunately, whole grains, the backbone of a healthy diet and the staple of virtually all traditional cultures, are very inexpensive. Yet even if it does cost a little more to eat healthy foods, it is well worth the expense. After all, as Benjamin Franklin put it, "There is no greater wealth than health." A diet rich in delicious, healthy foods is one abundance that we should not deprive ourselves of.

Move Your Body

The benefits of regular physical exercise are well documented. We know that regular physical exercise helps to increase circulation, improve respiration, balance hormones, reduce stress, enhance mood, tone muscles, improve posture, lower blood pressure, increase vitality and stamina, improve immune response, reduce weight, and deepen sleep. We will not belabor the point or detail the evidence supporting the benefits of exercise listed above. Unless you have been living your whole life in a cave, you know that regular exercise is good for you. Yet at this writing, only 15 percent of adults in the U.S. engage in vigorous regular exercise at least three times a week for twenty minutes or more.[5]

Clearly, telling people that exercise is good for them is not enough. Part of the problem, of course, is the modern lifestyle. Most of us get little exercise in our daily work. Therefore, we must make a point of scheduling it as a special activity. Often we turn exercise into a "have-to" activity, something we must force ourselves to do. It is especially difficult for those who view their workday as a "have to," to come home and begin another have-to activity.

If we are going to maintain a regular exercise program, it must become a "want to" in our lives. Often it is simply a matter of getting past the initial inertia and lethargy that results from sedentary lives. Once they break through this sluggishness, people often find that regular exercise is

Tell me what you eat, and I will tell you what you are.

ANTHELME BRILLAT-SAVARIN (1755-1826)

something they don't want to live without. If you resist exercise because you think that it must be painful and strenuous to be effective, you might want to consider alternatives to the weight training and aerobic model that prevails at local gyms and health clubs. Yoga, Tai Ch'i Chuan, simple stretching exercises, or brisk walking will help keep the energy circulating.

Rest Your Body

If we want to maintain health, vitality, and good cheer, it is essential that we get adequate amounts of deep, restful sleep. The Taoists concur with the old adage "Early to bed, early to rise." To rise with or before the light and to begin to settle down and sleep with nightfall—this is the natural order of things. It is the way human beings lived for countless ages. Today, bright electric lights seemingly turn night into day. Yet our bodies' natural rhythms remain tied to the sun and its light. In addition to the lights themselves, modern technology gives us so many things to do with them on. Most people spend their evenings with televisions, stereos, computers, video games, or other electronic gadgets that tend to excite the nervous system. This nervous excitement, combined with the general stresses of modern life, may make it difficult for us to go to bed early or even to sleep at all.

Try to wind down your activities so that you are ready to go to sleep between 9 and 10 P.M. I know this advice may seem difficult to follow for some. I was a night owl myself for many years. Especially when I was younger, I thought going to sleep early was boring and staying up late was fun and exciting. However, in more recent years, I find myself retiring early and naturally rising between five and six o'clock in the morning, the time which the ancient Chinese referred to as "the hour of arousal." Since changing my habits, I find that I feel more rested with less sleep.

The Taoists tell us that every hour we sleep before midnight is worth two hours after midnight. They believe that we do most of our dreaming between the hours of 1 and 5 A.M. We all know that while we are dreaming, our bodies do not reach the deepest levels of rest. Modern sleep researchers have confirmed that sleep becomes lighter as night progresses. Make your bedroom as dark as possible before you go to sleep. The general rule is: the darker the room, the deeper you will sleep. If you are in excellent health, have peace of mind, eat well, and retire early, six hours of sleep is plenty.

The best doctors in the world are Doctor Diet, Doctor Quiet, and Doctor Merryman.

JONATHAN SWIFT

Lacking any of these conditions, you will require more. How much more will depend on you. Be aware that you can sleep too much and that quality of sleep is as important as quantity.

Another aspect of getting adequate rest is taking time to do nothing, to just be. If you can find even twenty minutes a day to sit or lie quietly in a yard or park, gaze out a window, or lie down on a bed or couch with your eyes closed (without falling asleep), you will be amazed at the rejuvenating effects these brief interludes can bring. When we are doing nothing, we are resting not only our bodies but our minds and emotions as well. Take time to be still and listen to the quiet.

Master Your Emotions

The Taoists believe that while *ching,* or generative energy, is lost primarily through sexual desire and *shen,* or spiritual energy, is lost mainly through an overactive mind, *ch'i,* or vital energy, is lost principally through negative emotions. We can eat the right foods and get plenty of rest and exercise, but if we do not learn to master our emotions, both peace of mind and genuine health will elude us. Emotions such as fear and anger actually alter respiration, heart rate, and body chemistry and upset hormonal balance. Besides robbing our health and stealing the joy out of life, these emotions limit our effectiveness. We all know that we do not think clearly or make good decisions when we are upset. While we are knotted up in anxiety or consumed by anger, even the simplest of tasks can become a challenge.

> *For every minute you are angry, you lose sixty seconds of happiness.*
> —EMERSON

If you were to smoke *a* cigarette, you would be very unlikely to suffer any serious consequences. However, if you were to fill your lungs with two packs a day, day after day, year after year, you would be very unlikely to escape serious consequences. The same applies to the so-called negative emotions. If you are suddenly startled by a loud noise and momentarily respond in fear, that is one thing. If you are chronically and habitually fearful, going about with halting breathing and a knot in your stomach, that is quite another. If you momentarily get angry with people or events

Calmness is power.

JAMES ALLEN

from time to time and quickly let it go, the consequences will probably be minimal. On the other hand, if you hold onto grudges, are often consumed by jealousy or thoughts of revenge, or frequently explode in rage, it will be difficult indeed to escape the consequences. Remember, as Blake said, "Damn braces, bless relaxes." Let go of emotional defensiveness and, with it, the physical tension that gives rise to disease. Bless all, including yourself.

Because it breaks the cycle of fear and anger and puts the energy back into constructive circulation, forgiveness is the most essential skill to learn on the road to emotional mastery. Confucius said, "To be wronged is nothing unless you continue to remember it." What is it that makes us hold onto a perceived injury? And why is it that, as Aesop said, "The injuries we do and those we suffer are seldom weighed in the same scales"? These questions will be addressed in greater length in the next chapter. Here, let it suffice to say that to feel wronged, to cling to a perceived injury, is to misunderstand the situation. Many times we take offense when none is intended. Yet even when someone is deliberately trying to injure us, their actions are a reflection of their own pain and suffering. They are not trying to hurt us because they feel good about themselves. Indeed, all hate is ultimately self-hate.

To respond to hatred with hatred only fuels the fire and drags you down into the emotional hell that the other party was living in when he or she first thought to injure you. If you can resist the urge to fight fire with fire, if you can maintain your love and poise, you might be able to lift the other person up. Even if you can't lift the other, you can keep yourself from falling into an emotional abyss. As the Buddha said, "Hatreds never cease by hatreds; they cease by non-hatred; this is the primeval law." Or expressed in the vernacular: "Hating people is like burning down your own house to get rid of a rat."[6]

Meditate

Learning to meditate can do wonders for your life. It can lower your blood pressure, increase your energy, and bring you a sense of peace and deep relaxation. It also boosts your creativity by emptying and quieting your mind, allowing it to become a better, more subtle receiver set. The philosophy behind the practice of meditation is explained simply by the Taoists.

They tell us that in the normal course of events, our energy is constantly being directed outward through the senses. It is thus depleted and exhausted. When we meditate, we reverse the flow of energy, directing it back within ourselves, where it nourishes and strengthens our whole being—mental, physical, and spiritual.

> *When fire gives off light outwardly, the fuel is being used up; when the spirit's intellect is racing outwardly, wholeness is disintegrating.*[7]

The Taoists believe that *shen,* or spiritual energy, escapes through the eyes and is exhausted by mental excitement. To cultivate *shen,* focus your attention on the inner, or "third," eye (located behind and above the eyeballs) while meditating. Keep your body still and focus on your breath until your mind becomes quiet and your heart is at peace. The Taoists believe that while you are meditating, you are not only preserving and redirecting the flow of energy, but also enhancing your receptivity to the descending *ch'i* of Heaven. You are allowing yourself to be filled with the spiritual energies of the universe.

Simplify

The Taoist view of life is conservative in the truest sense of the word. It can be stated: Do only what is necessary; keep only what you need. What is necessary for you will depend to a great extent on your values. Simply asking yourself, What is necessary? may help you to eliminate a lot of wasted motion. It will keep you from being busy for busy's sake. Living, as we do, in a culture obsessed with material acquisition, we do well to remind ourselves that *the more we have, the more we have to worry about.* Here, by "worry about," I don't mean neurotic anxieties or greedy obsessions (though these, of course, compound the problem) but simply the responsibilities that attend ownership. Many people are seduced into buying things that may give them a few moments, hours, or days of satisfaction, only to find that they then must spend weeks, months, or years paying for them. This complicates life unnecessarily. Consider well the real cost of anything *before* you purchase it. One way or another, everything you buy is costing you time—time to earn the money to pay for it, time to use or enjoy it, time to care for it. Time is life and most precious. Don't sell it cheap.

Spend Time in Nature

In many traditional cultures, when one wanted to develop his or her spiritual life, he or she went into the forest. The word itself tells us what the forest is for: it is for-(r)est. A walk in the woods is a spiritual experience for any sensitive person. It energizes and harmonizes body, mind, and spirit. There is *ch'i*, life energy, in all living things. When you stand against or lie under a tree, you are exchanging energy with a living being. When you enter a forest, you are being touched on subtle levels by the life energies around you. The color and energy around you vitalizes and sensitizes you. If you live in an urban environment and it is difficult for you to get to the country, spend time in your city's parks. We spend so much time surrounded by mechanical and man-made objects that we forget what it means to be among living things. Yet even a little time in nature can make a big difference in the way we feel.

Cultivate an Awareness of Your Surroundings

We do not live in a vacuum. The physical space around us—its sights, scents, and sounds—are having an uplifting or depressing effect on our energies. Understanding this, the Taoists recognized the importance of *feng shui* (pronounced "fung schway"), the ancient Chinese art of placement. Most generally, feng shui is concerned with the selection of building sites, the design of buildings (architecture), and the arrangement of furniture and objects within the building (interior design). The idea is a simple one: to create harmonious and prosperous living environments by working with the natural principles of the movement of *ch'i*, or life energy. Again, proper circulation of energy is of paramount importance. The feng shui master's "skill lies in his ability to allow for the unhindered circulation of this energy *{ch'i}* in relation to the dwelling of the living and the dead."[8]

> *If a geomancer can recognize ch'i, that is all there is to Feng Shui.*
> —SARA ROSBACH

The selection of a site for a home, the positioning of a door in a house, or the arrangement of furniture in a room may block the flow of *ch'i* or serve to attract abundant vital energy. We all recognize that we feel better in some homes or buildings than in others. We know that we are influenced by the color scheme of a room, by the objects of beauty or the piles of clutter that may decorate it. Feng shui recognizes and manipulates these influences. More importantly, it takes into account subtle, even invisible, influences that affect the flow of *ch'i*. Some of its principles are simple common sense. For example, don't place a bed, couch, or office desk in a place from which you can't easily see the entry door. Other principles are more esoteric. For example, don't let the White Tiger (yang) energy overwhelm the Green Dragon (yin) energy in your home.

In addition to facilitating harmony and balance, feng shui can be, and most often is, used for attracting wealth and prosperity. In Hong Kong, a typical business person would no more think of starting a business without consulting a feng shui master than he would launch a new product without a marketing strategy. Today, feng shui is becoming increasingly popular in the West, and there are a number of excellent books available on the subject. You may want to investigate these or consult a feng shui master.

In a classic Tantric text, we read, "The quality of any space is determined by the sound." Sound is moving energy. This "sound *ch'i*" can have a harmonizing and vivifying or disconcerting and destructive influence. The effects of noise pollution on stress in the human body are well documented. On the other hand, certain kinds of music are known to enhance learning capabilities, reduce stress, and promote peace of mind. Incorporate sounds into your life that lift your spirit and charge your energy.

As with sound, so with scent. We all know that certain scents have the power to excite or calm, to agitate or disgust us. Researchers have demonstrated that the inhalation of certain essential plant oils actually alters brain wave patterns. While the exact mechanism is not well understood, studies indicate that scents act on the hypothalamus, which influences the hormonal system. This may account for the influence of scent on mood, metabolism, nervous tension, and sex drive. Aromatherapy is the art of using essential plant oils for healing and mood enhancement. Today, like feng shui, aromatherapy is becoming increasingly popular, finding its way not only into people's homes but into the corporate workplace as well.

This chapter explored how we can apply the principle of *ch'i* to enhance our experience of abundance. The next chapter will explore the principle of *Te*, the nature of authentic power, and how it relates to our sense of personal integrity and dignity.

*Happiness depends,
as Nature shows,
Less on exterior things
than most suppose.*

WILLIAM COWPER

Production, Speculation, and the Flow of Money

The basic law of the universe—as you sow, so you reap; as you give, so you receive—ultimately applies. If one, as Confucius put it, values his soul above his property, he will certainly keep it in mind. Yet on the financial level, there exist artificial constraints that impede the natural cycle of return. This is so since our society does not recognize a distinction between money made by producing real value and money made from mere speculation. Real wealth is generated by the production and distribution of useful goods and services. On the other hand, speculation is a means of increasing net worth without actually producing anything. The production process is as follows:

1. Identify a genuine need or human motivation to serve.
2. Create goods and services to address that need or motive.
3. Deliver goods and services in such a way as to provide maximum benefit.
4. Receive adequate payment for goods or services delivered.

This formula for the creation of wealth through production is the basis of all real wealth. In a true free-market economy, one's income and wealth would be in direct proportion to the value one adds, that is, the real benefit one provides to others. Such a system would allow for the free flow of energy and the unimpeded circulation of wealth. Yet in a highly controlled and regulated economy like our own, greater income can often be attained by means of speculation than by means of production. Speculation involves trading artificial abstractions of existing real wealth so as to realize monetary profit on them.

For example, farmers create wealth by growing, harvesting, and delivering so many bushels of corn. By speculating on the future price of the farmer's corn, commodity traders realize profits without creating any new real wealth. They make money without making anything else. Building contractors and laborers produce real value. They create the wealth of new or remodeled homes, which people may live in and enjoy. Real estate investors speculate on this actual wealth so as to maximize the return on their investments, often without adding any real value.

Corporations produce goods and services, some of which add real value, some of which do not. Investors then speculate on the value of these companies, in stock markets. Some companies may be overvalued in the stock markets, in which case the market assigns to them a value greater than their production and distribution merits. Other companies may go under because they are under-valued in stock markets. The value of the stock, though it may be related to the company's real value, does not depend on it. Thus, traders may speculate on it. Those who speculate on the value of a company often make a great deal more money than those who actually make the goods or provide the services the company offers.

Again, production, delivering real value, is the basis of all man-made wealth. Speculation, on the other hand, is essentially gambling on existing values. The existing legal infrastructure favors making money on money, which is to say, speculating, over making money by producing and delivering valuable goods and services (see chapter 5). Thus, the schoolteacher who provides real service to others may have a meager income, while the speculator who spends his days gambling on existing value makes millions. The Taoist would view such a system as fundamentally corrupt. From their perspective, human beings must express their innate gifts and provide real service to others in order to fulfill their individual destinies and bring about a just and harmonious society. In a society that rewards speculation, or gambling, above real service, people are likely to become dishonest and try to cheat one another.

Today, providing real value by producing goods and services typically supplies individuals with compensation in the form of income. Yet this resulting income, more often than not, does not translate into wealth as measured by net worth. In order to accumulate wealth of this kind, it is generally necessary to be involved in some form of speculation. Regardless of the real value that you provide through your work, speculation may be necessary as a wealth-building strategy if you want to achieve financial independence. Below are some basic rules to keep in mind for successful speculation:

1. Choose an existing value in which to trade, for example, real estate, stock, commodities, etc. Gain knowledge of the markets in which it is traded, as well as knowledge of the specific items you want to trade in.

2. Achieve control of that value for trading purposes, at the lowest possible cost in terms of dollars and hours.

3. Gain advantage by:
   a. Selling for profit
   b. Maximizing leverage
   c. Controlling the market

4. Reduce the negative consequences of winning, i.e., the bites of taxes and inflation.

5. Conserve some gains; reinvest the rest.

CHAPTER FIVE

Te

THE POWER OF ABUNDANCE

Our life is our own possession, and its benefit to us is very great. Regarding its dignity, even the honor of being Emperor could not compare with it. Regarding its importance, even the wealth of possessing the world would not be exchanged for it.
                                        —YANG CHU

This chapter explores the principle of *Te* and the natural dignity and power that results from living in the Tao. The Way of *Te* is really simple: Be what you are, follow your own nature. This will lead you to your destiny, including the work, relationships, and way of life that are naturally yours. Yet in its alienation, struggle, and resentment, the ego leads us from the path of Te. Instead of seeking our own way, we crave the approval and recognition of others. We attempt to find security and approval in conformity. Inevitably, this conformity provokes an inner rebellion. In reaction, we may try to exert coercive or manipulative power over others, or we may resort to self-destructive behaviors. This chapter explores the origins of the patterns of dependency that rob us of our innate dignity and power—and how these can be overcome once and for all. In addition to these inner impediments to authentic power, this chapter examines economic and social forces that make it difficult for us to follow the way of our own natures. In the related exercises at the end of the book, you will have the opportunity to chart a path to the realization of your inborn destiny.

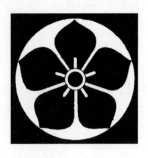

Chuang Tzu said: "That which things get in order to live is called *Te*." We can think of *Te* as the measure or portion of the Great Tao that each individual thing or being receives. The oak has its *Te*; the bird, its *Te*; the man, his *Te*. "Everything has its own Te, or virtue. Everything has its own proper nature. Everything is happy, if it is allowed to be in accordance with its own nature."[1] We can say that for each of us, *Te* is the full power, dignity, and ordinary majesty of being who we really are. It is not the self-conscious, controlling power of ego but rather the natural, preconscious, intuitive power of being.

The word *Te* is often translated "virtue." Yet this virtue is not a matter of adhering to an abstract code of ethical behavior. As the *Lao Tzu* instructs, "Inferior virtue does not let go of being virtuous and thus is not virtuous." Rather, *Te* more closely fits the meaning of virtue in the archaic sense of "effective force" or innate power, such as when we speak of the healing virtues of plants, or when we say that conductivity is a virtue of copper. We can equate the innate power of *Te* with dignity in the sense of "inherent nobility and worth."[2]

To say that *Te* is innate is not to say that it is automatically realized. There are indeed many diversions and distractions to be overcome on the way to the full flowering of our humanity and the development of our unique innate abilities. At any point, we may become sidetracked and miss the life we were born to live. Though Lao Tzu and Chuang Tzu posed them in different ways, they too were interested in the questions Jesus asked in the Gospel of St. Mark: "For what profit a man, if he gain the whole world, and lose his own soul? Or what shall a man give in exchange for his soul?"[3]

We could ask: For what will you sacrifice your *Te*? Will you lose it because you fear offending others and find it easier to conform? Will you trade it for money or fame, for lust or ambition, for cheap thrills or empty promises? When the poet Wordsworth says "Getting and spending, we lay waste our powers," he is talking about losing our *Te*. To preserve and develop your own natural ability and innate power is no easy task in today's commercial society.

The man or woman of Tao is fiercely independent and understands that, as Joseph Campbell put it, "social pressure is the enemy." Yet ultimately, social pressure only affects us to the degree that we allow it to. As Albert Einstein said, "While it is true that an inherently free and scrupulous individual [the man or woman of Tao] may be destroyed, such an individual can never be enslaved or used as a blind tool." As water requires cold to become ice, so outer social pressure requires an inner psychology of fear to become effective. We lose our *Te* when we value the approval of others too highly and sell the innate dignity and power of our own souls too cheaply. Regardless of how vast the riches, prestigious the honors, or overwhelming the approval we may earn, there is no genuine experience of abundance if these come at the cost of our souls. How much less if we sell out for chump change?

This chapter will explore some of the social pressures upon us today, and what we as individuals can do to break free of the inner psychology that makes us so susceptible to them. We cannot preserve or strengthen our *Te* without understanding how we deplete it. There is rain enough to fill the reservoir if we plug up the leaks. We have within us power enough to handle life as it presents itself, if we do not needlessly deplete it.

The Classical Taoists frequently referred to the "ancients" with reverence and veneration. They believed that humankind had fallen from a state of grace enjoyed by these highly intuitive and naturally powerful beings, into the artificiality and self-consciousness of the present era. They believed that as collective awareness of the Tao was lost, humankind fell into a degraded state. Today we see human beings engaged in a seemingly endless variety of degrading behaviors. We can put on our judge's hat and say, "This behavior is wrong; that one is bad. This we must condemn; that we must eliminate." We can create religious prohibitions and legal restrictions against such behaviors. The Taoists were not enamored with these kinds of sanctions. They viewed them as contrary to nature and thus needlessly burdensome and ultimately ineffectual. In the words of Chuang Tzu, "'Systems of right and wrong,' are human judgments and have nothing to do with nature. To see this is the very essence of Tao."

They were, rather, interested in understanding the cravings that give rise to the behaviors in the first place. Degradation begins in the heart and mind. Degradation is ultimately and only degraded, which is to say, incomplete or inferior, awareness. It may manifest in the worst forms of cruelty or self-destruction, or the slow rotting of a soul resigned to a life lived without joy or meaning. It is not enough to condemn the symptoms. If we are to heal as individuals or as a society, we must understand the root causes of our suffering. We must love the patient, whether it is ourselves or others, and recognize the innate dignity of all human beings, however far they have wandered from the Way.

The Dignity of Self-Reliance

He is his own best friend, and takes delight in privacy;
whereas the man of no virtue or ability is his own worst
enemy and is afraid of solitude. —ARISTOTLE

From the Taoist perspective, Heaven and Earth unite in the human being. The Earth principle suggests the way of nature *(hsing);* the Heaven principle, the way of destiny *(ming).* The essence of the Taoist philosophy is perhaps best encapsulated in the expression, *"hsing ming shuang hsiou,"* meaning *"to cultivate nature and destiny together."* The road to our divinity, which is to say, the realization of ourselves as spiritual beings, runs through our humanity (our nature). Efforts made to try to go above or around it are futile at best; at worst, wholly disastrous. In the Isha Upanishad, we read, "To darkness they are doomed who worship only the body [Earth], to greater darkness they who worship only the spirit [Heaven]." The wise, therefore, cultivate both body and spirit, nature and destiny.

If our spiritual life is to have real value, it must be grounded on the earth. It begins, not with a flight to escape the tribulations and the limitations of the body (the heartache and the thousand natural shocks that flesh is heir to), but with a descent into nature. It means identifying with the wisdom body—the universal intelligence that formed and maintains our bodies as well as all the bodies around us, including the one we whirl around the sun on. Acceptance of nature requires the acceptance of the human body and of the limitations that go with it.

Let's think about what it means to be a human being. As human beings, we are born into a long period of dependency and incompleteness. The moment the umbilical cord is cut, we are helpless. This physiological fact has a profound effect on our psychology. We develop a psychology of approval-seeking as a reaction (or protection) against our biological helplessness. The young child has the feeling, "I will die without approval," and there is a certain biological basis for this belief, for he or she is totally dependent on the support of others.

The formation of a psychology dominated by approval-seeking *is* an effective survival strategy. It helps ameliorate the two fundamental problems of the first stage of life, namely dependence and incompleteness. First, by seeking the approval of our parents or caretakers, we are more likely to win their protection, affection, and support. Second, the desire for approval provides powerful motivation for learning the skills we need to survive in the physical world and in human society. We say the words "da-da" or "ma-ma" and our parents give us praise or a smile. Their attention and praise encourages us to walk, to feed ourselves, and to learn many other essential physical and social skills. Likewise, parental disapproval is an effective tool in the process of social conditioning. Since we associate approval with survival, disapproval is experienced as a threat to our existence and as such becomes a powerful force in shaping behavior.

The process of social conditioning is necessary to our survival. Through it, we learn a great deal about the physical world and the society in which we live. However necessary and beneficial it may be, this conditioning process is experienced as restrictive and painful. Nietzsche compared the human being in the first stage of life to a beast of burden. He said we are like camels, getting down on our knees, accepting the weight and burden of social conditioning. In the first stage of life, the search for approval becomes our *raison d'etre*, deeply woven into the fabric of our subconscious minds and closely tied to our identity—our sense of who we are and what we are here to do. The quest for approval so dominates our inner lives that there is little psychic energy left for anything else. Again, this is a natural reaction to our biological condition and is perfectly appropriate and effective as a survival strategy in the first stage of life.

The problem comes when we try to carry this psychology over into adulthood. At this stage, an inner life oriented around approval issues is not only no longer useful; it is positively destructive. It robs us of our capacity to live our own lives. Whether we spend our lives conforming to win approval or rebelling because we think we can't get it (or more likely, alternating between conforming and rebelling), we are allowing ourselves to be controlled by issues inappropriate to the adult stage of life. Consequently, we spend our lives on the defensive. Incapable of real creative action, we can only react. Incapable of seeing things, ourselves, or others objectively, we get caught up in peripheral subjective issues. Unless we make a break as sharp and distinct as the cutting of the umbilical cord, we are likely to remain psychologically dependent creatures for the whole of our lives. The power, the virtue, the dignity, of *Te* will elude us.

To maintain one's human nature is the first step toward achieving divinity.

NARADA BHAKTI SUTRAS

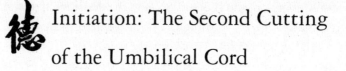 Initiation: The Second Cutting of the Umbilical Cord

When I was a child, I spake as a child
I understood as a child, I thought as a child:
But when I became a man, I put away childish things
—I Corinthians 13:11

Recognizing this problem, traditional cultures introduced initiation rites to aid the individual in making the inner transformation appropriate to the adult stage of life. While specific initiatory rites varied from culture to culture, all implicitly recognized the need to throw off the old infantile psychology and adopt a new one appropriate to adulthood. There must be a breaking point, a point of passage that reorients our inner lives to our new situation. We must undergo a transformation that brings our subconscious minds up to date with the fact that we are now biologically independent and socially adequate. This psychological rebirth was not only recognized as a necessity, but was richly and joyously celebrated in most traditional cultures.

Young people today may think: "Now, I'm 18. I've got my driver's license and my high school diploma. I can vote. Now, I'm an adult." Yet subconsciously, they haven't made the break. While the outer circumstances of their lives have dramatically changed, their inner lives remain essentially the same. Today, we have no socially recognized process for orienting the individual's psychology towards the responsibilities and possibilities of adulthood.

Should we be surprised, then, that we live in what Christopher Lasch called a "Culture of Narcissism"—a society of psychological children? There is perhaps nothing more sad or pathetic than to hear people in their seventies and beyond whining about what their parents did to them. We feel embarrassed for them, intuitively understanding that these are issues they should have resolved long ago. We recognize at once that they have missed their true calling in life and wasted vast amounts of their psychic energies playing the victim game. They have denied their natures and lost their *Te.*

The purpose of the initiatory rites in traditional tribal societies was to impress upon the individual's psyche the fact that he or she now had a new body. The typical ritual might go something like this: If the individual was a male, when he had reached the appropriate age, the menfolk in the society would come to take him away. His mother would put up a mock battle to hold onto him. All this was experienced symbolically, as an archetypal drama—the clinging mother representing the dependent child state; the men taking the boy, the new responsibilities and privileges of adulthood.

> *But now we are a mob. Man does not stand in awe of man, nor is his genius admonished to stay at home, to put itself in communication with the internal ocean, but it goes abroad to beg a cup of water from the urns of other men.* —EMERSON

The boy was brought to the men's lodge or ritual meeting place to be initiated into his new body. This was done through rites, often involving physical pain. There might be circumcision or some form of physical scarring. The pain and the change in physical appearance were intended to impress upon the individual's subconscious mind the fact that he now had a new body. The tribal elders were not sadists, capriciously or wantonly inflicting injury. They understood that the individual who remains psychologically a child will be a hopelessly unhappy neurotic and a danger to society. Before, during, or after initiatory rites, stories were told and rituals enacted to orient the initiate's psychology toward his new role in society. He learned the mythology of his people and what it meant to be a man in the tribe.

In some cultures, the girls as well were circumcised, scarred, or tattooed. More typically, at the onset of her first menstruation, a girl was taken by the womenfolk to a ritual hut, where she was to contemplate the meaning of the transformation her body was undergoing. Again, the womenfolk would tell the initiate stories and/or act out rituals designed to convey to her what it meant to be a member of her tribe and, particularly, to be a woman in it.

Following gender-specific rites, the male and female initiates would rejoin the group and the whole society would celebrate the new bodies and the changed status of the initiates. They were no longer viewed by themselves or others as children but were accepted by all as adult members of their societies. All would join in the feasting, dancing, and singing that marked the joyous occasion.

Nothing happens to any man which he is not formed by nature to bear.

MARCUS AURELIUS

In traditional cultures, initiation rites are performed on virtually everyone in the society. This kind of socially mandated initiatory process plays an important role, not only in the life of the individual, but also in maintaining harmony within a society and in relation to the environment. Yet this kind of process is most effective in small tribal communities, where roles are clearly defined and specialization of labor is minimal. While effective in achieving their aims of psychological adjustment, these kinds of rituals tend to be somewhat crude in their application. For example, while the psychological break is necessary for initiation—the administration of physical pain is not.

There is another, more esoteric initiatory process associated with mystery schools and mystic traditions around the world. Within these traditions, initiations were only available to qualified candidates who demonstrated the requisite character and moral strength. Pythagoras and Plato were said to be initiates of such mystery schools.[4] Both men and women were accepted as candidates and initiated into the same rites. Within these esoteric traditions, the initiation into adulthood was recognized as only the first in a series of initiations through which the qualified candidate might pass.

Because participants were sworn to secrecy under penalty of death, we do not know exactly what transpired during these initiatory rites. Yet from accounts written by their detractors, and through surviving ritual artifacts, we can surmise something of these rites.[5] Within the Eleusinian mysteries, the first initiation involved breaking the hold of the separated ego on consciousness by going beneath it, symbolically descending into the underworld. The objective was for the initiate to unite in consciousness with the sheer power and raw energy of nature—the Dionysian pulse of life in its destructive as well as its creative aspect.

The initiate would be stripped naked (even as he had entered the world) and given a hallucinogenic barley drink to intensify his experience of the events to follow and to impress them deeply on his subconscious mind. He would be led by an elder down into subterranean chambers, a symbolic underworld in which the all horrors of Hades would be portrayed in a vivid, ritualistic drama. He would see a scene not unlike Dante's Inferno, in which the soul in the afterlife remains consumed by the desires that gripped it on earth. He would learn that death is neither to be feared nor to be hoped for as an escape, but is simply another platform on which the play of the soul continues. At a critical turning point in the drama, the youth would be shown a mirror in which he would see an image of himself as an old man. He would come face to face with his own mortality. The message is clear: Only when we see things as they are, are we ready to put aside the trivial pursuits of youth, the egocentric quest for attention and approval. Only when we face, and indeed embrace, our death, are we ready to live.

The Classical Taoists approached the issue in a philosophical rather than a ritualistic way. Yet there can be no doubt that they viewed the underlying realization as essential to the Way. In chapter 5 of the *Chuang Tzu,* Lao Tzu gave it to a man named Toeless as the key by which to instruct others on the path of liberation. He said, "Why did you not lead him to see that life and death are one, and that right and wrong are the same, so freeing him from his handcuffs and fetters?"

Nature: The Good with the Bad

Thus, those who say they would have right without its correlate, wrong; or good government without its correlate, misrule, do not apprehend the great principles of the universe, nor the nature of all creation.
—CHUANG TZU

While our society recognizes neither traditional nor esoteric initiatory rites, we can nevertheless understand the important elements of the initiatory process and, in so doing, make the psychological journey into adulthood. It is not the rites themselves that are important but a deep recognition of the principles involved. Socrates was said to have refused initiation into the Eleusinian mysteries because the pledge of secrecy would have prevented him from discussing the principles revealed therein. The classical Taoists, especially Chuang Tzu, approached these matters at length and offer much insight into the nature of the problem and its resolution.

The lesson of the first initiation is to accept nature as it is—a mixed bag. Life *and* death, light *and* dark, creation *and* destruction, and so on. We are not to favor life over death, light over dark, but to say yes to the totality of existence. If we can accept the human condition at all, it is because we accept it as a mixed bag, taking that which we perceive to be the good with that which we perceive to be the bad. Accepting (all) our humanity re-quires that we accept the early biological state of dependency and the pain associated with it. In so doing, we open ourselves up to a new experience of life.

The study of other cultures and spiritual traditions helps us to appreciate the need to make the inner transit between the first and second stage of life as a universal human problem. It is not an individual problem, not John Doe's or Jane Smith's problem, not a religious, a Christian, Jewish, or Taoist problem, not a gender, a male or female problem, but a human problem. It is a universal human problem because it is based on human biology. The approval-seeking mindset is the psychological baggage we carry from our extended period of dependency. This baggage must be thrown off if we are to experience the innate dignity of our being and realize the full power of *Te* in our lives.

> *All things can do something, and can equally succeed. If one . . .*
> *struggles for what is beyond the most proper, doing not in accordance*
> *with one's natural ability, acting not with one's genuine feeling, one*
> *will surely get into trouble . . .* —KUO HSIANG

We make a mistake when we compare biographies instead of biologies. We err if we say, "I would have preferred so-and-so's biography to my own." The relevant comparison is not with other people but with other (non-human) species. You probably don't spend much time wishing you had been born an insect or a cow. Many animals are born independent and complete. Those born dependent are so for a few years at most. On the other hand, human societies generally do not recognize an individual as independent before the age of thirteen, and in some, not until they are eighteen or twenty-one.

In relation to other animals, human beings enjoy many advantages. Yet our increased consciousness, our capacity for learning, language, art, and culture come with a cost—a prolonged period of dependence. As with everything in nature, the bigger the front, the bigger the back. Because we have large brains and bodies and because we walk upright, we are all, in a very real sense, born premature. There is only so much of us that can fit through the small human birth canal. In consequence, we spend the greater part of the first year of our lives lying about sleeping and growing. We require many more years to develop into fully independent individuals.

The problem of childhood, or the first stage of life, is ultimately one of biological helplessness, not of our unique biographies or the particulars of

our early upbringing. It is difficult, if not impossible, to move into the full aliveness and joy that come with living our own lives until we recognize this fact. Many go through life feeling wounded by, and complaining about, the abuse or the neglect they suffered at the hands of their parents. Yet both of these problems ultimately come down to the helplessness and dependency of our early biology. When somebody acts in an unkind or abusive manner toward you as an adult, you have the choice of confronting them or leaving the scene. Likewise, as an adult, if you are feeling neglected, there are things you can do about it, including clearly articulating your feelings and/or making significant changes in your life.

As an adult, you have a variety of choices not available to you as a child. You have strength, ability, and knowledge you didn't have then. As a child, you were stuck with what your parents did. Yet ultimately the problem was not what they were or were not doing, but the fact that you were helpless to do anything about it—including leave. And that is not your fault OR their fault. It is simply biology. While you may have wished that your parents had acted differently, ultimately, the problem stems from your biology. Indeed, even if you had been blessed with the best parents in the world, you still would have had the problem of being born biologically dependent and incomplete. You still would have formed an approval-seeking psychology as a reaction against this condition. It is this general orientation to life, not simply the particular traumas of your childhood, that must be overcome. We can try to cut the weeds bit by bit, again and again, or we can pull them out by the roots, once and for all.

The first initiation, then, is to accept and embrace the human condition as your own. You can't run away from it. It isn't a matter of will, of saying, "I can't stand being dependent; I'll be independent." It doesn't work like that. It's a matter of acceptance, of going back and loving and accepting what you didn't before—your helplessness. You can only feel angry about your childhood if you are thinking it shouldn't have been the way it was. Yet since the pains of your childhood ultimately reduce to your helplessness, and since helplessness is a natural developmental stage for a human being, to say that it should not exist is to say that you should not exist as a human being. It is to reject yourself at the most basic level—as a human being. Then you might search the world over, looking for acceptance, yet never find it because you are denying it to yourself. Again, you cannot receive from others anything you are unwilling to give yourself. (See chapter 2.)

Acceptance is neither an escape nor a whitewash. It's not a matter of pretending that it was a wonderful experience to be helpless. To urinate and defecate in your pants; to try to communicate with coos, grunts, and screams; to rely on someone else to feed you or move you from place to place—all of this was indeed painful. Likewise, it was painful to feel yourself so dependent upon and controlled by the approval of others. Admitting this pain is the first step to freeing ourselves from it. Denying the pain of our helplessness or making it wrong only perpetuates the problem. It locks us into a pattern of dependency and rebellion—of desperately seeking approval and then tiring of this process and rebelling and reacting against it. While one's psychology is dominated by approval issues, one is not free to live his or her own life. There is no real possibility of cultivating *Te*.

Recognize that while still dependent and incomplete, you made some critical decisions about yourself, about life, about others, and about the kind of impact you could have upon the world. The fact that your reasoning powers had not yet fully developed and that you were under the influence of your desire for approval means that, in all likelihood, at least some of these were not the best possible decisions. For example, you might have decided that people can't be trusted or that you can't be happy or do what you want in life. Once you admit that you were dependent and incomplete when you made these life decisions, you are no longer stuck in the untenable position of defending the choices made while under this kind of duress. You do not have to go around for the rest of your life defending these decisions or pretending they were brilliant. Admitting and accepting your helplessness in the first stage of life will bring all the limiting decisions you've made and suppressed to the surface to be reexamined and released. They will be cleared simply and easily, for there is no longer any reason to suppress them. What had kept them in place was denying and suppressing the pain you felt about your early dependency.

The first umbilical cord was cut for you. The second, you must cut for yourself. Cutting the first was the beginning of your physical independence. Cutting the second is the real beginning of your spiritual life. Accept the human condition. It is the first step to cultivating the way of nature, and an indispensable part of fulfilling your destiny. Lao Tzu reminds us that everything grows according to its nature. Therefore, do not seek the approval of others, but value your *Te*; allow yourself to grow in your own natural way.

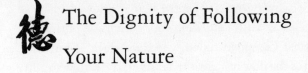

The Dignity of Following Your Nature

*A man's own natural duty, even if it seems imperfectly
done, is better than work not naturally his own even if
this is well performed. . . . Therefore, no one should give
up his natural work, even though he does it imperfectly.*

—BHAGAVAD-GITA

Te, real human dignity and power, can only be realized by following your own nature. Above, we spent a good deal of time discussing the need to free ourselves from the approval-seeking psychology of youth. This mindset can distort our lives in a variety of ways, including keeping us from doing the work we were born to do. Only when we free ourselves from the craving for approval can we really know ourselves for who and what we really are. Only when we accept how much we are like everyone else can we discover and express our unique gifts and abilities. In our work, as in our relationships (see highlight on page 146), and indeed the whole of our lives, the road to our destiny runs through our nature.

*The vocation, whether it be that of the farmer or the architect,
is a function; the exercise of this function as regards the man himself
is the most indispensable means of spiritual development, and as regards
his relation to society the measure of his worth.*

—ANANDA K. COOMARASWAMY

For most of us, our work is the primary channel through which we receive material abundance. Yet the experience of working itself is one that may enhance or diminish our experience of abundance. Following your nature or, as Joseph Campbell put it, your bliss, will lead you to the life you were born to live, and that includes the work that's right for you. He said, "If you follow your bliss, you put yourself on a kind of track, which has been there all the while waiting for you, and the life that you ought to be living is the one you are living."

There are two key elements here with respect to the Tao of Abundance: (1) Following your nature is the path of *Te*, of real power and genuine joy.

*Obey your own destiny;
it is often very difficult,
but it is the only means
of attaining serenity.*

CHUANG TZU

As Fung Yu-Lan put it, "Everything is happy, if it is allowed to be in accordance with its own nature." (2) Following your nature also puts you in the flow of the Tao—what Campbell called "the right track"—but what might be better imaged as the flow of a great river. As all rivers flow steadily and inevitably to the ocean, so following your inborn nature inevitably leads to your destiny.

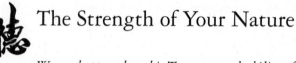

The Strength of Your Nature

We are happy when this Te *or natural ability of ours is fully exercised, that is, when our nature is fully and freely developed.*
— FUNG YU-LAN

If there is one essential principle of the Tao of Abundance, it is this: Follow your nature. Your nature is your strength. To deny it is to rob yourself of your own power, your *Te*. Many deny their talents, gifts, and abilities, then complain they can't be happy or successful in this world. This is like placing leg-irons around your ankles and then complaining that you can't run fast. Following your nature is a simple matter of doing what you are naturally good at. In his commentary on the *Chuang Tzu*, Kuo Hsiang wrote: "If by nature a man is a strong man, he will carry a heavy burden without feeling the weight. If one is by nature a skillful man, he can manage all sorts of affairs without feeling busy." Ease, joy, and power are natural by-products of following your nature, and need not be sought for themselves.

> *{One} who is naturally and constitutionally adapted to and trained in some one or another kind of making, even though he earns his living by this making, is really doing what he likes most, and if he is forced by circumstances to do some other kind of work, even though more highly paid, is actually unhappy.* — ANANDA K. COOMARASWAMY

Two men leave the same town at the same time, bound for the same destination. One rides a strong and willing stallion; the other takes a stubborn old mule, which he must drag, kick, coax, and cajole along. Who arrives first? Who has the more pleasant journey? Many people struggle unnecessarily by spending their lives doing work to which they are not naturally suited. Like the man with the mule, they kick, drag, coax, and cajole themselves through the day. Even if they do manage to achieve financial success, they miss the joy of developing their innate strengths. If the work you do every day of your life runs contrary to your nature, you are missing out on one of the great joys of living—one for which no salary, however great, could ever fully compensate.

 ## Moving in the Flow

One's place is where one can live happily.
—KAUTHILYA

Denying your gifts and abilities doesn't just limit your power, strength, and joy; it robs you of the guiding and motivating force that leads you to the life you were born to live. Following your nature puts you in the flow of the Tao. Remember, as Lao Tzu put it, "the Tao's principle is spontaneity." If you are suppressing your own nature every day in your work, you can hardly expect yourself to live spontaneously in any aspect of your life. Denying your nature deadens and dulls the senses and switches off your innate intuitive intelligence. It makes you feel heavy and doubt yourself.

On the other hand, as you give your gifts and express your inmost nature in the outer world, you attract to yourself the people, circumstances, and resources you will need to fulfill your destiny. You enter a field of experience that, from a conventional perspective, seems magical, but in fact is only the natural state of your being. Spontaneous, creative action and synchronicity in relationships and events become the order of the day. You find yourself being at the right place at the right time. It is not anything you are consciously doing; you are simply allowing your own nature to move you into the flow of the Tao.

We are seduced away from our spontaneous nature by the promise and illusion of security. The way of nature means embracing creative insecurity, moving with and effectively responding to, continuous and spontaneous change. By following the way of your nature and doing the work to which you are naturally suited, you enter the stream of your destiny. You have simply to flow with it. If, instead of following your nature, you choose your career to please your parents, to make more money, or to win social accep-

Craving For Approval Creates Relationships of Dependency

From the infantile, approval-seeking psychology, we do not see our own strength or appreciate our basic human dignity; rather, we feel isolated, lonely, and desperate. We mistakenly think that winning the approval of others will lessen our sense of isolation. Yet trying to win approval from another person is the surest way of avoiding real contact with them. While craving another's approval, we turn that person into an object. We are no longer seeing a living, breathing human being but a kind of substitute parent alternatively dispensing approval and disapproval. We try to control and manipulate the other person into giving us the approval we think we need.

We are not only turning others into objects; we are turning ourselves into powerless subjects. We become "subject" in several senses of the word. Our experience of the world becomes entirely subjective; we lose the capacity to see events, others, or ourselves objectively. "Me" and what's right and wrong with me and what people are doing for or against "me" becomes the primary subject or topic of interest. We become subject to or *at effect of* the approval or disapproval of others. In this way, we lose our natural *Te.*

One of the trickiest problems in intimate relationships arises from the unconscious tendency to turn our partners into parental figures, to project on them the unresolved issues of our childhood. Now, of course, a young child doesn't see a parent as he or she really is, that is, as a person with their own problems and issues. In a childlike way, we may confuse a partner's tiredness with indifference, we read our partner's pain or frustration as disapproval of us. We can get so caught up in trying to be what we think our partners need or want us to be that we miss opportunities to give them what they really do need or want. We become so focused on what we think we need from them that we lose the capacity to understand and feel genuine compassion for them.

We feel controlled by those whose approval we seek and perplexed by how easily and deeply they seem to affect us. Their responses, interpreted as signs of approval or disapproval, can alter our moods or even affect our sense of self-worth. While we are winning their approval, we feel manipulated; when we lose it, we feel hurt to the core. Ultimately, we come to resent those whom we get into a pattern of seeking approval from. In just this way, many relationships are weakened or destroyed. Yet often we fail to realize that it is not the other party but our own need that is controlling us. We may go on repeating the same pattern in relationship after relationship. This pattern may prevent us from finding the right partners in the first place, or cause us to muddle things up if we do. To break the cycle once and for all, we have to step back from the immediate situation, recognize that this is a pattern we have carried with us from childhood, and take the initiation into our adulthood. Healthy relationships are built on mutual respect, love, and understanding; confusing approval with love will surely get us into trouble.

tance, your destiny will escape you. Again, people often overlook their innate talents when making career choices, then complain that they don't know what they are here on this Earth to do. They often become sidetracked by peripheral issues.

For example, in the course of my career consulting work, many outwardly successful men have told me that they decided to become doctors, lawyers, business executives, or to enter other lucrative careers in order to "get the ladies." Sadly, they often end up feeling trapped in work to which they are not suited and which they do not enjoy, for fear of losing the approval of their wives or partners. Having "won" their partners on the basis of their earning potentials, they fear losing them, should they take time away from work for self-exploration or to enter less lucrative fields. They feel that they can't be themselves at home or at work, that they spend the whole of their lives masquerading as something they are not. By midlife, they often feel frustrated and resentful. This points out the danger of letting oneself be guided by ulterior motives. Choose work for the sake of the work itself. Any other course, however expedient it may seem at the time, is in the end fraught with great danger. As the Taoist would say, "The clever often end up outwitting themselves." Better to be simple and follow the way of your own heart.

Of course, it is a loss to the individual; but how much do we as a society lose when people do not follow their natures? If one person loses their *Te*, do we not all suffer a loss? What are the social costs when *most* people lose their way? Clearly, we have a responsibility, not only to ourselves, but to the broader society, to develop and fully express our unique abilities.

 ## Balancing Nature and Society

*Follow that will and that way which experience confirms
to be your own.*
—CARL JUNG

The ironic thing is that in today's world, it often takes more "efforting" to find or create a platform from which to do one's natural work than it does to do the work itself. This is largely a function of the way modern society is organized and the values that dominate it. Of course, conflicts between the agenda of society and the way of nature are not peculiar to modern times.

Still, understanding what we in the present era are up against can be a great help. Today's commercial society rewards those with ambitious, extroverted personalities, people who enjoy attracting attention to themselves and like to toot their own horns.

Of course, many people are not naturally like this. Yet unless they, in some way, come to terms with this societal predilection, they may miss the opportunity to do the work that is naturally theirs to do. If there ever was a time when building a better mouse trap would bring the world to your door, that time has long since passed. Unless one is born financially independent, she must find a way to market herself if she wants to do and go on doing the work that is naturally hers. Beyond getting the opportunity to do the work at all, real creative freedom usually requires considerable commercial success. A balance must be struck that will allow one to do work that is naturally his or hers to do, without allowing one's energies to be consumed by marketing hype. Devoting too little or too much effort to self-promotion may spoil our ability to follow our natures.

While we should not give in to social pressures, neither should we minimize them. They can greatly affect even the lives of highly conscious and gifted individuals. In his autobiography, philosopher and Zen writer Alan Watts wrote about the importance of showmanship as a requirement for success in today's highly commercial society. As he put it, "No one can succeed as an independent author or minister, without a flair for drama and coming on strongly as a personality, and by success I mean not only financial reward, but also effective communication."

What Watts didn't mention in his autobiography was the fact that he was an alcoholic. As his friends saw it, Watts was a sensitive man, a natural introvert who, in order to perform on stage in his lectures and to mix in a gregarious way at the cocktail parties that accompanied them, would drink to loosen up. "He would sweat blood before these events . . . Then one day he discovered that if he had two, maybe three martinis, he was not only comfortable, but the life of the party."[6] Eventually, his drinking became heavy and no doubt was a factor in his early death. His friend Chung-liang Al Huang saw in Watts's life a reflection of the imbalance in modern society, with its overemphasis on yang or masculine values taking their toll on a man who gave much to the world. Though playing the roles of in-demand lecturer and New Age celebrity helped Watts promote his ideas and support himself and his family financially, they also fed his ego and ran counter to his nature.[7] As Watts' story illustrates, social pressures do not evaporate, even when one does manage to make his outer daily work a reflection of his inmost nature. (In fact, they may be compounded.) One still has to decide how he or she will manage them.

The challenge of persevering and fulfilling your nature while earning a living in the modern world is a difficult one, to be sure. How to go about doing it is a subject we haven't time to adequately address here. I have covered the topic at great length in my books, *Zen and the Art of Making a Living* and *How to Find the Work You Love,* and would invite readers seeking to make a living that preserves and expresses their inmost natures to investigate these and other sources. I am encouraged by what I perceive to be a growing awareness within the modern culture of the need to make one's work a true expression of one's self and not simply a means to a paycheck. This burgeoning cultural awareness has within it the potential of a major social transformation. Yet we must also recognize that the individual doing the work that he or she loves and naturally excels at remains very much the exception. Today, this social movement, if it can be called that, is largely confined to the better educated and the more self-directed.

The remainder of this chapter explores some of the obstacles that the organization of modern society, and the values promoted by it, place in the path of the individual endeavoring to fulfill her nature. While the exploration must necessarily be brief, it is important to our present discussion for three principal reasons. First, market society defines life, society, human beings, the natural world, and the concept of abundance in an artificial, which is to say, unnatural way. Second, market society, for all its talk of freedom, is, in a variety of ways, oppressive to human nature, human relationships, and human dignity. Finally, one cannot in good conscience admonish people to follow their natures by doing the work they were born to, without acknowledging the difficulties that attend this task in today's world.

Live according to one's self, but not to others. If so, the integrity of one's nature will be preserved.

KOU HSIANG

 ## Dignity and The Rule of Society

When people do not pollute their innate nature and set aside their Te, then is there need for the government of mankind? —CHUANG TZU

The social environment in which people live may make it more or less difficult for them to cultivate their *Te.* As things stand today, it is not so easy. Tenzin Gyatso, the current Dalai Lama, put it like this: "If the feeling or attitude of most of your neighbors is just a competitive and selfish motive or some such atmosphere, then you will always feel isolated and also that there is no one that you can trust. This is very bad. Ultimately compassion and respect for others diminish, because you may be put in a position where you find that unless you defend yourself there is no alternative; then one naturally develops a selfish motive."[8]

Now the Taoists would say that people are not naturally selfish and defensive and that it is only when they have lost their *Te* that they become so. The classical Taoists also asserted that those who rule society have a responsibility to create an environment that fosters the cultivation of the Tao and most certainly *not* one that promotes greed and competitiveness. They contrast the natural, authentic power (*Te*) by which a craftsman is to perform his art or a leader to guide her people, with inauthentic, contrived, or coercive power. Inauthentic power arises, not from innate human dignity and ability (*Te*), but by deception or force of will.

When the leadership of society is established and maintained by means of this inauthentic power, great human suffering results. It becomes difficult for the people to preserve their natures, and degradations of all kinds abound. From the Taoist perspective, the sequence of events is as follows: Awareness of the Tao is lost in the society as a whole. Next, rulers establish themselves by means of inauthentic power. These rulers, in turn, organize society in ways that tend to further separate people from their true natures.

Far from being disinterested spiritual hermits, the classical Taoists were vigorous social critics and had much to say about the social order and political economy of their day.[9] The classical Taoists were not, as some have asserted, true anarchists. They accepted the need for leadership in the present era, but thought that leaders ought to rule with an extremely light touch, avoiding excessive regulations, laws, or interference, and refraining from placing heavy burdens on the citizenry. They thought that one should "govern a country as you cook a small fish."[10]

The Artificial Society

*The moment we allow the economic calculus to invade everything,
then nothing becomes worthwhile anymore.*

—E. F. SCHUMACHER

If there is anything we can call a guiding principle of Taoist ethics, it is this: What is in harmony with nature is to be pursued; what is contrary to nature is to be avoided. Naturalness fosters *Te*; artificiality breeds degradation. The Taoists criticized the advent of the feudal society in China because of the increased artificiality and oppression that resulted from it.[11] We can only imagine how they would have viewed today's market society. In any objective sense, it must be viewed as the most artificial society in the history of humankind, and the first truly global one. The market society is based on a kind of Orwellian doublespeak. It cannot function without the great mass of people accepting the fiction that labor, land, and money are commodities that can be bought and sold in markets.

Yet, as economic historian Karl Polanyi puts it, "Land, labor, and money are obviously *not* commodities; the postulate that anything that is bought and sold must have been produced for sale is emphatically untrue in regard to them. In other words, according to the empirical definition of commodities, they are not commodities. . . . *Labor* is only another name for human activity which goes with life itself, which in turn is not produced for sale but for entirely different reasons, nor can it be detached from the rest of life, be stored or mobilized; *land* is only another name for nature, which is not produced by man; actual *money*, finally, is only a token of purchasing power which, as a rule, is not produced at all, but comes into being through the mechanism of banking or state finance. . . *The commodity description of labor, land, and money is entirely fictitious.*"[12] (Emphasis mine.)

But what does it mean for us that we accept this fiction? It means, among other things, that our cultural conception of wealth and abundance is an entirely artificial one. It means that we have renamed the world and the people in it. In the mythic traditions of many cultures, there is a practice called "naming the land" in which the local environment is ritualistically "named" in terms of the local societies' concept of the sacred. Great power and magic are held to be in the naming of the world, for it orients

the imagination or inner psychic life to the external world. Today, this power has been expropriated by economists, who have named our world in terms of economic abstractions. Thus: *society* equals marketplace; *human beings* equal "units of marginal productivity," "labor costs," or "consumers"; the *natural world* equals "real estate," "raw materials," or "natural resources"; *time* equals money; and *viable* (literally "able to live") equals "economically successful." Where all of these terms (i.e., society, human beings, the natural world, etc.) once had a sacred referent and meaning, today they are defined in economic terms.

> *If names and realities do not correspond with each other,*
> *Then there will be fighting.*
> —THE CANON LAW (JING FA)

These economic definitions prescribe the social objectives of modern societies. Since people are defined as units of production and units of consumption, the goal becomes, on the one hand, to squeeze from them the greatest production at the lowest cost and, on the other, to induce them to consume the most they can with ready credit at interest to supplement their employment earnings. Economists become concerned with signs that people are not living up to these expectations. A "decline in productivity growth" or a "weakening of consumer demand" could spell disaster. Through their repetition in the commercial media, these ideas have become a commonplace, not only of social discourse, but of individual self-perception. People come to view themselves as "products for sale" and to measure themselves against their neighbors in terms of their consumption levels. In this way, we create a "healthy economy," if not a healthy society.

In the market society, human activity is valued to the extent that it can be sold, land is valued to the extent that a profit can be realized from it, and money reigns supreme. But, as Karl Polanyi points out, "Labor and land are no other than the human beings themselves of which every society consists and the natural surroundings in which they exist. *To include them in the market mechanism means to subordinate the substance of society itself to the laws of the market.*"[13] (Emphasis mine.)

"The commodity fiction . . . supplies a vital organizing principle in regard to the whole of society. . . . [It requires that] no arrangement or behavior should be allowed to exist that might prevent the actual functioning of the market mechanism on the lines of the commodity fiction."[14] In other words, no arrangement or behavior must be allowed to exist that gives lie to the fiction that labor, land, and money are commodities to be bought and sold. This gives the market society its missionary zeal and helps to explain why it has become the first truly global one.

Market society cannot brook the survival of any society in which the commodity fiction is not recognized as fact, that is, any society organized around something other than buying and selling. Existing organic cultures and the social relationships that sustained them had to be destroyed in order to "separate labor from other human activities and subject it to the laws of the market."[15] The effects of the annihilation of existing social structures, first in Europe and then around the world, included "the destruction of family life, the devastation of neighborhoods, the denudation of forests, the pollution of rivers, the deterioration of craft standards, the disruption of folkways, and the general degradation of existence including housing and the arts. . ."[16]

The artificial "laws of the market" provide the logic of the new global society. Consider Los Angeles and Mexico City, two giant metropolises, one in a desert basin, the other 7,000 feet high on a mountain plateau.[17] From the perspective of nature, their very existence in these locales is absurd. From the perspective of human society, they are equally absurd—frenetic, overcrowded, and dirty. Yet from the artificial "laws of the market," they make sense. The laws of the market mean that pharmaceutical companies stand in line to produce mood-altering pills to assuage the neurosis of the middle and upper classes in the developed world, while they will not produce an existing effective cure for malaria because its one-time use renders it insufficiently profitable. That millions die each year from malaria must be chalked up to the greater good of economic growth. We could cite endless examples of the perverse effects of applying the logic of the artificial "laws of the market" to human affairs. Yet space will not permit a full accounting of the costs to human life and dignity that it engenders.

The enormous inequality in the distribution of the wealth is appalling. The fact that three hundred fifty-eight people own as much as three billion is indictment enough of the market society.[18] But even this is not the central issue. We have replaced human activity organized around use with human activity organized around making money. It becomes more important that an organization make a profit than that it make anything useful. As Polanyi puts it, "The extreme artificiality of the market economy is rooted in the fact that the process of production itself is here organized in

the form of buying and selling."[19] What this means is that what gets done or left undone—what shapes and controls human activity today—is money.

Today, the success of any human enterprise is more dependent on having access to money than on any other single criteria. This makes it difficult, even for those who are determined to do so, to break free of the work-for-hire model and pursue their natural calling in life. As E. F. Schumacher wrote: "Some don't accept the First Commandment, 'Thou shalt adapt yourself to slots'; they say, I want to do my own thing, I've got ability and brains and hands, and I want to make something—and then you find you can't, because you haven't got the capital that is needed."[20] To follow your nature in a society in which respect for nature itself and respect for individual human dignity are subordinated to the artificial "laws of the market" is indeed a formidable task. Yet the consequences of not doing so are profound.

Adam Smith, author of *The Wealth of Nations* and the so-called father of economics, saw the tragic human costs of organizing society around the profit motive. Yet he saw this, and the ever increasing specialization of labor it fosters, as inevitable. He said, "The understandings of the greater part of men are necessarily formed by their ordinary employments. The man whose whole life is spent in performing a few simple operations . . . has no occasion to exert his understanding. . . . He naturally loses, there-fore, the habit of such exertion and generally becomes *as stupid and ignorant as it is possible for a human creature to become.* . . . But in every improved and civilized society this is the state into which the labouring poor, that is, the great body of the people, must necessarily fall. . . ."[21]

Today, criticism of the market system tends to focus on inequality in wealth distribution. Yet throughout much of the nineteenth century, Ameri-can political leaders and social philosophers argued against the increas-ing commodification of labor on spiritual grounds.[22] They were concerned about its degrading effects on the dignity and character of individuals and how these would affect society in the long run. They viewed wage work in much the same terms that we think of welfare today: best if not an enduring condition but a temporary one, brought on by the exigencies of circumstance. Work for hire was to be remedied as soon as possible by independent work, lest, like living on the dole, it would begin to weaken the self-esteem and character of the individual.

They argued that wage work would tend to separate the individual from himself, his natural gifts and spiritual aspirations, and weaken his sense of civic and social responsibility. It would also tend to dull his intelligence and turn him into an escapist, only too happy to give himself up to entertainments that might distract him from his true condition. Wage work, as a labor leader of the 1870s put it, "use(s) up in the service of others, the whole of the day, leaving us no time to comply with the public duties which we are having thrust upon us, or for the exercise of any personal gifts or longings for refined pleasures."[23] Though in time, the trade labor movement gave up the character argument in favor of the push for higher wages and better working conditions, this was originally conceived by men like Samuel Gompers of the American Federation of Labor as a short-term strategy for achieving what he called the "final emancipation" of workers. As he put it, "The way out of the wage system is higher wages." Of course, we know today that this strategy did not prove effective. Moreover, the entire debate over the effects of wage work on individual character and the civic society has all but disappeared from the public discourse.

It is the dreariness, unnaturalness, and dumbifying effect of so much of the work in the market society that causes us to seek escape in entertainments that further deplete our *Te*. Our desire to live for the weekends is "proof of the fact that most of us are working at a task to which we could never have been called by anyone but a salesman, certainly not by God or by our own natures."[24] This desire for escape is as well made to serve the "laws of the market" in the form of the banal and often degrading products served up by the entertainment industry. Moreover, it is this desire that fuels the acquisitiveness that defines life in today's commercial culture. People are not only being exploited when they are made to accept mind-numbing employment; they are also, as Alan Watts put it, "being exploited when they are persuaded to desire more and more possessions, and led to confuse happiness with progressive acquisition."

The organization of the whole of society on the principle of gain and profit must have far-reaching results.

KARL POLANYI

That soul-destroying, meaningless, mechanical, moronic work is an insult to human nature which must necessarily and inevitably produce either escapism or aggression, and that no amount of 'bread and circuses' can compensate for the damage done—these are facts which are neither denied nor acknowledged but are met with an unbreakable conspiracy of silence—because to deny them would be too obviously absurd and to acknowledge them would condemn the central preoccupation of modern society as a crime against humanity.

—E. F. SCHUMACHER

The desire for approval, discussed at length above, is made to serve the goal of ever-increasing consumption. Having failed to discover his or her own innate purpose in life, the individual has little choice but to follow the socially sanctioned model. Thus, in the market system, social responsibility and commitment to personal growth are abandoned in favor of the certainty of being told what to do both on the job and off. The individual becomes less concerned with contributing to his society than with fitting into it. Fitting in requires that he join the consumer society, and this, in turn, puts pressure on him to place income ahead of other considerations when determining career choice. This comes at a cost to individual human dignity and, in the aggregate, means that social responsibility is abdicated in favor of social conformity.

The human being, defined by the market system as a unit of production and as a consumer, is not expected or encouraged to fulfill his or her vocation or natural work or to otherwise develop his innate spiritual capacities, but only to keep the wheels of commerce turning. Yet all this turning and all of the marvelous "labor saving" devices that the market system has produced have not, in the words of E. F. Schumacher, "given people more time to devote to their all-important spiritual tasks; it has made it exceedingly difficult for anyone, except the most determined, to find any time whatever for these tasks."[25] Today, people have a difficult time pursuing their nature through their work and precious little time to cultivate it away from it. Truly, "getting and spending," we lay waste our *Te*; we subordinate our human needs to the market way.

The fact that the whole of society is organized around buying and selling destroys organic cultures, fosters mistrust and competitiveness, and diverts people from their natural vocations in life. Beyond this, the simple fact that it takes so much money to live puts enormous pressure on people. Even when they sacrifice their relationships, their peace of mind, and their true callings in life, the high tribute that people typically must pay means they are likely to struggle financially just the same. It is to this oppressive system of tribute payment that we will turn next.

The Rule of Money

Money is a new form of slavery, and is distinguishable from the old simply by the fact that it is impersonal—that there is no human relation between master and slave. —L. N. TOLSTOY

Since the beginnings of recorded history, we find in every civilization and in many nonliterate cultures, a privileged class, a select group who enjoy special prerogatives that distinguish them from the rest in their society. Always, the privileged class were held by themselves and those they ruled, to have obligations to the society as a whole and to those beneath them. In traditional societies, privilege was granted for the performance of a social role. The Chinese Emperor and the village chief, the priests of Sumer and the lamas of Tibet, the lord of the feudal manor—all had obligations to their subjects.

They may have abused their privileges or neglected their obligations; nevertheless, these were clearly defined and known to all. Many traditional societies established procedures for reigning in or removing higher-ups who neglected the responsibilities, or abused the privileges, of their positions. Beyond a social responsibility, privilege carried a responsibility to a higher cosmic power, in whatever way that power was conceived by various cultures. Myths and folk stories handed down from generation to generation reinforced the system of mutual obligations. The Greek tale of the Minotaur is a tragic tale of what happens when a king confuses his privileged role with his ego identity.

The Industrial Revolution, whatever else it did, created a new social order, one in which power and privilege were no longer a matter of noble birth, of political, military, or religious authority, but went with money. As the industrial and financial capitalists took over from the aristocratic nobility, they looked for ways to legitimize their new position of privilege. In the Old World, the new rich set about to buy or, as was the case with the Rothchilds, to extort, titles to confirm ancient legitimacy to their newfound privileged position. In late nineteenth and early twentieth century America, we had the spectacle of wealthy families such as the Vanderbilts marrying their daughters off to European nobility in need of ready cash.

These vainglorious shenanigans aside, the new system was unique in the degree to which privilege had become free of responsibility, either to

A man's true wealth is the good he does in this world.

MOHAMMED

society as a whole or to those below. The new moneyed class were not to be burdened with *noblesse oblige* (duty to those below) that had guided, at least in theory, the old aristocracy. The new rulers touted instead the principle of *laissez-faire* which was supposed to mean "let [people] do [as they choose]," but which in practice meant massive political and legal intervention on behalf of the new financial and merchant elite. As Polanyi points out, "The road to the free market was opened and kept open by an enormous increase in continuous, centrally organized and controlled interventionism . . . [The] *laissez-faire* economy was the product of deliberate state action. . . ."[26] "There was nothing natural about *laissez-faire;* free markets could never have come into being merely by allowing things to take their course."[27]

To this deliberate and "continuous, centrally organized and controlled interventionism," the classical Taoists would most certainly object. Were *lassiez-faire*, in fact, what it purports to be, it is fair to say that the Taoists would wholeheartedly embrace the principle. Yet the "laws of the market" cannot operate without the laws of the legislature that make them effective. Recognizing this, Western financiers were hesitant to invest in former communist countries until the "proper legal infrastructure" was in place. Once in place, the legal infrastructure codifies the preference for those who make money on money over those who produce goods and services in an endless variety of ways. This codified preference works through an elaborate and complex web of legal metaphysics, including corporate, banking, insurance, property, and tax law. These laws don't just establish the mechanism of the market; they make it possible for the economic elite to extract tribute from those below.

> *The more laws and restrictions there are,*
> *The poorer people become . . . .*
> *The more rules and regulations,*
> *The more thieves and robbers.*
>
> —LAO TZU

One of the long recognized privileges of power is the right to exact tribute. Even as the Roman emperor or the headman of the local village required tribute from their subjects, so the new privileged economic class came to exact its own tribute. In every society, the paying of tribute affirms and reinforces the position of the privileged class. When power changes hands, tribute is paid to the new rulers. For example, once the British East India company established effective military control over the wealthy Indian province of Bengal, they set up a system of "taxation" on the local population. It was, in fact, a system of tribute payment; local people could expect to receive nothing in exchange for these taxes. The wealth transfer that resulted from these kinds of arrangements helped to secure the capital concentration necessary to turn European nations into industrial giants. From India alone, "British colonialists derived a direct income exceeding 100,000,000 pounds."[28] Europe prospered as it milked tribute from its colonies in the form of slaves, taxes, gold, silver, and raw materials. Monopolistic trade practices further enriched the colonial powers. It was resistance to the colonial tribute system that helped launch the American Revolution.

Once free of the British, most white Americans in the first half of the nineteenth century enjoyed a period virtually free of tribute payment. Having come as serfs and peasants from Europe, they were determined not to accept the yoke of tribute that had weighed so heavily upon them in their native lands. Moreover, the vast expanse of the new continent meant that immigrants were able to claim "virgin" land on the frontier (once, of course, the native peoples had been exterminated or relocated). As a nation of independent farmers and shopkeepers, who paid no income tax and who had virtually no personal debt, America in the first half of the nineteenth century was a land free of an organized tribute payment system.[29] Of course, in the same breath, it must be said that during this time, millions of African Americans were subjected to a highly organized system of oppression that demanded the whole of their lives and culture as tribute to those who exploited them.

For the majority of Americans, the situation began to change in the latter half of the nineteenth century. As the available "virgin" land dwindled, as wage work replaced independent farming and retailing, as the tax burden grew, and as interest payments became a commonplace of everyday life, the yoke of tribute began to be felt by these once fiercely independent people. Compared with that of his counterpart in the first half of the nineteenth century, the portion of today's average American worker's productive effort that remains his own is small indeed. Today, workers are constantly being told that they must increase their productivity. Yet they understand that most of their productivity gains will not accrue to themselves but will be siphoned off as one form of tribute payment or another.

There is today in America a great deal of talk about the anxious middle

The protection of society, in the first instance, falls to the rulers, who can directly enforce their will.

KARL POLANYI

class and their fear of falling in their living standard and social status. Economists claim that their only hope lies in increased productivity. Yet in recent years, productivity gains have failed to keep pace with a burdensome tribute system. Despite productivity gains, real earnings for most American families have actually dropped.[30] This, despite the fact that Americans are working more hours per year than at any time in recent history.[31] Given the conditions of the poor around the world, it may seem frivolous to fret over the plight of the middle class in the developed nations. Yet there is real suffering involved.

For most, this suffering stems not so much from material lack as from the fact that the middle class are psychologically committed to the notion of measuring their worth in economic terms. They feel shame for not achieving the material level of their parents' generation. More than this, they are increasingly time-poor, having fewer hours to devote to noneconomic activities. Economic time pressures contribute to the breakdown of families and communities and to a growing sense of alienation and loneliness. Even people who manage to marginally improve their economic level, at the loss of time for anything else, are apt to feel not richer but poorer. This is especially true since most people do not feel psychologically enriched or creatively engaged by the work they do to earn a living. Many are apt to agree with Lily Tomlin's quip, "The trouble with the rat race is that even if you win, you're still a rat."

The individual may wonder why, though he seems to be spinning his wheels ever harder, he never seems to be getting anywhere. Unlike the peasant or serf, he may not even realize that he is paying tribute at all. Laws established at the behest of the privileged class both authorize and enforce the system of modern tribute payments. Interest, rents, and profits are all forms of tribute because they accrue to one solely because he possesses property, i.e., money, land, and capital. These are established by law as privileges of property and not as a result of productive effort on the property holder's part. Moreover, by law, the rights of tribute vary for different kinds of property. For example, the right to receive tribute on "intellectual property" (e.g., patents and copyrights) is extremely limited as compared to the rights of "real property." Patents and copyrights are returned to "the public domain" after so many years, while "money property" rights and "land property rights" are held for perpetuity through inheritance. All forms of property are not, it seems, created equal.

Today, the heavy tribute system helps to insure that those who have, get more and those who don't, stay poor. Again, because we have accepted the fiction of labor, land, and money as commodities, the markets for these, which is to say, wages, rent, and interest, become the real facts of our everyday lives. Even as the serfs were required to pay in tribute a portion of their productive fruits to the feudal lord, their modern equivalents are required to pay a large portion of their productive efforts in tribute.

When a individual takes a job, the lion's share of his productive effort goes as tribute to the property holder who has granted him the privilege of working on his property (capital). When that individual buys a home or car, another portion of his productive effort typically goes as tribute in the form of interest to the property holder who has given him the privilege of borrowing his property (money). If that individual rents a home, a portion of his productive effort goes as tribute to the property holder who has given him the privilege of borrowing his property ("improved" land). In all likelihood, a further portion of his productive effort will go to pay interest on various consumer goods—his car, furnishings, credit cards, and the like.

> In 1993 in households of [American] people under 65 making less than $200,000 per year, an average of 22.9% of after tax income went to service debt . . . .[32]

Finally, today's typical worker pays innumerable taxes, a large percentage of which will go to pay interest on privately held debt or to other policies that favor the privileged class. Because in America today, money is no longer created by the government (As per the United States Constitution: "Congress shall have the Power to Coin Money and Regulate the Value Thereof.") but by private banks who charge the government interest on the money it borrows, much of the tax bill represents another form of tribute payment to the moneyed class. The cost of interest on the government debt, which would be nonexistent if the formula prescribed by the Constitutional framers was followed, is, of course, passed on to the taxpayers. (Today, the average American works from January 1 to May 10 to pay his or her taxes, and more than one half of all federal personal income taxes go to interest on the national debt.)

More than this, by controlling the *volume* of money, private central banks (e.g., the Federal Reserve, The Bank of England, etc.) regulate the value of money. The constitutional framers who expressly reserved this power for Congress were well aware of the dangers of allowing the power to create money to fall into the hands of private bankers. As Thomas Jefferson wrote, "If the American people ever allow private banks to control the issue of their money, first by inflation and then by deflation, the banks and corporations that will grow up around them, will deprive the people of their property until their children will wake up homeless on the continent their fathers conquered."

Yet Jefferson's warnings went unheeded and it fell to another American president, Woodrow Wilson, to describe the aftermath: "A great industrial Nation is controlled by its system of credit. Our system of credit is concentrated. The growth of the Nation and all our activities are in the hands of a few men. We have come to be one of the worst ruled, one of the most completely controlled and dominated Governments in the world—no longer a Government of free opinion, no longer a Government by conviction and vote of the majority, but a Government by the opinion and duress of small groups of dominant men." What is the agenda of this "small group of dominant men?" Clearly, to make more money. But do they consider the welfare of those they rule? We are told that the wealth they "create" will trickle down to the masses. Yet something, somewhere seems to be blocking the flow. It bears repeating that three hundred fifty-eight people, who, incidentally, just happen to be billionaires, own as much wealth as the poorest half of the world's population—nearly three billion people.

 ## Banking on Inflation

It is only when the maker of things is a maker of things by vocation, and not merely holding down a job, that the price of things is approximate to their real value . . . . —ANANDA K. COOMARASWAMY

We pay tribute directly, in the form of wage work, rent, taxes, and interest, as well as indirectly, in the form of inflated costs for goods and services. Inflation is built into the current money system. The fact that central banks like the Federal Reserve are able to regulate the rate of inflation and with it the economy, by adjusting interest rates, demonstrates how central the concept of interest is to the current system of money rule.

At a 5 percent annual rate, inflation doubles the cost of things every twelve years. At this rate, taking into account no other factors, in twelve years, the $150,000 home costs $300,000; the $20,000 automobile costs $40,000, and so on. Inflation disproportionately affects the poor and middle class for two major reasons. First, they are less likely than the well-off to have investments that outearn the rate of inflation. Second, a family making $40,000 a year that loses 4 percent a year to inflation is losing $1,600 it needs for food, children's clothing, car maintenance, and so on. The $40,000 that a household making $1,0000,000 a year would lose at the same annual inflation rate will have a much less dramatic impact on their everyday standard of living (this, of course, in the unlikely event that they do not have investments that more than make up the difference).

The inflation tax constitutes the most retrogressive of all forms of taxation because it hurts the poor the most.

JACK WEATHERFORD

Most goods in 1900 were cheaper than they had been in 1800. In only a little over twenty-five years, between 1872 and 1897, "one dollar could buy 43 percent more rice than in 1872, 35 percent more beans, 49 percent more tea, 51 percent more roasted coffee, 114 percent more sugar, 62 percent more mutton, 25 percent more fresh pork, 60 percent more lard and butter, and 42 percent more milk."[33]

The credit money system puts pressure on corporations to seek excessive profits (and reduce wage costs), not only so they can repay their own loans at interest, but also to attract stock investors by outearning the prevailing interest rate. The stock markets, wherein shares in legally created fictitious "persons" or corporations are traded, have become the penultimate markets. Since a corporation's survival is dependent on the price of its stock in these artificial markets, the allegiance of corporate management is naturally to its shareholders, and most certainly not to its workers, its customers, or the greater public. And who are the shareholders? According to the Economic Policy Institute, "two thirds of the value of all stock is owned by the wealthiest 10% of households."[34]

We are completely dependent on the commercial banks. Someone has to borrow every dollar we have in circulation, cash or credit. . . . When one gets a complete grasp of the picture, the tragic absurdity of our hopeless position is almost incredible, but there it is. It is the most important subject intelligent persons can investigate and reflect upon. It is so important that our present civilization may collapse unless it becomes widely understood and the defects remedied very soon. —ROBERT H. HEMPHILL
(FORMER CREDIT MANAGER, FEDERAL RESERVE BANK, ATLANTA, GA.)

Because all money is created as loans at interest, there is never enough money to go around, and prices keep rising. When money is created in the form of loan deposits, the principal is circulated into the economy, but not the interest required to pay it back. For example, a thirty-year home mortgage loan of $150,000 at 8% interest requires a repayment of $396,230, or $246,230 more than the original loan amount. The $150,000 goes to the seller who presumably puts the lion's share of it back into circulation. This is not the case with the interest payments.

We might well say, yes, it is unfortunate that we must pay 2.5 times the cost of the house, but who has $150,000 lying about? What may not occur to us is that it is the system of credit money we live with today that inflates the price of the house in the first place. Throughout the nineteenth century and into the early twentieth century, it was common among ordinary Americans to buy or build a home without having to take out a mortgage loan. Now, as individuals, we are stuck: we pay the inflated price and the interest tribute, or we forget about the house.

Yet the government has the power to create money, a power it has long abdicated to private interests. When private banks loan hundreds of billions of dollars to the government, they are creating billions in interest debt, while recording these enormous loans as assets that enable them to lend still more money to other governments, corporations, and individuals.

> *If the Nation can issue a dollar bond it can issue a dollar bill. The element that makes the bond good makes the bill good also. . . . It is absurd to say our Country can issue bonds and cannot issue currency. Both are promises to pay, but one fattens the usurer and the other helps the People. . . . It is a terrible situation when the Government, to insure the National Wealth, must go in debt and submit to ruinous interest charges. . . .*
>
> —THOMAS A. EDISON

By "creating deposits," banks are, by statute, allowed to legally lend money that they themselves do not anywhere possess. And they do it every day. The following is a true story and helps to illustrate in a simple way how this system works. Some years ago, a man applied for a home equity loan on a $45,000 home and was granted a line of credit in the amount of $23,000. The bank, however, made a typographical error and instead credited the man with $230,000. He never notified the bank of their mistake and instead set about buying real estate with his expanded credit line. He purchased twelve properties and greatly increased his net worth, as well as raising his "standard of living." Even after he was found out and eventually paid back all the borrowed money, he came out ahead. This story illustrates a couple of important points.

(1) Money Makes Money: This man from a humble background and with little formal education was able to greatly increase his net worth, simply by acquiring a substantial line of credit. It was not an increase in education nor diligent hard work that increased his wealth but simply having access to more money. Yet what the man did was certainly dishonest and may have been illegal. After all, he was using ten times more money than his collateral reserves indicated he was "worth."

(2) The Rich Get Richer: Yet this is *precisely* what banks are legally allowed to do every day. The man had fraudulently borrowed ten times more than his collateral reserve. Yet a bank is permitted to legally lend even more than ten times its reserves, to earn interest on all of the borrowed money, and to count monies it has previously lent as a part of the reserve against which to lend still more. This all adds up. During the savings and loan crisis of the 1980s, one institution lost more than 800 times its net worth. The average citizen would be hard pressed to find herself in a situation where she could possibly lose 800 times her net worth. (The codified preference for those who make money on money insured that these losses were paid by the taxpayers and not by those who incurred them.) The banking privilege is granted by a government whose election is financed by wealthy special interests, which goes a long way in insuring that only those who are already well-to-do are legally allowed to play this game.

I could go on, but we don't want to get bogged down in the details of the financial flim-flam game—only to understand its effects on the world in which we live. Sir Josiah Stamp, a former president of the Bank of England (model for the U.S. Federal Reserve) understood these quite well, indeed. He wrote: "Banking was conceived in iniquity and was born in sin. The bankers own the earth. Take it away from them, but leave them the power to create deposits, and with the flick of the pen they create enough deposits to buy it back again. However, take it away from them, and all the great fortunes like mine will disappear, and they ought to disappear, for this would be a happier and better world to live in. But, if you wish to remain the slaves of the bankers and pay the cost of your own slavery, let them continue to create deposits."

Whoever controls the volume of money in any country is absolute master of all industry and commerce.

JAMES A. GARFIELD
20TH PRESIDENT OF
THE UNITED STATES

Men had their land and farms
But you (the feudal lord) now have them,
Men had their people and their folk
But you have seized them from them. . . .
You sow not nor reap,
Where do you get the produce of those three hundred farms?

—SHIH CHING

The Taoists warned that to place heavy tribute burdens on the people would be to bring social degradation and ruin. The privileged rulers should not think only of themselves but show compassion toward the people on whom their position depends. They should see to it that they do not interfere in the lives of ordinary people by placing undue burdens upon them. The Taoists warned that when the people begin to feel that there is no legitimate way for them to prosper, they are likely to turn desperate and resort to extreme measures. Conservative and liberal social commentators alike lament the breakdown of the social order, the increase in violence, the lack of respect for traditional institutions. For all of its vaunted freedom, America today has more people per capita in prison than any other country in the world.[35] Perhaps it is time that we listen to the message of the Taoists and at least begin to consider how we might lighten the burdens of the people.

The principal point for our discussion of the dignity of the Tao is the effect that this system of oppression has in diverting people from the natural course of their lives. The Taoist implicitly affirms the *Te,* the power and virtue of the authentic life lived in accord with one's own nature. As Chuang Tzu put it, "Let everything be allowed to do what it naturally does, so that its nature will be satisfied."

Now, if by force of arms, I make a man or woman a slave and compel him or her to do only as I choose, he or she is clearly not free to follow his or her nature. Likewise, if I arrange a worldwide system that compels a man or woman to earn large amounts of money just to survive, and if I limit the means by which he or she may earn that money, is he or she free to follow his or her own nature?

If a man, who is by nature an artist, is compelled to spend his life as a waiter or accountant, has not only the man but society itself lost a measure of its *Te?* Chuang Tzu said, "The duck's legs are short, but if we try to lengthen them, the duck will feel pain. The crane's legs are long, but if we try to cut off a portion of them, the crane will feel grief." All over the world, the oppression of the money system is trying to make ducks out of cranes and cranes out of ducks, and all are feeling the pain.

Nothing I have said here is in any way meant to imply or suggest that we as individuals should throw up our hands and resign ourselves to doing something other than what we are by nature born to do. On the contrary, I have dedicated the greater part of my adult life to helping people discover what it is that they are by nature born to do and how they can, in fact, make a living doing that in the world we live in today. I have seen hundreds firsthand, and heard from thousands more, who have managed to do so in their own lives. I encourage anyone and everyone to use their innate gifts and to persevere until they are able to create a platform that will allow for their full expression. Yet it is important for the individual to realize what he or she is up against, not as an excuse to give up or lash out, but to determine how to live the life he or she was born to live, despite the attendant difficulties.

Forewarned is forearmed, and in today's world, it is often a battle to be who you really are. As e. e. cummings put it, "to be nobody-but-yourself—in a world which is doing its best, night and day, to make you everybody else—means to fight the hardest battle which any human being can fight; and never stop fighting." Yet too often, we tend to ignore the oppressive effects of organizing a worldwide system around the "commodity fiction" and the massive interventionism needed to create and sustain it. Instead, we go on singing the praises of the "free market." The widespread acceptance of the myth of the free market based on individual initiative tends to insure that those who "fail" economically will internalize their frustration in the form of shame and/or act out in a self-destructive or violent manner.

If a person isn't "making it," it must be because he is too ignorant or too lazy, lacking the internal fortitude to grab ahold of his own boot straps and give a good hearty yank. This sense of shame not only affects the poor but helps insure that those in the better-educated middle class make career choices on the basis of economic criteria rather than their hearts' desire or real talents. The fear of shame and ridicule tends to keep people from pursuing the sometimes financially risky process of following their own natures. In my career work, I have seen, time and again, intelligent people who have never seriously asked what kind of work would be personally meaningful or provide for the best expression of their talents. They have

Bankers are just like anyone else, only richer.

OGDEN NASH

committed themselves to the idea of economic success without realizing, often until many years later, that doing a job every day that they hate or simply tolerate is hardly being free.

In conclusion, it seems clear that we cannot separate the individual from the society in which she lives. All of us must recognize our responsibilities to fulfill our own natures and to, in whatever ways we can, create a social environment that makes it easier for others to do so. We ought not be afraid to criticize the oppression and injustice we see around us, nor to consider our work done because we have done so. In following our natures, in preserving and strengthening our own *Te,* we help those around us find their way. In refusing in our own lives to put market values ahead of human ones, we affirm the dignity of all humankind.

In Whose Interest?

The power which money gives is that of brute force; it is the power of the bludgeon and the bayonet.

—WILLIAM CORBETT

Today we live by a credit economy. At its core is the practice of charging interest on money. So much a part of our daily lives is the practice, that we can hardly imagine modern life without it. Yet, as it affects the great mass of people, it is a very recent invention. Before 1915, middle-class Americans were loathe to purchase anything on credit.[36]

Though we seldom question it today, it is worthwhile to reflect on how those in other times and cultures viewed the practice of charging interest. Sounding much like a Taoist, the ancient Greek philosopher Aristotle condemned it as "contrary to nature." He said, "Very much disliked also is the practice of charging interest; and the dislike is fully justified, for the gain arises out of currency itself, not as a product for which currency was provided. Currency was intended to be a means of exchange, whereas interest represents an increase in currency itself. . . . And so, of all types of business, this is the most contrary to nature."

Through long ages, the practice of usury, or charging interest on money, was considered morally repugnant. To this day, it is still forbidden in a number of Islamic countries. Usury was wrong, went the traditional moral argument, not only because of its inflationary effect, but because people borrow money when they are in need—and to take advantage of someone's need is clearly wrong.

Interest is the invention of Satan.

—THOMAS EDISON

In a remarkable piece of intellectual archeology entitled *The Idea of Usury: From Tribal Brotherhood to Universal Otherhood,* Nelson Benjamin traces the historical development of the practice of loaning money at interest within the Western tradition. He begins his analysis with the Mosaic Law of the Old Testament Bible. Like the Babylonian Laws of Hammurabi (c.1792–1750 B.C.E.) upon which it is based, the Mosaic Law makes sharp distinctions in the way it treats those who are in the in-group versus those who are not. This sense of a different standard for "them" and "us" is prevalent throughout the Old Testament.

For instance, one of the Ten Commandments is "Thou shalt not kill"; yet in Deuteronomy 20:16-17, we read God's command: "But the cities of these people, which the Lord thy God doth give thee for an inheritance, thou shalt save alive nothing that breatheth." From the Biblical record, it seems clear that commands such as this were indeed carried out. In Joshua 6:21-24, we read: "they utterly destroyed all that was in the city, both man and woman, young and old, and ox, and sheep, and ass, with the edge of the sword . . . and they burnt the city with fire, and all that was therein." The message is clear: while it is wrong to kill your tribal brother, is perfectly to fine to kill the enemy.

In Deuteronomy, the same in-group/out-group distinction was applied to the practice of usury, or charging interest. "Thou shalt not lend upon usury to thy brother, usury of money, usury of victuals, usury of any thing that is lent upon usury. Unto a stranger thou mayest lend under usury: but not unto thy brother thou shalt not lend unto usury. That the Lord thy God may bless thee in all that thou setteth thy hand to. . . ."[37]

The early Christian fathers went even further in making explicit the connection between sanctioned killing and sanctioned usury. As the Roman Stoic turned Christian father, St. Ambrose of Milan wrote:

From him exact usury whom it would not be a crime to kill. He fights without a weapon who demands usury. . . . Therefore, where there is the right of war there is a right of usury.

Where there is a right of war, there is a right of usury: Now, upon whom does a nation, group, or individual have a right of war? Clearly, only upon the most egregious enemies, those whom the nation, group, or individual would destroy. According to the Old Testament as well as the early fathers of the Christian church, it was upon these alone that usury could be levied. So heinous a crime, so disastrous in consequences was usury considered to be that it must be withheld from use against all except the worst of enemies, those whom one could, in good conscience, kill. Today, this "weapon" is used indiscriminately upon friend and foe alike.

He fights without a weapon who demands usury. Countless millions suffer from a war waged against them with this invisible weapon. As the nineteenth-century American journalist and one-time presidential candidate Horace Greeley put it: "While boasting of our noble deeds, we are careful to conceal the ugly fact that by an iniquitous money system we have nationalized a system of oppression which, though more refined, is not less cruel than the old system of chattel slavery." Today, this "system of oppression" spans the globe.

Religion and the Branch of Commerce

For the ancient Chinese, agriculture was considered the root, and commerce the branch of life in society. "Root" activities were more highly esteemed than "branch" activities. For instance, gentlemen-farmers were esteemed above wealthy merchants. It was believed that employment in commerce tended to develop and/or accentuate undesirable qualities such as selfishness, dishonesty, and cunning.[17] A similar value system applied in traditional European culture as well. In Roman times, the gentleman-farmer was esteemed above merchants or financiers. So too in the medieval days, the lord of the feudal manor held a higher place than the merchants or money men.

Yet in the Italian trading cities where the modern world was born, a new ranking of occupations began to take shape. Here, not only was the branch favored over the root, but the higher one could get up into the tree, the better; and the closer one came to the earth—that is, to handling anything "natural"—the less esteemed his occupation. Like many Renaissance inventions, this idea quickly spread throughout the Western world.

In his excellent work *The Wheels of Commerce,* Fernand Braudel points out that already, by the seventeenth century, this new means of ranking occupations had spread to all the major trading centers of Europe. Braudel writes, "At the top of the pyramid were the proud ranks of those who 'understood finance.'" Next came the wholesale merchants, who were scorned by the financiers, but who in turn looked down on retailers as mere shopkeepers. "But the latter in turn looked down on the artisan-shopkeepers who worked with their hands."[38] Lower still on the social totem pole were those whose sole occupation was the manufacture or cultivation of items for sale.

This ranking reflects a logical extension of the religious world-view of the time. If the natural world is dirty, sinful, and corrupt, then those who interact with it directly cannot help but be corrupted in the process. On the other hand, if the world of ideation and abstraction is a closer approximation of the heavenly realm, then financiers, who deal in abstraction and the divine art of mathematics, are to be esteemed. Clearly, theirs is a more spiritual occupation than that of those who deal in more earthly affairs. Of course, the social hierarchy described above is one we recognize today. Yet by and large, we have forgotten the role that the anti-nature religious world-view played in its genesis.

CHAPTER SIX

Yin / Yang

The Harmony of Abundance

Life is the blended harmony of the yin and yang.

—Chuang Tzu

This chapter explores the concept of *yin* and *yang* and how we can balance these universal energies in our lives. For one living in the Tao, the world is a dance of these complementary energies. On the other hand, for one trapped in the confines of the ego, duality is a battle. The ego lives in a black and white world, marked by sharp divisions between right and wrong, good and bad, and so on. As we learn to reconcile the seeming pairs of opposites in our lives, we develop a new relationship with the duality of the universe. This not only yields a new understanding of life all around us, but it also fosters a deep sense of peace and a feeling of being at home in the universe. In the related exercises at the end of the book, you'll have a chance to identify places in your life where you may be unnecessarily battling against yourself, others, or the nature of life—and then to integrate and harmonize these elements in your life.

In his essay "Compensation," Emerson wrote: "An inevitable dualism bisects nature, so that each thing is half, and suggests another thing to make it whole; spirit, matter; man, woman; odd, even; subjective, objective; in, out; upper, under; motion, rest; yea, nay. Whilst the world is thus dual, so is every one of its parts. . . . There is somewhat that resembles the ebb and flow of the sea, day and night, man and woman, in a single needle of pine, in a kernel of corn, in each individual of every animal tribe." Long ago, the ancient Chinese recognized this dual "somewhat." They called it "yin and yang."

While the concept of yin and yang long predates even the classical Taoists, it is essential and implicit in the whole of Taoist philosophy and, indeed, in most traditional Chinese philosophy. The earliest surviving written reference to yin and yang is found in the *I Ching,* the oldest extant book of Chinese literature and perhaps the oldest book in the world.[1] It says simply, "One yin, one yang, that is Tao."[2] As expounded in the *I Ching* and a variety of other works, the yin/yang philosophy is profound in its depth and scope. One may devote a lifetime to the study of the yin and yang and continually gain new insights and understandings. This chapter will consider three basic elements of yin/yang philosophy and how we can apply these understandings to bring harmony and balance to the practical events of our everyday lives.

In ancient times, those people who understood Tao patterned themselves upon the Yin and the Yang and they lived in harmony. . . .

—CH'I PO

First, yin and yang are correlatives, meaning they have a reciprocal or complementary relationship. They are *not* to be conceived of as opposites. Indeed, yin and yang are two sides of the same coin or, quite literally, two sides of the same hill. The terms originally referred to the shady (yin) and the sunny (yang) side of a hill or mountain. The sunny, or yang, side is bright, warm, and dry, while the shady, or yin, side is dark, cool, and moist. From these initial observations, endless extrapolations were made so that by extension, yang came to be associated with motion, yin with rest; yang with the masculine, yin with the feminine; yang with Heaven, yin with Earth.

Second, yin and yang are not absolutes; each contains the seed or essence of the other within itself. Therefore, they attract and evoke as well as contrast one another. Third, the interaction of these two cosmic principles is everywhere manifest throughout the universe. Indeed, the physical universe itself is the result of this interaction, and all changes within it are governed by laws of the transformations of yin and yang. These three principles will be explored in greater depth below.

Fundamentals of Yin and Yang Philosophy

1. Complementary Poles: They are two sides of the same coin.
2. Nonabsolute: Each contains an element of the other.
   Magnetic: Yin attracts yang; yang attracts yin.
   Evocative: Strong yang evokes yin; strong yin evokes yang.
3. Dynamic: Yin transforms yang; yang transforms yin.

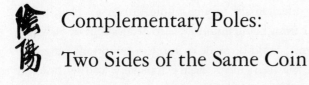 # Complementary Poles:
Two Sides of the Same Coin

Yang endows, yin receives; male and female need each other.
—THE TRIPLEX UNITY

Like light and dark, yin and yang depend upon one another—there is not (cannot be) one without the other. Yin and yang arise mutually, like the crest and trough of a wave, like the intaking and outgoing of breath, endlessly expanding and contracting. When we speak of yin and yang, we are speaking of sex, which is another way of saying, the relationships between polarities. These polarities might be man and woman, dry and wet, hot and cold, heaven and earth. Because man is attracted to woman and woman to man, children are born and the human race continues. Because dryness is attracted to wetness and wetness to dryness, water evaporates and the life-giving rains fall. Because Heaven is attracted to Earth, *shen,* or spiritual, energy descends; because Earth is attracted to Heaven, *ching* energy rises to open the heart and illuminate the brain.

From the perspective of yin/yang philosophy, the whole world is sexual. This "sexuality" can be seen not only in the obvious biological act of reproduction through which plants and animals sustain life but in the multiplication of cells, the bonding of atoms, indeed, throughout all the processes of organic and inorganic life. From this perspective, things are either preparing to copulate, copulating, or resting from copulation—only to begin the cycle all over again.

One yin and one yang is called the Tao. The passionate union of yin and yang and the copulation of husband and wife is the eternal pattern of the universe. If heaven and earth did not mingle, whence would everything receive life?
—CH'ENG TZU

It is not surprising that of all the great cultures of the world, we find the ancient Chinese culture to be the most developed and refined with respect to the sexual arts.[3] Joseph Needham wrote: "It was quite natural, in view of the general acceptance of the yin-yang theories, to think of human sexual relations against a cosmic background, and indeed as having intimate connections with the mechanism of the whole universe. The Taoists considered that sex, far from being an obstacle to attainment of *hsein-ship* (spiritual enlightenment), could be made to aid it in important ways."[4]

On the other hand, Western culture hasn't done very well with sex. It certainly never integrated it into the main currents of its three great culture-forming religions. Early Christian theologians, in particular, held an extremely dim view of sex. Origen of Alexandria castrated himself to avoid temptation. Arnobius called sexual intercourse "filthy and degrading"; Methodius, "unseemly"; Jerome, "unclean"; Tertullian, "shameful"; and Ambrose, "a defilement."[5] Sex was sanctioned for the common people, who could not resist its allure—but only as means of procreation. It was not to be enjoyed. Sex was evil *because* it was natural. As Tertullian wrote, "Even natural beauty ought to be obliterated by concealment and neglect, since it is dangerous to those who look upon it."[6]

What sexual iconography and mythology survived in the West from ancient pagan and Goddess religions was systematically rooted out over centuries of determined, and often brutal, attack. Nevertheless, we should recognize that explicitly sexual imagery played an integral role in the mythology and ritual life of many traditional cultures, including the Neolithic European culture. It would be a mistake to dismiss the whole of this sexual iconography as magical fetishes used by primitive peoples in association with fertility rites. In many cases, it represented an extremely sophisticated understanding of the cosmic polarity of the universe, symbolically expressed in the relationship between the masculine and feminine.

Even as traditional cultures did not separate the sacred from the profane, neither did they separate the spiritual from the natural, which is to say, the sexual. The *participation mystique* (the sense of conscious participation in the mysteries of nature), or the wisdom of the body, is a feminine intelligence that has been long suppressed in the West (see chapter 2). Consequently, Westerners tend to be rather squeamish when it comes to open and frank discussions about sex. Even today, Western intellectuals have a difficult time confronting and understanding the sexual dimension in the spiritual life of traditional peoples.

The much heralded sexual revolution notwithstanding, crateloads of explicitly sexual religious artifacts from a variety of cultures (including our own) remain, to this day, hidden away in museum basements and warehouses. (Were one to be given free reign of the British Museum, the Vatican Museum and Library, or the National Museum at Naples, among other places, she would certainly get an eyeful!) Apparently, their keepers still deem these artifacts too shocking for public view. It is this refusal to confront, let alone celebrate, the inherent sexuality in life that in large part makes the yin/yang philosophy seem strange to Westerners encountering it for the first time. One imagines that to our ancient or more "primitive" counterparts, it would not have seemed foreign at all but only a variation on a familiar theme.

To the extent that most Westerners are familiar with sacred sexual iconography at all, it is that which comes to us by way of India and Tibet. In Indian and Tibetan religion and art, the underlying unity of polarities is represented in images of male and female deities engaged in sexual intercourse or in icons of androgynous deities. Also common in India is the icon of the lingam and yoni, the united male and female sexual organs, representing the union of the cosmic polarities. In traditional Chinese culture, the cosmic polarities were not concretized into personal deities but were conceived of as impersonal forces, yin and yang.

Every part of our personality that we do not like will become hostile to us.

ROBERT BLY

Sex: A Battle or a Dance?

Man is a microcosmos that functions in exactly the same way as the
macrocosmos, and the sexual union of man and wife is a small replica of
the mutual interaction of the dual forces of nature. —R. H. VAN GULIK

Sexual polarity is altogether missing from the sacred iconography of the
orthodox Western religions. Indeed, Western religion waged war on it for
centuries. The Western battle against sex was responsible for infecting the
population with soul-draining shame, guilt, and fear in association with
one of the most natural of human functions. It also spawned a variety of
mental and physical ailments associated with sexual repression and perversion. These effects are not merely historical but linger in the psyche of
Western man and woman. Much has been made in recent years about the
social and psychological costs of pornography, which is purchased mostly
by men. Yet even a cursory reading of books such as *My Secret Garden* reveals that many women are equally obsessed with images of sexual perversion—though they are more likely to form the pictures in their minds than
to purchase them from a newsstand. (Many of the fantasies detailed in books
such as this would make all but enthusiasts of the most hard-core pornography wince.) Sexual repression, guilt, and perversion begins in the mind
and culture, and it is there that it must be healed. The Taoists would tell us
that efforts to legislate morality without consideration of the underlying
psychological motivations are doomed to failure.

In his important work *Sexual Life in Ancient China*, R. H. Van Gulik
summarized the ancient Chinese attitude toward sex and its effect on the
Chinese social and psychological development. He wrote, "Here I wish to
stress only one fact, namely that the Chinese considered the sexual act as
part of the order of nature, and the exercise of it the sacred duty of every
man and woman, it was never associated with a feeling of sin or moral
guilt. . . . It was probably this mental attitude together with the nearly
total lack of repression, that caused ancient Chinese sexual life to be, on the
whole, a healthy one, remarkably free from the pathological abnormality
and aberrations found in so many other ancient cultures."[7]

There can be no doubt that Taoist philosophy was instrumental in fos-
tering a healthy sexual life in ancient China. As Joseph Needham has written: "The recognition of the importance of woman in the scheme of things,
the acceptance of equality of women with men, the conviction that the

attainment of health and longevity needed the cooperation of the sexes, [and] the considered admiration for certain feminine psychological characteristics . . . had no counterpart in Confucianism or ordinary Buddhism."[8] No culture can have a healthy sex life without a healthy respect for both sexes. The Taoist's unique respect for the feminine, together with their profound understanding of yin/yang dynamics helped to create a climate for a healthy sexual life.

The battle against sex inevitably becomes the battle between the sexes. In our own culture, the battle between the sexes has long pitted men and women against each another. Historically, it has meant the subjugation of women and the diminishment of the feminine intelligences (see chapter 5). It has also meant that we have come to value doing and possessing above being and resting (a subject for the next chapter).

The battle against sex (the inherent polarity in life) becomes the battle to assert the *one* "right" way, be it reason, technology, capitalism, Marxism, fundamentalism, or whatever. We are always picking sides. We cling to life and deny death. We assert the value of reason and live in fear of the deep unconscious. We even take the French word for right (adroit) and call it "skillful." We take the word for left (gauche) and call it "clumsy and inept." It seems we can't help choosing sides.

To end the battle of the sexes, we must end the battle against sex itself. We must come at last to see all duality as part of a deeper underlying unity. This is the path to harmony revealed in the philosophy of yin and yang. There is no point in discussing whether man is better than woman or woman is better than man; there is only man/woman in relation. There is no point in discussing whether light is better than dark or dark better than light; there is only light/dark in relation—and so on, with life/death, hot/cold, and all bipolar relationships.

An important first step for an individual seeking greater harmony in her life is to become increasingly conscious of the way in which she experiences the inherent polarity or sexuality in life. In the West, it is especially important that we ask ourselves: Must it be a battle? Is antagonism implicit in polarity? The Taoists tell us most emphatically that it is not. They tell us to embrace the inherent sexuality in life. Yin and yang in all of their manifestations are not opposites but complementary poles of the same eternal stuff of life. With this recognition, we can move from the battle of the sexes to the dance of the sexes, appreciating how these polarities interact through all creation.

In repose {he} shares the passivity of the yin, in action the energy of yang.

CHUANG TZU

In the final analysis, we cannot transcend the battle of the sexes without altering our understanding of what the universe is. The way we view nature is the way we view ourselves. If nature is anything, it is sex. A war against sex must be a war against nature itself, including human nature. The battle of the sexes, at its most fundamental level, reflects our understanding of the universe and of God, the Tao, or Ultimate Reality. In the West, God is conceived of as the all-good who battles the all-evil (devil). So in the West, heaven is good; earth is bad. Light is good; dark is bad. Spiritual is good; natural is bad. Conscious is good; unconscious, bad, and so on. From the Taoist perspective, the Tao is conceived of as the "all" that contains the light and the dark, the good and the bad, man and woman, yin and yang.

It may help here to recall Carl Jung's notion of the ego and shadow, discussed briefly in chapter 3. The idea of the shadow is essentially this: What you avoid or resist, you will tend to see as evil. To the extent that an individual insists on only being aware of the light or the good, he or she will constantly be shadowed by the dark or bad. This applies not only to individuals but to whole cultures. If we deny our sexuality, we end up with repressed, perverted, or exploitative sex. If we deny our natural human aggression, it manifests in wars and senseless violence.

In *Parzival,* Wolfram Von Eshenbach's telling of the Quest for the Holy Grail, the Grail King—and here, as in many myths, the king is symbolic of the culture—is sexually wounded. The natural, sexual life energies have been held to be in opposition to spiritual life and have, therefore, been repressed. Written in the twelfth century, the *Parzival* can be conceived as a guide to the reintegration of spirit and nature, the yang of Heaven and the yin of Earth, within Western culture. Its message, for the most part, went unheeded. The integration of yin and yang remains our work today, both as individuals in our daily lives and collectively in the broader society. Like the classical Taoists, Von Eshenbach's classic *Parzival* tells us to put our faith in the universal life energies rather than in the man-made social laws or codes. Both encourage us to trust our spontaneous intuitive nature over mental concepts of what we should and should not do—to accept the body and embrace the natural energies and wisdom that lie within it. They tell us to go into the shadows, find the hidden things, and bring them to light.

Heraclitus said, "In the circle, the beginning and the end are common." We cannot understand the Tai Ch'i Tu without the circle (Tao) that enfolds

the yin and yang. Here, the two suggests the One (the Tao, or the underlying unity) as well as the three (the trinity of Tao, yin, and yang). From the perspective of orthodox Western religions, God is the white half of the circle, opposed not only by the dark half but even by the little black spot within. The one is missing and an otherworldly aspect runs through all elements of the three, or trinity (Father, Son, and Holy Spirit). The earth, or yin, element is not embraced.

Alchemy: Inner Union

{To} love all of the ten thousand things—
treat Heaven and Earth as one body.
—HUI SHIH

The Taoists recognized that the masculine and feminine polarities reside within the physical bodies and psyches of human beings as well as in the external world. Here again, harmony results from the acceptance and union of polarities. This inner union of polarities is a critical element of Taoist alchemy, which has many parallels with Western alchemy. C. G. Jung helped revive interest in Western alchemy, arguing against the popular belief that it was merely a primitive form of science and/or that its principal goal was the physical conversion of lead into gold. While it is true that in both the Western and Chinese traditions, there were alchemists who sought more materialistic goals (Westerners, wealth; and Chinese, physical immortality), at their best, both systems of alchemy were concerned with inner union and transformation. This in-  ner union required spiritual training and resulted in transformations of the physical body as well as the generation of a kind of spiritual body, which the Taoists called the "Immortal Fetus."

Sexual imagery is prominent throughout all systems of alchemy. Taoist alchemists speak of the copulation of the Green Dragon (yin) and the White

Tiger (yang) energies. In Western alchemy, the union of the inner masculine and feminine energies is often portrayed by the conjugal embrace of the solar king and the lunar queen. In the chakra system of Indian yoga, the second, or sexual, chakra is symbolically represented by the sexual union of male and female. A second couple in sexual embrace is depicted at the level of the heart chakra. This second union is symbolic of the uniting of the inner masculine and feminine. As the physical body is born from the union of male and female, so the second, or spiritual, birth requires the uniting of the inner masculine and feminine energies. For the Taoist alchemists, the culmination of this "inner sex" is the birth of the Immortal Fetus. In all three systems, the union of masculine fire and feminine water is essential. The theme is echoed symbolically in the Christian tradition with the baptism by water and the fiery descent of the Holy Spirit.

It should be pointed out that in both Western and Taoist alchemy, as well as in the Tantric and Buddhist yoga systems, the transformations sought and achieved through alchemy are not merely intellectual realiza-

tions but involve physical transformations of the body. All of these "alchemies" have their own symbolic languages and practical techniques, the description of which lies far beyond the scope of the present work. Yet there is a kind of alchemy that all of us can employ to bring greater harmony into our lives. It too is based on the principle of three, or the uniting of the polar dualities. The modern mystic and philosopher G. I. Guidjieff spoke of this threefold action in terms of the affirming, denying, and reconciling forces within the universe. Let's see how we can apply this understanding to the dynamics of everyday life.

Imagine a woman who has gotten the idea that she must always appear bright and happy. She resists any sadness she may feel about events in her life, as well as the inherent pain in life. She floats above her feelings and goes about with a counterfeit smile plastered across her face. For this individual, moving into grief would be an act of profound psychological growth. Indeed, if she were to allow the grief to become deep enough, which is to say, to transcend her personal troubles and unite with the suffering of all living beings, it would become the vehicle for a breakthrough experience—the birth of genuine compassion. This compassion, what the Buddhists call "karuna," in turn brings a new experience of happiness. Yet it is a far deeper one that reconciles and embraces the suffering in life.

Man always travels along precipices.
His truest obligation is to keep his balance.
—José Ortega y Gasset

Similarly, genuine nonviolence includes and transcends violence. It is not a matter of pretending it isn't there. Mahatma Gandhi repeatedly emphasized that the courageous but violent person is closer to the true spirit of nonviolence than the weak and timid person. As he put it, "There is hope for the violent man to be some day nonviolent, but there is none for the coward."[9] The apparent nonviolence of the timid is not nonviolence at all but subjugation to fear. On the other hand, the courageous person who can learn to conserve and transmute his or her anger has the potential to become truly nonviolent.

We should never identify ourselves with reason,
for man is not, and never will be a creature of reason alone. . . .
—Carl Jung

The principle of transcendence through the integration of seeming opposites applies equally to our experience of material abundance. The person who fears and resists poverty and with blind ambition devotes his life to the pursuit of money has no chance of experiencing true abundance, no matter how much wealth he may acquire. Only when he confronts his fear of poverty and, most likely, his hatred for the poor, has he any real chance at finding true prosperity. These examples may suggest ways in which you can reconcile seemingly antagonistic energies in your own life. (See the exercises at the end of the chapter.) Again, whether we view the duality inherent in life as conflict or as complementarity makes all the difference.

陰陽 Nonabsolute:

Yin Contains Yang; Yang, Yin

Rising and Passing,
Creation and Annihilation,
Birth and Death,
Joy and Grief,
They are meshed in one another.
—GOETHE

It is important to keep in mind that yin and yang are relative terms, which is to say that something is yin or yang relative to something else. The philosophy of yin and yang helps us to understand relationships rather than to assign identities. A look at Chinese medicine will illustrate. From *The Yellow Emperor's Classic of Internal Medicine*, we learn that the inside of the body is yin, relative to the outside of the body, which is yang. Within the body, the five viscera (liver, heart, spleen, lungs, kidneys) are yin relative to the "hollow" organs (the gall bladder, stomach, lower intestines, bladder, and the "three burning spaces"), which are yang.[10] While all of the viscera are yin, they are yin and yang relative to one another, so that the liver and heart are yang relative to the lungs and kidneys, which are yin. Within the heart, which is yin relative to the hollow organs and yang relative to the kidneys, we find yin and yang elements of the heart itself. If we were to dissect a portion of the heart, we would find yin and yang elements within that portion as well. This could go on *ad infinitum*, like opening a Chinese box inside a box, inside a box, inside a box . . . . At every level, from the most grand and cosmic to the most mundane and infinitesimal, the relationship between yin and yang persists.

We can say of yin and yang what the poet Rumi said of lovers: they "don't finally meet somewhere./They're in each other all along." Nothing is wholly yin, nothing wholly yang. Each contains the seed of the other. Man can relate to woman because there is something of woman within man. Woman can relate to man because there is something of man within woman. Were they absolutely different, they could not relate. So it is with all things in nature; all things contain the seeds of their apparent opposites.

This is not to imply that at any time yin and yang cannot be out of balance. Indeed, we have already discussed the extent to which our culture is in many respects excessively yang. From traditional Chinese medicine, we learn that an excess of yin in the body will lead to a slow or inadequate functioning of certain organs, resulting ultimately in a predictable set of ailments. On the other hand, excessive yang will bring an overexcitement of certain organs, resulting in a different, yet equally predictable, set of ailments. Within traditional Chinese culture, an appreciation of yin and yang and the importance of harmonizing the two pervades all aspects of life. From architecture to diet, from psychology to military strategy, from medicine to technology, from sexual life to the affairs of state, an understanding of yin/yang dynamics is paramount.

> *All of this is arranged so that Yin and Yang (complement each other)*
> *in front and back, inside and outside, as male and female element, and*
> *that they serve and respond to each other in order to conform with the*
> *Yin and Yang of Heaven.*
> —The Yellow Emperor's Classic of Internal Medicine

To take but one example of the application of the yin/yang theory in practical affairs, let us briefly consider the Taoist sexual arts. In the practice of these arts, the male learns to develop his yin, or feminine, receptive nature by learning to become a more patient lover and to gain control of the ejaculatory reflex. The female, in turn, learns to develop her masculine, or yang, aspect by asserting her sexuality and becoming, more often than not, the initiator of intimate congress. This "turning toward the other" actually accentuates the original polarity so that the male preserves and develops his yang strength while the female preserves and develops her yin potency. Recognizing the other within does not diminish but actually enhances one's primary sexual characteristics. On the other hand, the male who doesn't embrace the inner feminine will in time tend to become excessively yin, while the female who does not embrace the masculine within will in time tend to become excessively yang.

Anima and Animus: One Inside the Other

Jungian psychology recognizes a psychological parallel to the one-within-the-other principle in the concept of the *anima* and *animus*.[11] Jung believed that within the unconscious of men, there is a feminine psyche, which he called "anima," and that within the unconscious of women, there is a masculine psyche, which he called "animus." The anima gives the male the capacity for the relatedness and receptivity of the feminine (Eros). The animus gives the female the capacity for the reason and will of the masculine (Logos). Yet in their shadow aspects, anima and animus wreak havoc in the relationship between the sexes. In arguments between couples in relationship, the anima and animus in their negative, or shadow, aspects often dominate. These counter-sexual aspects, being part of the structure of consciousness, are archetypal and therefore, in their negative aspects, are dominated by the collective shadow.

The animus projection by the female onto the male and the anima projection of the male onto the female tend to follow prescribed patterns. The male in the grip of the anima becomes moody, overly sensitive, and seemingly impossible to please. The underlying message is: "You don't care about me." The female in the grip of animus takes the word (logos) as the sword with which to cut and berate, often employing sweeping generalizations (you never . . . you always . . . etc.), stated with the unquestioned authority of fact. She becomes seemingly impossible to console or reach through her rage. The underlying message is: "You don't respect me." Now, while a woman may do some particular thing that shows a lack of caring, or a man a may do some particular thing that shows a lack of respect (or vice versa, for that matter), one clear sign that the negative anima or animus is at work is if the upset partner rapidly slides from one issue or grievance to another.

The problem is compounded by the fact that the shadow anima and animus evoke one another. The woman in the throes of an animus "possession" rather quickly engages the male anima. Similarly, the male in the grip of the shadow anima rapidly triggers his partner's animus. The moment of mutual engagement is the instant arguments tend to get out of control, for now it is no longer *this* man and *this* woman discussing *this* issue, but two powerful elements of the collective unconscious reenacting an age-old drama. When the two have regained their balance, they may wonder to themselves, What was *that* all about?, implicitly recognizing that they have been caught up in a field of energy far bigger than themselves.

As these are archetypal energies, there is no getting rid of them. The only course to transcending their destructive elements is to become conscious of them. Jung stressed that anima and animus are more difficult to recognize and confront than the shadow in general. "Firstly, there is no moral education in this respect, and secondly, most people are content to be self-righteous and prefer mutual vilification (if nothing worse) to the recognition of their projections." If we are to free ourselves from the inharmony wrought by negative animus and anima, we must become aware of these effects, recognize them for the projections that they are, and take them back into ourselves. In relation to our partners, we must learn not to react when we feel we are not being seen (while the other is in the throes of projection, we are *not* seen) or unjustly vilified. The other's projections will more quickly fade if we do not react to them.

A final word about shadow animus and anima in relationships: Their illusory projections contain positive as well as negative distortions. Often, when people first fall in love, they project the image of their ideal man or woman onto their partner. Then, as they move deeper into the relationship, they discover that the other person is a human being and not the god or goddess they had imagined. Soon enough, the negative projections begin to surface. At this point, many people either physically or emotionally bail out and begin to search again—either in the external world or their imaginations—for the lover on which to project their idealized fantasies. Only when we have penetrated through the positive as well as the negative distortions of the anima and animus are we capable of creating and sustaining real harmony in our relationships. This we can only do when we have accepted and embraced the whole of life, including all aspects of the self.

From an Eastern perspective, spiritual "achievement" is not a matter of good destroying evil but the realization of emptiness. The "emptiness" to which the Taoists and later Ch'an (Zen) masters frequently referred is not empty-headedness or disengagement from the world. Rather, in the words of the Sixth Ch'an Patriarch Hui Neng, "Emptiness includes the sun, moon, stars, and planets, the great earth, mountains and rivers, all trees and grasses, bad men and good men, bad things and good things, heaven and hell; they are all in the midst of emptiness. Emptiness in human nature is also like this." In other words, it embraces all aspects of the self.

The greatest virtue between heaven and earth is to live.

I CHING

Dynamic: Yin Transforms Yang; Yang Transforms Yin

The ceaseless interplay of heaven and earth gives form to all things. The sexual union of male and female gives life to all things. This interaction of Yin and Yang is called the Way, and the resulting creative process is called change.

—I CHING

Now we come to the last of the three primary principles of yin and yang— the process of their transformations. The patterns of these transformations are most clearly and profoundly articulated in the *I Ching,* or Book of Changes. The *I Ching* is perhaps best known as a kind of oracle, a means of anticipating likely scenarios surrounding specific future events. Yet much more than a book of divination, the *I Ching* offers a practical philosophy for living a productive and harmonious life, as well as a symbolic language for representing universal archetypes of transformation.

Though most people in the West are unfamiliar with the *I Ching,* and few indeed could be said to have real understanding of it, we are all in its debt. The 1s and 0s that today drive our computers may have been derived from the solid and broken lines that represent yang and yin in the *I Ching.* The eighteenth-century philosopher William Gottfried Leibnitz, who developed binary arithmetic and is widely recognized as an intellectual progenitor of the computer age, was influenced by Chinese philosophy in general and by the *I Ching* in particular. Leibnitz was in close contact with Jesuit missionaries in China and remarked on the similarities between his own binary system and that of the *I Ching.* Regarding Leibnitz's Chinese connection, Joseph Needham writes: "It was thus no coincidence that Leibnitz, besides developing binary arithmetic, was also the founder of modern mathematical logic and a pioneer in the construction of calculating machines." The German philosopher Hegel, whose work influenced a number of later Western thinkers, including Marx, also studied and even lectured on the *I Ching.*

The *I Ching* describes the process of change. Understanding the nature and process of change, the interplay of yin and yang, not only helps us understand how we can more effectively and effortlessly achieve the results we desire but also helps us understand when we must let go and accept things that are beyond our power to change. It tells us when to advance with persistent effort and when to retreat.

In the West, we exalt change we ourselves have intended. We call it "progress." Yet we tend to fear change that comes at the behest of others or through "acts of nature." From the traditional Chinese view, change is a recurring cycle rather than a linear progression.[12] Moreover, unintended change is viewed more favorably than in the West. "Change is gushing life," proclaims the Great Treatise on the *I Ching*. This statement suggests the confidence with which the traditional Chinese mind embraced change of all kinds. Change is not chaos but is itself an expression of the natural *order* of things. Change is not the opposite of the Unchangeable but rather its manifestation. The Ten Thousand Things is the Nameless Tao made manifest.

The Western view of the world is in many ways a legacy of the ancient Greeks. While the Greeks were concerned with finding the ultimate substance, or stuff, the ancient Chinese were interested in understanding the patterns or relationships between things. Western culture is fascinated with matter; Chinese culture, with time. As much as a book, the *I Ching* can be conceived of as an elemental table of time or, more accurately, of the patterns of transformation within time. It is as natural and logical a result of the Chinese world-view as the table of chemical elements is the logical result of the Western (Greek) interest in understanding the essential components of matter. One view of the world is concerned with finding the final result or ultimate cause; the other, with understanding process.

While the European philosophy tended to find reality in substance, *Chinese philosophy tended to find it in* relation.

JOSEPH NEEDHAM

This difference in world-view prompted the best minds in each culture to look for different things and to see the same things differently. On one world-view, if a particle of matter occupied a particular point in space-time, it was because another particle had pushed it there; on the other, . . . it was taking up its place in a field of force alongside other particles similarly responsive. —JOSEPH NEEDHAM

The Western mind asks, What is the (ultimate) matter? or What is the cause? At a political level, this translates into, Who is the boss? and, at a more immediate or personal level, into, Who is to blame? The traditional Chinese mind asks, What is the relationship? or What is the pattern? At the political level, the emphasis on relationship translated into the communalism of the Taoists and the familial model of the Confucian political system.

These differences in world-view may be traced to differences in the structure of the two languages. Unlike English and other European languages, the Chinese language does not require a subject for every verb. Thus things may happen or be without reference to a causative agent. Moreover, while to the Western mind, a thing cannot both be and not be at the same time, from the perspective of traditional Chinese philosophy, things are either in the process of becoming or of "un-" or "de-" becoming. From this perspective (which, incidentally, more closely fits our current understanding of physics), nothing has a "solid" or stable identity; rather, everything is on its way to becoming something else. The signs (kua), or hexagrams, of the *I Ching* mark out the stages in the process of becoming and unbecoming.

From the perspective of the *I Ching,* all change is a function of the interaction of yin and yang. As read in the *I Ching,* "The Creative (Yang) and the Receptive (Yin) are the real secret of the changes." The dance of yin and yang, with its ceaseless merging and separating, separating and merging, suggests the double helix, a traditional yin/yang symbol. The double helix is also, as Watson and Crick discovered in the 1950s, the model for the human DNA molecule. They also discovered that the genetic code consists of 64 binary triplets, called "DNA condons." In 1973, a German philosopher named Martin Schonberger published a book entitled *The Hidden Key to Life*. In it, he detailed how (when written in binary order) the 64 DNA condons correspond exactly to the 64 kua (or hexagrams) of the *I Ching.* The *I Ching* is indeed a hidden key to life and one that warrants further study, not only by individuals seeking greater harmony and understanding in their own lives, but by Western philosophers and scientists as well.

Within the *I Ching,* a solid line (———) represents yang, while a broken line (— —) represents yin. These solid and broken lines are arranged in patterns of threes to form the eight primary signs, the Pa Kua (literally, "eight signs"), which appears below. The three lines represent Heaven, Earth and Man, the human realm. These eight signs (or trigrams) are combined to form the 64 signs (or hexagrams) of the *I Ching.* The 384 (64 x 6) lines of the *I Ching* are said to represent all possible combinations of yin and yang.

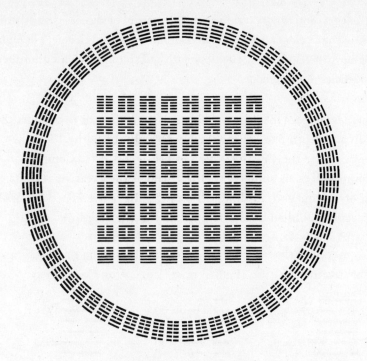

Pa Kua (Eight Signs)

Creative	Receptive	Abysmal	Clinging
Ch'ien	*K'un*	*K'an*	*Li*
Heaven	Earth	Water	Fire

Arousing	Joyous	Gentle	Keeping Still
Chen	*Tui*	*Sun*	*Ken*
Thunder	Lake	Wind	Mountain

The hexagrams of the *I Ching* are not to be viewed as static identities but rather as moving, dynamic patterns of change. What Richard Wilhelm wrote about the trigrams of the Pa Kua applies as well to the 64 hexagrams:

The eight trigrams . . . were held to be in a state of continual transition, one changing into the other, just as the transition from one phenomenon to another is continually taking place in the physical world. . . .

Attention centers not on things in their state of being—as is chiefly the case in the Occidental—but upon their movements in change. The eight trigrams therefore are not representative of things as such but of their tendencies in movement.[13]

There isn't space to adequately address the *I Ching* or to consider the 64 signs in any depth here. We will consider only three: the 1st, the 2nd, and the 63rd kua, or the Creative, the Receptive, and After Completion. The kua comprised of six solid (yang) lines denotes the Creative; the kua comprised of six broken (yin) lines denotes the Receptive. The kua for After Completion is formed by alternating the yin and yang lines.

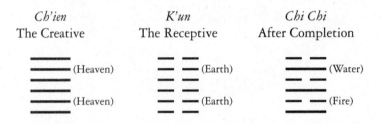

Ch'ien The Creative	*K'un* The Receptive	*Chi Chi* After Completion
(Heaven) (Heaven)	(Earth) (Earth)	(Water) (Fire)

The hexagrams Ch'ien and K'un, or the Creative and the Receptive, are formed by doubling the trigrams for heaven and earth respectively. They are considered the most important of all the signs, for all others are derived from them. From the Great Treatise on the *I Ching* we read: "The Creative is the strongest of all things in the world. The expression of its nature is invariably the easy, in order to master the dangerous. The Receptive is the most devoted of all things in the world. The expression of its nature is invariably the simple, in order to master the obstructive." From the Appendix, we read: "Heaven is high, earth is low; thus the Ch'ien and K'un are fixed . . . . The way of the Ch'ien is male, the way of K'un constitutes the female. The ch'ien knows the great beginnings; the k'un gives things completion. The ch'ien knows through the easy; the k'un accomplishes through the simple."

The sign After Completion is also called "Perfect Union." In *The True Classic of Perfect Union*, Lü Yen described it like this: "The upper trigram is *K'an* [water] and the lower, *Li* [fire]. *Li* represents the male. Its empty middle is true *yin*, therefore the male is *yang* on the outside and *yin* on the inside. K'an is the trigram that represents the female. Its full middle is true *yang,* therefore the female is *yin* on the outside and *yang* on the inside."[14]

This sign represents balance, or the union of yin and yang, on a number of the levels. It is seen not only in the symmetry of its arrangement, the alternating yin then yang lines, but in the placement of the trigram for water, which descends from heaven, above the trigram for fire, which rises from the earth. We can also view it horizontally in relation to the signs for the Creative and the Receptive.

Starting from the bottom to the top (which is the way hexagrams are read), we take a line from the Creative sign, followed by a line from the Receptive sign, another from the Creative, and so on.

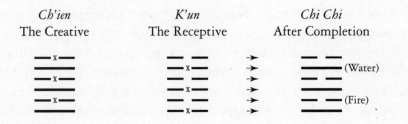

Ch'ien	K'un	Chi Chi
The Creative	The Receptive	After Completion

Synchronizing Inner and Outer

Carl Jung was fascinated by the *I Ching* and wrote the foreword to the Richard Wilhelm translation. Jung's concept of synchronicity gives insight into the way in which the *I Ching* works as an oracle. Synchronicity can be defined as a noncausal but meaningful relationship between events or states of mind within the human psyche and events in the outside world. More simply, we could call it the experience of "meaningful coincidence." We have all had experiences that we intuitively recognize as meaningful, though we would be hard pressed to explain them in rational terms. In fact, these "meaningful coincidences" are not coincidences at all but spontaneous realizations of the underlying interconnectedness of all things within the universe. As Heraclitus put it, "The unseen design of things is more harmonious than the seen." The *I Ching* is a kind of window that allows us a glimpse of this unseen design.

Our Western empirical science tends to look for patterns of events that are repeated and repeatable. In fact, validation of any scientific experiment is recognized only when its results can be successfully and consistently replicated. The "laws" of science (or at least of prequantum science) are concerned with things that always happen. Yet there is another category of events—things that sometimes happen. In other words, events that are subject to change. It is to this aspect of reality that quantum physics, with its probabilities, and the *I Ching,* with its hexagrams, seek to address. When we are seeking insight into future events, we are in this field of discontinuous or changeable events. We cannot say with certainty what *will* happen in the future. Yet we can suppose a meaningful relationship between the present, including our current state of mind, and likely future events.

One following the traditional method of consulting the *I Ching* first quiets the mind, then concentrates on a specific question, while performing a kind of ritual sorting of 50 yarrow stalks. The purpose of throwing the yarrow stalks is to arrive at one of the 64 cosmic archetypes represented by hexagrams of the *I Ching* and to ascribe significance to each of the six lines that comprise it. Because this procedure may take as long as half an hour, one's inner state of mind in relation to the question cannot help but permeate the activity that ultimately arrives at a specific hexagram from the *I Ching.* The ritual way in which the yarrow stalks are thrown (filled as it is with reminders of the cosmic order), combined with the element of chance, aids in synchronizing the individual's inner state of mind with the outside world of action and events in relation to the issue at hand. As Wilhelm puts it, "The manipulation of the yarrow stalks makes it possible for the unconscious in man to become active."

Skill in using the *I Ching* as a divinational tool is as much as anything a matter of one's ability to adequately interpret the "meaning" that the particular hexagram (and the individual lines that comprise it) has in relation to the events in question. The purpose in consulting the *I Ching* is not mere soothsaying or fortunetelling. Rather, the idea is to relate the present context to this possible future and thus to determine what action or inaction in the present represents the best course.

Whether or not we choose to consult the *I Ching,* synchronizing the inner and outer world, "making active" typically unconscious intelligence enhances our experience of harmony by increasing our sense of participation in nature. Traditional cultures sought, through a variety of means, to make the world of unconscious intelligence available to the conscious mind.

The purpose was to apply this intelligence in making decisions related to the welfare of the individual and the group. From the perspective of these cultures, to make important decisions on a strictly rational basis, without access to this deeper intelligence, was to operate in darkness. Not only arts of divination but rituals, trance dancing, fasting, mantras, and psychotropic drugs were used as means for accessing this deeper intelligence.

Trading Places

At its apex or zenith, yin transforms into yang, and vice versa. Things expand just so far, then they contract. (Keep blowing up a balloon and eventually it pops.) Endless growth or expansion is not possible. In the history of civilizations, as in life itself, we see birth, growth, and expansion, followed by decline, decay, and destruction. In biology, the out-of-control growth of what we call "cancerous cells" rapidly destroys the host, unless the growth is somehow checked. The understanding that things move toward their counterparts can be applied to a variety of circumstances in life. For example, from the perspective of yin/yang philosophy, the idea of perpetual economic growth is incongruent with the natural order of things, where loss follows gain; decrease, increase. Even if we were able to show uninterrupted growth in terms of the abstract measures of economic statistics, we would suffer loss in others ways (as indeed we have). The next chapter will examine the price we have paid in terms of the loss of leisure in modern life. In our collective struggle to end one kind of poverty (material), we have succeeded in creating another (time).

Carl Jung (following Heraclitus) called this phenomena *enantiodromia*, or "a running contrariwise." He said, "Every psychological extreme secretly contains its own opposite or stands in some relation to it." The worst crimes are committed in the name of fighting evil. The hero falls—defeated by his own hubris. One (person or country) humbly and diligently strives and ultimately achieves success. Yet soon, pride and laziness set in and, with these, the onset of decline. The *I Ching* instructs us to consider danger and misfortune when things are going well and to recognize, when events seem to be running against us, that "this too will pass." We find harmony, not by defeating evil once and for all, but by recognizing the relationship between good and evil and remaining psychologically in the middle, between the pairs of seeming opposites.

The yang having reached its climax retreats in favor of the yin; the yin having reached its climax retreats in favor of yang.

WANG CH'UNG

Danger arises when a man feels secure in his position. Destruction threat-ens when a man seeks to preserve his worldly estate. Confusion develops when a man has put everything in order. Therefore the superior man does not forget danger in his security, nor ruin when he is well established, nor confusion when his affairs are in order.
—I Ching

As we can needlessly and fruitlessly battle sex by making enemies out of the polarities in life, so too can we needlessly and fruitlessly battle change by viewing it as something separate from ourselves. Change isn't happen-ing to us. We are happening in a sea of change. We battle change with the fanciful hope that favorable circumstances will always prevail. We battle change when we resign ourselves to unfavorable conditions for fear that they will never change. The Taoists tell us not to battle change but to surrender to it—not in a sense of resignation but with a spirit of joy and thanksgiving.

Competitive Hostility

The cyclic flow is like a river: As all flowing rivers find peace in the ocean where they lose their name and form.
—Upanishads

The sexual battle described above is, of course, the ego's battle. For Freud, the battle to control the unconscious sex urge defines the ego. Yet there is another more basic sexual battle, the one established by the existence of the ego itself, in other words, by the me/not-me world-view. It is this duality that produces the feeling of competitive hostility, the desire to manipulate and control that which is not-me, be it other people or the natural world. In this "sexual" battle, who is on top is all-important.

It is only when we fail to recognize the reciprocal nature of polar rela-tionships that we delude ourselves into thinking that we can win at the expense of others. The classical Taoists referred to this as the desire to "lord it over" nature and others. Without the experience of our *Te,* our natural power and dignity, we seek inauthentic power and control. We abandon our innate dignity and become involved in a desperate search for attention and approval. What gives a hostile edge to this search is the simple fact that we see ourselves in competition with others to get it.

Once people get the idea that there isn't enough of something, they
begin to deprive one another to get it. —PHILIP SLATER

It is the ego's competitive hostility that, more than anything, destroys harmony in the lives of individuals and nations. It caused Cain to kill Abel, and it has killed millions since. When the Israelites took by force the land of milk and honey, when the Aryans overran Sumeria and India or the Mongols invaded China, we can be sure that (protestations of divine inspiration notwithstanding) competitive hostility marched alongside the conquering forces. When the people of one nation lusted after the lands and riches of another, competitive hostility blinded them to the humanity of their victims.

It is true that a relative few organized and engineered the extermination of millions of Jews during the reign of the Nazis in Germany. Yet it is equally true that in their hearts, millions of Germans harbored competitive hostility for a people whom they viewed as unfairly privileged and whose material, intellectual, and artistic accomplishments they resented. Blinded by competitive hostility, they pretended not to see, passively acquiesced, or actively participated in an evil that dwarfs all others. Sadly, it is only the scale and not the essential character of this event that marks it as unique.

Ask the Incas, Aztecs, or North American native tribes what competitive hostility can do to a people. The Sioux, who were dispossessed of their homelands time and time again, referred to gold as the thing that "makes white people crazy." Yet it is not the gold itself but lust for the power and approval that goes with it that makes people crazy. The fact that we do not kill, plunder, or loot doesn't mean that we cannot become just as crazy. Envy, self-righteousness, and the desire to win at all costs can bring devastation and ruin to our personal lives as surely as it has to the lives of peoples and nations.

As we have seen, competitive hostility is a universal ego tendency that cuts across time and cultures. Yet cultures can and do play a role in encouraging or mitigating this tendency (see highlight on page 199). In our own modern commercial culture, competitiveness is encouraged in virtually every aspect of life. Beyond the competitiveness of the commercial marketplace, our cultural obsession with "model" beauty, power, and material wealth fosters competitiveness in the relationships between the sexes as well as within the sexes. Modern advertising is constantly encouraging us to compare ourselves with others, to see ourselves in competition with the most

We go all wrong by
too strenuous a resolution
to go all right.

NATHANIEL HAWTHORNE

197

beautiful, the most famous, the most wealthy. We should want what they have and buy the things that will help us get it.

The next chapter will explore how competitive hostility, or the desire to be enviable, translates into the quest for material acquisition and control. This greedy chase, or rat race, robs us of the leisure we need to maintain our human-heartedness. Competitive hostility hardens our hearts and blinds our vision to our own true self-interest. The chapter that follows explores why we should, and how we can, find the leisure necessary to nurture and cultivate our humanity.

The Taoist World-view:
Live and Let Live

In contrast to our own, traditional Chinese culture was, on the whole, less competitive. This is perhaps best illustrated by the difference between the two cultures with respect to the issue of colonial expansion. More than fifty years before Vasco de Gama reached India, or Columbus sailed for America, enormous Chinese Imperial fleets sailed as far east as Java and as far west as the mouth of the Red Sea. The Chinese were skilled navigators who had invented the magnetic compass. They perfected the design of multiple masts that made large oceangoing vessels possible. Indeed, their ships were far larger and more seaworthy than their European counterparts of the day. With a flotilla of 317 ships, some up to 444 feet long, and crews numbering some 37,000 men, the Chinese Imperial fleet could easily have been employed to establish a great worldwide colonial empire. It was without question vastly superior to anything the Europeans possessed at the time. The Chinese also developed gun powder, which the Europeans used to subdue native peoples in distant lands.

While the Chinese had the technical and organizational wherewithal necessary for global dominance, they lacked the desire to conquer and impose their wills upon the people and territories of distant lands. Moreover, they lacked the conviction that they were blessed with the one true religion and, therefore, the missionary zeal to spread it to the ends of the earth. As the noted historian Daniel Boorstin put it, "the Chinese had quite another view of religion, a tradition of live and let live."[15]

"[M]odern agriculture, modern shipping, the modern oil industry, modern astronomical observatories, modern music, decimal mathematics, paper money, umbrellas, fishing reels, wheel barrows, multi-stage rockets, guns, underwater mines, poison gas, parachutes, hot air balloons, manned flight, brandy, whisky, the game of chess, printing, even the essential design for the steam engine, all came from China."[16]

Typically, Western historians explain European colonial expansion and eventual global dominance in terms of the West's superior technology. Yet this argument is not supported by the evidence. (See *The Genius of China: 3,000 Years of Science, Discovery and Invention,* by Robert Temple.) It could be advanced for so long only because most Western historians were, and in many cases still are, ignorant of Chinese scientific and technological developments. Moreover, Western historians have neglected adequate consideration of the role that a culture's collective consciousness or world-view plays in shaping the events of history. The interesting question, given China's tremendous technological advantage in the fourteenth and early fifteenth centuries is, "Why did it not seek to expand its influence around the world?" In the most general terms, the answer lies in cultural elements that restrained competitive hostility, and in this, the Taoist role was significant.

CHAPTER SEVEN

Jen

THE LEISURE OF ABUNDANCE

Every man knows how useful it is to be useful.
No one seems to know
How useful it is to be useless.

—CHUANG TZU

This chapter explores the principle of *jen,* or "human-heartedness," and how it can be maintained and cultivated in the midst of today's fast-paced society. It takes time to be, grow, and relate. It takes time to care for ourselves and others. In short, it takes time to be human. Leisure is one of the great abundances in life. No one, no matter how financially successful, can be said to enjoy real abundance if his or her life is lived at a frenetic pace, devoid of leisure and the opportunity to cultivate the finer feelings in life. Yet in our drive to be productive and our obsession with consumption, we've lost an appreciation for the value of leisure in determining quality of life. Today, in the midst of great material affluence, many feel "time poor." This chapter explores the social and psychological dynamics that contribute to time poverty, and what we can do to turn the situation around in our own lives. In the related exercises at the end of the book, you'll have the opportunity to evaluate your financial needs and goals in light of their time costs, and to determine your own time priorities, based on your values.

Of course, leisure isn't *necessary* for human survival. Yet it is necessary to preserve and develop our humanity. It is for this reason that we relate leisure to the Chinese term *jen. Jen* is often translated "benevolence" or "kindness," but "human-heartedness" gives a better sense of the meaning. It refers to the innate compassion of our authentic human nature. The character *jen* is formed by combining the character for a human being with that for "two." *Jen,* then, is concerned with the human being in relation.

Admittedly, the term *jen* is more closely associated with the Confucians than the Taoists. In fact, *jen* is one of the four cardinal virtues of the *Ju,* or Confucian, philosophy.[1] Yet we should remember that the concept of the Tao predates those whom we call "Taoists," and that it informs the whole of traditional Chinese philosophy, including the Confucian. Confucius was particularly interested in the Tao, or Way, in human affairs. When we are discussing *jen,* we are talking about the Tao of Humanity, the human being's innate sense of compassion for and identification with his or her fellow beings. In a hurried life without leisure, it is difficult indeed to maintain our natural human-heartedness.

But what is leisure? My dictionary defines leisure as "freedom from time-consuming duties, responsibilities, or activities."[2] Yet the length of time consumed by an activity is not the critical factor in determining whether or not it provides a sense of leisure. One could spend hours watching clouds roll by or become lost in a creative project for days or weeks at a time, yet retain a leisurely ease throughout. What sets leisure activities apart from others is the sense of losing the awareness of time while engaged in them. Thus, for purposes of this discussion, leisure will be defined as "activity free of time remembrance." To forget time is to forget ourselves, to lose self-consciousness. This loss of self-consciousness is simultaneously relaxing and invigorating. It is the essence of leisure.

Since leisure is not distinguished by the special nature of the activities involved, or even by a lack of activity, but by a state of mind free of time awareness, one's daily work or household chores can be leisure activities. On the other hand, a hyperorganized "vacation," where every minute is crammed with scheduled activities, may provide anything but leisure. When you lose yourself in a good book, this is leisure. On the other hand, watching television may or may not be a leisure activity. If you settle in to watch an engaging movie or a thought-provoking interview or documentary without interruption, this can provide leisure. Yet most commercial television is so broken up with advertising breaks that you can hardly lose track of time.

Losing yourself in your partner while making love can be an ecstatic form of leisure. On the other hand, hurried or goal-oriented sex is something else again. Sitting by a mountain stream, watching the water break over the rocks certainly seems like a leisure activity. Yet if all the while, you are fretting over the worries and problems in your life, the element of leisure is missing. I will not belabor the point, except to say again: the hallmark of leisure is the loss of awareness of the passage of time.

12 Contrasting Ideas of Enjoyment and Abundance

The ideal society of the Taoists was cooperative, not acquisitive.
—JOSEPH NEEDHAM

In the West, we typically define abundance by the quantity and quality of our possessions. For the Taoists, leisure is the essence of abundance. A look at Chinese and Western paintings from roughly the same period reveals these two distinctly different views of abundance. To illustrate, I have selected two paintings: one from the Chinese painter Liu Chüeh, entitled *The Pure and Plain Pavilion* (1458); the other, from the German painter Hans Holbein, entitled *The Ambassadors* (1533).[3] In the Chinese painting, we see a broad view of a mountainous landscape in which the man-made environment (the buildings and bridge) as well as the human figures themselves are small, yet fully integrated elements. The interior man-made environment is open and blends seamlessly into the exterior natural setting. In the Western painting, we see an enclosed man-made environment, filled with man-made objects. The only reference to the wider world is the globe on the table, which suggests a relationship of domination rather than harmony. The heavy draperies in the background create the illusion of a stage upon which the men, in all of their finery, have made their entrance.

In viewing the Chinese painting, we have the sense of stumbling onto a serene scene. The figures, in plain dress, are engaged in their own lives. They show no signs of being observed. We see two men seated face-to-face, presumably engaged in conservation, while a third man gazes out at the beauty of the surrounding scenery. In the painting by Holbein, we have a

The superior man loves his soul, The inferior man loves his property.

CONFUCIUS

The Ambassadors,

HANS HOLBEIN (1533)

sense of being confronted by the men and their objects. The two men are not relating to one another but are on display, along with their objects, before us—the spectator-viewers. The important relationship is not to each other but to us as viewers. The *Ambassadors* seem to be saying, "Here, look at us. Look at what we've got. See how important we are!"

These two paintings are representative of countless others from their respective cultures. In the post-Renaissance era, aristocrats and wealthy merchants, surrounded by their material possessions (or simply the possessions themselves), were popular subjects for Western art. In an era before photography, wealthy merchants were anxious to record their status as confirmed by their possessions and so commissioned the greatest number of paintings.[4] By the same token, there are hundreds of surviving Chinese paintings (undoubtedly, a small fraction of the total produced) similar to the one shown here. In these paintings, we might see a lone figure carrying a stick as he ambles along a mountain trail, or a hermit in a little hut on a mountain cliff or on a bit of island in the midst of a river or stream. In still other paintings, we see companions passing the time in quiet contemplation of their surroundings, in the enjoyment of a cup of tea, in the practice of calligraphy or painting, or in philosophical discussion. Always, the land-

The Pure and Plain Pavilion,
LIU CHÜEH (1458)

scape dominates; human beings, their possessions, and creations take a subordinate role. In later Chinese paintings we often see couples engaged in leisurely love dalliance. This too shows a Taoist influence.

As evidenced in the paintings, the Taoist takes pleasure in the contemplation of nature, in the enjoyment of a cup of tea, in the practice of art (principally calligraphy and painting), in relationships with equally refined friends, and in loving partnership with his or her mate. We cannot help but notice in these paintings a highly refined, richly opulent lifestyle that is virtually devoid of the material goods that we associate with wealth. We see in these paintings the celebration of a lifestyle that has all of the flavor and substance of abundance, but none of its trappings. The emphasis is on relationship, beauty, and humanity (human-heartedness), not on possession.

It is this avid and ambitious desire to take possession of the object by the owner or even the spectator which seems to me to constitute one of the outstanding original features of the art of Western civilization.
—CLAUDE LÉVI-STRAUSS

Both the Taoist- and Ch'an (Zen)-inspired Chinese brush stroke paintings and the merchant-commissioned Western oil paintings represent an ideal view of the world, a model for emulation by the members of their respective societies. Each suggests an ideal of enjoyment, and with it, a quality of relationship with the natural world. Each represents a kind of opulence: the first, of time; the second, of things. These differences follow naturally from the Greek interest in matter and the Chinese interest in time, discussed in the previous chapter. It is worth noting that the rebirth to which the Renaissance refers was, in large part, a result of the rediscovery of, and renewed interest in, the spiritual, artistic, and intellectual legacy of the Greeks.

Returning to the two paintings we are examining here, we notice that in the Chinese painting, the figures, though physically distant, seem close to us in their humanity. We identify with them. In the Western painting, the men appear physically close, yet psychologically distant. They seem intimidating. This effect of physical immediacy and psychological distance is one that has been carried over to the present day. It is used time and again in modern advertising. We all have seen countless images in magazine and newspaper ads and on television of the beautiful, sexy model who appears physically close, yet psychologically distant and aloof.

Paintings like *The Ambassadors* as well as many modern advertising layouts are designed to make us feel impressed by the principal subjects and their possessions. Yet there is a difference. In their display, the Ambassadors are affirming their position. They ask from us only that we acknowledge their status. On the other hand, the advertising model is selling something. She is inviting us to participate in the glamorous world in which she resides. The implicit message in the advertising image is that we can approach the model, that we can bridge the psychological gap between her world and our own, by buying what she is selling.

*One does not always lose
if he has to do without.*

GOETHE

Yet the model is not really selling herself or even the product she represents. She is selling us an idealized image of ourselves. If we buy the product, we too will become glamorous. We too will become enviable. Of course, what we have said about the advertising model applies equally to the celebrity sports figure or any other "enviable" icon used to move merchandise. In every case, we are being asked to buy into the idea that we can buy happiness. And we are being asked incessantly. By the time the average American is twenty years old, he or she will have seen a million advertisements. By the time he or she is ready to leave this Earth, the average American will have spent an entire year of his or her life watching television commercials.[5]

> *I heard from my master that those who have cunning devices use cunning in their affairs, and that those who use cunning in their affairs have cunning hearts. Such cunning means the loss of pure simplicity. Such a loss leads to restlessness of the spirit, and with such men the Tao will not dwell.[6]*

In 1983, during the early years of Microsoft's meteoric rise, Bill Gates courted a man who had worked as a marketing executive for a cosmetics firm, to serve as his first vice-president of corporate communications. The man, C. Rowland Hanson, had little experience with computers at the time and wondered why Gates was interested in him. Gates reportedly asked him to describe the difference between a moisturizer that sells for a dollar an ounce and one that sells for a hundred dollars an ounce. Hanson replied, "Nothing. It all has to do with the brand halo that has been created." Gates replied, "That's it exactly and what this industry doesn't understand."[7] I once had a conversation with a man who owns a large California vineyard. The man sells some of his grapes to wineries that use them to produce wine that sells for two hundred dollars a bottle. He sells the very same grapes to different wineries that use them to make wine that sells for ten to twelve dollars a bottle. When asked to describe the difference between the ten dollar bottle of wine and the two hundred dollar bottle, he replied in one word: "Merchandising."

It is only among people whose minds have been weakened by a sort of mesmerism that so transparent a trick as that of advertising could ever have been tried at all.
　　　　　　　　　　　　　　　　　　　　　　　　　—G. K. CHESTERTON

We have been merchandised not only on specific products but also on the idea of merchandising itself. Our cultural obsession with consumption is no accident, but part and parcel of a commercial value system that is constantly being reinforced by those who stand to profit from it. (This will be explained in greater depth below.) Yet we should recognize our own complicity in this state of affairs. We respond to the ego's craving for approval, and its competitive hostility, by becoming greedy. We lust after things not simply for use or enjoyment but for the social approval and personal clout that we imagine comes with them. In accepting the consumption model of abundance idealized in post-Renaissance oil paintings and carried over in modern advertising, we have substituted the glamour of possession for the experience of actual enjoyment. We have chosen enjoyments of consumption over those of leisure. We have come to value the freedom to possess things over the freedom to determine how we use our time.

There is a story about Confucius and a group of his pupils that contrasts these two views of abundance. Confucius asked each of his pupils to tell him his ambitions in life. One wanted to be minister of war; another, minister of finance; a third, a ceremonial officer in the prince's court. Tseng Tien, the remaining pupil, made no reply, but quietly strummed his lute. When Confucius asked him for his answer, Tseng Tien said that in springtime, he would like to go to the river bank with his friends. There he would bathe in the river, enjoy the breezes, and return home singing. Confucius was most pleased by Tseng Tien's answer. The message is clear: to value simple enjoyments and preserve human-heartedness, to choose living for its own sake, over the acquisition of things or positions.

Like leisure, consumption beyond the basics of food, shelter, and clothing is unnecessary for survival. Whether we choose the preponderance of our enjoyments in leisure or in consumption makes a difference in terms of the quality of life we enjoy as individuals. Even more, it makes a difference to our collective survival in the twenty-first century. Environmentalists have long warned that if the rest of the world were to adopt the consumption patterns of North Americans, the consequences on the environment would be catastrophic. Yet each year, millions more are coming to embrace the consumption-based paradigm of abundance—and buying accordingly.

> *It is impossible to give the whole world the kind of lifestyle you have here {in America}, that the Germans have, that the Dutch have . . . and we must face this reality.* —JOSÉ LUTZENBURGER, FORMER SECRETARY OF STATE FOR THE ENVIRONMENT, BRAZIL

Yet, as the images from the Taoist-influenced paintings suggest, in recognizing the limits of consumption, we needn't sacrifice abundance. On the contrary, true abundance is first and foremost an abundance of time and the freedom to choose what to do with it.

12 Modern Society and the Decline of Leisure

Time is the new poverty.
—ROBERT HEILBRONER

It is a profound irony that in the most affluent country in the world, in the most materially and technologically advanced culture in the history of humankind, we are so time poor. Since 1950, Americans alone have used more natural resources than all the human beings who ever lived on earth before them, combined.[8] The United States, with 5 percent of the world's population, consumes 30 percent of its resources. The average American uses five times more of the world's resources than the average Mexican, ten times more than the average Chinese, and thirty times more than the aver-

*Man has become the tool
of his tools.*

THOREAU

age Indian.[9] Between 1978 and 1998, per capita consumption in America increased by 45 percent.[10] Yet this increased material affluence has not produced corresponding increases in happiness. In fact, the number of Americans who consider themselves "very happy" peaked in 1957.[11]

Clearly, material affluence cannot be equated with happiness. In fact, beyond a certain point, it may actually detract from the experience of abundance. Back in 1970, in a book ironically entitled *The Harried Leisure Class*, Staffan Linder warned of a link between increasing material affluence and the stress associated with time scarcity. At the dawn of the twenty-first century, time scarcity and stress are the daily experience of the vast majority of working Americans and hundreds of millions more throughout the world.

Today, millions of Americans are living in retirement for fifteen years or more, a phenomenon that would have been unimaginable only one hundred years ago.[12] Yet the vast majority of those in their working years actually enjoy less leisure than human beings from other times and cultures, despite unprecedented material affluence. Several key factors contribute to the decline of leisure in modern life. First, we work many more hours per year than our counterparts from other times and cultures. Second, we work by the clock, not by the work, which is to say, we are much more conscious of time in the way we work. Third, our time away from work is occupied with fewer time-forgetting activities.

While it's true that in the early days of the Industrial Revolution, many factory workers worked longer hours than we typically do today, at the time, most people were still living an agrarian lifestyle and were not so employed. Moreover, the twelve- to fourteen-hour days of the sweatshop era represented a major departure from humanity's traditional working patterns. For example, in ancient Rome, there were 175 public festival days per year. In medieval England, holidays comprised about one third of the year. French workers under the *ancien régime* were guaranteed ninety rest days and thirty-eight holidays, in addition to work-free Sundays.[13] Anthropological studies of so-called primitive cultures have found that people in these cultures typically worked far fewer hours than we do today. For example, the Ohlone of the California coast were able to supply their basic living needs by working only two hours per day.

Labor laws have limited the number of hours people may work and have generally improved conditions over what they were in the sweatshop era of the nineteenth century. Nevertheless, the amount of time American workers spent on the job rose significantly in the second half of the twentieth century. In one twenty-year period in the 1970s and 1980s, worktime increased by an additional month per year. Today, full-time workers are working more hours per week than at any time since the Second World War. Americans work more hours per year than the people of any other major industrialized nation.[14]

As noted economist Robert Heilbroner puts it, "lack of time is the new poverty."[15] Many today feel that their lives have come to revolve around work. Corporate downsizing has left remaining employees with heavier workloads and, in many cases, more hours on the job. Moreover, more is being demanded from workers today in terms of the responsibilities they are being asked to assume and in terms of the pace at which they are expected to learn new skills and incorporate new knowledge on the job. As a result, people often must take their work home with them or take additional training or courses in their "off" hours. Since it now takes the combined efforts of both adult members of a household to make the same amount of money (actually less in real dollars) than just one earned thirty years ago, people have less time to spend with their families or to do a variety of other things they enjoy.[16]

Beyond the time that we spend on the job, getting ready for, and commuting to and from it, there is still much work to be done. In a traditional agrarian society, the pace of life and the sharp division of labor between the sexes meant that when work was done—it was done. Today, when we finish working for others, we still have our own work to do. Paying bills, shopping, laundry, cooking, cleaning, and caring for children must be done on our own time (which is to say, after an average forty-nine-hour workweek).

12 The Big Time Spilt

As capitalism grew, it steadily lengthened worktime.
—JULIET SCHOR

Yet the lack of leisure results from more than the sheer number of hours we work today. It has even more to do with the way we experience time. In the preindustrial era, time was measured, not in minutes or hours, but by the sun and its daily and seasonal cycles. While the peasant or serf was required to give up a portion of the fruits of his labors to the lord of the manor, there wasn't a clear demarcation between his own time and that of the lord. What division of time there was, was related to the cycles of nature. For example, long hours during planting and harvesting times were followed by a long season of relative inactivity during the winter months. The custom of the afternoon nap time, or siesta, which survives today in Spain, Southern Italy, and many Latin American countries, was once common in the Northern European countries as well. Today, the pace of life is constant. We have little regard for the effects of the seasons on our bodies, or the time of day on our biorhythms.

Whatever else it did, capitalism bifurcated time. It divided the sixteen waking hours into the "owner's" or employer's time and the worker's time. The time-on/time-off, work-time/free-time pattern we all know so well profoundly altered the human experience. Today, it has become so much a part of the common sense of things that a recent television commercial selling cheap weekend phone rates matter-of-factly stated that: "Weekends are the time for catching up on the life you missed during the week." This division of time provides the motive force behind the two great themes of modern commercial culture, namely, the drive for ever greater productivity and the drive for ever greater consumption. Together, these two have made it increasingly difficult for ordinary people to find any leisure in their lives.

仁 The Drive for Efficiency

It is not enough to be busy, so are the ants.
The question is, what are we busy about?
—THOREAU

The dramatic increases in production achieved during the Industrial Revolution would not have been possible without a profound transformation of attitudes toward work. This shift in attitudes was at least as significant as the new technologies and new methods of organizing work that are more often credited with paving the road to industrialization. Workers initially resisted the long working hours and the patterns of regular employment that were, and remain, hallmarks of life in industrialized societies. Early factory owners were often frustrated when workers would leave the worksite after they had earned the amount of money they needed to maintain the standard of living they had grown accustomed to. The offer of additional money with which to buy more goods proved insufficient to entice workers to remain on the job. While there was still a possibility of earning their living in traditional ways, males in particular resisted full-time employment. Women were first brought into the factories because they were considered more submissive to authority and therefore more likely to remain on the job. The widespread use of child labor had a similar motivation. Moreover, it helped condition a new generation of male and female workers to long hours of regular employment.

Conform and be dull.

JAMES FRANK DOBIE

Once people had grown accustomed to continuous employment, the emphasis shifted to exacting ever greater efficiency from them. The factory owner saw it as in his interest to break down time into ever smaller units and to squeeze the greatest production out of his employees for every minute they were under his control. Increasingly, time pressure became synonymous with work. The typical worker was no longer an agrarian, working by the sun but an urbanite, working by the clock. Though mechanical clocks (yet another Chinese invention) had been around in Europe since at least the middle of the fourteenth century, they had little influence on the lives of ordinary people until the late eighteenth and early nineteenth centuries.

Working by time and for money changed the human experience in ways that are difficult for us to fully appreciate. In the 1880s, Frederick Taylor's time and motion studies launched an era of increased emphasis on hyper-efficiency in the workplace. As one historian has written, "With his stopwatch, a further encroachment of time on physical movement, Taylor proposed . . . the absolute subordination of 'living labor' to the machine. . . ."[17] This subordination of man to machine put new strains on the human nervous system. In 1884, George M. Beard published a book entitled *American Nervousness* in which he chronicled the effects that emerging time stresses associated with industrialization were having on the human body and psyche. "Modern nervousness is the cry of the system struggling with its environment," wrote Beard.[18] He argued that simply making the effort to be on time puts stress on the human body. He also believed that modern inventions such as the railroad and the telegraph put additional nervous strain on the human body.

We can only imagine what Beard would have to say about air travel, freeways, traffic jams, telephones, fax machines, pagers, and E-mail, not to mention the increased drive for productivity in the workplace. Yet we should imagine, which is to say we should consider, the effect that these modern marvels, and the frenetic pace of life they engender, have upon our nervous systems and on the way we relate to one another. Our situation recalls the familiar story of the frog in the hot water. Put a frog in a pot of hot water and it will quickly jump out. Yet if you slowly raise the temperature, the frog will remain in the pot until the heat overcomes and kills it. It's overstating the case to say that time pressure is killing us. Yet it *is* transforming us in a variety of ways. We are not, we cannot be, fully conscious of the effects of living in a society where the pace of life is constantly accelerating—where the drum beats ever faster and faster and the trumpet blares ever louder and louder.

> *It is a great evil, perhaps the greatest evil, of modern industrial society that, through its immensely involved nature, it imposes an undue nervous strain and absorbs an undue proportion of man's attention.*
>
> —E. F. SCHUMACHER

Of course, we are familiar with the impact of stress on the human body. Today, forty million Americans suffer from some kind of sleep disorder.[19] Some forty-five million take prescription psychiatric drugs on a regular basis.[20] Many millions more are addicted to alcohol and illegal drugs.[21] Americans by the millions overeat to the point of obesity in a desperate attempt to fill their sense of emptiness and to control their anxiety. As women have entered the workplace in mass numbers, they are experiencing increased incidences of heart disease, long the bane of the driven male executive. All of these and many more are symptoms of the toll that the time stresses of modern life take on our psyches and bodies.

Yet beyond these, time pressure affects our human-heartedness, the way we relate to ourselves, to others, and to the world around us. In response to the hyperactive pace of modern life, we tense up and shut down to the world around us. Many of us find it hard, not only to let go and deeply relax, but also to concentrate for extended periods of time. The fact that so many of us need the nervous stimulation of caffeine simply to handle the pace of an ordinary day should tell us something. Time pressure doesn't just shorten our attention spans. It makes us short with one another. Today, social commentators of every hue and stripe lament the breakdown of civility in our social discourse and in the way we interact with one another. Yet we seldom probe the underlying social pressures, including time stress, that contribute to this breakdown.

As the Taoists offer us a contrasting view of abundance, so too they offer an alternate view of productivity. The Taoist's approach to productivity is revealed in this simple dictum: Do what is needed, leave undone what is not. Today, we measure productivity in the abstract terms of economics. In economic terms, the intrinsic value of a thing or event is less important than its capacity to generate profits. Of course, monetary value and real value may correspond. Yet they need not and often do not. As we have seen, a thing's monetary value is often more a function of the way it is merchandised than of its intrinsic value. In practice, this means that many things are made and done that are neither useful nor valuable, but are highly profitable. The Taoists would tell us that regardless of the profits made from these kinds of enterprises, they are *not* productive. Rather, by any real standard of value, they are a wasteful misuse of the natural resources and human energy required to sustain them.

There is enough for everybody's need but not everybody's greed.

GANDHI

Today, one is considered productive to the extent that she generates monetary profit for herself or others. In the determination of her social standing, her intelligence, innate talents, and service to others are secondary to her earning capacity. In practice, this means that individuals choose their work on the basis of what will pay rather than on what will give them the most enjoyment and provide the greatest service to others. Again, the Taoists would not see this as productive, for it limits human happiness and leaves many needed things undone, while we scurry about doing things of little real value.

If a man has important work, and enough leisure and income to enable him to do it properly, he is in possession of as much happiness as is good for any of the children of Adam. —R. H. TAWNEY

Today, the efficiency values that dominate in the workplace have been carried over into all aspects of life. We feel the need to pack our free time with entertainments. The fact that most of us spend the bulk of our lives working for others on things that have little personal meaning leaves us with the desire to cram as much as we can into our free time. More than anything, we fill it with shopping (see below). To be sure, our obsession with shopping affords the diversion of a temporary "high"; yet in the end, it only helps ensure that we continue on in work that offers little in the way of personal fulfillment or social value. A popular bumper sticker sums up what many feel as their principal motivation for going to work: "I owe, I owe, so off to work I go."

12 The Drive for Increased Consumption

Entertainment has replaced its most potent rival for human emotion, religion, as the opiate of the masses. —JOHN MALTHEVITCH

To be sure, the emphasis on efficiency in the workplace has resulted in tremendous increases in productivity. Yet productivity gains have not been translated into increased leisure but have instead gone into increased consumption. In her excellent book, *The Overworked American*, Juliet Schor notes that if Americans today enjoyed the same standard of living they had in 1948, they could work every other year or take six months off.[22] Today, we have a variety of "labor-saving" devices and entertainments unknown to earlier generations. In 1948, Americans didn't own dishwashers, home air conditioners, microwaves, or automatic dryers. They didn't have televisions, computers, compact disc players, or VCRs. Fewer Americans owned their own homes, and the typical single-family dwelling was smaller (roughly the size of today's three-car garage). Yet we could well ask if the material things and comforts we have gained in the last fifty years are worth six months of the year, or half of the time of our lives.

At the very least, we should ask how things might be different if we had opted for more free time rather than greater consumption. It is pretty clear what things we wouldn't have, but what would we have that we don't have now? Would marital relationships be stronger? Would our children be better cared for and feel more secure? Would we have greater opportunities to express ourselves creatively? Would communities profit from increased participation in their social, cultural, and political life? Would we feel more relaxed and enjoy the simple things of life more fully? Would we be friendlier and take more interest in our neighbors? Would we be healthier in body, mind, and spirit?

Of course, these are hypotheticals that cannot be definitely answered. Nevertheless, there is something to be gained by raising the questions. Even more important, we might well ask what we would like to do with the productivity gains that will likely result in the next half century. Should these too be channeled into increased tribute for the elite and increased consumption for the masses? Or should they come back to workers in the form of increased free time? Certainly, the new technologies and toys that we will be invited to buy and enjoy will fascinate and stimulate the senses. Yet we should also consider their effect on our human-heartedness. New gadgetry that comes at the expense of peace of mind or human relationships cannot be considered progress.

We expect that workers will be financially compensated for increases in their company's productivity (though, as discussed in chapter 5, wage increases have not kept pace with productivity increases, this expectation has, to some extent, been met). Yet we could ask: Why haven't employers at least offered workers the option of taking more time off in exchange for productivity increases? Juliet Schor argues that collectively, employers have a vested economic interest in keeping a large pool of unemployed people, while at the same time extracting long hours from those in their employ. It helps keep the cost of labor low (and the fear of being laid off, high). On the other hand, pay increases are likely to be spent, and at least a portion of this additional spending is likely to find its way back to the pockets of employers.

Whatever the real reason, today we hear two principal arguments against allowing ordinary people more free time. The first flows from the prevailing concept of human nature, the idea that people are essentially selfish and greedy. If they have more free time, they will only get into more mischief. They can't be trusted to use their time well. (For more on this, see the highlight on pages 237–239.)

Here, we will concentrate on the second and more popular argument—namely, that the economy (and with it, the social fabric) would fall apart if "consumer demand" were allowed to significantly taper off. The logic behind this argument essentially asks us to believe that we are captives of our own productive success. Any significant slowdown in the work-and-spend cycle—like that which would result from more leisure time—might cause the house of cards to collapse. How to keep it all going has been the principal concern of economists and the governments of market-economy countries for many years now.

The first economic problem, the one that concerned Adam Smith and other pioneers in the field, was the problem of physical scarcity: How to overcome what he called "nature's stinginess"? How to produce sufficient

Money-making and the kind of advantages which a money-making society provides are not enough to satisfy humanity . . .

EDMUND WILSON

goods to supply people's basic needs? In the later part of the nineteenth century, interest in this problem began to fade as a second problem came to dominate the thinking of economists: How to overcome the problem of overproduction?, or alternately stated, How to increase consumption to insure sustained demand for ever-increasing production? The answer lay in tapping into what was conceived as an endless resource—the human emotion of greed.

Already, in the 1920s, a government report proclaimed what by this time had become the conventional wisdom. "Economists have long declared that consumption, the satisfaction of wants, would expand with little evidence of satiation if we could so *adjust* our economic processes as to make dormant demands effective."[23] In practice, "making dormant demands effective" means making people want things they don't even know they want. An ancillary process is the one John Wannaker, an early department store magnate, called turning "luxuries into commodities or into necessities."[24] This too was rightly viewed as a powerful tool for overcoming the problem of overproduction.

Today, the process of "making dormant demands effective" is commonly referred to as "developing markets." Market development takes two major forms. The first is a matter of creating a new product and then convincing people that they ought to want and buy it. This is a process with which we are all intimately familiar. The push to buy the latest in electronic gadgetry is perhaps the best example. Yet this form of market development has included everything from electric toothbrushes and specially processed microwave foods to designer fragrances. In the latter case, the name and marketing pitch for the fragrance are often produced long before the perfume has ever been formulated, let alone manufactured.

The second way to "develop markets" is to move into "developing countries" with existing products and convince the local people that they need and want something that they have gotten along without for thousands of years. At this writing, markets for American candy bars are "being developed" in Russia, while in India, the market for American fast food is being primed. To view these "developing markets" from the classical economic "law of supply and demand" is clearly absurd. Are we to believe that the demands for Snickers bars in Russia and hamburgers in India have lain dormant for thousands of years, but are suddenly now awakening?

Global market development is a threat, not only to the environment, but to any meaningful cultural diversity. We risk the homogenization of the world and, with it, the loss of cultural legacies—vast stores of wisdom and knowledge accumulated over thousands of years. Recently, a Japanese national attending graduate school in America remarked to me that she likes eating at McDonald's because it reminds her of home. Today, you can sip Pepsi, drink Starbucks coffee, or eat Kentucky Fried Chicken in Beijing. You can stay at the Holiday Inn in Lhasa, Tibet, once the most remote capital in the world. You can visit a Pizza Hut in over eighty countries. You can buy posters of American movie stars, pop music stars, and sports heroes in small African villages and Chinese provincial capitals.

Do you want to make a people active and hard-working? {O}ffer them amusements that make them love their condition, and prevent them from enjoying a more pleasant one. —JEAN JACQUES ROUSSEAU

Today, it seems the whole world is trying to keep up with the Joneses. Yet the dynamics of ever increasing production and new market development ensure that we will never reach the promised land of consumptive parity. When new products are developed, they are not equally distributed among all economic sectors. Unequal distribution breeds envy, which in turn, fuels further growth. Two examples, one from the developed world and one from the developing, will illustrate. At a cost of around $7,000 a unit, today, only the wealthy can afford the new high definition television sets. Yet the fact that some people have them excites others to desire them. This envy creates demand and helps to insure that (if the market development for HD-TV follows the pattern of similar consumer products) by the time the price becomes more affordable, the market demand will be strong.

In many Asian countries, the pattern of "development" in transportation has been one of moving from foot and animal transportation to bicycles, then motor scooters, then larger motorcycles and tiny cars, and finally to larger automobiles. As late as the mid-1980s, there were but a few thousand privately owned automobiles in the whole of China. Since then, the number has grown dramatically, and with a population of over a billion people, the market potential for autos in China seems virtually limitless. Again, the more people have cars, the more those who don't, want them.

Most people understand that their work is managed by someone else; few understand the extent to which their consumption is also managed by

Nothing was any longer good or bad, only either premature or out of date.

ALBERT CAMUS

others. In the late nineteenth and early twentieth centuries, department stores created the mass-market fashion industry. From the beginning, women were its primary targets. One early "fashion expert" recognized in fashion a means of greatly enhancing consumption and, in so doing, helping to alleviate "the problem of overproduction." "The way out of overproduction," he wrote, "must lie in finding what the woman at the counter is going to want. Make it and then promptly drop it, and go onto something else, to which fickle fashion is turning her attention."[25] "Constant change," wrote another, "through the entire gamut of material, color, design, is essential to the prosperity alike of producers and distributors."[26]

It is our job to make women unhappy with what they have.
—B. EARL PUCKETT, FORMER HEAD
OF ALLIED STORES CORPORATION

Amos Parrish, who ran an influential consulting firm and held regular classes that were attended by representatives of hundreds of retail stores, wrote in 1929: "Nothing is going to stop fashion. It wears things out. And industry wants things worn out in order to make more things to build bigger businesses, to pay larger dividends. Things must grow. Fashion is the one thing in the world that will do it. And without fashion it won't be done. But it will be done."[27] "Fashion," as one retailer put it in 1908, "imparts to merchandise a value over and above its intrinsic worth and imbues with special desirability the goods which otherwise create only languid interest."[28]

Today, men as much as women, and children as much as adults, are targets of fashion appeals. Moreover, principles of merchandising first developed by the fashion (clothing) industry were later effectively applied to automobiles, appliances, electronics, home furnishing, entertainments, travel, the recording industry, even to the so-called "diet industry." Already, by 1930, one fashion merchandiser could write: "There is not a commodity today that escapes fashion; there is fashion in furniture, cars, washing machines, tires, and so forth. Fashion makes things live and people buy."[29] And buy we do! Today, shopping is the number one entertainment activity for Americans. Seventy percent of Americans visit a shopping mall at least once a week.[30]

Today, we take the consumptive society for granted. Yet significant resistance had to be overcome before it could take root. Even as traditional values had to be altered in order to fuel the engines of production, so too they had to be changed to fuel the engines of consumption. In the nineteenth century, middle-class Americans were loath to buy anything on credit. Usury was still suspect, thrift was valued, and to buy things you could not afford was considered sinful by many. The shift to a buy-now-pay-later attitude toward purchasing decisions is a recent one. Historian William Leach writes: "Many middle class people in 1915 still disdained installment buying; by 1925 their reservations were fast withering. Consumers of all classes bought automobiles 'on time'—and then, the ice broken, washing machines, refrigerators, and dishwashers. After 1920 a new banking system for consumers, similar to the one functioning in the world of production, fed the growth of consumer credit."[31]

In the 1950s, the Diners Club introduced the first credit card in the United States. Today, Americans alone have over a billion credit cards. Less than one third of card holders pay off their balances each month. Excluding real estate loans, Americans carry over a trillion dollars in personal debt. In 1996, more Americans filed for bankruptcy than graduated from college.[32] The incitement to envy and the social pressure to consume can overwhelm our human-heartedness and better judgment in a variety of ways. When a middle-class marriage ends in divorce because the couple got caught up in trying to live beyond their means and ended up being mean to one another, and when an eleven-year-old kid from the inner city kills a companion in order to get his expensive basketball shoes, the same inner dynamics are at play.

I don't read advertisements; I would spend all my time wanting things.

GEORGE CAREY,
ARCHBISHOP
OF CANTERBURY

> *These are my three treasures,*
> *Compassion, frugality, and humility*
> *Being compassionate one has courage,*
> *Being frugal one has abundance,*
> *Being humble one becomes the chief of all vessels.*
> —LAO TZU

Lao Tzu said, "Being frugal one has abundance." In a society in which social standing and even personal worth are measured by our possessions, frugality is hardly a value. Yet if we trace the origin of the word, we find that it is derived from the Latin *frux,* or fruit. To be frugal is to be fruitful. To save, to conserve, to mend, to repair, to do without what is unneeded— surely these are virtues. Yet Madison Avenue has convinced us that these behaviors are neither sexy nor desirable. We go 'round and 'round in a cycle of work and spend, in the interest of preserving the social, which is to say, the economic order.

To those who say that society would fall apart if people thought a little more before they bought, or bought a little less, we could well ask if it is not already showing ample signs of breakdown? We could ask what our commitment to ever-expanding production and consumption are doing to our humanity. Moreover, sooner or later, we are going to have to face the fact that there are limits to the earth's capacity to support runaway growth. Better that we confront and deal with this problem now than cover our eyes and wait until we are forced by major ecological and economic crises to face it later on. It's up to all of us to explore alternative visions of abundant living, with a view toward creating a social order that is ecologically responsible and committed to preserving, and indeed nurturing, human-heartedness.

仁 An Abundance of Leisure

Joy is not in things; it is in us.
—Charles Wagner

In his bestselling book *The Seven Habits of Highly Effective People*, Stephen Covey emphasized the critical difference between the urgent and the important in life. The urgent things are those we must deal with. It's an urgent matter to pay your rent or taxes when they are due. The important things are those that reflect our values and sense of purpose in life. Too often, we let the urgent overwhelm the important. Many of the truly important things in life require a quality of leisure. While in economic terms, leisure is only productive to the extent that it generates profit for the tourist, entertainment, or recreational industries, from the standpoint of cultivating our human-heartedness, leisure is highly productive (see below).

As much as time management, we need time awareness, to examine the way we use our time in light of our values and priorities. Growing numbers of people are doing precisely that and, in the process, defining for themselves what abundance means to them. In increasing numbers, they are coming to reject the scorecard of the financial bottom line and material possessions as the critical criteria for measuring abundance. They are seeking ways to reduce their living costs and are placing time above money in their priorities.

A poll conducted for *Time* magazine reported that 69 percent of Americans say they would like to slow down and have a more relaxed lifestyle.[33] The Trends Research Institute estimates that by the year 2005, 15 percent of the population in the developed world will be in some way practicing voluntary simplicity.[34] Many are discovering that the less invested they are in the pursuit of material acquisition, the more latitude they have in deciding what kind of work they do. In fact, they often feel a greater sense of control in determining how they will use all of the time of their lives. Whenever we expand the sense of freedom and control in our lives, we naturally feel more abundant.

After all, if we haven't the time to spend with our children and mates or to participate in the life of our communities, if we haven't time to think, to learn, or to express ourselves creatively, if we haven't time to experience the wonders of life, to play, or just simply be still once in a while, then certainly, the experience of abundance has eluded us, no matter how materially affluent we may be. The section below considers some of the abundances of leisure, why it is important that we reclaim them, and how we can.

You might well ask, "Where will I find the time to engage in these leisures?" Even without a major restructuring of your life, a downshift or move to voluntary simplicity, it's a good bet that you can find some time if you are willing to make some adjustments in the way you appropriate it. For example, the average adult American spends twenty hours a week watching television. While there is nothing wrong with watching television, chances are that taking time to enjoy some of the leisures explored below will provide more interesting, enriching, and rewarding experiences.

The Leisure to Be	The Leisure to Grow	The Leisure to Relate
Time to Idle	Time to Think	Time for Our Mates
Time to Play	Time to Learn	Time for Our Children
Time to Experience	Time to Express	Time for Our Communities

亿 Leisure to Be

If you want to be happy, be. —HENRY DAVID THOREAU

Time to Idle

As young children, we were oblivious to time. We lived in a world dominated by the immediacies of the moment and by subconscious mental processes. As we grew older, we had to submit to the exigencies of time. Our
awareness moved out of the immediacy of the moment, into hopes and
anxieties for the future, and nostalgia and regrets for the past. While at
leisure, we recapture the time-free world of our youth. It is for this reason
that we say that leisure "makes you feel like a kid again."

> *When people wish to see their reflections, they do not look into running
> water; they look into still water. Only that which is still can hold other
> things still.* —CHUANG TZU

We have mentioned several times the value of meditation. Simply sitting still and listening to your breath provides deep refreshment. Meditation is a real vacation—one in which we vacate the cares, worries, and
troubles of the time-bound world and drink the Bliss of Pure Being. And it
doesn't cost a dime! But we don't need to meditate to kill time.

When was the last time you watched the clouds roll by or gazed into a
fire for hours on end? When was the last time you watched the unfolding
splendor of a night sky? When was the last time you sat on a beach or
lakeshore and watched the waves roll in and out, or closed your eyes and
merged with the sound of the waves breaking against the shore—until you
were no more? How long has it been since you lay beneath a tree and watched
the leaves dancing in the wind or took a leisurely walk on a winter's night
just to watch snowflakes fall in the moonlight? Take time to do nothing.
And do it well.

Time to Play

Abundant living includes time to play. Play reminds us that life itself is a game and keeps us from taking it and ourselves too seriously. In countless ways, our daily routines tend to deaden and dull our senses. Through play, we recapture the sense of wonder and the exuberance for life we knew as children. In this spirit of wide-eyed innocence, we are able to see things in a fresh way, to make combinations and connections we might otherwise miss. To play in a childlike way is to let go of self-consciousness, to drop the armor of ego defenses, to give up our pretenses and be what we are, pure and simple.

Besides being fun and relaxing, play can give us insight into ourselves and even into the nature of the universe. The great psychologist C. G. Jung loved to play in the mud. One day, when he was an old man, Jung stood on the shore of a riverbank, turning over mud with a shovel as he had many times before. Suddenly, he realized: this was what his whole life had been about. He had spent it turning over the mud, looking into things hidden beneath the surface of the conscious mind.

Michael Faraday imagined living the life of an atom. He went on to discover electromagnetic theory. Albert Einstein imagined himself flying through space at the speed of light. Einstein credited his discovery of the theory of relativity to just this kind of play. As he put it, "Play seems to be the essential feature in productive thought." In the beginning, the telescope was just a toy for Galileo. Isaac Newton said, "I do not know what I may appear to the world; but to myself I seem to have been only like a boy playing on the seashore, and diverting myself in now and then finding a smoother pebble or a prettier shell than the ordinary, whilst the great ocean of truth lay all undiscovered before me."

The insights of Newton, Galileo, Einstein, and Faraday have, to a great extent, shaped our view of the world. These giants of modern science weren't afraid to play. Yet many of us think it silly or undignified to really let go. We fear that others will think us foolish if we show too much joy, excitement, or playfulness. We keep a tight reign on our imaginations, lest they wander too far off the beaten path. Especially while at work, we tend to take a serious, nose-to-the-grindstone attitude. We have gotten the notion that to be "grown-up" is to act stiff and "dignified." We fear that others will not take us seriously if we allow them to see us acting silly or in an overtly playful manner.

For such is our nature, that cannot stand long bent, but we must have relaxations of mind, as of body.

H. PEACHAM
ENGLISH RECREATIONS, 1641

Without this playing with fantasy, no creative work has ever yet come to birth. The debt we owe to the play of the imagination is incalculable.

C. G. JUNG

Our commercial culture, with its "bottom-line" orientation, has little use (or time) for play for its own sake. To the extent that we value play at all, it is as an escape from the drudgery of the daily grind. Instead of enjoying it for its own sake, we tend to view play as a reward for spending so much of our lives doing things we don't want to do. This, in turn, brings a goal-directed, or driven, quality to our play, which robs it of the refreshment it might otherwise give. When you find yourself turning play into something serious, step back and remind yourself that your only goal is to have fun.

As important as it is to take time to play, it is equally important to nurture our innate playfulness. Playfulness is a way of life, not a special quality we exhibit while engaged in certain activities. We can be playful with our children, mates, and friends and, if we have the right kind of job, at least some of the time with our co-workers, bosses, or subordinates. Playfulness moves us out of the conventional and automatic and into the now moment—and it's contagious. With humor or affectionate teasing, with singing or dancing, or just by goofing off now and then, we can remind others of their playful natures. We can even remind ourselves when we are all alone, simply by stopping every now and then to have a good laugh—at ourselves.

Time to Experience

The French novelist Collette said, "What a wonderful life I've had! I only wish I had realized it sooner." We all have wonderful lives, if we can but realize it. We have wonderful lives because life itself is filled with wonder. Simply to breathe or to walk is a wondrous event. To watch a sunset or the play of light on a leaf, to experience the taste of our food or the movements of our bodies is to be in the presence of a mystery.

The pace of life today puts many of us in a hyperactive frenzy from which we never fully unwind. Consequently, we miss so much of the life around us. Taking time to experience simply means slowing down enough to pay attention to what we are doing. Take eating, for example. For the most part, Americans have lost the art of dining, and we are on our way to losing the art of preparing food. We gobble down fast, frozen, or microwaved food, often while driving, working, or watching television. We hardly take the time to notice what we are eating, let alone how it tastes. Similarly, we are losing the art of conversation. People today feel so pressed for time that they are often talking at, rather than really listening to, one another. Whether it's in our interpersonal relationships or the broader public discourse, we seem to fear that if we listen to others, we won't have time to get our own points across.

Taking time to meditate, to play, to get a massage, or just do nothing at all, can help slow us down enough to actually experience the life in front of us. We can live our lives in a sacred, fully conscious manner, or we can allow ourselves to go on autopilot. From a sacred perspective, the daily events of life—eating, talking with a friend, making love, or doing our work, are profound rituals to be celebrated and enjoyed. All it takes is what the Buddhists call "mindfulness," paying attention in each and every moment.

12 The Leisure to Grow

Change and growth take place when a person has risked himself and dares to become involved with experimenting with his own life.
—HERBERT OTTO

Time to Think

Leisure allows us to access parts of ourselves we might otherwise miss altogether. Aspects long suppressed or neglected may come bubbling to the surface when given the time and psychic space to emerge. We can heal old wounds, discover new interests and abilities, and see ourselves and our situations with new clarity. This, in turn, affords the possibility of making significant changes in our attitudes or life directions.

Much has been written about the dumbing down of America. Certainly, little in popular culture challenges us to think deeply or to seriously examine our own lives. Commercial television is by and large a mind-numbing wasteland. In recent years, we have seen serious books pushed off the shelves in favor of celebrity memoirs. We've seen the respect once reserved for serious thinkers transferred to talking-head experts, skilled at reducing their messages to thirty-second sound bites. We are used to being spoon-fed predigested arguments and canned conventional wisdom, tailor-made to fit specific, and often hidden, agendas. Yet, like the muscles of our bodies, our thinking muscles get sluggish without regular exercise. It's often easier to go along with the life program laid out for us by society, our parents, or our peers than to think for ourselves and make our own decisions. Especially if we are not used to it, we must make a considerable effort to overcome this inertia, or resistance, to self-directed thinking. This takes time, patience, and commitment.

We require leisure to think beyond the box of our immediate survival and daily personal concerns and consider our responsibilities to the world in which we live. It takes time to work out for ourselves our personal and social values and life priorities—to determine who we are and what we want our lives to be about. Joseph Campbell often recommended that people drop out of society for a period of time and devote themselves to a self-directed course of study, serious thought, and reflection—as he himself had done. While all may not find this practicable or desirable, we can all profit by taking some time for reflection and introspection.

It takes time to sort through our personal and societal conditioning and become conscious of our own thought processes. Yet only when we have become aware of the impact that our conditioning has on the way we view and react to the world can we freely determine our own values. Only when we have chosen our own values can we make intelligent and truly free choices as to what to do with our lives.

In addition to time for contemplation and for determining the direction we want our lives to take, it helps to take time to analyze how we use our time every day. We want to ensure that the way we use time truly serves our values, visions, and goals, and not allow it to be haphazardly frittered away on unconscious routine. Time management experts speak of the rule of one-to-four and the 80/20 principle. The rule of one-to-four states that for every four hours of work (or activity), one hour of planning is required to ensure the most effective use of this time. The 80/20 principle states that, as a general rule, only 20 percent of what we do is really effective, while the remaining 80 percent yields proportionally fewer results.

The key is to reflect on how we use our time and to become aware of the 20 percent and, by highlighting and expanding this, not only achieve greater results, but also make more time for other pursuits. By bringing awareness to how we spend our time, we have the opportunity to break out of the mold of routine and consciously choose how we will use the most precious resource we have—the time of our lives.

Time to Learn

Our word *leisure* comes to us by way of the French and originates in the Latin root *licere*, meaning "license." Leisure went to the aristocracy by right of birth and was licensed to a certain number of artists and intellectuals. These were given pensions, freeing them from the need to provide for their sustenance, and thus allowing them to concentrate on their music, art, writings, or studies. Throughout the nineteenth century, many hoped and believed that the technological advances of the Industrial Revolution would one day give the common man and woman the leisure to develop spiritually, intellectually, and culturally, and to participate more fully in the civic life of their communities. They looked forward to a cultural rebirth, which would inevitably come as people's attention would begin to shift away from the harsh struggle for economic survival, toward more creative and enriching pursuits.

Of course, as we discussed above, the expected increase in leisure failed to materialize. In fact, people actually have less time for self-betterment than they did thirty years ago. Understandably, many view learning and personal growth as a kind of luxury that has little to with their daily struggle to make ends meet. Moreover, if we follow the prevailing cultural pattern, we are more interested in acquiring stuff or in seeking entertainments than in developing ourselves intellectually, culturally, or spiritually.

The highest happiness of man as a thinking being is to have probed what is knowable and quietly to revere what is unknowable.

GOETHE

In antiquity men studied for their own sake; nowadays men study for the sake of {impressing} others. —CONFUCIUS

Where learning *is* valued, it's as a vehicle to "better" ourselves in market or economic terms. The application of market values to higher education has meant the decline of departments devoted to philosophy, art, and the humanities in general, in favor of business, science, and engineering, curricula, considered more likely to contribute to the economic growth of the community and the economic advancement of the individual. While much has been made of the historical and cultural illiteracy of today's youth, it seems clear that they are simply responding to the messages we've given them about what is important. Increasingly, learning is being viewed as a kind of commodity to be purchased in order to get ahead rather than something to be pursued for its own sake. This effects the society as much as the individual. The range of knowledge within the culture is diminished as,

229

time and again, individuals forego learning about what they are interested in, in favor of what will pay.

While the Taoists were not enamored with collecting knowledge for its own sake, they were very much interested in learning and experimentation. In fact, Joseph Needham credits the Taoist world-view with playing a significant role in the extraordinary scientific achievements and advances made by the Chinese.[35] The modern Indian philosopher J. Krishnamurti said, "Learning is the very essence of humility. . . ." It is in this spirit that we can speak of the Tao of Learning. The point of learning is not to become walking encyclopedias or to impress others with what we know. Indeed, learning is opening into new insights, sensitivities, vistas, and possibilities. This is always an essentially humbling, and most certainly *not* an ego-puffing, process. As Einstein put it, "The more I learn, the more I realize I don't know." The moment of learning is a creative awakening—an "aha"—that fills us with awe and wonder. Lifelong learning and a vigorous spirit of exploration helps keep us young and keeps life interesting and fresh.

The term *curriculum vitae,* which today is as used as sophisticated synonym for career résumé, literally means "a course of life study." Life itself is the great classroom, and the lessons we learn from it are the most significant. There is much we can learn without course fees, professors, or books. Indeed, we learn as much or more by intuition as by tuition. If we can learn to mine our own experience—detaching from and reflecting on the events of our lives—we will surely find nuggets of wisdom, life lessons more precious than gold.

The Taoist approach to inquiry begins with stilling the mind, then observing and penetrating into the essence of things, be they the physical forms and events of the natural world or the processes of our own minds. The Taoist approach assumes the intelligence of the universe. Its emphasis is on making ourselves more sensitive and receptive to the world around us rather than on collecting and analyzing data. This more feminine approach to inquiry requires leisure, a relaxed and patient state of mind that allows things and events to suggest their own organic solutions. Cultivating this awareness can help us face the challenges of the new millennium by bringing fresh insights into the issues that confront us. Take time to study, research, and meditate on subjects that arouse your curiosity and interest—take time to learn about yourself and your world.

Time to Express Yourself Creatively

The poet Wallace Stevens (who, incidentally, made his living as an attorney) said, "It is necessary to any originality to have the courage to be an amateur." It is often just this courage that we need to express ourselves creatively. Many of us have had few opportunities for self-expression and little encouragement for our innate creative capacities. Yet humans are naturally creative beings and, as such, require outlets for creative self-expression in order to be happy. If creativity is not already a way of life for you, if you don't make your living by expressing your innate gifts—dare to be an amateur!

> {Creativity is} like driving a car at night, you never see any further than your headlights, but you can make the whole trip that way.
>
> —E. L. DOCTOROW

At a minimum, try to make some time to allow yourself some form of creative self-expression several times a week. Your vehicle for expression might be writing in a journal, taking photographs, singing, or sailing. It could be painting or writing poetry, woodworking, or some kind of craft. It might be home decorating, gardening, bird-watching, or marathon running. The important thing is that it's something that's really you—something you love to do.

In my work as a career consultant, I have worked with many who have found in a hobby or leisure activity what turned out to be their true calling in life. Often, the road to a new career opens when we begin experimenting with new interests in our free time. We're able to gain confidence, skill, and experience, without the pressure of turning a new interest or skill into a moneymaking proposition. Leonardo da Vinci said: "To enjoy—to love a thing for its own sake and for no other reason." Do the things you enjoy, the ones you love for their own sake, even if you can't find a way to make them pay the bills. Your love will provide the motivation to do it well. When you excel at something, you are likely to get paid for it—sooner or later.

One financially successful, but very unhappy, man came to me in desperation. He took a somewhat defiant approach and was adamant throughout the exploratory exercises that all he wanted to do was sail his boat. Once I determined that he was sincere, we began to develop a plan for how he could make a living from this passion of his. Eventually, he moved to Ha-

Do not attempt to be a particular type of person, but be many types simultaneously.

CHUANG TZU

waii, bought a larger sailboat, and began taking tourists out for jaunts around the islands. Of course, he took a significant pay cut, and admittedly, his work was not a great humanitarian service. Yet too often, we fail to recognize the value of simple happiness. A happy person cannot help but spread happiness, even as a miserable person cannot avoid spreading gloom.

In the best of all worlds, the way you love to express yourself the most is the basis of your career. Yet even if you never do (or never can) make a living from them, do the things you love. Follow the impulses of your heart. If you love to sing but know you will never become a professional singer, SING ANYWAY. If you love to write but can't imagine how you will ever get published, WRITE ANYWAY. Whatever it is that you love to do—DO IT.

仁 The Leisure to Relate

We are all born for love. . . . It is the principle of existence and its only end. —BENJAMIN DISRAELI

Time for Our Mates

If the family is the foundation of society, then the relationship between the adult family members is the foundation of the family. The strongest families are those in which the adult partners are loving and devoted friends. Parents are role models, and the way that they relate to one another will shape their children's relationships with the opposite sex for years to come. We communicate far more to children by our example than in any other way. Yet too often, we may be giving them the wrong message. Today, when the average American working couple spends just twelve minutes a day talking to each other, it is probably not surprising that over 50 percent of marriages end in divorce.[36]

The time and money pressures of modern life put tremendous strain on relationships between couples. In 90 percent of divorces, arguments about money play a significant role. This no doubt is due, in part, to the pressures couples feel to conform to social standards related to consumption. The physical and psychological stress associated with the time crunch shortens tempers and makes people more irritable than they might otherwise be. The breakup of extended families and the loss of real neighborhoods isolates the nuclear family and puts additional stresses on couples. Overtaxed relationships often have unrealistic expectations placed on them; too often we expect our partners to fulfill all of our needs and solve all of our problems. Moreover, our relationships with our partners provide the only forum many of us have to vent frustrations we feel about a wide range of topics, from specific issues related to work or childrearing to more generalized feelings of loneliness or alienation. This venting can damage our relationships if we don't take enough time to nurture and strengthen them in positive and supportive ways.

The market values of the commercial culture are often carried over into our relationships. We are encouraged by the popular culture to see ourselves and our potential partners as commodities in a kind of mate market. This affects the choices we make when selecting prospective partners. A look at popular men's and women's magazines gives us the idea that relationships are more about negotiating the best deal than finding true love. If we accept this negotiation model, we are more likely to give up on a relationship if we see it failing to gratify our needs. After all, if we view our partners as commodities, we can always return to the marketplace and try to negotiate a "better deal."

While we often expect too much from our relationships, we are likely to invest too little of ourselves in them. The time stresses and the emphasis on personal achievement that pervade our culture cause us too often to leave our relationships until everything else is done. Determine to give your relationship with your spouse or partner the quality time it deserves. At a minimum, your relationship deserves that you take time:

- to share with one another your individual values, visions, and goals
- to share with one another your fears, doubts, and concerns
- to discuss with one another the events of the day
- to maintain a quality of romance and an exciting sex life
- to be affectionate
- for shared activities
- to develop shared goals
- to play with one another and be silly

Time for Our Children

The so-called "men's movement," which began to surface in the late 1980s and early 1990s, was widely ridiculed in the media and became the butt of many popular jokes. Nevertheless, important issues were raised by some of the more thoughtful leaders associated with this "movement." Robert Bly, for instance, asked us to consider the impact on the psychology of the individual and on society as a whole that attended the shift from an agrarian to an industrial economy. The family structure changed in a dramatic way as the male typically became the sole breadwinner in a home he was now physically absent from for long periods of time. Often, the father's "absence" was more than physical, more than missing the emotional bonding that comes with consistent prolonged daily interaction. Long hours of tedious, spiritually and psychologically draining work often rendered fathers emotionally absent, even when they were at home.

For Bly, a lack of trust between men is a direct result of the removal of the father from the home. There is, of course, no great mystery in this: people tend to trust what they know and distrust what they are unfamiliar with. Men who don't intimately know their own fathers are less likely to trust other men. Similarly, women who don't know their fathers are less likely to trust men. Recognizing and understanding the significance of this is especially important to us at this time, as we are undergoing another great historic change in working patterns and thus in home life. The dramatic increase in the number of women in the workplace over the last several decades has yielded the first generation raised with "absent mothers" as well as absent fathers.

It would be wrong to conclude that in every case, young children of parents who both work outside of home suffer psychologically as a result. There is much that parents can do, and indeed that many parents are doing, to mitigate these effects. Yet counteracting them requires an awareness of the potential problems associated with parental absence, and a conscious effort to counteract them. This is an awareness that many lack and an effort that many are either unwilling or unable to make. The problem is compounded by the fact that the nuclear family is much more isolated today. A century ago, extended families living in the same household were common; today, they are extremely rare, and parents alone must do all of the childrearing.

Since the time that many of us can spend with our children is limited, giving them our full and undivided attention when we are available makes

a big difference. It helps to designate some time at least once a week for each parent to spend alone with every child in the family. This is in addition to regular family evenings and weekend outings. Spending quality time with our children helps, yet it too recalls the efficiency model of the marketplace. We are likely to discount the value that our mere physical presence has in making a child feel nurtured, loved, and secure.

According to Jessie O'Neill, author of *The Golden Ghetto*, "The average working woman plays with her children forty minutes a week and shops six hours."[37] The juxtaposition of these two statistics makes the case for a redefinition of our cultural values in a striking way. While in recent years, fathers have begun spending more time with their children, it still only amounts to seventy minutes a week on average.

Balancing family and career is certainly a challenge in today's world and one that we are only beginning to address as a society. For some couples, home-based business provides at least a partial solution to the problem. Others are deciding that it is essential for one parent to remain at home with the children, at least through the preschool years. Of course, this often means making some financial adjustments. Many who decide to restructure their lives and simplify their material requirements are motivated to do so by their desire to spend more time with their families. They reason that if they made more money but, as a consequence, suffered a divorce or allowed their children to grow up without getting to know them, it would be a very bad bargain indeed.

Time for Our Communities

The word *community* comes from a Latin root meaning "common." The classic Taoists advocated small human settlements because they believed it helped to maintain our human-heartedness, a feeling of sharing a common experience with others. In a major city, we can step over the body of a homeless person lying on the sidewalk as if that human being were just so much debris. This simply wouldn't be possible in a small community, where everyone knew one another. Yet it is not only the large urban centers that have lost the sense of community; in many ways, suburban life can be even more isolating.

Where once the experience of community was part and parcel of being born into human society, today we must deliberately seek it out. And many are doing just that. In the 1990s, America underwent a unprecedented demographic shift as population growth began to move away from urban centers and their environs, toward small towns and rural communities. Here, living costs are cheaper, the pace of life is slower, and people are more likely to know and relate to one another. People are looking for a sense of community and belonging. Where they are unable to find it in their local neighborhoods, many are finding it in association with like-minded individuals.

In facilitating life's work development seminars and support groups, I have seen firsthand how group dynamics can empower individuals. As people come to recognize that they are not alone—that others share the same aspirations, doubts, and challenges—they often feel a profound sense of relief. Instead of wasting energy wondering if they are strange for wanting more, or castigating themselves for not already having made greater progress, they are able to focus on the issue at hand with renewed vigor and commitment. Moreover, people in this kind of group setting have the opportunity to exchange ideas and information and to feed off of one another's energy and enthusiasm.

While others may inspire us, we can only find sustained motivation within ourselves. Yet here, too, the group experience can play a significant role. As people begin to view their own individual quests in relation to a broader social context, their personal search takes on new meaning. They begin to feel that in confronting and solving their own problems, they are participating in something bigger than themselves. Beyond these obvious benefits, there is an intangible component to the group experience. Each group takes on a life of its own—a creative synthesis emerges out of the interaction of the individuals in specific groups.

People are finding these same benefits—self-affirmation, information exchange, inspiration, motivation, and creative synthesis—in groups dedicated to a variety of purposes. From enhancing spiritual awareness or artistic development to advocating social action or public policy, from enjoying shared interests like gardening or nature walks to simply sharing meals and outings—people today are building a sense of community and shared experience through associations. Truly, as Aristotle said, "Man is a social animal." It is important for all of us to find ways to experience a sense of community in the fractured and often chaotic world we live in. Our human-heartedness depends on it.

The Philosophy of Greed

Economics is being taught without any awareness of the view of human nature that underlies present-day economic theory.

—E. F. SCHUMACHER

Through the ages, human beings have advanced a variety of social philosophies, or ideal visions of human society. Modern economics began as a branch of social, or what was then termed "moral," philosophy. The peculiar "moral philosophy" advanced by early economists (and largely embraced by their successors) assumes, first, that there is a universal human nature. Second, it assumes that this human nature is rooted in selfishness, greediness, or in polite terms, "self-interest." Third, it assumes that this greedy human nature is essentially fixed and incapable of transformation. Finally (and in this respect, it is most unique), it argues that greedy human nature is without the need of transformation, that greed itself is a high moral virtue.

Today, many challenge the concept of human nature. They argue that human behavior varies to such a degree as to preclude any judgment about what is natural. Of those philosophical traditions that do recognize a general human nature, many (including the Taoist) assume that human nature is essentially good and that to act in a greedy or selfish manner is to act in a manner inconsistent with one's "original nature." Of those moral philosophies—for example, the Christian—that hold man's original nature to be sinful and corrupt, most hold that this corrupt or carnal nature is capable of transformation and, indeed, ought to be transformed. One made "new in Christ" is capable of loving his enemies, blessing those that curse him, and being generous and forgiving. Finally, no other social philosophy of which I am aware elevates greed to the status of a moral virtue.

The impact of this strange new moral philosophy was profound. Of course, greed was nothing new to the world. Yet it was an impulse that traditional cultures had sought to keep in check. What was new was the elevation of greed, or self-interest, to the status of a moral virtue, and indeed *the critical virtue,* on which an entire culture was to be based. Karl Polyani writes: "The true criticism of market society is not that it is based on economics—in a sense, every and any society must be based on it—but that its economy was based on self-interest. Such an organization of economic life is entirely unnatural, in the strictly empirical sense of *exceptional.*"[38]

In the late eighteenth century, Adam Smith, the "father" of modern economics, put forth in his classic work *The Wealth of Nations* the theory that the "propensity to barter, truck or exchange one thing for another" was the overriding human motivation and that it had been responsible for elevating man from the primitive, or savage, state to that of civilization. This theory was to have a profound effect on the modern world. As Karl Polyani writes: "No misreading of the past ever proved to be more prophetic of the future. For, while in Adam Smith's day, that propensity had hardly shown up on a considerable scale in any observable community . . . a hundred years later, an industrial system was in full swing over a major part of the planet which . . . implied that the human race was swayed in all of its economic activities, if not also in its political, intellectual, and spiritual pursuits, by this one propensity."[39]

Never has there been a better example (or at least one of such scale) of the power of a self-fulfilling prophecy. As more people came to see human nature as Adam Smith had envisioned it, Western culture was remade in the image he had laid out. It's difficult for us to fully realize the significance of the cultural transformation that this new economic theory of human nature wrought and its impact on our daily lives. In the words of John Maynard Keynes, arguably the most influential economist of the twentieth century: "The *ideas* of economists and political philosophers, both when they are right and when they are wrong are more powerful than commonly understood. Indeed the world is ruled by little else. Practical men who believe themselves to be quite exempt from intellectual influences are usually the slaves of some defunct economist." (Emphasis mine.)

The moral philosophy advanced by modern economics is unique among all others, not only with respect to its unusual view of human nature, but also in its global reach and dominance. In the history of mankind, no other social philosophy has penetrated a more diverse range of ethnic and national groups, nor held so many under its influence. Perhaps even more extraordinary is the speed at which this philosophy swept across the globe.

Originally, the theory of economic self-interest or the "natural" greediness of human beings was used to explain social inequality and to justify the status of the new rulers of the moneyed class. Why were a few so obviously better off than the rest? The gist of the philosophy expounded by early economists such as Ricardo and Malthus was that while everyone was greedy—some were more successful than others. This was as it should be, indeed, the way God, or later nature (genetics), intended it. Herbert Spencer, who coined the term "survival of the fittest," attempted to apply Darwin's theory of evolution to the economic domain. For him, the rich became so because they were biologically superior, more naturally fit, human beings.

Philosophies such as these naturally held a certain charm for the well-to-do, but did little for the common man beyond explaining why his betters were better. He was too busy struggling to survive. Of what use was his own greedy nature if he had so little opportunity to exercise it? Many of the working poor, particularly in the industrial sector, rejected the theory of the innate superiority of the company owners and organized themselves for what were often long and difficult labor struggles. Common people, including the majority of the American middle class, tended to stick with traditional religious morality and were largely untouched by the values of the economic self-interest theory of human nature throughout the first three-quarters of the nineteenth century.

Then, in the late nineteenth, and early twentieth, centuries, American commercial interests, recognizing that traditional values were impeding maximum economic development—particularly mass consumption—developed powerful new systems for maximizing and mechanizing consumption. A variety of new technologies (including advertising, consumer credit, the entertainment and fashion industries, mass media, and chain stores), were developed with the aim, not of increasing production, but of increasing consumption.

These new systems were extremely successful in altering the prevailing moral climate to favor greater consumption. In the process, they democratized greed. For the first time, this new moral philosophy had real popular appeal. Around the world, profound cultural change occurred as traditional values were tossed aside in favor of the newly democratic social philosophy of the commercial culture. With the promise and the reality of more material "goodies," the mass of people began to accept and to internalize the new economic values. For now, as liberals are fond of saying, they had "a stake in the system."

Having accepted the moral philosophy of greed and having elevated it to the status of the organizing principle of economic and political society, is it surprising that we see today a breakdown of religious, ethical, community, and family values? All of these values require that the individual check, restrain, or somehow mitigate his or her self-interest. Religious, political, and academic commentators decry the breakdown of the family and the loss of community. Yet isn't this breakdown a natural result of building a culture on the moral foundation of greed and economic self-interest? A look at traditional peoples undergoing rapid economic development in their native lands, or at immigrants to the United States, makes clear the impact of the modern economic system on moral life. Within a single generation, religious, ethical, community, and family values of long duration are severely weakened, and by the second generation, economic self-interest comes to dominate all other values. The peculiar moral philosophy advocated by the early economists is today the single-most powerful social philosophy on the face of the Earth.

The simplest way of understanding any social philosophy is to ask, "What does it have to say about human nature?" The social philosophy of modern commercial culture assumes that human beings are basically and inevitably greedy. In other words, we are acting naturally when we are motivated by economic self-interest. Of course, even economists recognize that people do at times act with compassion, generosity, and selflessness, but this is considered an aberration. For the Taoists, man's "original nature," or natural state, is one of harmony with the universe. There is no original sin that must be overcome. Selfishness and greed are not our natural state but only symptoms of having lost the "way."

CHAPTER EIGHT

Li

THE BEAUTY OF ABUNDANCE

A thing of beauty is a joy forever:
Its loveliness increases; It will never
Pass into nothingness.

—JOHN KEATS

This chapter examines the principle of *li* and the beauty of the Tao revealed in the natural order of the universe. The organic patterns within nature, the collective human consciousness, and the life of each of us as individuals reflect the natural order in life. For one living in the Tao, these organic patterns serve as essential guideposts on the path of beauty. The role of art is to orient the human imagination to these patterns and to show us in them a reflection of the wholeness, harmony, and rhythm of the universe. Today, art has largely been taken over by commercial interests whose purpose is not to lead us to transcendence or the path of beauty but to sell us things. This chapter will consider the effect this subversion of art has in promoting a lack of consciousness in the broader culture, and steps we can take to mitigate the influence of these effects in our lives. It will also explore a variety of practical ways in which we can sensitize ourselves to the beauty in life all around us. In the related exercises at the end of the book, you will have the opportunity to consider how you can bring more genuine beauty into your life.

If we were to look at human beings in any sort of objective way, taking into account the vast span of their existence, we would have to say that beauty is a fundamental principle of human life. To get a sense of this, we needn't travel the world or even visit art museums with large international collections. A visit to a local natural history museum with a solid cultural anthropology collection will suffice. Here we find that the artifacts of daily life in prehistoric and so-called primitive cultures were things of remarkable beauty.

Moreover, "as anthropologists deep in the study of primitive life have repeatedly pointed out, it is by no means clear that the necessary came before the beautiful."[1] Indeed, the beautiful arose together with the necessary and perhaps, in some cases, even before it. As human beings made things, they made them beautifully. Making no distinction between sacred and profane, they endowed the tools, artifacts, and means of individual adornment of their everyday lives with aesthetic value and spiritual meaning as well as functional utility.[2] This sense of beauty in the making of everyday objects was carried forward in more technologically advanced civilizations through the tradition of the artisan and craftsman. Lewis Mumford writes, "The craftsman, like the artist, lived in his work, for his work, by his work; the rewards of labor were intrinsic to the activity itself, and the effect of the art was merely to heighten and intensify these natural organic processes—not to serve as compensation or escape."[3]

Beyond this, beauty has long been fundamental to the human experience, for the simple reason that people lived in nature. Whether they lived high in the mountains or nestled in river valleys, in dense jungles or on wind-swept deserts, they could not help but be struck by the beauty of the natural world. Today, for most of us, the natural world is no longer a part of our everyday experience. Nature has become "other," a place to visit on the weekends or on holiday. Moreover, the mechanical mode of manufacture places little value on aesthetics or spiritual meaning in the objects of everyday life. For us then beauty is a choice.

Like leisure, beauty isn't really necessary to our survival. If we are merely units of production and consumption, then beauty has no intrinsic value. It is only a commodity like any other, to be sold at a price the market will bear. If, on the other hand, we are spiritual beings, beauty is fundamental to our existence. Beauty is nourishment for our souls—as necessary to our spiritual growth and well-being as food is to our physical sustenance. Surely, an abundant life is one rich in inner and outer beauty. Yet, as we will dis-

We are immersed in beauty but our eyes have no clear vision.

EMERSON

cover, we needn't possess great material wealth to live a beautiful life. For beauty is *not* a commodity but part and parcel of the inherent structure of the universe, and as such, it is revealed in the natural expressions of those who are motivated by love. This chapter will examine what beauty is, why it's important to us, and how we can cultivate it in our lives. We will begin by exploring the Chinese concept of *li*.

The Principle of Beauty

The concept of li *is actually much more inclusive than either the Christian concept of {God's} law or the Indian concept of* dharma. —WEI MING

In the context that it is used here, *li* is usually translated "principle" or "pattern."[4] In ancient times, it was noticed that fields under cultivation, laid out in conformity with the natural contour of the land, formed visible patterns. It was to these patterns that *li* originally referred. Later, the term was used to indicate naturally occurring patterns such as markings in jade, the grain in wood or bamboo, the texture of muscle fiber, and so on.

Still later, *li* came to mean the "organizing principle," or "inner law," of things. For the Neo-Confucian Chu Hsi (1130–1200 C.E.), who was influenced by both the classical Taoist and Buddhist philosophies, every physical thing in the universe has both *li* and *ch'i*.[5] As he put it, "If there were no Ch'i, Li would have no way of manifesting itself and no dwelling place." Conversely, "The activity of Ch'i depends absolutely on that of Li."[6] *Li* is the invisible (nonmaterial) inner organization or organic pattern of a thing made manifest by *ch'i*. A thing's *li* exists prior to its taking form in the material world, that is, before it is animated by *ch'i*.

Gathered up, all things are unified in one supreme Principle of Being. Separated from one another, every one of them has its own Principle of being. —CHU HSI

Chu Hsi referred to *li* as the principle or organic pattern of each separate thing, as well as the cosmic principle of organization that pervades the natural world. While from the perspective of the Taoists, things arise without a causative agent (or Creator), the pattern of their interaction is not random but conforms to the cosmic order, or *li*, of the universe. It is in this sense that *li* is referred to as the "inner law of things." This cosmic *li* runs through all levels of Being, including the human being. As Chu Hsi puts it, "Principle [*li*] is not some separate thing in front of us; rather it's in our minds. People must discover for themselves that this thing [*li*] is truly in them, then everything will be okay."[7]

Thus, we can conceive of *li* in three broad dimensions: First, there is the *li* of each individual thing; second, the *li* within the human consciousness; and finally, the cosmic *li*, which in a sense is the grand pattern of patterns. It is this three-fold understanding of *li* that we will use to elucidate our discussion of beauty. *Beauty is the revelation of the organic patterns, the underlying cosmic principle of organization in and of things.* The principle of *li* will help us to appreciate the Beauty of (or Tao in) the whole universe, the Beauty of (or Tao in) the individual thing, as well as the Beauty of (or Tao in) the human consciousness.

 ## The Rhythm of Beauty

> *Art, as far as it is able, follows nature,*
> *as a pupil imitates his master; thus your art must be,*
> *as it were, God's grandchild.* —DANTE

Whether we are talking about the cosmic *li* of Heaven (*T'ien-li*), the *li* of the human psyche, or the *li* of a specific thing, we are talking about a principle of organization that reveals itself in rhythmic patterns. We know that all apparently solid objects are actually organized patterns of vibrating atoms. These patterns in turn endow the object with its specific characteristics. The characteristics as well as the vibratory patterns that underlie them reflect the innate intelligence, or inner law *(li)*, of the thing itself.[8] So, too, on a cosmic level, individual things fit together in a grand pattern, the cosmic *li*, reflected in the rhythmic interaction of all things within the universe.

This suggests the image of a grand patchwork quilt in which each of the separate and unique individual designs fit together in a grand design. Yet this image is too static. A better metaphor is the Hindu image of the Net of Indra. In this grand net, a reflective gem is placed at each cross-stitch, such that each gem reflects all the others, as well as itself within the others—on and on. Together, all of these reflecting reflections create the grand tapestry of light that is the whole. These three: wholeness (the net), harmony (the reflective quality of the gems), and rhythm (the movement of light) are the constituents of Beauty.[9]

Earlier, we said that all peoples consciously living in nature live in Beauty. The definition above (i.e., wholeness, harmony, rhythm) helps us understand how this is so. Virtually without exception, for peoples living in nature, the portion of the natural world they themselves occupy suggests a larger *whole*, a more expansive world than that of their immediate environment, as well as an underlying ground of being, back of it (i.e., Tao, God, Great Spirit, etc.). They recognized the interdependent relationship of all things and thus, deeply felt a need to be in *harmony* with the occupants of the visible world around them as well as with the beings, powers, or forces of the invisible realm.

Finally, all nature is *rhythm*, and manifestly so for those who live in it. Whether it is in the beating of the human heart, the inflow and out-go of breath, the patterns of a leaf, the sound of a stream, the migrations of animals, or the cycles of days or seasons, the pulse of life is rhythmic. Virtually without exception, traditional peoples celebrated the "whr" (wholeness, harmony, and rhythm) of the universe in festivals and rituals with chanting, singing, and dancing—in other words, in rhythmic expressions. We could say that the structure of human consciousness is a rhythmic pattern that reflects, responds to, and recreates (through ritual, myth, and art) the rhythmic patterns of the universe.

The term Tao refers to the vast and great, the term li *includes the innumerable vein-like patterns included in the Tao.*

CHU HSI

> *Beauty is before me*
> *And beauty is behind me*
> *Above and below me hovers the beautiful*
> *I am surrounded by it*
> *I am immersed in it*
> *In my youth I am aware of it*
> *And in old age I shall walk quietly*
> *The beautiful trail.*
>   —NAVAJO PRAYER

When we say that all nature is beautiful and that those who truly live in it live in beauty, we are of course speaking of a Beauty that transcends the beautiful and the ugly. Beauty is not merely the attractive or agreeable. The destruction, death, and inherent violence in nature reveal as well the wholeness, harmony, and rhythm in life. They are as much a part of its Beauty as the serene quietude of a mountain lake on a warm spring day. "Beauty is," as the Japanese artist Sōetsu Yanagi has written, "that which has been liberated—or freed—from duality." We could say that Beauty is the human apprehension of Eternity, or more poetically, the beatific vision of God. It is in this sense that we can say with the poet Keats, "Beauty is truth, truth beauty,—that is all/Ye know on earth, and all ye need to know."

The fact that most of us no longer live in nature doesn't mean that we can't participate in its beauty and mystery. Like the Taoists before them, eighteenth-century European Pantheists like Goethe and nineteenth-century American transcendentalists like Thoreau advocated the contemplation of nature as a path to transcendence.[10] Their writings exhort us to take the natural world as our temple and find in it the revelation and Beauty of transcendent Mystery. When Goethe said, "Do not look beyond the Phenomena [the Ten Thousand Things]; they are the Doctrine {li}," he showed an understanding that runs parallel with that of the Taoists. The part reveals the whole and points to the Mystery in, through, and back of it all (Tao). Again, Goethe: "If the entire is to feed thy soul, / "Then in the littlest thou must see the whole."[11]

Is it really remarkable that those who live in nature—be they ancient Chinese Taoists, eighteenth-century Native Americans, or nineteenth-century naturalists like John Muir—so often said essentially the same things? For example, when Muir said, "When we tug at a single thing in nature, we find that it is attached to the rest of the world," it could have been Chuang Tzu or Chief Seattle speaking. Wisdom is inherent in nature and reveals itself to people of any nation, race, or time if they will open themselves up to it. We too can avail ourselves of this wisdom by making time to spend in nature.

While few of us have the opportunity (or even the desire) to retreat into the woods for a couple of years like Thoreau did on Walden pond, we can enjoy shorter outings in nature. Backpacking into remote areas or even camping away from the crowds can be a rejuvenating and potentially life-changing experience. Spending extended periods of time in nature allows our bodies to slow down to the rhythms of nature, and to begin to feel at one with them. Our senses become more acute and our attention spans elongate. We begin to notice things on the third or fourth day that we might have overlooked on the first. In this state of grace, we can begin to more fully appreciate the transcendent wisdom that abounds in nature.

> *To see a World in a grain of sand*
> *And a Heaven in a wild flower,*
> *Hold Infinity in the palm of your hand,*
> *And Eternity in an hour.*
> —WILLIAM BLAKE

The characteristics of beauty in nature (wholeness, harmony, and rhythm) are as well the essential elements of art (more on this below). It is in this that art imitates nature. Art imitates nature, not in the production of likenesses (poor copies of originals), but by evoking in its patterns a window on the underlying pattern of the universe. Our word *art* comes from the Greek *artunien,* meaning "to arrange." Art is a fortunate arrangement that, through its wholeness, harmony, and rhythm, becomes transparent to the transcendent reality. Art provides a window through which we may gaze upon the invisible. Yet the fact that a window exists does not mean that everyone will want to look through it, nor that everyone who does will really be able to see.

> *The Kingdom of Heaven is spread upon the earth and men do not see it.*
> —THE GOSPEL ACCORDING TO THOMAS

Still, the contemplation of art, like the contemplation of nature, provides a vehicle for the revelation of Mystery. If the eye of intuition is open, we may travel either path and find that it leads to the same transcendent reality. If not, all bets are off. When Blake said, "A fool sees not the same tree as a wise man," he was giving us essentially the warning vis-a-vis the contemplation of nature that the Chinese painter Ching Hao expressed with reference to art. Ching Hao said, "There is an appearance which may not be mistaken for the true reality. . . . Unless this is understood, one will draw a mere likeness, but *not* capture the real essence. . . . A likeness is what you get when you portray a thing's form and miss the spirit. *Chen* [reality] means when you have captured both the form and the spirit. When spirit is left out, the form is dead."[12]

So it is with our daily existence; it too becomes dead when the spirit is left out. The likeness that is devoid of spirit in art corresponds to the idea of maya or glamour in the world of human events. *Glamour* means "a magic spell: bewitchment"; and *maya*, "magic: illusion." To see the ego as the final term of the self is a form of bewitchment; to see the physical world as a random collection of solid, static, and separate parts is to be under a kind of magic spell. We overcome the magic as we penetrate the veil of forms and unite with the consciousness that pervades all—within and without. We break the spell as we come to realize that within and without, higher and lower, better and worse, sacred and profane, and so on are all distinctions of the mind and not characteristics of reality. Coming to this realization seems to happen as a result of a process, or spiritual journey, that frequently requires a great deal of time and effort. Yet, all the while, this awareness resides within, a part of the structure of human consciousness. Again, as Chu Hsi put it, "Principle [*li*] is not some separate thing in front of us; rather it's in our minds."

 ## The Pattern of the Mind

The pattern of man's behavior is not to be found in any code, but in the principles of the universe, which is continually revealing to us its own nature. —ANANDA K. COOMARASWAMY

The Jungian term *archetype* gives insight into Chu Hsi's expression that *li* is within our minds. Of course, we must realize that here, by "mind," we do not mean the limited cerebral function or individual personality, but the entire intelligence of the human organism. To say that *li* is within our minds is to say that there is a definite pattern or structure to human consciousness, which transcends the idiosyncratic conditioning of the individual as well as the social conditioning, customs, and mores of the local group. This pattern or structure is revealed in the archetypes of the collective unconscious. In Jung's words, "The archetypes are the numinous [spiritual], structural elements of the psyche and possess a certain autonomy and specific energy which enables them to attract, out of the conscious mind, those contents which are best suited to themselves." We can think of archetypes as principles of organization (*li*) within the human consciousness, through which the transcendent reality (Tao) makes itself known to us.

What Jung called "archetypes," Adolf Bastian before him had referred to as "elementary ideas."[13] Specific local groups represent these elementary ideas in their own unique ways, which Bastian called "ethnic ideas." For example, the concept of a transcendent reality is a universal elementary idea appearing in a wide variety of cultures across time and place. In many cultures, this elementary idea or archetype was personified as a local deity (e.g., Yahweh or Indra). In other cultures, it was represented as an impersonal force (e.g., Tao or Brahman). These are all ethnic or cultural manifestations of a universal elementary idea. The specific content, whether manifested in the myth of a culture or in the dreams and visions of the individual, gives concrete form to the preexisting archetype in much the same way that *ch'i* gives concrete form to the *li* of a thing in the physical world. The specific content (e.g., a cultural myth) makes the underlying archetype visible, even as *ch'i* (matter/energy) makes the underlying *li* of a thing apparent.

> *Innate Ideas are in Every Man, Born with him; they are truly Himself.*
> *The Man who says that we have No Innate Ideas must be a Fool & Knave,*
> *Having No Conscience or Innate Science.* —WILLIAM BLAKE

Whether we are speaking of elementary ideas, archetypes, or the *li* within the mind, the specific content is less important than the underlying structure or principle of organization. It was just this understanding that allowed Joseph Campbell to recognize, in the myths of peoples from vastly different times and cultures, the same essential structure or pattern. From the vast range of human societies across the sweep of human history (and prehistory), Campbell identified four pedagogical models, or cultural paradigms. He called these: the Way of the Animal Powers, The Way of the Seeded Earth, The Way of Celestial Lights, and The Way of Man.[14] While the cultural content varies a great deal, taking on, according to time and place, its own ethnic inflection, the elementary pattern or structure is essentially the same for all societies within each of these groups. This kind of classification is not unlike literary genres, which are recognizable because they follow identifiable story patterns. Though these mythological "genres" vary in form, they all refer to the same underlying reality or elementary idea.

The organizing principle (*li*), of things proscribes their potential outcomes. For example, the fact that the human being stands and walks erect shapes his experience in a variety of ways. Chapter 5 briefly examined how this affects childbirth and development, which in turn has reverberating effects on the psychology of the individual and on the organization of hu-

When one approaches the Wonderful, one knows not whether art is Tao or Tao is art.

HUI TS'UNG

man societies. Beyond these effects, standing erect permits the free use of the hands. (In fact, one of the earliest hominoid types is called *homo habilis*, literally "handy man.") Our erect posture determines (quite literally) the way we see the world and has numerous other effects I haven't space to explore here.

In much the same way that the structure of the human body shapes human behavior, the underlying structure of human consciousness shapes the archetypes of the collective unconscious and their manifestations. It is certainly remarkable, for example, that in so-called primitive cultures as remote from one another as Africa, North America, and Polynesia, we find essentially the same myth as to the origin of a primary vegetal food source (though in each case, the plant itself is different). Where do these myths come from? What Jung or Campbell would say is that they come from the realm of dreams or the nonrational wisdom of the body. They would argue that, in a sense, the structure of human consciousness is shaped by the structure of the human body.

Yet both the body and the consciousness associated with it are manifestations of an underlying energy (*ch'i*) and intelligence (*li*) that pervade the manifest universe and yet exist prior to it (Tao). Moreover, the image or symbolic representation of transcendent reality—whether conceived as the impersonal Tao, or Brahman, or as the personal Yahweh, Allah, or Shiva— is but a metaphor of a transcendent reality that is beyond human capacity to render in anything other than symbolic language.

We can (if we can) recognize what the classical Taoists were saying— even though we are not Chinese and even though some two thousand years have passed since their words were first recorded—because the capacity for this recognition is part of the organic pattern (or *li*) of human consciousness. Yet the reality to which the term *Tao* or *God* points is not to be confused with the term used to convey the idea to human consciousness. (The name that can be named is not the real name.) While we in the West tend to take God as a literal fact and therefore to accept or reject religious teachings on literal grounds, in the East, deities are commonly understood to be metaphors.

> *We are the deities, . . . there has never been a time even in our most black and vicious moods when the deities and their qualities were not fully actualized by us and fully exemplified by our every thought and action.*
> —TARTHUNG TULKU

For example, in Indian and Tibetan mythology, a given deity is recognized as a *representation* of some kind of power, be it transcendent, cosmological, natural, or psychic. The deity is not viewed as the power itself but as a representation of it to human consciousness. Thus, in art, a deity may be interchangeably represented as an icon (an anthropomorphic symbol), a *yantra* (a geometric symbol), or as a *mantra* (an auditory symbol). Whatever level or aspect of power the particular deity represents, the symbol is used to awaken awareness of that power in the consciousness of the beholder of art. The power is worshipped, recognized, or identified with, through the vehicle of the deity, which in turn is represented through the vehicles of icons, yantras, and mantras as well as through dance, storytelling, theater, and so on. The deity, to say nothing of the means through which it is worshipped, is never to be confused with the reality it represents. Moreover, it is never to be viewed as something separate from the human being. Among the Tantrics of India, there is a familiar saying that makes this clear: "By none but god shall a god be worshipped."[15]

It is not Arts that follow & attend upon Empire, but Empire that attends upon & follows the Arts.

WILLIAM BLAKE

Religion and art are thus names for one and the same experience— an intuition of reality and of identity.

—ANANDA K. COOMARASWAMY

There is an interesting area of ongoing medical research, which by way of analogy can help us understand how the principle of organization of the whole can exist within the part. It has been known for some time that embryonic stem cells have the capacity to become the cells of various organs. Recently, researchers have devised means of triggering stem cells into becoming liver, bone, bladder, or various other kinds of cells.[16] This could only be possible because the organic pattern of the whole organism is already contained within the part. By analogy, we could say that the human being is a kind of stem cell of the entire living organism of the universe. The human being is a part that contains, within the structure of its consciousness, innate knowledge of the organic pattern of the whole. It is possible to create an environment in which the human cell becomes conscious of the whole organism. This is the task of art and the "purpose" of the spiritual path.

The Role of Art

Degrade first the Arts if you'd Mankind Degrade.
—WILLIAM BLAKE

In the last chapter, we briefly explored how the commercial ethic—call it greed or economic self-interest—has come to dominate the collective imagination. This is critical since cultures are not formed or transformed by reason but by the human imagination. As the great historian Arnold Toynbee saw it, civilizations are born as a result of a series of creative responses to various challenges that beset a given people at a particular time and place. These creative responses are the products of the human imagination—and symbols, not facts; metaphors, not metrics, are the language of the imagination.

Cultural battles are neither fought nor won in the realm of reason and ideas. They are waged in the human imagination. This is evidenced in our culture by the fact that so many excellent criticisms of commercial culture seem to have had so little effect in transforming it. Now and again, an astute thinker comes along with a brilliant and seemingly devastating analysis of prevailing culture. His or her analysis may for a time attract attention and stimulate debate; yet things go on as before. Indeed, if anything, the commercial culture takes hold of ever greater numbers of the world's population and penetrates into those remaining areas of society that heretofore have proved most resistant to its ethic.

> *When nations grow Old,*
> *The Arts grow Cold*
> *And Commerce settles on every tree.*
> —WILLIAM BLAKE

Writers and thinkers may speak to our intellects and, if they are passionate enough, even to our hearts, but the commercial art dominates our imaginations. Alternative world-views, be they traditional or visionary, are up against a powerful commercial art form. Alternative views may win in intellectual debate, but until or unless they are somehow translated into images capable of permeating the collective imagination, they have little hope of effecting significant cultural transformation. We need a new art, a reintegration of the spiritual and artistic values that call us to a richer experience of life than that proscribed by the one-dimensional, commercially dominated view of life.

> *In order to survive in this image-glutted world, it is necessary for us to devaluate the symbol and to reject every aspect of it but the purely sensational one.*
> —LEWIS MUMFORD

We have heard a great deal about information overload, yet we have as well an imagination overload. As much as our left-brain thinking capacities are overwhelmed by the sheer volume of facts to which we are exposed today, our right-brain creative faculties are drowning in a sea of images. The very number of images to which we are exposed, and their seemingly endless repetition, dulls our sensitivity to the artistic or spiritual impulse. As new technologies fill our heads with ever more images, our imagination muscles grow flabby for want of use. When we read a novel, we must form pictures in our minds, based on the author's descriptions of settings, characters, and events. We must exercise our imaginations in a way that is not required when the images come ready-made in a movie or television show. Children who grow up watching a lot of television and playing video and computer games may have little opportunity to develop their own imaginative abilities. The quick-cut style of editing—first widely introduced in MTV music videos and since picked up in movies, television programs, and commercials—crams more images into a second than we used to see in minutes, thus adding to the overload.

Today, television commercials freely appropriate symbols from art and religion. A commercial for a computer software company employs Mozart's *Requiem* as background music; another for an auto maker uses the "Ode to Joy" from Beethoven's Ninth Symphony for the same purpose. A third (another ad for a car manufacturer) opens to the sound of Tibetan monks chanting. Yet another flashes, in rapid succession, images of the Buddha, of monks, ritual costume and dance, and sacred architecture from around the world. It is not until the end that we realize that this is an ad for a business software company. The sounds and images expropriated in these ads are symbolic referents to transcendent reality. They are the products of deep levels of consciousness and hold the capacity to open us to a breakthrough experience. It is the very power that these symbols hold to arrest and open the mind that makes them attractive to advertisers.

To send light into the darkness of men's hearts— such is the duty of the artist.

ROBERT SCHUMANN

The effect of repeated exposure to these symbols in this fashion is a kind of double inoculation against their transforming influence. First, the sheer volume of images to which we are subjected necessarily numbs us to the effects of any single image. The proliferation of images today makes it difficult for us to appreciate the effect that images of art, or of any kind, once had on people living in less image-intense environments. Imagine, for example, a simple peasant entering one of the great Gothic cathedrals at Chartres or Amiens. He would have at once the sense of entering a space totally unlike any other he encountered in his daily life, an environment in which the sounds, and the images in exquisite stained glass and stone, addressed him as a spiritual being. The environment was intended to, and was no doubt effective in, pitching the consciousness of the beholder out of his mundane concerns and into a qualitatively different field of awareness.

Even commercial advertising art once held far greater sway on the minds and emotions of people than it does today. In 1914, Joseph Huneker, a writer living in New York, complained about the power a particular poster had in seducing him to go to Coney Island after he swore he'd never go again. "But that poster, ah. If these advertising men only knew how their signs and symbols arouse human passions, they would be more prudent in giving artists full swing with their suggestion brushes."[17] Today, we may take a certain pride in being indifferent to the suggestive power of commercial art. Yet in erecting defenses against this image onslaught, we have not only lost a measure of our innocence but have necessarily dulled our perceptive abilities in the bargain.

The second effect of the use of sacred symbols in the kind of advertising described above is to vaccinate us against the specific sacred symbol or image used in the advertising message. Instead of being first revealed to us while we are in a meditative and psychologically receptive state (as it was intended to be received), the image is thrust before us for a fleeting few seconds before it disappears. The symbol is not being used to arrest our minds but to hook them and attach them to something else, i.e., the product being sold. Moreover, this kind of advertising has the effect of trivializing significant sacred images, symbols, and sounds, placing them on a par with the often inane scenarios and ridiculous images that populate television commercials.

Certainly, artists of all kinds bear a unique responsibility for the sounds and images they eject into the collective consciousness. We remember that

Plato thought that, in shaping the character of a society, the musicians were more important than the political leaders. Yet ultimately, the problem stems as much from the led as from their leaders. The Vaisnava Hindus say that if an individual has the desire to awaken from the spell of maya, or illusion, the god Krishna helps him to awaken and remember who he truly is. If, on the other hand, he has a desire to forget his spiritual nature and enjoy the pleasures of maya, Krishna helps him to forget. As many as there are who may want to awaken, many more want to forget. In this book, we've considered some of the difficulties that the current social order places on those who seek to live as free and self-realized beings. While we cannot deny the special responsibility that those in leadership bear for the state of society, we must keep in mind that ultimately, the problem stems from the fact that most don't want to remember who they really are and thus easily fall prey to those who use art to deceive—be it for political or commercial gain.

There is a Buddhist myth that beautifully illustrates. One day, the Lord Avalokitesvara looked down from his celestial abode at countless beings suffering in Hell. So moved was he that at once he descended into Hell and rescued all the beings residing there. Yet by the time he had returned to his abode and looked back down on Hell, he could see that once again, it was filled with suffering souls. It is said that a tear of compassion ran from his eye, and that tear became the Goddess Tara, compassionate protectoress of spiritual aspirants. Those who would seek to bring enlightenment into the world do well to remember this story. Do not presume that you can save anyone from themselves. Yet all, whatever their state of depravity or enlightenment, are worthy and deserving of your love and compassion exactly as they are. In the words of Christ, God "maketh his sun to rise on the evil and on the good, and sendeth rain on the just and on the unjust."[18]

Those who seek to uplift others should keep in mind these words from Albert Schweitzer: "Anyone who proposes to do good must not expect people to roll stones out of his way, but must accept his lot calmly, even if they roll a few more upon it." The way of life is the way of sacrifice. Sacrifice is not self-denial but literally "to make sacred," to consecrate one's life to something beyond the momentary desires of the ego. To live as an artist is to consecrate your life and embrace your true vocation, come what may. The poet Robert Graves put it like this, "You chose your jobs because they promised to provide you with a steady income and leisure to render the Goddess whom you adore valuable part-time service. Who am I, you will

Symbols have the capacity to touch us not just on an intellectual level but on behavioral and emotional levels as well.

ALBERT EINSTEIN

ask, to warn you that she demands either whole-time service or none at all?"[19] The genuine artist realizes that self-liberation is not freedom *for* the self but freedom *from* the self. Her task is to become a vehicle through which transcendent consciousness can make itself known in the human experience.

Those who make it their profession to create the symbolic image-food on which the human soul feeds have a special responsibility. We know what motivated Bach, Mozart, and Beethoven. In the words of Beethoven, "There is no loftier mission than to approach the Godhead more nearly than other mortals and by means of that contact to spread the rays of the Godhead through the human race."[20] We know what motivated Dante, Goethe, and Blake. In Dante's words, "The purpose of the whole [work] is to remove those who are living in this life from a state of wretchedness and lead them to the state of blessedness." We know what motivated the great Chinese painters of the landscape tradition. In the *Chieh Tzu Yüan*, we read, "When painting has reached divinity [*shen*], there is the end of the matter."[21] Historically, all of the art forms, from painting to poetry, from theater, music, and dance to grand architecture, were born of the desire to relate the human consciousness to some higher power.

> *The greatest productions of art, whether painting, music, sculpture or poetry, have invariably this quality—something approaching the work of God.*
> —D. T. SUZUKI

What, we may ask, motivates today's artists? If it is not the desire for money or fame, it is often a desire to involve others in a kind of public therapy session or to advance a particular political agenda. Now, these things have their place, but if we allow them to supplant authentic art, we are in big trouble. The motivation for art is, as Thomas Mann wrote, "the natural instinct toward humanization, that is, toward the spiritualization of life...." To give to works that spring from an entirely different set of motives the place once reserved for art is the worst form of idolatry.

Historian Arnold Toynbee wrote: "Idolatry may be defined as the intellectually and moral purblind worship of the part instead of the whole; ... of Time instead of Eternity; ... [It] accomplishes the perverse and disastrous miracle of transforming one of the 'ineffably sublime works' of God into an 'abomination of desolation, standing where it ought not!'" He goes on to say in his great work *A Study of History* that when civilizations fall victim to this kind of idolatry, they are already on the road to ruin.[22] Inevitably, we must confront the question: What is art about? In response to just this question, Ananda K. Coomaraswamy wrote: "Let us tell them the painful truth, that most of these [traditional] works of art are about God, whom we never mention in polite society."[23] Extending the notion of God beyond that of personified deity, we can say that all genuine works of art are about spiritual Reality.

Where the spirit does not work with the hand there is no art.
—LEONARDO DA VINCI

This notion is not only consistent with the traditional view of art the world over but also with that held by a number of our own modern artists. The German Expressionist Max Beckman wrote: "In my opinion, all important things in art since Ur of the Chaldees, since Tel Halaf and Crete, have always originated from the deepest feeling about the mystery of Being. Self-realization is the urge of all objective spirits. . . . Art is creative for the sake of realization, not for amusement; for transfiguration, not for the sake of play." Today, all too often, we confuse entertainment with art.

Entertainment is escape, and there are times when we may want to escape from the pressures and cares of our lives. Yet art has another purpose. The purpose of art is to provide not an escape from the world but an intensification and illumination of our experience of it. It isn't that ordinary life is so tedious and drab that we must insulate ourselves by constructing an artificial world filled with pretty pictures and beautiful sounds. Genuine art is not pushing away the world; nor is it pulling us to desire and possess its fruits. We do not want to eat the apples in Cezanne's still lifes, nor do we desire in a sexual way the nudes in his *Bathers*.

Where entertainment makes us forget the world and advertising makes us want to possess it, art awakens an awareness that we *are* it. At one point in his career, Vincent van Gogh said that his goal was to make the ordinary people in his paintings emanate the radiance of the Buddha. In a sense, this is the goal of all art: to show the Buddha nature, the Tao, the spirit manifest in the Ten Thousand Things. This is the Beauty in art.

Even as the work of art does not cause us to desire or possess the objects it represents, neither does it cause us to run from them in fear or disgust. This is so, even though the sensations we experience in an encounter with art are not necessarily pleasurable ones. A work such as Shakespeare's *King*

All that is true, by whomsoever it has been said, has its origin in the Spirit.

THOMAS AQUINAS

257

Lear can take us into the darkest corners of the human experience. It is not merely the tragedy of Lear's life that we feel but the tragedy of our own. To be sure, peeling away the veils of illusion can be a wrenching experience. Yet the poignancy and frailty of the human experience reveals its ultimate beauty as much as noble or heroic action. This too is the beauty in art.

As a society, we've lost respect for the culture-building role that genuine art plays in society and the soul-nourishing effect it has on the life of the individual. We have as well lost respect for the artist, confusing celebrity with merit, confusing popularity with value. Today, we are caught up in celebrity and credentials, in who is famous or esteemed as a "bona fide" expert. In other words, we rely on others to tell us who and what to believe and to judge what is and is not valuable. We've lost confidence in our own abilities to discern the truth in arts or letters. If a thing is true, it matters not who said it; if a work of art has real value, it stands on its own. On the other hand, the learning, honors, or fame of a speaker or writer will not make the false true; nor will the technical virtuosity of a painter or musician transform mere entertainment into art.

Another less religious-sounding way of saying that a work of art is about God is to say that it is "inspired." The work of art is conceived *in* the spirit (in-spir-[it]-ation). The artistic intuition is a breakthrough experience. This breakthrough may result from a disciplined spiritual training or may seem to arise spontaneously of itself.[24] As Kandinsky said, "Construction on a purely spiritual basis is a slow business. . . . The artist must train not only his eye but also his soul. . . ."[25] Without this breakthrough into Mystery, there is no art, no matter the grandeur of the conception or the virtuosity of the technique employed.

The way of art, both in its perception and in its expression, is the revelation of the transcendent Mystery. The artist makes the breakthrough beyond time, into the eternal; out of the personal mask, into the universal. The modern German artist Oskar Kokoschka gives us a sense of the means to the breakthrough: "If we will surrender our closed personalities so full of tension, we are in a position to accept this magical principle of living. . . . For we set aside the self and personal existence as being fused in a larger experience. All that is required of us is to RELEASE CONTROL."[26] This statement is of course consistent with the teachings of the classical Taoists—indeed, with the esoteric teachings of all the world's great religions. The key to the experience of transcendence is found in letting go of mental control and uniting with a higher order of intelligence.

The work of art addresses the whole person: body, mind, and spirit. The artist appeals to the body, engaging the senses with color, sound, or movement, etc. She arranges these colors, sounds, or movements in rhythmic patterns that concentrate and focus the mind. Yet, if she doesn't go the final step and arrest the mind, if her work doesn't make the breakthrough into the transcendent realm of the spirit, it is not art.

The artist's task, then, is by no means an easy one. In the words of Ananda K. Coomaraswamy, "What . . . we do not yet understand is the heroism of art, that exhausting and perpetual demand which all creative labor makes alike on body and soul. The artist must fight a continual battle for mastery of himself and his environment; his work must usually be achieved in the teeth of violent, ignorant and often well-organized opposition, or against still more wearing apathy, and in any case, even at the best, against the intense resistance which matter opposes to the moulding force of ideas. . . ."

 ## The Creative Life

It is for purely accidental reasons that the fine arts have been singled out to be almost identical with Art.

—IRWIN EDMAN

Friedrich Nietzsche said, "Art is the proper task of life." Yet what of those of us who do not see art as the task of our lives? While we may not all work with the symbolic tools that shape the human imagination, we all leave our mark on the world and the people in it. Moreover, it would be a mistake to limit our conception of art to the fine arts. This is a very recent distinction and one that first came to prominence as the industrial model of mechanical manufacture began to replace the work of artisans in a variety of fields. Now, only a few, the fine artists, would be concerned with beauty, and the rest would themselves become interchangeable parts in the machinery of mass production. Yet we all have within us the "natural instinct toward humanization . . . toward the spiritualization of life," and each of us has the capacity to express in our own unique way this universal instinct. If the motive is appropriate and the execution well made, we may all work as artists, regardless of the fields we work in. Each can bring Beauty to life by following the organic pattern of his or her own life.

For man is by nature an artist.

TAGORE

Earlier, we discussed *li* in terms of the organic pattern of human consciousness. Yet there is another way that we can speak of an organic pattern (*li*) within the human being. Beyond the archetypal dimension that we all share, there is an organic pattern for the life of each individual human being. Each of us is born with an organizing principle for our lives, a natural way of expressing ourselves and fulfilling our unique destinies. The real beauty in life comes in being what we are.

In my career consulting work, I've noticed that people often have profound realizations with regard to their career directions simply by changing the questions they are asking. The question isn't, What do I want to be? The question is: Am I being what I am? Of course, that inevitably leads to the question, What, or rather, Who am I? Leaving aside the deeper issue of ultimate identity, this question presupposes that you are indeed something already. The question, What do I want to be? assumes that what to be is a matter of choice, if not whim. For the Taoists, what you are is already built in. Self-actualization begins not with choice but with self-discovery and self-realization.

Chuang Tzu was once asked, "Can one get the Tao so as to have it for one's own?" He replied, "Your body is not your own, it is the delegated image of heaven [*ch'ien*]. Your life is not your own, it is the delegated adaptability of heaven." To say that your life is the "delegated adaptability of heaven" implies that it has both innate purpose and innate capacities. To say that your life is not your own suggests inherent responsibility. You can think of your natural gifts and abilities, even your deepest interests, as manifestations of the organic pattern (*li*) of your life. These (your gifts, etc.), in turn, are recognized by the *ch'i,* or life energy, associated with them. Early on in my career work, I observed that when people hit upon something pointing to the right path, they would display a noticeable change in their energy. Their eyes would light up, their cheeks would flush, and the sound of their voices would ring with a new strength and enthusiasm. In short, they would come alive. It was as though some inner chord had been stuck and was now reverberating through their beings.

Applying the concepts of *li* and *chi* gives new understanding to the formula, "Follow your bliss." Follow the energy (*ch'i*), for where you find the deepest source of energy in your life, you will find the key to its organic pattern (*li*). The idea of an organic pattern for your life suggests a natural order. It is the same order we see everywhere in nature—not something imposed from the top down, but rather growing from the inside out. It is not a rigid order asserted by mental control and will, but a fluid order that embraces change as its fundamental dynamic. Again, your energy is the guide to tapping into this organic pattern.

Yet if you have been living without regard to this natural order, as you begin to move toward it, you may find that your life actually seems more chaotic. The ground must be torn up and turned upside down before the new crop can be planted. Similarly, to clean out and reorder a closet, you must first make a bigger mess. So it is with bringing your life into the natural order of your *li*. Having grown accustomed to the stultifying comfort of rigid routine, moving with the spontaneous impulses of intuition may at first seem frightening and disconcerting. Yet in time, you will learn to trust the intuitive impulses, as your own experience proves them out time and again. Indeed, you will find that far from producing chaos, these impulses seem to lead you on toward some kind of preordained destiny.

When he was in his sixties, Arthur Schopenhauer wrote that as he looked back on his own life, he recognized an order, a pattern so intricate that it suggested the narrative of a well-written story. He noted as well that often, what had seemed at the time to be only minor or unimportant events turned out to be major turning points in the story. So every life well lived reveals a pattern that can only be recognized in hindsight, but must be lived in each now moment. The organic pattern, the *li,* of our lives is there all the while, whether we choose to ignore or embrace it.

 ## The Beauty of Excellence

> *O Excellence! How narrow are thy paths, how arduous*
> *thy ways! Happy the man who climbs thy paths and can*
> *tread thy ways.* —GOTTFRIED VAN STRASSBURG

Beauty is seen in excellence—in bringing love and wisdom, care and attention to detail—to the things we do and make. Can we respond to the spontaneous impulse of intuition and yet maintain the commitment and persistent effort necessary to achieve excellence? Chapter 3 examined the principle of *wu-wei,* or effortless action. Effortless action must never be confused with slipshod work or with a careless or indifferent attitude toward what we are doing. Chuang Tzu was a wheelwright who obviously took great care in his work. When we consider the arts inspired by the Taoist vision, we see great attention to detail and an abiding commitment to excellence.

Ease is often hard won. In the work of a master calligrapher or painter, a great musician or dancer, we see a naturalness and ease of expression. Yet we often forget how many long hours of tedious practice have preceded the wondrous manifestations we behold. As Michelangelo said, "If people knew how hard I worked to get my mastery, it wouldn't seem so wonderful after all." We remember the injunction of the Chinese painter: "Meditate on bamboo for ten years, become bamboo, then paint yourself." Nothing careless or slipshod about that.

How do we then resolve the seeming contradiction between the pursuit of excellence and the idea of effortless action? We find it in the dedication of a love that transcends love and hate, in other words, liking and disliking. The ease of *wu-wei* is not a matter of taking the easy way out but of not resisting things as they are. One thing we must not resist is that it takes patience, love, and commitment to do things well. As the great Indian poet Tagore put it, "Work, especially good work, becomes easy when desire has learnt to discipline itself." Ease comes in embracing discipline, not in rejecting it. We think of the creative life, the life of the artist as all inspiration. Here it is, now it's gone, when will it return? Yet art is as much aspiration as it is inspiration. If inspiration is being in the spirit, then aspiration is moving toward the spirit, bringing form to that conceived in the spirit. To bring your inspirations to life, you must give them yours.

 ## Walk in a Beauty Way

What the human being sees, what is poured into his environment, becomes a force in him. In accordance with it, he forms himself.
—RUDOLF STEINER

As much as those who create the image-food on which the human imagination feeds have a responsibility for the quality of the "food" they produce, so each of us has a responsibility for what we ingest. Today, as a society, we are obsessed with diet and dieting. Many worry over whether they are eating the right foods or eating too much. Of course, there are good reasons to pay attention to the foods we eat (see chapter 4). Yet how many pay equal attention to what they put in their imaginations? Though what we feed our minds affects the quality of our lives as much, if not more, than what we feed our bellies, it seldom gets the same attention. It is worthwhile to examine your imagination diet and see if it is rich in the nutrients you need to sustain a healthy and creative life.

When I speak of your imagination diet, I'm not talking about ideas, about what you read and think about. I'm not talking about the need for positive thinking or even what the Buddhists call "right thinking." This is important, for our thoughts *do* shape our lives. Yet what we see is even more important than what we think. This is so because the forms and images of our environment penetrate into our subconscious minds and make deep impressions on the way we view ourselves and our world. Even more, it usually does so without our even being aware of the effect these forms and images are having on us.

Chapter 2 examined the desensitizing effects that the mechanical means of production and the loss of human touch in manufacture have on us. The craftsman or artisan made the objects with a love, care, and attention that today workers hardly have a chance to impart to their work. The great architects once built monuments to please God or, at the very least, the church leadership. Today, architects who work on a grand scale must please banks, insurance companies, or commercial real estate barons, for whom aesthetics seem an afterthought at best.

While a few American cities do have areas of architectural interest—New York, Chicago, Boston, Philadelphia, New Orleans, Washington, and San Francisco come to mind—few of the buildings added to these cities in the last fifty years could honestly be called aesthetic improvements. The city centers of metropolitan areas that have seen the greatest growth in the last half century—places like Denver, Los Angeles, Orlando, San Diego, Houston, and San Jose to name a few—are dominated by rectangular glass towers and bland, windowless boxes. The suburbs, where most of us live, are an architectural wasteland. While there is little that we as individuals can do to transform this soulless environment, being aware that it is affecting us can stimulate us to make an effort to counterbalance this influence by more actively cultivating beauty in other ways.

There *are* many areas of our lives where we can regulate what we allow into our imaginations. When it comes to regulating our imagination diets, the same principles that apply to food for the body apply to food for the

Painting is not self-expression but an expression of the harmony of Tao.

MAI MAI SZE

soul. Eat high-quality foods, and don't eat too much. Most of us are image obese and could certainly benefit from scaling back on our consumption. For most of us, watching less television or at least fewer commercials would be a good first step toward lightening up our diets.

Yet the quality as well as the quantity of images we ingest affect us. If the images and symbols of art have the power to lift us into a transcendent experience, it is not hard to imagine that other images could be equally powerful in creating negative effect. Protect your imagination, and don't imagine that you are immune to influences on it. Bring an awareness of these influences into your everyday choices and decisions. For example, before you go to see a movie or watch a television program, ask yourself what effect it is likely to have on your imagination. Will it be an uplifting, enriching, and ennobling one? Or will it fill your mind with things you would rather not have in it?

This is not to suggest that we become puritanical or that we close our eyes to the suffering or ugliness in the world—rather, that we pay attention to what we view. As the body weakens and degenerates on a diet of junk food, so too the spiritual power of the individual is exhausted by a steady diet of junk image-food. Even as it takes more effort to find and prepare delicious nutrient-rich foods than it does to pick up fast food on the go, so too it takes more effort to create a high-quality diet for your imagination. Yet it is an effort well worth making. The beauty we put into our lives will go on feeding and enriching them.

Beauty in the Little Things

In all things that we say or do or think or feel,
our mind leaves its mark. —HSIEH HO

In our everyday lives, we have innumerable opportunities not only to recognize but to express and participate in the beauty in life. We can make beautiful arrangements in the home, garden, or yard. While it takes time and a great deal of effort to achieve excellence in our work, it needn't take a great deal of time or money to add beauty and a sense of grace to our lives. Americans tend to think that a beautiful home must be an expensive home, something worthy of *Architectural Digest*. We tend to think of beautiful things as expensive things. In Europe and many other parts of the world, ordinary people seem to have a better sense of how to live with a sense of beauty and grace without spending a fortune.

With a little creativity and effort, we can bring beauty into the little things in our lives. Turning off the television and listening to beautiful music is a simple step most anyone can take. Some people enjoy the sounds of waterfalls in their homes or wind chimes around the house. In many communities, you can find inexpensive cut flowers at the local farmer's market. Fresh flowers add color, fragrance, and a touch of nature to the home. Living plants can give you a sense of connection with nature, even if you're living in an urban jungle.

While the urban-dweller has fewer opportunities to commune with nature, she generally has much better access to art than her rural counterpart. She can attend concerts and dance and fine art performances and see the best in the world execute their craft. Many smaller cities and towns that can't support a performing arts center have excellent arts and lecture programs available through local universities. Visiting museums is another inexpensive way urban dwellers can add beauty to their lives. A museum can serve as a kind of secular temple, a place to go for contemplation and to recharge the spirit. I find it best to go at odd times or to more obscure museums. This allows you the opportunity to really savor what you see, without the rush and hubbub of the crowds.

There are so many ways we can add beauty to our lives. We can even find inspirational, enriching, and informative programs amidst the television wasteland if we take the trouble to seek them out. There are thousands of fine films and documentaries available on video and in other formats. I have an extensive collection of art books and enjoy spending a leisurely evening looking at photographic reproductions of art images from around the world. (In fact, it was this practice that many years ago first convinced me of the universality of the archetypes of the collective unconscious.) The point is, there are many ways to add beauty to your life; find the ways that work for you. The possibilities are limited only by your imagination.

A few well-chosen pieces of art in your home can make a world of difference. If you can't afford original pieces, excellent reproductions are available today. Keep your space free of clutter. One beautiful piece, nicely placed, is usually more appealing than a smattering of tacky things or even a number of very beautiful pieces competing for the eye's attention. Chapter 4 briefly discussed *feng shui* and the effect that the placement of objects in the home has on your energy. Objects of beauty radiate uplifting vibrations that act on your consciousness.

We know as well that the various colors represent frequencies of energy that define the spectrum of light. Color affects our mood and energy level. Consciously using color in your home can be an inexpensive way to add beauty. In Mexico, many simple homes are brightly and beautifully painted. The same applies to the clothing we wear and the way we prepare and present food. To do things beautifully needn't require great expense, just a little care and attention.

Life: A Beautiful Gift

The only lasting beauty is the beauty of the heart.
—RUMI

The Taoists tell us that life is the gift, and everything beyond that is gravy. No matter how bad it is or how bad we think it is—life is a gift. This feeling of gratitude can only come from identifying with the energy of life. If you try to force it from the mind—telling yourself that you should be grateful—you'll get stuck in the pairs of opposites. Trust the energy *(ch'i)* and organic pattern *(li)* of your life. Life has its own intelligence; it's much smarter than you or me as separate little egos. So then, how do you stay identified with life, with the wisdom of the body? Give it your attention. Focus on it. Go out of your mind once in a while. Turn off that mental chatterbox that's always yacking away—so anxiously worrying about everything. It doesn't know a thing about living. It's got nothing to do with life. It's all about the then and there, the past and future. But life is happening here and now.

The doubt and confusion of the mental chatterbox give rise to the twin emotions that open a Pandora's Box on all that is ugly. These twins are named "Envy" and "Self-pity." Ever notice how when you get caught up in thinking in an envious or self-pitying way, you feel ugly? How the world and the people in it begin to look ugly to you? This ugly is called Hell, and we don't have to die to go there. Neither do we have to go anywhere to find the Beauty of Heaven. We see beauty in the overcoming power of the human spirit, in a love that transcends the pairs of opposites. Whether in art or humanitarian service, in relationships, the spiritual life, or the ordinary sufferings in life, where we see an overcoming spirit, we find beauty. As much in the small things as in the great, we find beauty in this overcoming spirit.

Thoreau said, "However mean your life is, meet it and live it; do not shun it and call it hard names . . . The faultfinder will find faults even in paradise. Love your life, poor as it is." The abundance and beauty of life are here now for those who will embrace them. The purpose of life is to live it. So many want to change the circumstances of their lives, but how many will freely change their attitudes? You can see that your attitude toward things makes all the difference. You can see that if you more consistently bring the energy and focus that you are capable of to what you do, the immediate circumstances of your life will improve. Similarly, you can imagine that you can—with enough patience, love, understanding, and persevering action—handle all of the internal and external obstacles of your life. So what does it take to do that?

Eliminate self-pity. That's all there is to it. If you don't bring yourself down, you don't have to raise yourself up. After all, what are you identified with? Your spirit is transcendent—eternal. It is untouchable. Tap into that . . . it's a relief and a release, far beyond the transitory ups and downs of life. How can you pity an eternal spirit? The Taoists tell us that all the conditions of the universe, and therefore all the conditions of our existence, have arisen together with us. Therefore, nothing can be against us.

From a Western perspective, we can talk about this problem from the standpoint of the soul. What is the soul as distinct from spirit? The soul can be conceived as a kind of body that contains the memory of all the experience one has gained through countless lifetimes. Through all of these incarnations and the experiences they afford, one is learning to love more deeply and completely. Each soul, depending on its experience and evolutionary level (how long it's been at it and how quickly it learns) has its own unique challenges to face, obstacles to overcome, lessons to learn. From the standpoint of ultimate reality, to see yourself as a soul moving through time, gaining experience is still an illusion. Yet it's a more expanded view of life than one gets from identifying with the personality AND it puts an end to self-pity.

Think of a soul entering the human body. It's as though it takes a nap in the mother's womb—and when it wakes (at birth), it has forgotten all of its experience and with it, its life lessons. Because of this amnesia, we often

. . . a first-rate soup is more creative than a second-rate painting.

ABRAHAM MASLOW

get involved in personality objectives that run directly counter to our soul objectives. Let's say a soul wants to learn patience and acceptance, but the personality is driven to have it all now. The soul is trying to learn its lesson, while the personality fights it every step of the way.

If we are to face the lessons of our lives square on, we must start by admitting that we know what they are. We have to embrace them. In so doing, we can find a totally different experience in exactly the same conditions. Since you know that there is something for you to learn, master, or overcome, why not say, "Okay, that's what I want to do." Since it is there, it *is* what you want to do. Whether you think you want to or not. You don't have to go through life at odds with yourself. Your experience has lessons for you. You can say, "Okay, let me get on with it," or you can resist. Resisting takes more energy, makes it more of a struggle, and postpones your learning the lessons. You never get the lesson by struggle; finally, you have to embrace it. The only thing you can get from struggling is to become so exhausted that you finally have to give up—and let go.

Melting in the Snow

Once in the early spring, I fasted for forty days in the mountains of Yosemite National Park. There, with only a sleeping bag, I enjoyed the solitude of nature. I had the rare opportunity to confront myself. If I was not happy, I alone was to blame. There were no people around to confuse the issue, no projects to be accomplished, no books to read, no experiences to lust after. No distractions. Nothing existed except that which was before me. Like the snow around me, I began to melt with each passing day. Each day, I moved deeper into myself and into an appreciation of the world around me. I stared transfixed for untold hours at the patterns in leaves. I watched fat black ants scrambling over leaves and twigs and marveled at what a thing a creature is. I laughed with the sounds of woodpeckers hammering trees in the distance. Like a giddy child, I followed a butterfly as it flittered about, landing here and there. I hugged the stones and heard the "sermons" in them. I felt the earth breathing.

Many people have asked me about this experience and what stood out most for me while on this fast. I sensed that they wanted to hear about supernatural phenomena and mystic visions of light and transcendent rapture. Indeed, I did see light and more, but those were not most important to me. Two experiences have never faded from my awareness and have changed me forever. I will try to recount them, though I doubt that either I or the language are up to the task.

Returning from my mountain solitude to Yosemite Valley, I boarded one of those little buses that take tourists around to the valley floor. Next to me on the bus were a group of fat and frumpy tourists making anxious conversation about their travel plans, what sights they should see while in Yosemite, and how far they might have to walk. While I was aware of their conversation, it seemed faint and distant, for I was in absolute awe of their beauty. Mind you, these were not specimens that would ever grace the covers of *GQ* or *Vogue,* yet I was dazzled. It was as though I had never really seen a human being before. How amazing the flesh of their hands, the warmth of their bodies, the shine in their eyes. I wanted to stand up and hug each and every one and ask them if they knew how extraordinary they were. Yet I sat silently, the joy welling up inside of me until I thought my heart would burst.

Without knowing them or being attracted to them by their looks, intelligence, personality, or views; without liking them or disliking them; without making any judgment of them in the affirmative or negative; without relating to them on any other level than their very existence as human beings—I felt a profound love for them. I cannot say it was my love, for there was no volition, no effort, no sense of self involved. When I got off the bus, still in ecstasy, I lay on a grassy spot. I closed my eyes and, with a vividness I cannot describe, I saw how love moves the universe. How it is love that spins the galaxies, love that moves the lion in the hunt, love that ultimately gives rise to *every* act we call evil and good. I felt completely safe and at home in the world. Should someone have come along in that moment to injure or destroy my body, I knew it would be love that moved them. Truly, as Lao Tzu said, "Tao is a mystery in all things."

THE TAO OF ABUNDANCE WORKBOOK

All of life is an experiment.
The more experiments you make, the better.
—RALPH WALDO EMERSON

The following pages contain opportunities for you to integrate the Taoist principles you have read about in the previous chapters into your everyday life. Life is an unfolding organic process, and one best enjoyed when we participate in it with full consciousness. The exercises that follow will encourage you to experiment with new ways of seeing, thinking, feeling, and doing. They will assist you in creating your own experience of true abundance.

* The exercises that follow are intended to provide the opportunity to apply the philosophical principles discussed in this book. They are not intended to serve as psychological counseling or as financial advice nor to substitute for these. Anyone in need of psychological counseling or financial planning is encouraged to seek the services of a qualified professional.

CHAPTER 1

◆

Your Vision of Abundance

Write a brief essay describing your vision of abundance. What does living abundantly mean to you? In addition to your concept of financial prosperity, be sure to include the kind of work you do, your spiritual life, home life, relationships with family, friends, and community, etc.

Describe where you would like to be in relation to your vision of abundance, in five years.

What major changes will you have to make to bring this about? What specific action steps will you take to effect these changes?

Defining Your Terms

In creating your own vision of abundance, it is worthwhile to define for yourself terms related to wealth and prosperity. It is interesting to note that, in their origins, none of the terms below made reference to money or economics. Read the word origins that follow, then define for yourself what each term means to you.

Abundance: Derived from Latin *abundāre*, meaning "to overflow"
Wealth: Derived from the Old English *wel* or *wela*, meaning "well" or "well-being." Well (weal) is to wealth as heal is to health.
Prosperity: Derived from the Latin *prosperāre*, meaning "to render fortunate."
Affluence: Derived from the Latin *affluēns*, meaning "flowing."
Rich: Derived from the Old English *rice*, meaning "strong," "powerful."

To me, abundance is:

To me, wealth is:

To me, prosperity is:

To me, affluence is:

To me, rich is:

Playing the Game Called "Life"

A successful longtime actor took on the task of directing his first film. A fellow actor and friend asked the novice director how it was that he was doing such a magnificent job his first time out. He replied that he was acting the part of the kind of director he always wanted to work with. This story illustrates an important lesson that all of us can apply, namely, to consciously act the parts we are playing. We are all playing so many roles in any case, we might as well play them well. After all, the greatest abundance in life is bringing the full measure of who we are to every aspect of our lives.

A wonderful benefit of not identifying with the roles we play is that it leaves us free to actually play them better, that is, with greater consciousness. The following exercise will help you to play your roles more skillfully.

List all the roles you play in the course of your life. For example: mother, wife, aunt, daughter, boss, co-worker, mentor, friend, citizen, etc.

Then, for each role, indicate how you want to play it and what you can do to improve your performance. For example: What kind of mother/father do I want to be? What kind of wife/husband do I want to be?

Role	How I want to play it?	How can I improve my "performance"?
1.		
2.		
3.		
4.		
5.		

CHAPTER 2

◆

The Source of Your Supply

The beliefs, attitudes, and ideas that we hold—whether conscious or unconscious—can deeply affect our experience of abundance or lack. In this exercise, you'll have the opportunity to explore ways you may be creating lack by holding onto limiting beliefs about the ways you can receive the abundance of the universe.

1. The Taoists tell us that the abundance of the universe is immediate and of-itself-so. In what ways might you be blocking your experience of this by holding onto beliefs that something must happen first? For example: Before I can receive abundance, I must earn a certain degree in school. Before I can receive abundance, I must become a partner in my firm. Before I can receive abundance, I must have a perfect credit report.

2. What self-judgments are blocking or limiting you from receiving the natural abundance of the universe? For example: If I were a better person, I would be more deserving of receiving abundance. If I were more intelligent, more talented, or had better looks, etc., I would be more deserving of receiving abundance.

3. In what ways are you limiting your experience of abundance by holding onto limiting beliefs about the channels through which it may come to you? For example: The only way I can make money is by doing things I don't like to do; the only way I can experience greater abundance is if my boss gives me a raise, etc.

4. To trust in the Tao is to live in abundance; to trust in the ego ultimately ties us to lack. What ego qualities are you attached to as the source of your supply? For example: My will is the cause of my supply; my charm is the cause of my supply, etc.

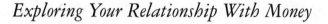

Exploring Your Relationship With Money

Write a brief essay entitled "What I Learned about Money from My Parents." Include your parents' attitudes toward earning, spending, saving, and investing money. Also describe the financial circumstances you were born into and how they changed as you grew older. Then answer the questions below. (Answering these questions can be valuable, even without writing the essay.)

The most powerful messages about money that I received from my father were:

The most powerful messages about money that I received from my mother were:

How are these ideas shaping your attitudes toward money today? For example: your parents often worried about paying the bills, and now you do as well; or your parents had basically healthy attitudes toward money, which you have adopted, etc.

In what ways are you reacting against parental beliefs about money? For example: your parents were very conservative, thrift-conscious, and future-oriented in their approach to money; in reaction, you adopted an immediate gratification, buy-now-pay-later approach.

List beliefs you have about money, that may be limiting your supply. For example: money is dirty; money is the root of all evil; only bad, greedy, selfish (etc.) people have plenty of money; money is hard to get and harder to hold onto, etc.

Next, challenge these beliefs. For example:

Belief: Only greedy, selfish people have plenty of money.

Challenge: Poor people can be as greedy and selfish as affluent people. People with a lot of money can do great good as well as harm; ultimately, it's the awareness and character of an individual that matters, not how much money they have.

Belief:

Challenge:

Belief:

Challenge:

In what ways would you like to change your ideas about money?

With regard to money and financial matters, what new behaviors would you like to adopt?

Which existing behaviors would you like to eliminate?

Behind the Mask: Creating Personality

A personality is only a mask, and we can wear many different ones. There is a Zen saying: Show the poet your poem, show the warrior your sword. Freedom comes when behavior arises spontaneously and is not conditioned by memory. Self-confidence comes when we can meet a variety of different kinds of people where they are. Playing counter to your usual personality traits now and then reminds you that your personality is your own creation and that it exists to serve you, not the other way around.

In the cinema or theater, a good actor is one who has the ability to play a wide range of roles, not one who can only be typecast into playing essentially the same character over and again. Similarly, to be a good actor on the stage called "life," it helps if we have a wide-ranging personality that will allow us to perform well in a variety of circumstances. We don't want to limit our concept of who we are to a narrowly defined set of behaviors and attitudes that we identify with our personalities. This will tend to leave us feeling frustrated, bored, and old before our time. Frustration is a feeling that arises from holding the thoughts "I want it" and "I can't have it" simultaneously. Often the reason we can't have it is because we can't get or receive it with the personality traits we cling to.

1. Indicate ways you have limited yourself by narrowing the personality traits you have identified with. For example, you want to go into business for yourself but feel that you could never sell or market yourself; you spontaneously feel a desire to give a person a hug, yet feel inner constraint because you are "not that kind of person," etc. Frame these in terms of "want it" and "can't have it" statements below.

Want It	*Can't Have It*
I want to go into business for myself.	I can't because I am not one of those outgoing people who can sell or market themselves.
I want to be more affectionate, to reach out to people and hug when I feel like it.	I can't because I've always acted reserved.

	Want It		*Can't Have It*
1.			
2.			
3.			
4.			
5.			

2. List five new behaviors and attitudes that will help you better play the roles you want to play.

	Behaviors		*Attitudes*
1.		*1.*	
2.		*2.*	
3.		*3.*	
4.		*4.*	
5.		*5.*	

◆   ◆   ◆

More Blessed to Receive

Recognizing that receiving is an intentional act, in what ways have you limited or blocked your ability to receive?

I have limited my ability to receive love by:

I can receive more love by:

I have limited my ability to receive joy by:

I can receive more joy by:

I have limited my natural intuitive ability by:

I can open to receive and act on my intuitions by:

I have limited my ability to receive wealth by:

I can receive more wealth by:

Next, write statements that affirm what you are now ready to receive. For example:

I am now ready to receive all the love in the universe.

I am now ready to receive and acknowledge the inspirations and intuitions that come to me and to act on them.

Creating a Vacuum

Nature abhors a vacuum. As we let go of things we no longer use or enjoy, as well as old grudges and habitual ways of doing and relating, we make room to experience more of what we truly want in our lives.

1. **Out with Old Things:** Create a vacuum for receiving by giving away things you no longer need, want, or use. Make a list of such things and determine what you'll do with each. For example: donate this item to a local charity, give that to a friend you know will appreciate it, etc.

    Item   *What you will do with it*

    1.

    2.

    3.

    4.

    5.

2. **Out with Old Grudges and Grievances:** Make a list of grudges and grievances that you have been holding onto but are now ready to let go of.

    1.

    2.

    3.

    4.

    5.

3. **Out with Old Limiting Ideas:** Identify, examine, and let go of limiting beliefs you have about life, yourself, work, and others. List limiting beliefs below for each category. Next, identify how that limiting belief is hurting you and why you are ready to let it go (assuming you are). For example . . .

LIFE

Belief	*How this belief hinders me:*	*Why I am ready to let it go:*
Life is a struggle	It makes things harder than they have to be.	I want more joy and fun in my life.

Belief	*How this belief hinders me:*	*Why I am ready to let it go:*
1.		
2.		
3.		

WORK

Belief	*How this belief hinders me:*	*Why I am ready to let it go:*
Work is something you have to do to pay the bills.	It keeps me from finding and doing something I would enjoy.	I'm tired of the rut I'm in.

Belief	*How this belief hinders me:*	*Why I am ready to let it go:*
1.		
2.		
3.		

SELF

Belief	*How this belief hinders me:*	*Why I am ready to let it go:*
I don't have enough energy to do the things I want to do.	It keeps me from taking risks and making commitments.	It makes my life seem boring.

Belief	*How this belief hinders me:*	*Why I am ready to let it go:*
1.		
2.		
3.		

OTHERS

Belief	*How this belief hinders me:*	*Why I am ready to let it go:*
You can't trust people.	It isolates me and makes me paranoid.	I'm tired of feeling lonely and defensive.

Belief	*How this belief hinders me:*	*Why I am ready to let it go:*
1.		
2.		
3.		

4. **Out with the Old Ways of Doing Things:** Make a list of habitual behaviors you know you want to break out of. For each, list ways you can change your routine to add more here-and-now moments to your life. For example: finding different ways to do things you always do, trying things you haven't done before, putting yourself in new situations that require that you be totally present, etc.

Habitual Behavior	*Alternatives*
1.	1.
2.	2.
3.	3.
4.	4.
5.	5.

CHAPTER 3

◆

Meditation on Ease

When we see ourselves as arising out of the universe, we begin to recognize that the universe is *for* us. To get an experience of this, try this simple meditation:

Seated wherever you are, begin thinking to yourself or saying aloud: This (or my) body is for me, the floor is for me, the house is for me, the chair is for me, the table (or other objects of furniture) are for me, this telephone is for me, and so on. Or try walking down the street, thinking or quietly saying to yourself: The sidewalk is for me, this fence is for me, these flowers are for me, these trees are for me, the sky is for me, this building is for me, this person who just walked by is for me. Don't limit your statements to what you think of as pleasant or beautiful objects or events. Include whatever is around you—this trash can is for me, these noisy cars are for me, this policeman is for me, and so on.

This meditation can be very energizing. It may also help you become aware of tension or defensiveness in the way you more typically experience the world.

◆ ◆ ◆

Look, It's for Me!: Gratitude List

1. **Having:** List all the things that you own or use that you are grateful for. For example: a warm place to sleep, a car that runs, a computer to work on, a stereo to listen to, etc.

2. **Being:** List all of the experiences in your life that you are grateful for. For example: the sun on your face, birds singing in the morning, breathing, being able to move about, etc.

3. **Relating:** List all of the people in your life that you are grateful to, and for each, state why.

4. **Achieving:** List all of the things you have been able to do or accomplish in your life that you feel grateful for. These needn't be grand accomplishments; they can include anything from learning how to walk or ride a bike to graduating from school.

Easy Approach to Problems

When we meet difficulties, problems, or setbacks in life, we can apply the "this is for me" approach. This exercise can help you step back from problems that seem immediately devastating as well as those that have long seemed insurmountable. It can allow you to see situations in a new light and to approach them in a new and less combative way.

First, state the problem in the "for me" context. For example: this physical pain is for me, this obstacle or disappointment is for me.

Next, ask yourself, What is this situation or event trying to teach me, or rather, What am I trying to teach myself through this experience? For example: to trust more, to be more patient, to accept myself, to embrace life more deeply, etc.

Eliminating the Struggle of Self-sabotage

We create unnecessary struggle through self-sabotage, which is to say, acts that intentionally or subconsciously thwart or obstruct a given purpose or set of purposes that we have identified for ourselves. Becoming aware of how and why we sabotage ourselves can help us eliminate struggle.

1. Describe a specific objective or personal goal and how you have sabotaged yourself in regard to achieving or realizing it. For example, sabotaging an important relationship, messing up an opportunity to work in a career you love, or performing below your ability at a task or event that was meaningful to you, etc.

2. What limiting subconscious beliefs were you holding that produced this self-sabotage? For example: "I'm not good enough," "I don't deserve to succeed," "I don't deserve love."

3. What did you secretly enjoy about creating this sabotage? (There is some kind of psychological payoff, even if it's only that of recreating a familiar pattern and so, not having to deal with change.)

4. When did you realize that you were going to commit this sabotage? Recognize that we generally have inner warnings or alarm bells that go off well before we actually fail.

5. Who supported you in sabotaging yourself? In what ways? Why? Who encouraged you to realize your goal? How?

6. How would you rewrite this script if you had the opportunity to do it all over again?

7. Why do you believe you will not need to sabotage yourself in a similar situation in the future? How have you learned and grown from your experience?

Creating with Ease

Often we push and struggle to make things happen when we could make things much easier for ourselves by going with the natural flow. Below, we explore two important ways of doing this. First, go with the inspirations you receive: they are at one with the universal and all-pervasive intelligence of the Tao. Second, visualize the results you seek. Mentally rehearse the outcomes you seek before you put physical effort into making them happen.

GO WITH YOUR INSPIRATIONS

Make a list of the inspirations you have received, ideas you have about things you would like to do or accomplish.

Next, select from your list the three inspirations that have the most energy for you at this time.

1.

2.

3.

List steps you can begin taking right now to put them into action.

Inspiration   *Steps I will take:*

1.

2.

3.

Next, visualize these inspirations as final or completed results in the real world. We are all constantly visualizing. However, most of our visualizations are subconscious, and often, they actually run counter to the purposes we have in mind. Athletes, entertainers, and successful people from all walks of life have long used the power of consciously directed visualization to make things happen. Below is a simple, easy-to-use formula for effective visualization.

How to Use Visualization

1.   **Deserve:** Be willing to create the picture exactly as you want it.

2.   **Focus:** See the picture and hold your attention on it. Don't let your mind wander.

3.   **Relax:** Don't tense or strain; pretend you're watching an enjoyable movie.

4.   **Desire:** Let yourself feel your desire for what you see. Pour your feelings into the image.

5.   **Detail:** Step into your picture and see the detail—the grain in the wood, the dew in the grass.

6.   **Include:** If you want the object of your visualization, be sure to include yourself in the picture.

7.   **Enjoy:** Feel good about what you see. Express gratitude for receiving it. Let it go. Know that it *is* done.

◆   ◆   ◆

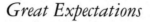

Great Expectations

Once you have identified and begun focusing on your creative inspiration, examine your expectations. Your expectations can be even more important than your desires or efforts. When there is a conflict between desire and expectation, you get what you expect, not what you want. Writing affirmations is a simple and easy way to get your head to agree with and support the inspirations of your heart. It helps to ensure that negative programming in your subconscious mind won't keep you from your soul's desires. The subconscious mind works much like a computer. You can't execute a task on your computer that the program you are running isn't designed to handle (e.g., sophisticated graphics on a word-processing program). Yet when you install a program that supports the outcomes you are after, you can do it easily. It works the same way with your mind.

In your subconscious mind, which is to say, at the level of your expectations, *you believe what you hear repeated.* (Think of how a song sticks in your mind after repeated hearings.) Most of all, you believe what you repeat to yourself. The most powerful way to use the affirmation process is to say *"I am"* before that which you want to be, do, or have. The words *I am* form the primary link to your self-image and should be used with great care. Be careful not to link negative thoughts with the words *I am, I, me,* or *mine,* or these negative thoughts will attach to your self-image. Below, write affirmations for things you want to be, do, or have. For example:

Be	*Do*	*Have*
I am healthy, happy, and in great shape.	I am successfully writing and publishing my first book.	I am now living in the perfect home for me.

Be	*Do*	*Have*
1.	*1.*	*1.*
2.	*2.*	*2.*
3.	*3.*	*3.*
4.	*4.*	*4.*

"I Am" Diary

It helps not only to affirm what you want but to pay attention to how you may be canceling it out by repeatedly affirming something contrary to it. Keep a notebook or journal with you and record negative off-hand comments or statements you make about yourself in the course of a week. For example: I'm no good at that, I'm getting old and ugly, I can't deal with that, etc. If you are like most people, you may be surprised at how often you are working against yourself. Becoming more aware of how you knock yourself will help you to knock it off.

Say It Again, Sam

The process that follows will help you to create a dialogue with your subconscious mind, enabling you to see where you stand with regard to your objective. State an affirmation of an outcome you desire, and then beneath it, write whatever response comes into your head. In the beginning, what comes to mind is likely to be negative and disbelieving. Yet as you continue, what you hear in your head will become increasingly at one with your affirmation.

Affirmation: I am now enjoying a wonderful and exciting career as a public speaker.

Response: Oh, yeah sure. What a joke.

Affirmation: I am now enjoying a wonderful and exciting career as a public speaker.

Response: I'm not sure I have anything worthwhile to say.

Affirmation: I am now enjoying a wonderful and exciting career as a public speaker.

Response: How would I ever market myself?

Affirmation: I am now enjoying a wonderful and exciting career as a public speaker.

Response: It's too competitive. I can't make a living doing that.

Affirmation: I am now enjoying a wonderful and exciting career as a public speaker.

Response: This is something I've always wanted to do.

Affirmation: I am now enjoying a wonderful and exciting career as a public speaker.

Response: People are always telling me I'm a natural.

Affirmation: I am now enjoying a wonderful and exciting career as a public speaker.

Response: I have a great idea for a seminar I want to give.

Affirmation: I am now enjoying a wonderful and exciting career as a public speaker.

Response: It wouldn't be that hard to organize it into a presentation.

Affirmation: I am now enjoying a wonderful and exciting career as a public speaker.

Response: Yeah, why not? I can do it.

Affirmation: I am now enjoying a wonderful and exciting career as a public speaker.

Response: I am going to be so excited when I give my first professional seminar.

◆   ◆   ◆

CHAPTER 4

◆

General Circulation Assessment

Rate each of the following areas of your life in terms of how well the energy is or is not flowing ("one" being the most stuck; "ten," the most free flowing).

	Energy Is Stuck					*Energy Is Flowing Freely*				
1. Career	1	2	3	4	5	6	7	8	9	10
2. Health	1	2	3	4	5	6	7	8	9	10
3. Finances	1	2	3	4	5	6	7	8	9	10
4. Relationships	1	2	3	4	5	6	7	8	9	10
5. Creativity	1	2	3	4	5	6	7	8	9	10
6. Sexuality	1	2	3	4	5	6	7	8	9	10
7. Spiritual life	1	2	3	4	5	6	7	8	9	10
8. Intellectual life	1	2	3	4	5	6	7	8	9	10
9. Emotional life	1	2	3	4	5	6	7	8	9	10
10. Family life	1	2	3	4	5	6	7	8	9	10

Answer the following questions for the areas in which the energy is most blocked:

What limiting beliefs might be holding you back in this area?

What specific behaviors could you adopt or eliminate to help you get the energy moving again?

Circulating Your Talents and Gifts

1. What are your natural talents, your strongest innate abilities and real gifts? List them below.

    If you don't know immediately, answering the questions that follow will help to bring this out.

    *   What do you naturally enjoy doing?

    *   What do you naturally enjoy thinking about?

    *   What do you naturally enjoy learning about?

    *   What do you enjoy doing as a process, in others words, for extended periods of time?

2. Once you have identified your strongest natural talents, ask yourself, Am I expressing these fully in my everyday life? If not, why not?

    *   In what ways could you begin expressing more of these talents now? Within your existing job or work? Outside of your job?

    *   In the longer term, how could you restructure or change your career to allow for fuller expression of your talents at work?

The Circulation of Wealth

Spending with Joy: What bills or debts do you resent paying, and why? How can you mentally reframe this situation so as to eliminate resentment? For example: you may be angry at yourself for spending beyond your means; you may resent having to pay taxes or other bills, etc. How is this anger or resentment affecting your own happiness and feeling of abundance? Can you find a way to truly feel gratitude about this situation?

Investments: What investment could you make that would make money for you, while helping others?

Networks: How could you increase your circulation with regard to your networks? For example, making new contacts, joining groups or associations, taking classes, etc. Who are some key people with whom developing a new or improved relationship would be particularly beneficial to your career or other goals?

Marketing Products and Services: How can you increase the circulation of your existing products or services? What new products or services could you put into circulation?

Tithing: How can you put positive energy into circulation by supporting people, groups, or causes that are providing services that are in alignment with your spiritual or ethical values? What charities would you like to support?

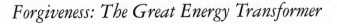

Forgiveness: The Great Energy Transformer

Confucius said, "To be wronged is nothing unless you continue to remember it." Things people say and do can hurt. Yet unless we have been physically injured, the only reason the pain from these incidents continues to affect us is that we hold onto a memory of it in our minds. It's as though it were a photographic image stuck in a film projector. The exercise that follows is designed to help you release this image and, in so doing, get the mental and emotional energy it monopolizes, into circulation again.

Screenwriters, directors, and actors use the term "back story" to indicate that a character's actions and motivations in the slice of life that is the movie do not come out of nowhere but flow from habits and attitudes formed by circumstances and events that took place prior to the time with which the movie is concerned. Considering your own as well as the other person's back story moves your mental focus off of the painful scene and puts it in a wider context. It can shed new light on painful memories and help give you the understanding from which forgiveness flows.

Make a list of incidents or scenes of past emotional pain that you continue to hold onto. Next, review your list and select the one that tends to bother you the most at this time. Then, answer the following questions with regard to this scenario.

1. Briefly, and as objectively as you can, describe this incident as though it were a scene in a movie—what you did or said and what the other person (or persons) did or said. At this point, stay away from your feelings about the situation and from ascribing motivations to yourself or the person (or persons) involved. Simply describe the scene.

2. What do you now understand about the situation that you didn't understand at the time?

3. What in the other party's back story helps to make their behavior more understandable? Include immediate stresses, long-standing fears, patterns in his, her, or their psychological make-up, etc. Remember, the understanding and forgiveness we give to others is the understanding and forgiveness we give to ourselves.

4. Often, we have difficulty forgiving others because we are, perhaps unknowingly, judging ourselves. What in your back story helps to make your own behavior more understandable? What immediate stresses, pressures, or fears were weighing on you at the time? In what ways does this situation remind you of painful incidents from your childhood? Are there significant parallels between this incident and past experiences of pain? Describe.

Remember the maxim: "Forgive or relive." We are likely to go on attracting to ourselves incidents that recall painful experiences that we have failed to forgive.

Joy Is in the Circle

What goes around comes around. The energy we put out is the energy we get back. What we give to others, we give to ourselves. What we give to ourselves, we give to others. The following series of questions will help to ensure that what is going around is what you want to come around.

GIVE WHAT YOU WANT TO GET

1. Make a list of things you want more of from your mate, family, friends, boss, coworkers, or others who are important to you. For example, you might want attention, patience, acceptance, acknowledgment, encouragement, moral support, etc.

2. How can you give more of these qualities or attributes to yourself? For example, if you want more acceptance, how can you accept yourself more? If you want to be acknowledged, how can you acknowledge yourself more, etc.?

3. Now, consider how you can give more of these qualities or attributes to others. For example, if you want more praise or attention, give more praise and attention to others.

DON'T GIVE WHAT YOU DON'T WANT TO GET

Keep in mind that what you give to yourself, you tend to attract from others. For example, being self-critical attracts criticism from others, and critical people, into your life. List self-judgments that you would like to eliminate, and thus, no longer attract from others.

The Communication Cycle

Communication problems result from a lack of circulation. We are either having difficulty expressing what is on the inside or we are having difficulty letting in and really receiving messages from the outside—sometimes both. Communication problems involve a block in expression or a jamming of reception.

Fear of Expression: What do you want to express that you are afraid to express? Make a list. Then select one item from your list and answer the questions that follow in relation to it.

Recognize that most likely, the fear is related to winning the approval of others, though this manifests in different ways, depending on the emphasis. Either you are afraid of how others will respond or you are afraid of how you will look to them. Write down which of these best applies to you in this situation. It may be that both apply. Depending on your response, answer the applicable questions that follow.

Intimidation: What is it that you fear others will do or say if you express yourself in this situation? For example: get angry with you, fire you, abandon you, etc. Is this a rational fear, which is to say, is it really likely to occur?

If so, how could you structure your presentation so as to mitigate the reaction you fear? Are you anticipating or assuming a negative response? How would you feel or act differently if you were anticipating a positive response? How is this likely to affect the response you receive?

It may not be necessary to confront the person directly. Clarify your thoughts and feelings about this issue by writing a letter to this person. You may never send the letter or even discuss the issue with the other person. You may determine that it would be better if these things were never said. Nevertheless, expressing yourself in this way will start circulating the mental and emotional energy stuck on this issue.

Loss of Approval: How do you fear others will view you if you express how you honestly feel about this situation? Are you afraid that they will see you as weak, vulnerable, neurotic, petty, demanding, controlling, etc?

Are these accurate perceptions of how others will view you or are they self-judgments that you are projecting onto others?

If these are your own judgments, why are you being so hard on yourself? How can you see yourself in a more constructive manner?

If these are likely to be the responses of others, are you going to let your life and behavior be controlled by what other people think of you?

Fear of Inadequacy: Fear of inadequacy is the fear that the people or events in your life will make you confront things that you feel unwilling or unable to deal with. What things have others told you about yourself that you have avoided dealing with? Additionally, what things about yourself have you become aware of that you haven't fully accepted or integrated into your life?

What seems painful about this situation?

Up to now, what has led you to believe that you can't handle this pain? Recognize that if you felt uncomfortable when confronted about this situation, it is likely because you weren't ready to deal with the pain behind it. Why didn't you feel ready?

What other painful or difficult circumstances have you already dealt with and overcome in your life?

What can you apply from the way you handled these circumstances, to the present one?

What new skills, information, or insights would help you to better handle this issue?

How, where, and when will you get these?

◆   ◆   ◆

Cultivating Ch'i

CHEERFULNESS

List ways that you can bring more joy into your life. How can you make a point of being cheerful? For example: smiling at strangers, laughing, being playful, facing difficulties with grace, etc.

The Inner Smile: Practice this method to relax and revitalize your body. Visualize an inner smile in the parts of your body that feel tense, e.g., your stomach, neck, shoulders, or back. Let the smile relax and calm you and put you in touch with the joy of being alive.

BREATHING

Awareness: Sit still in a comfortable position and pay attention to your breathing. Don't try to change it in any way; just be aware of the way you naturally breathe. Stop after five minutes and record your observations. For example, is your breathing fast or slow? Shallow or deep? Does it come through your nose or mouth? Does it start in your belly, chest, or neck?

A Simple Breathing Exercise: Now sit on the floor with your legs crossed and your back straight but relaxed, or, if it's more comfortable, sit on the edge of a chair with your feet firmly planted on the ground, again, keeping your back straight. (If you have back pain, sit back into the chair). Breathe through your nose, with your mouth closed. Now touch the palate of your mouth (the roof) with the tip of your tongue. Relax and notice your breath. Then, slowly and gently begin lengthening your breath so that your diaphragm naturally contracts on the inhale and expands on the exhale. Do this for ten minutes. Then record how you feel afterward and what you observed during this exercise.

Continue this practice each day, gradually lengthening the time, until you are breathing for twenty minutes to half an hour each day. For a more advanced practice, try focusing your eyes on the tip of your nose while placing your attention in the third eye area up from and behind the eyeballs. Record your observations.

DIET

Keep a diet diary. Record everything you eat and drink for one week.

Review your diet. What are its best and worst elements? How can you improve the nutritional value of your diet? For example: eating out less, reducing or eliminating "junk foods," taking cooking or nutrition classes, putting in a vegetable garden, buying organic produce, etc. For additional tips on balancing your diet, see the exercises for chapter 6.

EXERCISE AND MOVEMENT

Are you currently exercising on a regular basis (at least three times a week)? If so, are you satisfied with your current routine? What could you do to improve, vary, or supplement it? If not, why not? e.g., time, money, lack of energy or desire.

If you would like to be exercising but aren't, perhaps you haven't found something that suits you. Remember, there are so many options to choose from: martial arts, yoga, Tai Ch'i, aerobics, jogging, weight training, simply walking for twenty minutes, or doing stretching exercises in the morning. Determine to find something that works for you.

If, for whatever reason, you decide that you don't want to begin a regular exercise program at this time, consider ways that you can dovetail a little exercise into your everyday routine. For example, walking to your neighborhood market instead of driving, taking the stairs instead of the elevator, doing housework at a rapid pace, taking the dog for a lengthier or more vigorous walk. Jot down some ways that will work for you:

REST

Overall, are you currently getting enough rest? How long do you generally sleep each night? It is deep and restful sleep or troubled and intermittent? If you are not getting adequate rest, what steps could you take to improve the amount or quality of rest you get?

Early to bed, early to rise: While it may not make you healthy, wealthy, and wise, following this maxim will put in you tune with the rhythms of nature. Remember, the Taoists say every hour of sleep before midnight is worth two hours thereafter. How can you make this principle work for you?

Take time during the day to do absolutely nothing. Quality "nothing" time provides a rest to our minds and psyches, as well as our bodies. Look at ways you can take twenty minutes of "nothing time" each day to give yourself an energizing boost in the middle of the day. List below:

MASTERING YOUR EMOTIONS

Step One: List four ways in which you tend to emotionally react, and in the space to the right, indicate circumstances, individuals, or events that tend to illicit those reactions. For example:

	Emotional Reaction	*Circumstance*	*People*	*Events*
1.	Fear	lack of money	the boss	public speaking
2.	Anger	freeway traffic	the in-laws	paying taxes
	Emotional Reaction	*Circumstance*	*People*	*Events*
1.				
2.				
3.				

Step Two: In the space provided below, match your emotional reactions with effective behaviors for overcoming them.

Emotional Reaction	Effective Behavior
1.	1.
2.	2.
3.	3.
4.	4.

Remember to relax and breathe whenever you find yourself beginning to react emotionally.

Step Three: In the left column, list the benefits of adopting the new behavior, in the right column, put the consequences of continuing the old pattern.

Benefits	Consequences
1.	1.
2.	2.
3.	3.
4.	4.

SPEND TIME IN NATURE

How often do you spend time in nature? Do you have a favorite spot near where you live where you can go and enjoy a natural setting? If you live in an urban environment, how often do you visit city parks?

What about camping or backpacking? If these interest you, how often do you go? When and where would you like to go next?

CULTIVATE AN AWARENESS OF YOUR SURROUNDINGS

Space: Consult a *Feng Shui* master or an authoritative text, and determine how the energy is moving in your current surroundings. Next, make a plan to make changes accordingly.

Intuitively (i.e., without the aid of Feng Shui and without making a major overhaul of your living space), what simple changes could you make to create a more harmonious and prosperous living environment? For example, changing the color scheme of certain rooms in your house, adding artwork, removing excess and clutter, etc.

Sound: Remembering that, as much as anything, the quality of any space is determined by the sound: What sounds can you add or subtract from your environment to make it a more life-enhancing one? For example: adding a freestanding home waterfall, a white noise machine (if you live in a noisy city), soft background music, turning off the television if you are not actually watching it, muting commercials, etc.

Scent: How could you use scent to uplift your home environment? For example, you could use incense, aromatherapy diffusers, scented candles, or potpourri burners. You might want to include fragrant plants in your home such as sweet violets, winter-blooming jasmine, or gardenias.

◆　◆　◆

CHAPTER 5

◆

Self-Reliance vs. Approval Seeking Index

Rate yourself on a one-to-ten scale for the following criteria. Be as objective as possible.

Self-Reliance					*Approval-Seeking*				

Self-acknowledging   Strives to be acknowledged by others

1	2	3	4	5	6	7	8	9	10

A leader, whether active or silent   A follower, or bully

1	2	3	4	5	6	7	8	9	10

Self-controlled   Easily seduced

1	2	3	4	5	6	7	8	9	10

Stands up to intimidation
without being combative   Gives in easily to intimidation
or reacts with hostility

1	2	3	4	5	6	7	8	9	10

Perseveres in the face of difficulties
and obstacles   Gives up easily

1	2	3	4	5	6	7	8	9	10

Respects others equally   Esteems some people more and
others less than self

1	2	3	4	5	6	7	8	9	10

Works for love of the work   Works for rewards and the recognition
of others

1	2	3	4	5	6	7	8	9	10

Clear, specific, self-defined purposes
and objectives

| 1 | 2 | 3 | 4 | 5 | 6 | 7 | 8 | 9 | 10 |

Lack of clear goals: direction defined
by others

Primarily concerned with the present

| 1 | 2 | 3 | 4 | 5 | 6 | 7 | 8 | 9 | 10 |

Concerned with the past, fearful of
the future

Participates in society while
maintaining self

| 1 | 2 | 3 | 4 | 5 | 6 | 7 | 8 | 9 | 10 |

Hides in groups or withdraws into
isolation

Emotionally honest

| 1 | 2 | 3 | 4 | 5 | 6 | 7 | 8 | 9 | 10 |

Lives in denial and therefore guilt and fear

Accepts responsibility for one's actions
and their consequences

| 1 | 2 | 3 | 4 | 5 | 6 | 7 | 8 | 9 | 10 |

Blames others or beats up on self for
mistakes

Self-initiating

| 1 | 2 | 3 | 4 | 5 | 6 | 7 | 8 | 9 | 10 |

Waits to be told what to do

Takes risks

| 1 | 2 | 3 | 4 | 5 | 6 | 7 | 8 | 9 | 10 |

Seeks security in the status quo

Thoughtful and patient; considers
options before acting

| 1 | 2 | 3 | 4 | 5 | 6 | 7 | 8 | 9 | 10 |

Acts impulsively, without careful
consideration of consequences

Commands respect, without being
self-obsessed or petty

| 1 | 2 | 3 | 4 | 5 | 6 | 7 | 8 | 9 | 10 |

Becomes a doormat or puffed up in
oneself

Commitment to excellence

| 1 | 2 | 3 | 4 | 5 | 6 | 7 | 8 | 9 | 10 |

Does enough to get by

Determines views on the basis of intuition and experience									Determines opinions on the basis of what others say
1	2	3	4	5	6	7	8	9	10

Reserved in one's judgments									Tends to be easily impressed
1	2	3	4	5	6	7	8	9	10

Evaluates self objectively in terms of personally relevant criteria									Compares self to others
1	2	3	4	5	6	7	8	9	10

Encourages others to be self-reliant individuals									Encourages others to conform or be dependent
1	2	3	4	5	6	7	8	9	10

Optimism that springs from faith in life and self									Pessimistic and often discouraged
1	2	3	4	5	6	7	8	9	10

Expresses feelings easily									Difficulty in communicating feelings
1	2	3	4	5	6	7	8	9	10

Follows nature spontaneously									Waits for "something better" to turn up
1	2	3	4	5	6	7	8	9	10

Enjoys life									Worries a lot
1	2	3	4	5	6	7	8	9	10

What were your strongest areas?

What were your weakest areas?

What can you do to improve these?

Breaking Out of the Approval Trap

1. In what ways has the desire for approval limited or controlled you? Specifically, how has it affected:

Your relationships: For example, choosing the wrong kind of partners, not standing up for yourself and being overly dependent and resentful as a result, etc.

Your work life: For example, choosing the wrong career, not advancing as rapidly as you could, getting stuck with the tasks no one else wants to do, etc.

Your self-esteem: For example, valuing the ideas and opinions of others over your own, being anxious and afraid to take risks, etc.

2. In what ways have you reacted against the desire for approval and/or your failure to get it? For example, shutting down emotionally, becoming cynical, playing sour grapes, developing a hostile or "take no prisoners" attitude.

How has this affected:

Your relationships:

Your work:

Your self-esteem:

Initiation: Cutting the Cord

BIOLOGY OR BIOGRAPHY?

Identify the ways in which being psychologically committed to your biography, that is, the story of your life, creates limitations in your life. For example: I'm a shy person because my parents were withdrawn or controlling, or because the kids used to laugh at me in school, etc. I'm an undisciplined person because my parents were permissive and I didn't learn to stick with things when I was young. I don't trust people because I was jilted by a lover, etc.

I'm _____ because _____

I'm _____ because _____

I'm _____ because _____

I often _____ because _____

I tend to be _____ because _____

I don't _____ because _____

EMPOWERING THE CHILD WITHIN

The following exercise can help you to release psychological attachment to painful elements of your biography. Recall a painful incident from your childhood. Relive the experience in your mind's eye.

Next, imagine you are full-grown in this same scenario. How would you have responded differently than you did as a child?

What would you say or do as an adult that you couldn't or didn't say as a child?

What insight or understanding would you have brought to the situation as an adult that you didn't have as a child?

How would you have better protected yourself?

Would this incident have been less traumatic or painful if you had done all of these things? How so?

Does this help you to realize that ultimately, the root of this pain stems from your human biology and not your individual biography? Explain.

Accepting Your Parents

List things, events, or circumstances you still blame or resent your parents for. Be honest. For example, favoring another sibling, specific incidents of physical or verbal abuse, parental fighting or divorce, parental neglect or lack of affection, being overly controlling or dominating, manipulating you with guilt or fear, not buying you things other kids had, not putting you through college, etc.

Next, for each item on your list, indicate how many years ago this occurred.

Has holding onto this blame or resentment helped you? In what ways?

Has it hindered you? In what ways?

Remember, as Longfellow said, "If we could read the secret history of our enemies, we should find in each person sorrow and suffering enough to disarm all hostility." If this is true of our enemies, how much more forgiving can we be of our own parents, who, for whatever else they may have done, have made possible our very lives in this world? Are you now ready to let it go and forgive your parent(s)? Why?

If not, what steps can you take to be more ready to do so? For example: go into psychological counseling, talk with your parents and try to better understand why they might have reacted the way they did, etc.

Power Attitudes

In chapter 5, we distinguished authentic natural power from inauthentic coercive power. What does being powerful mean to you? For example: does it mean bossing people around? always being in control? being true to conscience? contributing to the lives of others? or something else?

My idea of a powerful person is someone who:

The most powerful person I know is_____. Why?

Indicate below any negative or limiting ideas you have about power. For example, do you believe you will lose love if you are more powerful? Do you believe that you must become a meaner or more unethical person in order to become a more powerful one?

Next, challenge these beliefs. For example:

Belief	*Challenge*
I will lose love if I become more powerful.	I may lose approval, but I cannot lose love, for the love I feel is up to me and no one else. If I am true to myself, I will be happier and so, a more lovable person.
Belief	*Challenge*

Following Your Nature

Are there any aspects of your life where you feel you have compromised your dignity? For example: selling out your values or natural talents to make money, marrying for money or security, doing things you don't believe in because of peer pressure.

Why did you do so? What were you valuing over your own dignity and worth?

What steps can you now take to correct this mistake?

What purpose and objectives does the work you do every day support?

Are these in alignment with your own values and sense of purpose or mission in life?

If not, what could you be doing that would be more in keeping with these? If you are unclear, you might want to consult *How to Find the Work You Love, Zen and the Art of Making a Living* by the same author, or other books of this kind to help you clarify.

Tribute Payments; or, Where Does All the Money Go?

Use the form below to figure the costs of the tribute payments you are making. Once you have filled these out, answer the questions that follow.

INTEREST:

Home mortgage _____

Auto loan _____

Credit cards _____

Installment buying _____

School loans _____

Other loans _____

TAXES:

Local:

Property taxes _____

Sales taxes _____

Mandated fees _____

Tolls _____

Special assessments _____

Other _____

State:

Sales _____

Income _____

Excise _____

Mandated fees _____

Other _____

Federal:

Income _____

Social Security _____

Excise _____

Gift _____

Inheritance _____

Mandated fees _____

Capital gains _____

Rent:

Housing _____

Office _____

Other _____

Inflation tax: To figure your inflation tax, multiply your annual income by the current annual rate of inflation. For example, if your income is $100,000 and the annual inflation rate is 5 percent, your annual inflation tax is $5,000 ($100,000 x .05).

Employment tax: First, figure the difference between the net value of what your efforts bring to your employer and the net value of what you receive. (In some fields or occupations, this will be straightforward and easy to figure; in other fields and occupations, you might have to make a subjective assessment.) Next, if applicable, subtract from this figure the cost of being in business for yourself. This represents your employment tax.

Calculate that total cost of the tribute payments you are currently making, both of actual dollar amounts and as percentage of yearly income.

What changes can you make to keep more of what you earn?

Confronting Social Pressures

Recognizing that, as e. e. cummings said, "to be nobody-but-yourself—in a world which is doing its best, night and day, to make you everybody else—means to fight the hardest battle which any human being can fight; and never stop fighting"—in what ways have social pressures kept you from being or expressing who you are? Include major turning points in your life when you based an important decision on social pressure rather than on the dictates of your heart.

Were you aware of pressure at the time? If so, how did you respond?

If you had a strong sense of your own direction and caved in, answer the questions that immediately follow. If you let social pressure push you because you didn't know where you wanted to go, answer the question on the line below. What did you do to resist these pressures? What were the critical factors that forced you to give in?

If so, why were you unsure of yourself? Have you since become clear about your own direction?

What price were you unwilling or unable to pay to resist social pressure?

What did it cost you to give in?

What strategies can you employ to better handle this kind of pressure in the future?

CHAPTER 6

◆

Yin/Yang Balance

1. Examine your life in terms of yin/yang balance.

A. Psychic Balance: Make a list of values and qualities that you associate with the masculine and a second list of values and qualities that you associate with the feminine. (You may want to refer to the chart below.) Rate yourself in terms of each of these qualities. Also, be aware that how you feel about masculine or feminine qualities may reveal something about the state of your own inner yin/yang balance. A person who is overly yin will tend to fear even healthy yang (e.g., assertiveness or assertive people), while a person who is overly yang may look with disgust at healthy yin (e.g., intuition or intuitive people).

FEMININE		MASCULINE	
Quality	*Extreme*	*Quality*	*Extreme*
Affectionate	Clinging	Assertive	Dominating
Receptive	Timid	Active	Hyperactive
Nurturing	Smothering	Enduring	Stubborn
Serene	Lazy	Logical	Calculating
Devoted	Martyrlike	Goal-directed	Blindly ambitious
Compassionate	Hypersensitive	Analytical	Cold
Intuitive	Superstitious	Powerful	Cruel

B. Physical Balance

The information below gives you preliminary information with which to assess your physical health with respect to yin and yang balance, along with some strategies for making adjustments.

Indications of Excessive Yin:

- Excessive coldness
- Slow metabolic activity
- Sluggish or inadequate functioning of organs or physiological processes
- Decreased resistance to stress or infection (for example, frequent colds)
- Weakness or disease in internal organs or inner aspects of organs, including but not limited to:

heart	liver	kidneys	inner ear
brain	bones	spinal cord	inner genitals
lung	spleen	deep vessels & nerves	lining of body cavities

Indications of Excessive Yang:

- Excessive heat
- Accelerated metabolic activity
- Hyperfunction of organs or physiological processes
- Increased reaction to stress
- Weakness or disease in external organs or aspects of organs including but not limited to:

skin	ears	tendons	joints
hair	nose	ligaments	breasts
nails	mouth	joints	anus
eyes	teeth	muscles	outer vessels or nerves

Below are some ways you can adjust the yin/yang balance in your body.

Increase Yang through these foods:

Cereal grains, such as brown rice, wheat, millet, buckwheat.
Legumes.
Root vegetables, including carrots, onions, daikon radish, & garlic.
Goat cheese.
Seeds and nuts.
Meat, eggs, salty fish.

Avoid these ☞

Drink less fluids.

Strength training and aerobic exercise.

Meditate at mid-day.

Rise early.

Spend a lot of time outdoors.

Increase Yin through these foods:

Fruits, especially citrus.
Soft or watery vegetables, such as eggplant or tomatoes.
Dairy products.
Frozen foods.
Refined oils.
Most fish.

The following are extremely yin and should be consumed sparingly:
Stimulants: coffee, caffeinated tea, etc.
Intoxicants: alcohol, drugs, etc.
Table sugar or sugary drinks or foods.
Processed foods, including white flour, preservatives, chemicals, and pesticides.

Drink more fluids.

Stretching exercises, such as hatha yoga, Tai Ch'i, etc.

Meditate in the evening.

Stay up late.

Spend a lot of time indoors.

Of course, the information above is necessarily incomplete. You may want to further investigate yin/yang theory as it relates to health in general and diet and nutrition in particular. See books such as: *Macrobiotic Diet* by Mishio and Aveline Kushi (Japan Publishers, 1993), *Macrobiotics: The Way of Healing* by George Ohsawa (George Ohsawa Macrobiotic Foundation, 1984), and *The Complete Book of Chinese Health and Healing* by Daniel Reid (New York: Barnes and Noble, Inc., 1994).

Inner Alchemies

The purpose of this exercise is to help you gain awareness of places where you may be battling against things as they are, and to help you come into a deeper acceptance of yourself, others, life, and society.

1. Identify places in your life where you are battling against human nature.

    a) Places where you are making yourself wrong, such as:

    Sex: I should be sexier or more attractive.
                 I shouldn't have those kinds of (sexual) thoughts or feelings.

    Anger: I should be in control at all times.
                 I shouldn't react to this or that.

    Desire: I should be satisfied with what I have.
                 I shouldn't want this or that.

    Weakness: I should be strong at all times.
                 I shouldn't admit or show vulnerability, fear, or inadequacy.

    b) Places where you are making others wrong, such as:

    Greed: People (he/she/you) shouldn't be so selfish and greedy.

    Apathy: People shouldn't be so lazy and indifferent.

    Fear: People shouldn't be so timid and cautious.

    Pettiness: People shouldn't be so petty and shallow.

Recognize that battling against human nature is futile and only leads to frustration and resentment. For example, feeling guilty or being angry at yourself for getting angry will tend to make you a more, not less, angry person. Now take each of the statements you wrote in part one of this question and write an affirmation of acceptance. For example:

I'm an imperfect human being, and that's okay.
People are often selfish and greedy, and that's okay.
I'm a sexual being, and that's okay.
Things irritate me from time to time, and that's okay.

2. Next, identify places in your life where you are battling against nature or society. Then write affirmations of acceptance as you did in the previous step.

   Nature: Change is a part of life, and that's okay.

   I can't stand winter . . . . Seasons are a part of life, and that's okay.

   I don't want to die . . . . Death is a part of life, and that's okay.
   I will live my life and let my death take care of itself.

   I don't want to get old . . . . Getting old is a part of life, and that's okay.

   Society: Social rules and conventions are a part of life, and that's okay.

   The social order is hierarchical and unjust . . . . Throughout the history of human civilizations, all societies have had their flaws, some may have been more egalitarian and fair-minded, some much less so. It's up to me to make my life where I live.

   Society values income and wealth over achievement, character, or human-ity. . . . This is unfortunate, yet I am free to choose my own values and to act accordingly.

Anima/Animus Dynamics

Being aware of the yin/yang dynamics of anima and animus can do much to bring harmony into your intimate relationships. Answering the questions in the following exercises can help you to become aware of how these dynamics play out in your relationships.

Recall a time when you had a fierce argument with an intimate partner of the opposite sex. Be aware that, in all likelihood, this exchange involved an encounter between anima and animus. (If you are not currently in a relationship, use examples from the last time you were.)

Determine whether or not your anima or animus was already activated prior to this encounter with your partner. Be honest. For a man: Were you already feeling moody and as though people didn't care about you? For a woman: Were you already feeling irritated and as though people didn't respect you?

Determine whether or not your partner's anima or animus was activated prior to this encounter. For a woman: Was he already feeling moody? For a man: Was she already feeling irritated?

If you were not already engaged in your anima/animus, determine what your partner said or did that triggered you.

If your partner was not already engaged in his/her anima/animus, determine what you said or did that triggered him or her.

* *Remember: a telltale sign of an anima or animus possession is jumping rapidly from one issue to another.*

Now, recall a time (or times) when your partner was engaged (in the anima/animus) and you didn't react. Did you view your partner differently than when you reacted? In what ways? How did the way you viewed your partner shape the way you responded?

Now recall a time when you were engaged (in your anima/animus) and your partner didn't react in kind. How did he or she respond? How did it make you feel?

How can you apply what you learned in your answers to these questions to help reduce or eliminate potential future conflict in your relationship?

CHAPTER 7

◆

Buy and Buy: Habits of Consumption

How much are you influenced by the commercial culture in your habits of consumption? Rate yourself on a one-to-ten scale, one being totally unlike you; ten, exactly like you.

I often buy things to impress others.

1	2	3	4	5	6	7	8	9	10

I feel pressured to "keep up with the Joneses."

1	2	3	4	5	6	7	8	9	10

I feel that designer brands or labels are intrinsically superior.

1	2	3	4	5	6	7	8	9	10

I would feel as though I were somehow less of a person if I drove an older car or lived in a less desirable part of town.

1	2	3	4	5	6	7	8	9	10

I use shopping as a way of giving myself an emotional lift.

1	2	3	4	5	6	7	8	9	10

I often make purchases on a buy-now-pay-later basis.

1	2	3	4	5	6	7	8	9	10

I feel as though I must follow the latest models, fashions, styles, or trends.

1	2	3	4	5	6	7	8	9	10

Time and Money

Time is *not* money, but it usually does take time to make money. The series of questions that follows is designed to help you evaluate your spending in terms of the time costs involved. It will help you figure out if the time you put into things is really paying off. First, review your monthly expenditures and determine how much you are actually spending each month in the following areas.

MONTHLY SPENDING PATTERNS

Essential Spending	*Dollar Amount*	*Cost in Hours*
Groceries:		
Rent/mortgage:		
Clothing:		
Auto (payments, gas, repairs, etc.):		
Telephone:		
Utilities (telephone, electric, cable, etc.):		
Child care:		
Insurance (health/auto/home/life):		
Household supplies:		
Household furnishings:		
Household repairs:		
Laundry/dry cleaning:		
Health care:		
Taxes:		

Discretionary Spending	*Dollar Amount*	*Cost in Hours*
Dining:		
Entertainment:		
Travel:		
Recreation:		
Nonessential consumer goods:		
Miscellaneous:		

Now, for each item above, indicate what it costs you in terms of time. Determine your after-tax monthly income and divide by the number of hours you typically work in a month. This is your (after tax) hourly wage. Next, determine how many hours of income each item costs. For example, if your hourly wage is $20 and your rent is $1,000 a month, it costs 50 hours a month (1000 ÷ 20), if you spend $170 a month eating out, it costs you 8.5 hours, and so on. Households with more than one breadwinner can figure a combined hourly wage or compute separately on the basis of their individual contributions to each item.

Which expenditures strike you as the best values for the time invested to earn them?

Which expenditures strike you as poor values for the time invested to earn them?

What kinds of specific spending cuts might you be able to make? Include large and small cost-cutting items. For example: moving to another city where housing costs are significantly less, or simply eating fewer meals out.

In what ways could you generate additional income that would not require a large time commitment? For example: investments, selling products, etc.

Are you currently practicing any form of voluntary simplicity? If so, describe. If not, would you be willing to reduce your level of consumption in exchange for more free time?

Weekly Time Diary

Examine how you use the time of your life. Keep a time diary for a typical week and note how many hours you spend:

Activity	Hours Per Week
Working	_____
Preparing for work	_____
Commuting to and from work	_____
Housekeeping	_____
Doing yard and home maintenance	_____
Doing household or work-related errands	_____
Alone with your mate	_____
Alone with your children	_____
With the whole (nuclear) family	_____
With extended family (in person or on the phone)	_____
With friends (in person or on the phone)	_____
In community activities	_____
Watching television	_____
Learning	_____
Exercising	_____
Idling	_____
Playing	_____
In forms of creative self-expression	_____
Meditating	_____
In nature	_____
Planning	_____
Reading and thinking	_____
Sleeping	_____
Paying bills or attending to other financial matters	_____
Other	_____
Other	_____
Other	_____

What are your thoughts and feelings as you reflect on your time diary?

Did anything surprise you? If so, what?

What adjustments would you like to make to the way you use time?

What activities do you spend the bulk of your time and money on?

Do these reflect your personal paradigm or vision of abundance?

Are there ways in which you can make your actions better fit with your values?
Describe.

◆ ◆ ◆

The Leisure of Your Life

Rate each of the following types of leisure in terms of their relative value in your life.

1. Time to idle _____   *5.* Time to express _____
2. Time to play _____   *6.* Time for your mate _____
3. Time to think _____   *7.* Time for your children _____
4. Time to learn _____   *8.* Time for your community _____

How can you see to it that these important values in your life are not overwhelmed by the urgent necessities of working and making a living? What activities could you eliminate or reduce (e.g., watching television) that would free up time for these personally meaningful pursuits?

LEISURE TO BE

Time to Idle: When was the last time you made a point of doing nothing, when you weren't feeling tired or exhausted? What was the setting? What effect did it have on you? Did you feel rejuvenated, or did it make you feel uncomfortable or guilty? How can you make the time to spend even a few hours a week doing nothing at all?

Time to Play: What is your attitude toward play? Do you view it as a reward for work well done? Something reserved for the weekends? Do you see it as an integral part of your everyday life?

List ways that you can bring more play into your life. For example: singing, dancing, affectionate teasing of a loved one, goofing off, laughing, etc.

LEISURE TO GROW

Time to Learn: What do you want to learn?

About life: For fun:

About yourself: About the world and the people in it:

For your career: About other things of interest to you:

Time to Think: How much time do you take to reflect upon issues not related to your immediate survival or daily personal concerns?

In this regard, what do you like to think about? For example: the nature of reality, the structure and direction of society, means of better symbolizing, conceptualizing, doing, or organizing things, etc.

Do you feel you are at the mercy of unconscious forces within you and/or larger social forces without?

How could you bring greater awareness into these dynamics?

Planning: Most of us could save a lot of time by more effectively managing the way we use it. A little forethought and planning in the way we do things will make more time for the things that are important to us. Remembering the 80/20 principle and rule of one to four (see chapter 7), how can you employ these techniques to better organize the way you use time?

Time for Creative Self-expression: What vehicles for creative self-expression are you currently engaged in?

What new forms of self-expression would you like to take up? What immediate steps can you take to begin? For example: purchase art supplies and begin painting or take a painting class; begin keeping a journal or take a writing class, etc.

Vehicles for Creative Expression	*Action Steps to Implement*
1.	
2.	
3.	
4.	
5.	

LEISURE TO RELATE

Time for our Mate: Evaluate quality time you spend with your mate, with "one" being almost no time; "ten," being enough time.

Time sharing with one another your individual values, visions, and goals.

| 1 | 2 | 3 | 4 | 5 | 6 | 7 | 8 | 9 | 10 |

Time to share your fears, doubts, or concerns.

| 1 | 2 | 3 | 4 | 5 | 6 | 7 | 8 | 9 | 10 |

Time discussing the events of the day.

| 1 | 2 | 3 | 4 | 5 | 6 | 7 | 8 | 9 | 10 |

Time for romance and an exciting sex life.

| 1 | 2 | 3 | 4 | 5 | 6 | 7 | 8 | 9 | 10 |

Time for affection.

| 1 | 2 | 3 | 4 | 5 | 6 | 7 | 8 | 9 | 10 |

Time for shared activities.

| 1 | 2 | 3 | 4 | 5 | 6 | 7 | 8 | 9 | 10 |

Time to develop shared goals.

| 1 | 2 | 3 | 4 | 5 | 6 | 7 | 8 | 9 | 10 |

Time to play and be silly.

| 1 | 2 | 3 | 4 | 5 | 6 | 7 | 8 | 9 | 10 |

What were your strongest areas?

Your weakest areas?

How can you improve on these?

Time for the Children: How much time do you spend with your children as a family? Alone with each child?

What additional activities or experiences would you like to share with your children?

How can you create the time to make these happen?

Time for Our Communities: What issue or issues in your community, nation, or world are you most concerned about?

What are you currently doing about these issues? What more could you be doing?

How can you bring more of a sense of community into your life? Participate in community activities? Organize neighborhood events? Develop an informal social group, organized around an area of interest?

List ways that you can bring play to your life. For example: singing, dancing, affectionate teasing of a loved one, goofing off, roaring laughter, etc.

CHAPTER 8

◆

Watching Your Imagination Diet

CUT DOWN ON JUNK FOOD

In what ways can you significantly reduce or eliminate "mental junk food" that drains your energy and saps your imaginative power? For example: watching less television, being more selective in the films you watch and the music you listen to, etc.

What lifestyle changes are you willing to make in order to keep your mind free of draining and deadening distractions?

EAT HIGH-QUALITY FOOD

What positive, uplifting "food" would you like to add to your imagination diet? (Consider art, literature, theater, music, philosophy, spiritual reflection, etc.)

What are some ways that you could expose yourself to art in the coming months? (Consider museums, galleries, concerts, films, books, music, etc.)

Li and Ch'i at Work: Exploring Career Options

The exercise that follows can serve as a way of exploring what career options might be best for you. (Again, for a much more in-depth approach to finding the right work for you, consult books such as *Zen and the Art of Making a Living, How to Find the Work You Love*, and other books of this type; or see a career professional.)

1. Make a list of career options you have considered.

2. **Wisdom of the Body:** For the second part of this exercise, ask a friend to help you. Give the friend your list of career options and ask him or her to ask you the questions that appear below. Feel your energy as you answer the questions and ask your friend as well to note how your energy changes as you discuss the various career options. Remember where you find the deepest source of energy (or *ch'i*) in your life, you will find the key to its organic pattern (*li*). Do not prepare for this exercise. Answer spontaneously. Don't worry about how articulate you are—pay attention to the energy. For variations on this exercise, you might want to videotape your question-and-answer session and review it later, or you could simply write your answers while feeling the energy in your body.

Why do you want to be a _____?

How does this career fit with your purpose in life?

In what ways does this career utilize your natural talents and gifts?

3.   Overall, which career option elicited the most energy and excitement?

     According to your friend   According to you

4.   What immediate steps can you take to keep the energy moving into this new
     career? For example: conducting research, interviewing people in the field, taking
     classes, etc.

Defeating the "Evil Twins"

The Taoists tell us that life is a beautiful gift. Yet ingratitude can blind us to the inherent beauty in life. Ingratitude comes in two varieties: Envy and Self-Pity. Both of these orient our consciousness on lack, and the more we focus on lack, the more it seems to expand in our lives.

ENVY

1.   List all of the things you envy in others.

Next, with regard to each item, ask yourself, Why am I making what others have or are more important than what I have and am? Remember, you can't envy others without making yourself, and indeed the whole mutually-arising universe, wrong.

2.   Often envy arises when we see other people having pleasure or enjoying life in ways that we are denying ourselves. Envy can be a useful tool for increasing self-awareness in that it often indicates what we really want, not what we think or hope we want, but what we actually *do* want. By exploring what makes you feel envious, you can gain a clearer understanding of your true desires and where you feel blocked or stuck in your own life.

Whom do you envy the most? List the first three people that come to mind.

For each of these individuals, list three reasons why you envy them. Pay particular attention to the qualities they exhibit or express that seem to be lacking in your life.

What can you do to bring these or similar qualities or aspects into your own life?

Now construct goals that will allow you to transform your feelings of jealousy into the expression of aspects of yourself that you may have blocked or denied.

SELF-PITY

List all of the ways you let self-pity creep into your life.

What things do you complain about most?

In what ways do you see yourself as a victim of others?

In what ways do you see yourself as inadequate to the challenges of life?

Attitude Adjustment: Your attitude toward the people, things, events, and experiences in life makes all the difference. If you trust in life and see all things as having mutually arisen with yourself, you recognize that you are never given a situation in life that you can't handle. With this in mind, how can you view the situations you listed above in a way that shows that you recognize life itself is a gift?

Beauty in the Little Things

List ten things that you can do to add beauty to your life that cost very little or no money.

What simple things can you do to make your home a more beautiful and attractive place? Your work space?

In what ways can you bring touches of nature into your living space? Your work space?

In what ways can you bring greater beauty into the work you do every day? For example: putting increased care and attention to detail into the things you do and make, radiating cheerfulness and love to those around you, sharing wisdom when and where appropriate.

Recall a time when you were in nature and you felt yourself slowing down to its natural rhythms. What were the most memorable sights and sounds?

What scenes in nature do you find most beautiful? For example: mountain streams, ocean cliffs or beaches, meadows, forests, deserts, lakes, rolling hills.

How long has it been since you enjoyed such scenes? When will you again?

AFFIRMATIONS

◆

CHAPTER 1

I am one with the natural abundance of the universe.

I am one with the creative intelligence of the universe.

I am at one with the process of the universe.

I am at one with this experience. What is happening now is meant to be.

What I admire is not better than me, what I detest is not worse than me, nothing is better, worse, or different from me.

My body is the same stuff as the flowers and trees; my mind is one with infinite galaxies.

Without my possessing anything, all things are mine to enjoy.

CHAPTER 2

The Creative Intelligence of the Universe (Tao) is the source of my supply.

I am now willing to receive love without struggle.

I am now willing to receive money without struggle.

I am open and receive the creative inspirations meant for me.

I am open and receive all the blessings meant for me.

Nothing must happen first before I can receive the love of the universe.

Nothing must happen first before I can receive the abundance of the universe.

CHAPTER 3

I attract love with ease.

I attract money with ease.

The Universe is for me and so is everything else.

_____ is for me and so is everything else.

I am for me and so is everything else.

Everything is for me and so is everything else.

I see the results I desire within my mind and they become manifest in the world.

CHAPTER 4

The energy is now flowing freely in all areas of my life.

The energy is now flowing freely in my body.

Money is flowing freely in my life.

I bless money and money blesses me.

I forgive all and all is forgiven me.

I am enjoying an abundant supply of energy in my life.

I have energy enough for all that is important to me.

I breathe easily and deeply, my breath energizes me.

The more good I do for others, the more good comes back to me.

CHAPTER 5

I am a naturally powerful and competent being.

I handle all that life presents to me with dignity and grace.

I trust my intuition and it guides me to my destiny.

I am doing the work I was born to do.

I have the courage to follow my destiny wherever it leads.

I am a naturally powerful person.

CHAPTER 6

I am at one with the dual forces in nature.

I am enjoying a happy, healthy, and exciting sex life.

I am moving toward ever greater harmony, balance, and acceptance in my life.

I embrace my dark side and it turns to light.

I am always at the right place at the right time.

CHAPTER 7

I make time for all the things that are important to me.

I am a playful being, so I make time to play.

I am a spiritual being, so I make time to be and to celebrate the mystery of life.

I am a social being, so I make time to relate to the people who are important to me.

I value time and use it well.

I value my humanity over any material thing.

CHAPTER 8

I live in beauty and beauty lives in me.

I see the beauty in myself and beauty blesses me.

I see the beauty in others and others bless me.

I see the beauty in nature and nature blesses me.

I see the beauty in art and art blesses me.

I allow the natural organic pattern of my life to unfold.

I am at one with the natural rhythms of life.

CHAPTER NOTES

THE FIVE FINGERS OF THE TAO

1. Chuang Tzu, quoted in Fritjof Capra, *The Tao of Physics* (New York: Bantam Books, 1984), 17.

2. This interpretation (the "five fingers") is my own and does not follow that of any particular Taoist school.

3. John Heider, *Tao of Leadership* (Atlanta, Ga.: Humanics Publishing Group, 1986). Nothing said here is meant to in any way disparage books of the sort mentioned above or the undoubtedly valuable information in them.

4. Chuang Tzu, quoted in Fritjof Capra, *The Tao of Physics,* 15.

5. Over the years there has much discussion and debate among scholars about whether Lao Tzu was in fact a historical figure or merely a legendary one, and about whether or not the *Tao Te Ching* can be attributed to any *single* author. The reader should be aware that when I use the expression "Lao Tzu said," I am using a literary convention and not implying authorship by a single historical person. I could have chosen to say "the Lao Tzu says," which would be more technically correct but unwieldy to use. The device used here is not unlike saying "Jesus Christ said," though no one believes that he wrote any of the gospels.

6. See Aldous Huxley, *The Perennial Philosophy* (New York: Harper & Row, 1944, 1945, 1970, 1990), and Frithjof Schoun, *The Transcendent Unity of Religions* (Wheaton, Ill.: Theosophical Publishing House, 1984).

7. *The Song of God: Bhagavad-Gita* trans. Swami Prabhavananda and Christopher Isherwood with an introduction by Aldous Huxley (New York: Penguin Books USA, 1972), chapter 13.

8. Joseph Campbell with Bill Moyers, ed. Betty Sue Flowers, *The Power of Myth* (New York: Doubleday, 1988), 130, 131.

9. Anne Baring and Jules Cashford, *The Myth of the Goddess* (New York: Arkana, 1991), 8, 9.

10. *Chuang Tzu,* chapter 2, quoted in Martin Palmer, *The Elements of Taoism* (Rockport, Mass.: Elements Books, 1991), 6.

11. Joseph Needham, *Science and Civilisation in China,* vol. 2 (New York: Cambridge University Press, 1991), 162.

12. Chuang Tzu, quoted in Joseph Needham, 87.

13. Michael H. Kohn, trans., *The Shambhala Dictionary of Buddhism and Zen* (Boston: Shambhala, 1991).

14. Thomas Merton, *The Way of Chuang Tzu* (New York: New Directions, 1965), 40.

15. Chuang Tzu, quoted in Benjamin Schwartz, *The World of Thought in Ancient China* (Cambridge, Mass.: Harvard University Press, 1985), 233.

16. Karlfried Graf Dürckheim, trans. Vincent Nash, *Zen and Us* (New York: E. P. Dutton, 1987).

17. *Chuang Tzu,* chapter VI, quoted in Fung Yu-lan, *Chuang-Tzu* (Beijing: Foreign Languages Press, 1989).

18. *Chuang Tzu,* chapter 25, quoted in Martin Palmer, *The Elements of Taoism*, 7.

19. R.G.H. Siu, *Tao of Science* (Cambridge Mass.: M.I.T. Press, 1990).

20. See *The Structure of Scientific Revolutions* by Thomas Kuhn (Chicago: University of Chicago Press, 1970).

21. *Chuang Tzu,* chapter 29, quoted in Joseph Needham, *Science and Civilisation in China,* vol. 2 (New York: Cambridge University Press, 1991), 102.

22. Albert Schweitzer, ed. Thomas Kierman, *A Treasury of Albert Schweitzer* (New York: Gramercy Books, 1965), 65.

INTRODUCTION

1. Lila and Dale Truett, *Economics* (St. Paul: West Publishing Company, 1982), 6. In *The Making of Economic Society,* economist Robert Heilbroner is emphatic on this point: "If there were no scarcity... economics . . . would cease to exist as a social preoccupation." Robert Heilbroner, *The Making of Economic Society* (Englewood Cliffs, N.J.: Prentice Hall, 1962), 5.

2. This and all the Buckminster Fuller quotes following are from *Critical Path* by R. Buckminster Fuller (New York: St. Martin's Press, 1981), 198.

3. See *Earth, Energy and Everyone* and *Ho-ping: Food for Everyone,* both by Medard Gabel. For more up-to-date information, visit the World Game Institute website at www.worldgame.org.

4. R. Buckminster Fuller, *Critical Path.*

CHAPTER ONE

1. Lao Tzu, quoted in Joseph Needham, *Science and Civilisation in China,* vol. 2 (New York: Cambridge University Press, 1991), 113.

2. Albert Schweitzer, ed. Harold Robles, *Reverence for Life* (San Francisco: Harper San Francisco, 1993).

3. Lao Tzu, quoted in Brian Walker, *Hua Hu Ching: The Unknown Teachings of Lao Tzu* (San Francisco: Harper San Francisco, 1995).

4. Lao Tzu, *Tao Te Ching,* chapter 25, quoted in Martin Palmer, *The Elements of Taoism* (Rockport, Mass.: Elements Books, 1991), 43.

5. Chuang Tzu, chapter 2, quoted in Martin Palmer, *The Elements of Taoism,* 6.

6. Kuo Hsiang, quoted in Fung Yu-lan, *Chuang-Tzu* (Beijing: Foreign Languages Press, 1989).

7. *Chuang Tzu,* chapter 2, quoted in Chang Chung-yuan, *Creativity and Taoism* (New York: Harper and Row, 1970), 36.

8. Ch'eng Hao, quoted in Chang Chung-yuan, *Creativity and Taoism.*

9. William Shakespeare, Hamlet.

10. Lao Tzu quoted in Martin Palmer, *The Elements of Taoism* (Rockport, Mass.: Elements Books, 1991), 1.

11. J. Krishnamurti, *The Awakening of Intelligence* (New York: Avon, 1973).

12. *The Way of Life: Lao Tzu,* trans. R. B. Blakney (New York: The New American Library, 1955).

13. Chuang Tzu, chapter 4 quoted in Chang Chung-yuan, *Creativity and Taoism,* 129.

14. Lu Hsiang-shan, quoted in Chang Chung-yuan, *Creativity and Taoism,* 83.

15. Joseph Needham, *Science and Civilisation in China,* 124.

16. Lao Tzu, quoted in Brian Walker, *Hua Hu Ching: The Unknown Teachings of Lao Tzu.*

17. Fung Yu-Lan, *A Short History of Chinese Philosophy* (New York: MacMillan, 1948), 18.

CHAPTER TWO

1. Wang Pi, quoted in *Lao-tzu and the Tao-te-Ching,* eds. Livia Kohn and Michael LaFargue (Albany, N.Y.: Suny Press, 1998).

2.   *Man models himself after earth*
    Earth models itself after heaven
    Heaven models itself after the Tao
    Tao models itself after so-being.   (*Tao Te Ching,* chapter 25)

3. Chuang-Tzu, quoted in Fung Yu-lan, *Chuang-Tzu* (Beijing: Foreign Languages Press, 1989), 12.

4. T. C. McLuhan, *Touch the Earth: A Self-Portrait of Indian Existence* (New York: Simon and Schuster, 1971), 99.

5. Quoted from the *Los Angeles Times,* 26 December 1993, sec. A.

6. Richard J. Barnet and John Cavanagh*, Global Dreams: Imperial Corporations and the New World Order* (New York: Simon and Schuster, 1994).

7. Alan Thein Durning, "Can't Live without It: Advertising and the Creation of Needs," *World Watch Magazine,* May/June 1993.

8. *Los Angeles Times,* 17 July 1996, Business section.

9. Quoted from the *Los Angeles Times,* 5 March 1998, sec. A, 21.

10. Henri Maspero, *Taoism and Chinese Religion,* trans. Frank A. Kierman Jr. (Amherst, Mass.: University of Massachusetts Press, 1981).

CHAPTER THREE

1. I will use the term *wu wei* as synonymous with effortless action or unforced action. This is a device used for simplicity's sake. We actually mean *wei wu wei* (literally, act-not-act) or "enacting nonaction."

2. *The Book of Lieh-tzu,* trans. A. C. Graham (New York: Columbia University Press, 1990), 90.

3. Chuang Tzu, quoted in *Tao: The Watercourse Way* by Alan Watts (New York: Pantheon Books, 1975), 80.

4. Benjamin Pang Jeng Lo, with Martin Inn, Robert Amacker, and Susan Foe, *The Essence of T'ai Chi Ch'uan* (Berkeley: North Atlantic Books, 1985), 54.

5. Quoted in *Coming to Our Senses*, by Morris Berman (Seattle, Wash.: Seattle Writers' Guild, 1998), 41.

6. Quoted in *The Power of Myth*, by Joseph Campbell with Bill Moyers, ed. Betty Sue Flowers (New York: Doubleday, 1988).

7. Chuang Tzu, quoted in *Chuang-Tzu* by Fung Yu-lan (Beijing: Foreign Languages Press, 1989).

8. Quoted from *Practical Taoism*, trans. Thomas Cleary (Boston, London: Shambhala, 1996), 46.

9. Lao Tzu, from Gregory C. Richter, *The Gate of All Marvelous Things: A Guide to Reading the Tao Te Ching* (South San Francisco, Calif.: Red Mansions Publishing, 1998), 66.

10. Quoted from *Practical Taoism*, trans. Thomas Cleary, 32.

11. See *The Secret Life of Plants* by Peter Tompkins and Christopher O. Bird (New York: HarperCollins, 1989).

12. Yuantong, quoted in *Zen Lessons* by Thomas Cleary (Boston: Shambhala, 1993).

13. Sun Tzu, *The Art of War,* trans. Thomas Cleary (Boston: Shambhala, 1988), 127.

14. *Practical Taoism*, trans. Thomas Cleary, 35.

CHAPTER FOUR

1. We have chosen to use *ch'i*. The reader new to Taoist writings should be aware that it is also romanized from the Chinese as *Ji, Qi, Chee, Chi, Chhi.*

2. Fung Yu-Lan, *A Short History of Chinese Philosophy* (New York: MacMillan, 1948).

3. The concept of karma was fully integrated by later Taoist schools. During the Southern Sung Dynasty (1127-1279) "Action and Karma" Taoism, a fusion of Buddhist, Confucian, and Taoist concepts, flourished in the south. The teaching of karmic responsibility was a central component of this popular Taoist religion.

4. As I mentioned in a previous footnote, Ch'i is also romanized Ji, Qi, Chee, and Chi. Similarly, kung is also romanized gung or gong. Ch'i Kung and Chee Gung and Qi Gong all refer to the same practice which can be loosely translated as "energy work."

5. Centers for Disease Control and President's Council on Physical Fitness and Sports, "Physical Activity and Health: A Report of the Surgeon General," *Chronic Disease Notes and Reports* 9, no. 2 (fall 1996).

6. Harry Emerson Fosdick, *On Being a Real Person* (New York: HarperCollins Publishers, 1977).

7. *Practical Taoism*, trans. Thomas Cleary (Boston, London: Shambhala, 1996), 53.

8. Joanne O'Brien with Kwok Man Ho, *The Elements of Feng Shui* (Rockport, Mass.: Element, Inc., 1991), 32.

CHAPTER FIVE

1. Fung Yu-lan, *Chuang-Tzu* (Beijing: Foreign Languages Press, 1989), 9.

2. *The American Heritage Dictionary: Dictionary of the English Language,* 3rd ed. (Boston: Houghton Mifflin Company, 1995).

3. Mark 8:36, 37.

4. See Edouard Schuré, *The Great Initiates: A Study of the Secret History of Religions* (San Francisco: Harper and Row, 1961).

5. The following is drawn largely from the work of Joseph Campbell and Manly F. Hall. See *Transformations of Myth Through Time* by Joseph Campbell (New York: HarperCollins, 1990) and *The Secret Teachings of All the Ages* by Manly P. Hall and Augustus Knapp (Los Angeles: Philosophical Research Society, 1999).

6. Roger Somers quoted in *Genuine Fake: A Biography of Alan Watts* by Monica Furlong (London: Unwin Paperbacks, 1986), 167.

7. See Alan Watts, *Tao: The Watercourse Way* (New York: Pantheon Books, 1975). Chuang-liang Huang's view seems to have been shared by Watt's friend Gary Synder. "I told him as best I could to get off of it [the drinking] but by this time he was stuck with an enormous alimony payment, and he was having to take far more gigs than anyone in their right mind would want to do just earning money, and he was also spending more money than he had to." Quoted in *Genuine Fake: A Biography of Alan Watts* by Monica Furlong, 166.

8. Tenzin Gyatso, *Universal Responsibility and the Good Heart* (Kanga, India: Library of Tibetan Works and Archives, 1980), 33.

9. See Joseph Needham, *Science and Civilisation in China,* vol. 2 (New York: Cambridge University Press, 1991), especially sections 10 (f) and 10 (g).

10. Lao Tzu, *Tao Te Ching*, chapter 60, quoted in *Tao: The Watercourse Way* by Alan Watts.

11. Joseph Needham, *Science and Civilisation in China*.

12. Karl Polanyi, *The Great Transformation* (Boston: Beacon Press, 1944), 72.

13. Ibid., 71.

14. Ibid., 73.

15. Ibid., 128.

16. Ibid., 133.

17. The population of Mexico City is already over twenty million people. According to a study commissioned by the Southern California Association of Governments, the six-county greater Los Angeles Metro Area will have a population of 22.35 million by 2020. Reported in the *Los Angeles Times*, 8 May 1998.

18. Even in an affluent country like the United States the top one percent of households now have more wealth than the entire bottom 95 percent. See Chuck Collins, Betsy Leondar-Wright and Holly Sklarr, *Shifting Fortunes: The Perils of the Growing American Wealth Gap* (Boston: United for a Fair Economy, 1999.)

19. Polanyi, *The Great Transformation*, 73.

20. E. F. Schumacher with Peter N. Gillingham, *Good Work* (New York: Harper and Row, 1979), 128.

21. Adam Smith, *Wealth of Nations,* vol. 1 (London: Methuen and Company, 1950).

22. Michael J. Sandel, *Democracy's Discontents: America in Search of a Public Philosophy* (Cambridge, Mass.: Harvard University Press, 1996).

23. Ibid.

24. Ananda K. Coomaraswamy, *Christian and Oriental Philosophy of Art* (Mineola, N.Y.: Dover Publications, 1956), 15.

25. E. F. Schumarcher with Peter N. Gillingham, *Good Work*, 25.

26. Polanyi, *The Great Transformation,* 140, 141.

27. Ibid., 139.

28. Arnold Toynbee, *A Study of History* (New York: Crown Publishers, 1988).

29. There were, of course, white indentured servants and especially in the South, tenant farmers.

30. "Median family income in 1994 was still $2,168 lower than it was in 1989." Lawrence Mishel, Jared Bernstein and John Schmitt, *The State of Working America 1996-1997* (Ithica, N.Y.: Cornell University Press, Economic Policy Institute, 1997).

31. See Juliet B. Schor, *The Overworked American* (New York: Basic Books, a division of HarperCollins Publishers, 1991).

32. Quoted in *New York Times,* 28 March 1994.

33. Jack Weatherford, *The History of Money* (New York: Three Rivers Press, 1997), 205-206.

34. Mishel, Bernstein and Schmitt, *The State of Working America 1996-1997.*

35. According to the United States Justice Department's Bureau of Statistics as of June 30, 1997, 1.7 million, or one in 155 Americans, was incarcerated. Reported in *the Los Angeles Times,* 5 March 1998.

36. William R. Leach, *Land of Desire* (New York: Pantheon Books, 1993).

37. *Deut. 23: 19-20.*

38. Fernand Braudel, *The Wheels of Commerce* (Berkeley: University of California Press, 1992).

CHAPTER SIX

1. The root text of the *I Ching* which describes the hexagrams and their lines is much older than the commentaries added later by Confucians. The root text is said to date from either the mythical Emperor Fsu Hsi (circa 3000 B.C.E.) or King Wen (circa 1150 B.C.E.) and his son Duke Chou. The commentaries were added some seven centuries later.

2. Richard Wilhelm and Cary F. Baynes, trans. *The I Ching* (New York: Princeton University Press, 1967), book 5, chapter 2.

3. See *Sexual Life in Ancient China* (New York: Barnes and Noble Books, 1961), by R. H. van Gulik and *The Art of the Bedchamber*, trans. Douglas Wile (New York: State University of New York Press, 1992). The Indian and Tibetan Tantra sexual arts were apparently heavily influenced by sexual teachings of Chinese origin. Joseph Needham and R. H. van Gulik point to the end of the seventh century as the time when Taoist sexual arts were introduced into India.

4. *Hsein*, literally "mountain man" is usually translated "Immortal." The process of hsein-ship is essentially one of creating a subtle immortal body.

5. Reay Tannahill, *Sex in History* (New York: Stein and Day Publishers, 1982), 141.

6. Ibid., 148.

7. R. H. van Gulik, *Sexual Life in Ancient China*, 50-51.

8. Joseph Needham, *Science and Civilisation in China,* vol. 2 (New York: Cambridge University Press, 1991), 151.

9. Eknath Easwaran and Michael N. Nagler, *Gandhi the Man* (Petaluma, Calif.: Nilgiri Press, 1977), 87.

10. See Ilza Veith, *The Yellow Emperor's Classic of Internal Medicine* (Berkeley: University of California Press, 1949).

11. This discussion draws from chapter 6 of *The Portable Jung* by Joseph Campbell (New York: Viking, 1976), 148-162.

12. See Joseph Needham, *Science and Civilisation in China*, 340-345.

13. Richard Wilhelm and Cary F. Baynes, trans. *The I Ching, l.*

14. Douglas Wile, trans., *The Art of the Bedchamber*, 133.

15. Daniel Boorstein, *The Discoverers* (New York: Random House, 1985).

16. Robert Temple, *The Genius of China* (London: Prion Books Limited, 1986).

CHAPTER SEVEN

1. The others are *Chih*, wisdom; *Yi,* righteousness or duty; and *Li,* the practice of rites and ceremonies. Not to be confused with *li,* as it is used in the next chapter where it refers to organic patterns or principles of organization.

2. *The American Heritage Dictionary: Dictionary of the English Language,* 3rd ed. (Boston: Houghton Mifflin Company, 1995).

3. Hans Holbein, *The Ambassadors* (1533), National Gallery, London; Liu Chüeh, *The Pure and Plain Pavilion* (1458), National Palace Museum, Taipei.

4. John Berger, *Ways of Seeing* (New York: Viking Press, 1995).

5. Michael F. Jacobson, "Commercialism in America," address at a meeting of the National Association of Consumer Agency Administrators, June 16, 1992.

6. See Joseph Needham, *Science and Civilisation in China, vol. 2, History of Scientific Thought* (New York: Cambridge University Press, 1956, 1991), 124.

7. This story and the quotes used from it appeared in an article by Elizabeth Lesly Stevens entitled, "Making Bill," in *Content* magazine September 1998, 106.

8. Alan Thein Durning, *How Much Is Enough? The Consumer Society and the Future of the Earth* (New York: W.W. Norton & Co, Inc, 1992), 38.

9. Sandy Bauers, "Study: Save Earth; Have Fewer Children," *Philadelphia Inquirer,* 17 January 1990.

10. Jessie H. O'Neil, *Golden Ghetto: The Psychology of Affluence* (Pleasant Valley, Minn.: Hazelden Educational Materials, 1996).

11. Alan Durning, "Asking How Much Is Enough," in Lester R. Brown et al, *State of the World 1991* (New York: W.W. Norton and Co. Inc., 1991), 156.

12. It would be wrong to conclude that longevity corresponds directly with economic and technological development. U.S. and U.K. longevity rates are similar to those in Sri Lanka and China. See *The Gaia Atlas of Green Economics* by Paul Ekins, Robert Hutchinson, and Mayer Hillman (New York: Anchor Press, 1992).

13. Juliet B. Schor, *The Overworked American* (New York: Basic Books, a division of HarperCollins Publishers, 1991), 47.

14. In 1991, employed Americans worked 163 more hours per year than they did in 1969. Ibid., 29.

15. Robert Heilbroner quoted in Ann Kathleen Bradley's, "Is Less More?" *New Age Journal,* July/August 1997, 86-146.

16. According to the Economic Policy Institute, median family income is less today in real dollars than it was in 1974. According to United for a Fair Economy, weekly wages for average workers in 1998 were 12% lower than in 1973, adjusting for inflation. *See Shifting Fortunes: The Perils of the Growing American Wealth Gap* by Chuck Collins et. al (Boston: United for a Fair Economy, 1999).

17. Alan Trachtenberg, *The Incorporation of America: Culture and Society in the Guilded Age* (New York: Farrar, Straus and Giroux, 1992).

18. Ibid.

19. An additional 20-30 million experience intermittent sleep-related problems. Source: U.S. Department of Health and Human Services, *Wake up America: A National Sleep Alert.* Report of The National Commission on Sleep Disorders Research, January 1993.

20. The number of visits during which a psychotropic medication was prescribed increased from 32.73 million in 1985 to 45.64 million in 1994. Harold Alan Pincus, et al., "Prescribing Trends in Psychotropic Medications: Primary Care, Psychiatry, and Other Medical Specialities," *JAMA, The Journal of the American Medical Association,* 18 February 1998, vol. 279 no. 7, 526(6).

21. More than twenty-five million abuse alcohol and illegal drugs. Cited in Peter R. Breggin, *Toxic Psychiatry* (New York: St. Martin's Press, 1994), 367.

22. Juliet B. Schor, *The Overworked American.*

23. Quoted in William R. Leach, *Land of Desire* (New York: Pantheon Books, 1993).

24. Ibid.

25. Ibid.

26. Ibid.

27. Ibid.

28. Ibid.

29. Ibid.

30. Reported on the PBS television program *Affluenza* produced by John de Graaf and Vivia Boe for KTCS/Seattle and Oregon Public Broadcasting, 1998.

31. William R. Leach, *Land of Desire.*

32. In 1998, 1,436,924 filed for personal bankruptcy.

33. Janice Castro, "The Simple Life," *Time,* 8 April 1991, 58.

34. Reported in Ann Kathleen Bradley, "Is Less More?" *New Age Journal,* July/August 1997, 86-146.

35. Adam Smith in the *Wealth of Nations* (London: Methuen and Company, 1950), had predicted precisely this outcome.

36. See Joseph Needham, *Science and Civilisation in China,* and Robert Temple, *The Genius of China* (London: Prion Books Limited, 1986).

37. Jessie H. O'Neil, *Golden Ghetto: The Psychology of Affluence.*

38. Karl Polyani*, The Great Transformation* (Boston: Beacon Press, 1980), 249.

39. Ibid., 43-44.

CHAPTER EIGHT

1. Irwin Edman, *Arts and the Man* (New York: W. W. Norton and Company), 37.

2. Some have argued that critical technological breakthroughs such as the wheel and the ox-drawn plow were first used as part of religious rituals and only later adapted to everyday use.

The wheel was everywhere a religious symbol—even among peoples that did not put it to physical use, such as those in the great civilizations of South America and Mesoamerica. It was the Sumerians who first put the wheel to work, and when they did, it would be drawn by an animal sacred in India, Egypt, Old Europe, and Mesopotamia, the ox. Lewis Mumford writes: "It is significant that the first known harnessing of cattle to sleighs or wagons was in religious processions; just as the earliest vehicles that have survived were not farm wagons or even military chariots, but hearses, which are found buried with draught animals and human attendants in the royal tombs at Kish, Susa, and Ur." The use of animal power, then, may well have been inspired by religious motivations and later adapted to augment—and in some cases replace—human labor.

Mumford (following John Hocart) also suggests that the plow was first "a purely religious instrument, drawn by a sacred ox, held by a priest or later king, penetrating Mother earth with its masculine tool, getting ready the soil for fertilization: so that gardens and fields, opened actually by digging stick or pickaxe, as yet never worked by any plow, might benefit by the ritual." See Lewis Mumford *The Myth of the Machine* (New York: Harcourt Brace, 1966), 153.

3. Lewis Mumford, *Art and Technics* (New York, London: Columbia University Press, 1952).

4. Note: the romanized term *li* can refer to a variety of meanings, from "fire" to "strength," "civility," and more.

5. While the theory of *li* was developed by the Chu Hsi, the term has connections to the classical Taoists. It was used some 35 times in the *Chuang Tzu.*

6. Chu Hsi with translations and commentary by Daniel K. Gardner, *Learning to Be a Sage* (Berkeley: University of California Press, 1990), 124.

7. Joseph Needham, *Science and Civilisation in China,* vol. 2 (New York: Cambridge University Press, 1991), 480.

8. Again, according to Chu Hsi this *li* exists prior to the thing taking form in the physical world.

9. This closely follows Aquinas' aesthetic ideal as given in James Joyce's *A Portrait of the Artist as*

a Young Man (New York: The Viking Press, 1964), viz.: wholeness (*integritas*), harmony (*consonantia*), and radiance (*claritas*).

10. Goethe described himself as a polytheist with respect to poetry, a pantheist with respect to science, and theist with respect to morals.

11. Frederick Ungar, ed. and Heinz Norden, trans., *Goethe's World View* (New York: Frederick Ungar Publishing Co., 1963).

12. Quoted in *The Chinese Theory of Art* by Lin Yutang (New York: G. P. Putnam's Sons, 1967), 64, 65.

13. Joseph Campbell, *The Masks of God: Creative Mythology* (New York: Arkana, 1995), 653.

14. Joseph Campbell, *Historical Altas of World Mythology,* vol. II, part 1 (Harper and Row, New York, 1988), 74.

15. Joseph Campbell, *Inner Reaches of Outer Space: Metaphor as Myth and As Religion* (New York: HarperCollins Publishers, 1988), 67.

16. See "Special Report: The Promise of Tissue Engineering," *Scientific American* April 1999, vol. 280, no. 4.

17. Quoted in William R. Leach, *Land of Desire* (New York: Pantheon Books, 1993), 46.

18. Matthew 5:45.

19. Robert Graves, *The White Goddess* (New York: Farrar, Straus and Giroux, 1948), 14-15.

20. David Tame, *Beethoven and the Spiritual Path* (Wheaton Illinois, Quest Books, 1994).

21. This translation appears in *The Transformation of Nature in Art* by Ananda K. Coomaraswamy, (New York: Dover Publications, 1934*), The Chieh Tzu Yuan Hua Chuan* or *Mustard Seed Garden Manual of Painting* was first published between 1679 and 1701.

22. Arnold Toynbee, *A Study of History* (New York: Crown Publishers, 1987).

23. Ananda K. Coomaraswamy, *Christian and Oriental Philosophy of Art* (New York: Dover, 1956).

24. From a Hindu perspective, an unstudied or "natural" artistic genius is one who has acquired great skill and merit in previous lifetimes.

25. Wassily Kandinsky, *Concerning the Spiritual in Art* (New York: Dover, 1977).

26. Robert L. Herbert, *Modern Artists on Art* (New York: Macmillan General Reference, 1964). (emphasis in original)

For more information, resources, and links
on creating abundance, finding the right
career, and more, visit:

THE CENTER FOR

CREATIVE EMPOWERMENT at

www.empoweryou.com

FOR THE BEST IN PAPERBACKS, LOOK FOR THE (penguin logo)

In every corner of the world, on every subject under the sun, Penguin represents quality and variety—the very best in publishing today.

For complete information about books available from Penguin—including Puffins, Penguin Classics, and Compass—and how to order them, write to us at the appropriate address below. Please note that for copyright reasons the selection of books varies from country to country.

In the United Kingdom: Please write to *Dept. EP, Penguin Books Ltd, Bath Road, Harmondsworth, West Drayton, Middlesex UB7 0DA.*

In the United States: Please write to *Penguin Putnam Inc., P.O. Box 12289 Dept. B, Newark, New Jersey 07101-5289* or call 1-800-788-6262.

In Canada: Please write to *Penguin Books Canada Ltd, 10 Alcorn Avenue, Suite 300, Toronto, Ontario M4V 3B2.*

In Australia: Please write to *Penguin Books Australia Ltd, P.O. Box 257, Ringwood, Victoria 3134.*

In New Zealand: Please write to *Penguin Books (NZ) Ltd, Private Bag 102902, North Shore Mail Centre, Auckland 10.*

In India: Please write to *Penguin Books India Pvt Ltd, 11 Panchsheel Shopping Centre, Panchsheel Park, New Delhi 110 017.*

In the Netherlands: Please write to *Penguin Books Netherlands bv, Postbus 3507, NL-1001 AH Amsterdam.*

In Germany: Please write to *Penguin Books Deutschland GmbH, Metzlerstrasse 26, 60594 Frankfurt am Main.*

In Spain: Please write to *Penguin Books S. A., Bravo Murillo 19, 1° B, 28015 Madrid.*

In Italy: Please write to *Penguin Italia s.r.l., Via Benedetto Croce 2, 20094 Corsico, Milano.*

In France: Please write to *Penguin France, Le Carré Wilson, 62 rue Benjamin Baillaud, 31500 Toulouse.*

In Japan: Please write to *Penguin Books Japan Ltd, Kaneko Building, 2-3-25 Koraku, Bunkyo-Ku, Tokyo 112.*

In South Africa: Please write to *Penguin Books South Africa (Pty) Ltd, Private Bag X14, Parkview, 2122 Johannesburg.*